The
State of
Working
America

The
State of
Working
America

1992–93

Lawrence Mishel
Jared Bernstein

Economic Policy Institute

Recommended citation for this book is as follows:
  Mishel, Lawrence and Jared Bernstein, *The State of Working America,
  1992-93*. Economic Policy Institute Series. Armonk: M. E. Sharpe, 1993.

ISBN: 1-56324-211-7 (Cloth) 1-56324-212-5 (Paper)

Printed in the United States of America

MV (c) 10 9 8 7 6 5 4 3 2 1
MV (p) 10 9 8 7 6 5 4 3 2 1

To my mother, Geraldine Baron

L.M.

To my family and to Beth

J.B.

TABLE OF CONTENTS:

CHAPTER 4:

Jobs: Worsening Underemployment 215

CHAPTER 5:

Wealth: Losses for Most, Gains for Few 251

CHAPTER 6:

Poverty: High Rates of Poverty Unresponsive to
Economic Expansion 271

CHAPTER 9:
International Comparisons: The United States is
Falling Behind 419

CHAPTER 7:

Regional Analysis: The Differences in Growth by Region and Residence 315

CHAPTER 8:

Losing Access to Basic Necessities: Education, Housing, Health Care, and Child Care 357

The State of Working America

Executive Summary

Using a wide variety of data on family incomes, taxes, wages, unemployment, wealth and poverty, *The State of Working America: 1992-1993* closely examines the impact of the economy on the living standards of the American people. The story we tell is one of great disparities.

The economic recovery of the 1980s was unusual in that the vast majority of Americans were, in many ways, worse off at the end of the recovery in 1989 than they were at the end of the 1970s. In 1989, for instance, many families were working longer for less money, many fell deeper into poverty, and many lacked access to basic necessities such as health care and housing. Meanwhile, a small group of American families at the top of the income scale benefitted extensively from the recovery. As this edition goes to press, the economy is somewhere between a protracted recession and an anemic recovery, wherein the economic problems of the 1980s have been exacerbated in the early 1990s. At this point in time, even the wealthy and highly educated are experiencing the income deterioration which has plagued the majority of Americans throughout the 1980s. The following is a summary of the economic realities that characterize the state of working America.

The economic recovery of the 1980s was unusual in that the vast majority of Americans were, in many ways, worse off at the end of the recovery in 1989 than they were at the end of the 1970s.

1

Family Incomes: Slow and Unequal Growth

The slow rate of income growth between 1979 and 1989 did not affect all families equally. The incomes of families at the top of the income scale—the richest 1%—grew 62.9% from 1980 to 1989. The bottom 60% of families actually experienced a decline in income.

Between 1979 and 1989, family income grew more slowly than in any other business cycle since World War II. In 1989, the median family's income was only $1,528 greater than it was ten years earlier. In the 1967-1973 period for example, family income rose that amount every 22 months (1.8 years). From 1989 to 1991, as the economic downturn began, the average family's inflation-adjusted income fell by 4.4%, a $1,640 drop.

The slow rate of income growth between 1979 and 1989 did not affect all families equally. The incomes of families at the top of the income scale—the richest 1%—grew 62.9% from 1980 to 1989, capturing 53.2% of the total income growth among all families. The bottom 60% of families actually experienced a decline in income. Such uneven growth led to a substantial increase in the wealthiest families' share of total income (their income share grew by 4.4 percentage points between 1980 and 1989, to 51.8%) and equally dramatic losses for everyone else, reversing the entire post war trend toward lessening inequality.

What income growth there was over the 1979-1989 period was driven primarily by increased work hours at lower wages. In fact, the only family type to experience positive income growth was married-couple families, whose incomes grew due to the increased earnings of wives. Among married couples with children, the average wife was employed 32.3% more hours in 1989 than in 1979, the equivalent of nearly seven weeks of full-time work.

In addition, families headed by someone aged 25 to 34 in 1989 had incomes $1,715 less than their counterparts did 10 years earlier in 1979. There is strong evidence that most families headed by someone born after 1945 will not achieve the same incomes in middle-age as achieved by preceding generations.

Finally, the economic downturn beginning in 1989 saw growth rates turn negative as the typical family experienced an income loss of 4.4% between 1989 and 1991. The character of this recessionary decline was unusual in that the incomes of the wealthiest families fell the most: between 1989 and 1991, the inflation-adjusted income of the richest 5% of families fell by 9.3%, twice the income loss of middle class families. Part of this income decline reflects adverse trends that developed in the late 1980s, preceding the onset of the recession, such as the decline in wages for white-collar and college-educated workers and in higher income regions such as the Northeast.

Taxes: A Further Cause of Worsening Inequality

Our tax system has not ameliorated the growing income inequalities examined in Chapter 1. In fact, recent tax changes have worsened the distribution of after-tax income by taxing the middle class and the poor more heavily while giving large tax cuts to the richest 1% of taxpayers. The average federal tax burden on the wealthiest families fell by 4.9 percentage points between 1980 and 1989, an average decrease of $27,430. Over the same period, the federal tax burden on the bottom fifth of families grew by 1.2 percentage points, an *addition* of $100 to their federal tax bill. These trends contributed to a 26.0% increase in the after-tax income of the average family in the top fifth, compared to a 1.7% increase for the average family in the bottom fifth.

Overall, taxes have increased little and the total U.S. tax burden (federal, state, and local) remains one of the lightest among the Western industrialized countries. While the U.S. tax burden gradually edged up during the postwar period, it has held relatively constant since 1973, staying between 31% and 32% of Gross Domestic Product (GDP). However, while the federal burden grew by only 1.4% of GDP since 1959, the state and local burden grew by 4.5% of GDP. Since state and local taxes are more regressive than federal taxes, the effect of this shift in the tax burden is to widen inequality.

Wages: Working Longer for Less

Declining wage trends are arguably the primary determinant of the slow growth of family income and the greater income inequality we have experienced in the 1980s. Between 1979 and 1989, the hourly wages of 80% of the

Recent tax changes have worsened the distribution of after-tax income by taxing the middle class and the poor more heavily while giving large tax cuts to the richest 1% of taxpayers.

3

workforce declined, with the wage of the typical (median) worker falling 4.9% between 1979 and 1989. However, wage loss varied dramatically by education and gender.

Toward the end of the recovery, weakening demand for white-collar workers began to place downward pressure on the wages of workers who had previously escaped wage erosion. White-collar workers lost 2.1% of their total compensation (wages and benefits) between 1987 and 1992; the hourly wage of college-educated workers fell by 3.1%, 1987-1991.

The most severe wage reductions, however, have been for entry level jobs for young, high school graduates, a group comprising two-thirds to three-fourths of all young workers. In 1991, the wages paid to young male and female high school graduates were, respectively, 26.5% and 15.4%, less than the wages their counterparts received in 1979. Over the 1973-1991 period, the wages of entry level college graduates have also fallen by 9.8%. Thus, young workers face a job market providing far lower wages than what comparably educated young people faced two decades ago.

The wages of women grew faster (or fell more slowly) than those of men over the 1980s. Between 1979 and 1989, the average (median) male hourly wage fell by 11.7% while the average female wage grew by 5.3%. These trends led to a narrowing of the gender wage gap, mostly due to the fall in male wages (72%). However, the recession reversed the growth of the female wage, and between 1989 and 1991, the average female wage fell by 2.8%, so that in 1991, it was only 1.1% higher than in 1973.

There has also been an expansion of jobs that, even with full-time work effort, do not pay enough to lift a family of four out of poverty. In 1989, 28% of the workforce earned poverty level wages, up from 25.1% in 1979 and 21.4% in 1973. By 1991, during the recession, 31.2% of the workforce was employed at poverty level wages.

A significant cause of this widespread wage decline is a shift to lower paying industries. The overall shift in the composition of employment, between 1980-1989, led to a 3.4% decline in total compensation. Other causes of wage decline include a lower minimum wage, increased import competition, technological change, and fewer and weaker unions. All of the evidence suggests continued wage erosion in the future.

Jobs: Worsening Underemployment

Over the course of the 1980s recovery, a rising number of workers experienced labor market distress, due to: un- or underemployment (involuntary part-timers and discouraged workers), low pay, or overemployment (multiple job holders, working more than one job to compensate for falling incomes). The unemployment rate in 1989 was a relatively moderate 5.3%, but the total underemployment rate was a much higher 9.8%.

The recession of the early 1990s differed from prior post war recessions in several important ways (based on the assumption that the recession ended in the second quarter of 1992). The recent recession lasted at least 22 months, twice as long as the 11-month average length of earlier downturns, but unemployment rose by far less than in the recessions of the mid-1970s and mid-1980s. Nevertheless, the recent recession involved roughly the same amount of *permanent* (versus temporary) job loss—a rise of 1.6%—as in recent, heavier downturns. The recent recession was also uncharacteristic in that it prompted an unusually large rise in white-collar unemployment coupled with historically slow growth in white-collar employment.

As noted above, there has been a growth in underemployment due to more people working part-time who want full-time jobs. The share of part-time jobs increased from 16.6% in 1973 to 18.1% in 1989, an increase almost entirely due to the increased rate at which workers are working part-time *involuntarily*. By 1991, over one-fourth of the part-time workforce was comprised of involuntary part-timers. A related phenomenon is the increase in the use of temporary workers, as the share of the workforce employed in the personnel services industry (consisting primarily of workers hired through or working for temporary agencies) doubled between 1982 and 1989. These trends reflect the increased use of "temps" and part-timers by employers and not the preferences of the workforce for shorter hours.

The recent recession was also uncharacteristic in that it prompted an unusually large rise in white-collar unemployment coupled with historically slow growth in white-collar employment.

Wealth: Losses for Most, Gains for Few

Stagnant incomes and falling wages tell only part of the story of rising inequality. The distribution of wealth also plays an important role in determining a family's living standards.

Wealth is even more concentrated at the top than income: in 1989, the top 1% of families earned 14.1% of total income, yet owned 38.3% of total net worth and 50.3% of net financial assets. The wealth distribution has also become more unequal over time. The wealth holdings of the richest 0.5% of families grew by one percentage point over the entire 21-year period, 1962-1983, but grew by four times as much in just six years between 1983 and 1989. Meanwhile, the bottom 60% of families had lower wealth holdings in 1989 than 1983.

The main cause of greater wealth inequality was the growth of financial assets—the stocks and bonds owned primarily by the wealthy—which grew at an annual rate of 2.9%, 1979-1989, about six times the growth rate over the previous business cycle, 1973-1979. Tangible assets— homes, cars and appliances—did not grow at all, 1979-1989, in marked contrast to the annual growth of tangible assets (between 4.2% and 4.3%, annually) throughout the 1950s, 1960s and 1970s. Since tangible assets are spread out more evenly than financial assets, their stagnation mainly affected the bulk of the population who are not wealthy.

The concentration of financial assets at the top implies that American businesses are owned and financed primarily by the richest families. In 1989, for example, the wealthiest top 0.5% owned 37.4% of all corporate stocks, while the bottom 90% owned only 16.1%. The top 0.5% also owned 64% of bonds, while the bottom 90% owned only 6.0%.

The gap in average wealth between minority and white households is even larger than the gap in income, with the average wealth in non-white families being just 19% of that in white families in 1989. There was, however, significant progress in lessening racial wealth inequality in the 1962 to 1983 period as non-white mean wealth grew from 13% to 24% of white mean wealth. In contrast, the racial wealth gap widened between 1983 and 1989.

The wealth holdings of the richest 0.5% of families grew by one percentage point over the entire 21-year period, 1962-1983, but grew by four times as much in just six years between 1983 and 1989. Meanwhile, the bottom 60% of families had lower wealth holdings in 1989 than 1983.

Poverty: High Poverty Rates
Unresponsive to Economic Expansion

Despite the growing economy between 1983 and 1989, poverty rates were high by historic standards, averaging 13.6% over the 1980s. In fact, those in poverty in 1989 were significantly poorer than the poor in 1979. For example, 8% more poor persons had incomes at 50% of the poverty line in 1989 than in 1979. Furthermore, these high rates are not sensitive to different measurement choices; poverty was a significant problem over the decade, given any accepted definition.

Minorities and children were especially vulnerable to the high poverty rates. The poverty rates of blacks have been at least three times that of whites since 1979, reaching 32.7% in 1991. The Hispanic rate has climbed from 21.9% in 1973 to 28.7% in 1991. Child poverty grew in all racial categories between 1979 and 1991. By 1991, more than one out of every five children was poor. For children under six-years-old, the rate was even higher, reaching 24.6% in 1991. Perhaps the most alarming statistic in the chapter refers to young black children: in 1991 more than half of black children (51.7%) under six were poor.

The conventional explanations for high poverty rates—the formation of mother-only families, the failure of the poor to exploit labor market opportunities—do not hold up under close scrutiny. The growth of families headed by a female slowed over the 1980s compared to the previous decade, and that growth contributed less to the rising poverty rates of the 1980s than in other periods. Regarding work effort, the percentage of the poor who worked grew over the decade, and those who worked increased their hours.

The reasons poverty rates remained high despite the recovery have to do with wage decline and the failure of the "safety net," i.e., the government's system of taxes and transfers designed to ameliorate poverty. Over the 1980s, the already low wages of low-income workers fell 15.9% for male and 6.8% for female workers in the bottom 20% of the earnings' distribution.

The failure of the safety net led to an additional 1.1% of the population on the poverty rolls, 1979-1989, including an additional 8.2% of persons in single-headed families with children.

Despite the growing economy between 1983 and 1989, poverty rates were high by historic standards, averaging 13.6% over the 1980s. The reasons poverty rates remained high despite the recovery have to do with wage decline and the failure of the "safety net."

7

Regional Analysis: The Differences in Growth by Region and Residence

While average wages for the college educated rose only slightly on a national basis from 1979 to 1989 (1.8%), regional analysis reveals that this positive growth was almost exclusively driven by the Northeastern region.

Economic growth was quite uneven on a regional basis over the 1980s. The Northeast region, comprising New England and the Mid-Atlantic divisions, did comparatively well in terms of greater income and wage growth, and lower unemployment. Conversely, the 1980s economy in the Midwest and the Western regions was characterized by relatively flat or negative income growth over the 1980s, rising poverty, and significant wage loss. The South experienced somewhat more mixed results over the 1980s, but did sustain high rates of poverty (particularly for children) and unemployment, and a surge in income inequality.

This pattern of uneven growth has left winners and losers in its wake. In 28 states, the average income of families in the lowest fifth fell over the 1980s, with dramatic losses in the Midwest and South. On the other end of the income spectrum, Northeastern families in the top fifth experienced dramatic income gains over the 1980s.

Although the Northeast experienced the most growth between 1979 and 1989, it was "hit" the hardest during the recent recession. Between 1989 and 1991, the median family in the Northeast saw a dramatic 7.2% drop in its income, the largest regional loss. Median family income also fell in the Midwest (3.3%), and fell steeply in the South and West (4.7% and 5.2%, respectively).

While average wages for the college educated rose only slightly on a national basis from 1979 to 1989 (1.8%), regional analysis reveals that this positive growth was almost exclusively driven by the Northeastern region, where the wages of college-educated workers grew by 5.9%. The only other region with positive growth for this group was the West, where wages grew less than half as fast.

The average hourly wages of college-educated men in the Northeast grew by 4.6%, 1979-1989, and fell by 3.6%, 1989-1991, leaving it practically flat (0.9% growth) over the full 1979-1991 period. College-educated workers also saw significant wage loss in the other regions during the recession, again denoting the end of the 1980s "white-collar" boom and the white-collar nature of this recession. In the South and West, even workers with post-graduate educations saw a slight decline overall between 1989 and 1991.

Shifting from regions to residence (urban versus rural), we find evidence of a downward shift in the rural income distribution over the 1980s, as 5.0% of rural families shifted from the middle- and upper-income class to the lower-income class. Rural areas also experienced higher unemployment than urban areas. However, despite this rural shift, the highest increase in poverty by residence was in cities. By 1989, 2.4% more city than rural residents were poor.

Losing Access to the Basic Necessities: Education, Housing, Health Care, and Child Care

Another dimension of the well-being of American families involves access to those basic necessities that have a vital impact on our living standards.

Education: Americans place a high value on equal access to quality education, yet we are far from providing it. The United States devotes fewer public resources to public education than most other industrialized countries, and our expenditures are unequally distributed, contributing to wide differences in the test scores of children from different economic backgrounds. Access to higher education, an important factor in lifetime earnings, is notably restricted for students from minority and low-income families and increasingly inaccessible overall due to rising costs. For example, the expected family contribution to private college tuition was over three and a half times the average income of low-income families in 1987.

Housing: The cost of owning or renting a home rose quickly in the early 1980s, both in real terms and as a percentage of income. In the period between 1974 and 1979, the typical first-time home buyer made a housing expenditure that was 29.9% of his or her income; in the period between 1980 and 1989, that percentage was 37.2%. Though home ownership costs fell in the latter part of the decade, the proportion of families owning their own homes also fell over the decade, with young, large, and low-income families facing the most difficulty in the housing market.

Access to higher education, an important factor in lifetime earnings, is notably restricted for students from minority and low-income families and increasingly inaccessible overall due to rising costs.

9

> *Even a full-time job, does not guarantee the provision of health insurance. In 1990 almost one-half of the uninsured were connected to the full-time/full-year workforce.*

The high proportion of income that many families had to expend on housing meant that many families' budgets were severely constrained after paying housing costs. We find that in 1989, one-third of families are "shelter poor," meaning that these families did not have enough to pay for a minimum amount of non-housing necessities, as defined by the U.S. Bureau of Labor Statistics. Housing problems became particularly severe for low-income households. In 1970, there were 200,000 more low-income units than low-income households; by 1989, there were 4.1 million more low-income *households* than low-income *units*. One result has been the highly visible problem of homelessness.

Health Care: Americans spend more on health care than any other nation in the world, over $650 billion in 1990. Yet we still lag behind most other countries, according to important health indicators. Our health care system is plagued by inflated costs and the serious problem of uneven health insurance coverage. Over 35 million Americans were without health insurance in 1991, a number that has grown steadily since 1987.

In 1989, we spent 11.8% of our Gross Domestic Product (GDP) on health care, well above the industrialized nations' average of 7.6%. Hospital costs, the most expensive component of our health care bill, rose 355.7% on a per capita basis, 1960-1990. The average American family now pays close to 12% of its income on health care, up from 9.0% in 1980.

Despite our high expenditure level, the U.S. ranks increasingly poorly on basic health indicators. The U.S. was situated 19 out of 23 countries in 1989 on infant mortality rates. Regarding life expectancy, the U.S. position was 17 for females and 19 for males in 1989 (again, out of 23).

Approximately 34.6 million Americans, 13.9% of the population, were without health insurance in 1990. In addition, having a job, even a full-time job, does not guarantee the provision of health insurance. In fact, in 1990 almost one-half of the uninsured were connected to the full-time/full-year workforce, and a minority of persons in each year were non-workers. By 1990, 49.3% of the uninsured were full-year, full-time workers or their dependents. One factor contributing to the high rates of those who are employed and uninsured is the rapid job growth in industries that are less likely to provide their employees with health insurance, primarily low-paying jobs in the service sector.

Child Care: By 1991, two-thirds of women with children had entered the labor force, creating the need for an essential corollary to mothers' workforce participation: child care. Lack of affordable, high-quality child care is found to be a significant constraint, keeping mothers either out of the workforce or working for fewer hours than they would prefer.

Most families with children under five (57%) were paying for child care in 1990, and wealthy families were paying a smaller percentage of their income than middle- and low-income families. In fact, low-income families spent as much as one-quarter of their income for child care, significantly constraining their family budgets, while families with incomes over $50,000 spent on average, only 6.2% of their income on child care.

International Comparisons: The United States is Falling Behind

While Americans still have the highest per capita income as measured by relative purchasing power, the U.S. is falling behind on many important economic indicators. Our productivity growth rate was 67% of the average of the industrialized countries on an annual basis, 1979-1989. Our wage growth was stagnant while other countries saw strong wage growth. U.S. production workers (non-managerial and non-supervisory) in manufacturing saw their hourly compensation fall at a rate of 0.6% per year, 1979-1989, while hourly compensation generally grew in other advanced countries.

The inequality in income and wealth is more evident in the U.S. than in other countries. Data from the mid-1980s show the U.S. to have the largest low-income class, the smallest middle class, and the third largest high-income class in a study with eight other comparable countries.

However, the relatively large size of America's low-income class is *not* driven by relative differences in market outcomes. In fact, prior to taxes and transfers, poverty (measured as 40% of median family income, adjusted for family size) is higher in most other countries. The American rate, 19.9%, was lower than the rate for France, Ger-

While Americans still have the highest per capita income as measured by relative purchasing power, the U.S. is falling behind on many important economic indicators.

11

> *American poverty, at 13.3%, is well above all the other countries. The American safety net became less effective at reducing poverty, while other countries' system of taxes and transfers expanded to ameliorate the increased rates of market-generated poverty.*

many, Sweden, and others. Yet after taxes and the transfer of government benefits, American poverty, at 13.3%, is well above all the other countries. Furthermore, over the course of the 1980s, as all countries generated higher poverty rates, the American safety net became less effective at reducing poverty, while other countries' system of taxes and transfers expanded to ameliorate the increased rates of market-generated poverty. Finally, U.S. poverty is the most persistent. In a three-year study tracking families in poverty, 14.4% of U.S. families were poor for the duration of the study, a higher percentage than any other comparable country (the German rate was 1.5%, the French rate was 1.6%).

One area where U.S. economic performance has been highly touted is job growth. It is true that from 1979 to 1989, millions more jobs were created in the U.S. than in other countries. However, the U.S. should be expected to have the largest absolute number of jobs, as it is by far the largest country with the greatest population growth. A better indicator is the *rate* of job creation. U.S. employment in 1989 was only 18.7% greater than in 1979, compared to increases of 26.5% in Australia and 20.1% in Canada over the same period. Furthermore, the U.S. is among the smallest spenders on job training and placement, increasing the likelihood that other countries will continue to outpace us on productivity and wage growth.

Introduction

The State of Working America presents a comprehensive statistical portrait of recent trends in the various factors that make up the standard of living of America's working families. The data show that the economy is failing most Americans and not simply because of the early 1990s recession: we are in the midst of a long-term erosion of incomes and opportunities.

Current income problems can be pictured as having two phases. The *first phase* emerged in the early 1980s and was concentrated in the wage deterioration experienced by the 75% of the workforce lacking a college degree. Family income problems essentially flowed from this wage erosion. By 1987, prior to the onset of the recent recession, a *second phase* of income problems emerged. As the white-collar boom of the 1980s ended, the wages of white-collar and college-educated workers fell behind inflation and women's wages and labor force participation stalled or fell. The peculiarly white-collar nature of the early 1990s recession has contributed to low consumer confidence and the generalized economic fears that the younger generation will not fare as well as their predecessors. As we show in Chapter 1 there is fire beneath that smoke.

Unfortunately, it has taken a lengthy and painful recession for most Americans to recognize both the shortcomings of the unbalanced growth of the 1980s and the fundamental problems that are limiting their ability to improve their standard of living. The economy is not now generating higher real wages for either blue- or white-collar work-

> *The economy is failing most Americans, and not simply because of the early 1990s recession: we are in the midst of a long-term erosion of incomes and opportunities.*

13

ers or for either college-educated workers or those without a college degree. On our present trajectory, little relief is in sight. In the short-term, the anemic recovery from the early 1990s recession will not reestablish the wage growth necessary to achieve significant improvements in income. Our analysis of long-term employment trends suggests that, without major policy changes, the 1990s will be a period of historically slow growth in skilled, high-wage jobs (Tables 3.51 and 3.52, meaning the 51st and 52nd tables in Chapter 3).

The End of the White-Collar Boom

In our view, a second phase of income problems emerged in the late 1980s, around 1987, *prior to the onset of the recent recession*. In this *second phase* of economic hardship many of the labor force groups that had previously enjoyed wage growth (white-collar, college-educated and women workers) also experienced an erosion of wages. These new income problems reflect a broadening of income difficulties and not the substitution of some new for some older problems.

The defining development in the second phase is the post-1987 wage setbacks for white-collar and college-educated workers. Between 1987 and 1991, for instance, the real wages of college-educated workers fell 3.1%, with a 4.9% fall among male college graduates (Table 3.19 and 3.20). There was a similar fall in white-collar hourly wages and compensation (wages and benefits) fell, respectively, 3.5% and 2.1% from 1987 to 1992 (Table 3.4). This second phase of income problems is the consequence of the end of the 1980s white-collar employment boom. Starting in 1987, economic difficulties in a wide variety of white-collar intensive industries such as retailing, finance, real estate, insurance and banking led to a slackened growth in white-collar jobs and the consequent cutback in wages. "Lean and mean" strategies or "restructuring" in manufacturing, and to a lesser degree in the service sector, have also led to diminished white-collar employment opportunities and wages.

This contraction in white-collar opportunities was evident in the early 1990s recession, when white-collar employment grew much slower than in earlier recessions. Moreover, there was a greater rise in white-collar than

In this second phase of economic hardship many of the labor force groups that had previously enjoyed wage growth also experienced an erosion of wages.

14

blue-collar unemployment in the recent recession (Table 4.6). In the prior five recessions the rise in white-collar unemployment was at most 53% of the rise in blue-collar unemployment. Further, the income declines in the recession have been most severe at the top of the income scale, an unusual pattern that reflects the upward expansion of wage and income problems.

There was also an economic reversal for women in this period, as the 2.8% wage decline from 1989 to 1991 (Table 3.7) wiped out half of the gains of the prior ten years. The wage reversal among women combined with a leveling off of growth of women's labor force participation meant that one of the main engines of family income growth in the 1980s—increased women's employment and earnings—had stalled in the early 1990s.

The First Phase Problems

The first phase income problems, which began in the early 1980s and *are ongoing*, consist of the wage reductions experienced by blue-collar workers and workers without a college degree (particularly men and younger workers), growing poverty and the "squeeze" on middle-class incomes. The defining development in the first phase was that incomes fell for the bottom 60% of families, while there was an extraordinary 63% income growth among the best-off 1% of families (Table 1.9). This same disparity can be seen in wealth trends, as the wealth (i.e., ownership of assets) of the upper 1% of families grew 54% over the recovery (1983-1989), while the net worth of the bottom 60% of families actually declined (Table 5.8).

During the first phase, only married-couple families achieved income growth, while families headed by single parents, male or female, fell. Moreover, the income growth among married couples was almost entirely fueled by the increased employment and hours of the wives in these families. For instance, the average wife in a married-couple family with children worked 32.3%, or 268 hours, more in 1989 than in 1979 (Table 1.24). Without this increased work effort the incomes of the bottom 80% of married-couple families with children would have fallen (the bottom 60%) or not risen (the upper-middle) from 1979 to 1989 (Table 1.26).

The defining development in the first phase was that incomes fell for the bottom 60% of families, while there was an extraordinary 63% income growth among the best-off 1% of families.

15

These first phase problems were characterized by the dramatic erosion of wages among noncollege-educated men, particularly those in their twenties or thirties. The group of noncollege-educated male workers who suffered serious wage declines in this period comprised three-fourths of male employment (Table 3.20). For instance, the real wages of male high school graduates fell 12.7% from 1979 to 1989. Men with "some college" had a somewhat lesser wage decline (8.3%) from 1979 to 1989 while male high school dropouts suffered much more (18.2%). In contrast, men with a college degree achieved a 2.8% wage gain from 1979 to 1987. The greatest wage gains among men were the almost 10% growth for those with at least two years of schooling beyond college.

Wage erosion was most severe for younger workers, particularly those without a college degree. A young male (female) high school graduate earned 22.4% (13.5%) less in 1989 than in 1979 (Table 3.23).

The group of non-college-educated male workers who suffered serious wage declines in this period comprised three-fourths of male employment.

Falling Wages

The cumulative effect of these two phases of income problems has been stagnant or falling incomes in the middle class, rising poverty, and rapidly expanding incomes and wealth for only the very richest families. In our view, these income developments stem from the failed performance of the economy as reflected in the erosion of wages among nearly all groups and the deterioration in the types of jobs available. As we will discuss below, wage and job trends have been driving both the slow growth in incomes and the surge in income inequality. We discuss other factors that have led to greater income inequality below.

The extent of the labor market's failure to provide decent earnings and adequate employment even at the peak of the business cycle is illustrated in **Table A**, which shows the number of workers and the percent of the labor force that was affected by various types of "labor market distress" in 1989. Overall, there were more than 30 million workers, nearly a third (31.5%) of the workforce, experiencing at least one of these types of labor market distress in 1989 (i.e., eliminating any double counting). Thus, at the end of the 1980s recovery and in a year of low unemployment, 1989, the economy was failing to provide adequate

16

wages and employment to a large segment of the workforce.

For instance, some 10.3% and 5.8% of the workforce experienced at least four weeks, respectively, of unemployment and involuntary part-time work (had only part-time work even though wanting full-time work) in 1989. Another 1.8% of the workforce were discouraged workers, people who wanted to work but felt that no jobs were available. Additionally, a sizeable 22.2% of the prime-age workforce earned poverty level hourly wages, a wage that was insufficient for a year-round, full-time worker to support a four-person family beyond the poverty standard. We view this as a conservative estimate of the number of people being failed by the poor performance of the labor market and the economy. This analysis is limited to prime-age workers (ages 25 to 64 years old) in a year of low unemployment. Moreover, this measure of labor market distress excludes a sizeable number of workers affected by less easily measurable types of distress: temporary or contract workers wanting a permanent position; people who are "self-employed" for lack of a decent job opportunity (Table 4.24); the nearly 3.0% of the workforce that work at least two-jobs because pay on the first job was insufficient to meet expenses (Table 4.16); workers experiencing job-

There were more than 30 million workers, nearly a third (31.5%) of the workforce, experiencing labor market distress in 1989.

TABLE A
Number and Share of Workforce Experiencing
Labor Market Distress in 1989

Type of Labor Market Distress*	Number (000)	Share of Labor Force
Earn Poverty Level Wages	21,205	22.2%
Discouraged Workers	1,711	1.8
Involuntary Part-time at Least Four Weeks	5,543	5.8
Unemployed at Least Four Weeks	9,799	10.3
Total with Labor Market Distress**	30,143	31.5%

*Based on a sample of civilian wage and salary workers ages 25-64 who worked, were unemployed or were a discouraged worker in 1989.
**Counts each person once even if subject to more than one type of distress.

17

related illnesses, injuries or death; workers who are not covered by any employer-provided (and partially paid) health insurance from their own or even a spouse's employer (Chapters 3 and 8); and, workers affected by wage and/or benefit reductions (Chapter 3). A more inclusive measure would clearly show that the labor market is failing to provide adequately paid, safe and steady employment for a much broader group of the workforce.

Unfortunately, data limitations prevent us from consistently estimating "labor market distress" in earlier or later years. It is certain, however, that much more of the workforce was adversely affected by labor market trends in 1991—the average number of unemployed, involuntary part-time, and discouraged workers rose 24% from 1989 to 1991 (Table 4.1) and the share of the workforce earning poverty level wages rose 11% at the same time (Table 3.9).

Underemployment grew from 1979 to 1989 and was raised further in the early 1990s recession. The largest labor market failure has been the deterioriation of wages.

Underemployment grew from 1979 to 1989 and was raised further in the early 1990s recession (Chapter 4). However, the largest labor market failure has been the deterioriation of wages, as we discussed earlier (and extensively in Chapter 3). There are a number of factors driving these changes in the wage structure. One was the quickened shift of employment from well-paying to low-paying employment: a trend where most of the new jobs were created in the lowest-paying segments of the service sector. This industrial job shift particularly affected the level of benefits paid to the average worker. The forces driving this adverse job shift were a rising trade deficit and slow growth in service sector productivity (especially relative to manufacturing).

International trade has directly, and adversely, affected earnings as workers whose jobs were displaced by imports or by a fall in exports were forced to accept jobs at lower wages. But there have also been indirect, or spillover, effects of trade that have had an even larger effect. The loss of good jobs because of higher imports and fewer exports has forced trade-displaced workers and young workers (who might have obtained a good job in an earlier period) to compete against similarly skilled workers for a more limited set of jobs, thus lowering wages for the entire workforce without a college degree. Trade pressures have also affected wages by limiting nominal wage growth or forcing wage concessions on workers who remained in trade-sensitive industries.

18

The weakening of unions and the erosion of union membership has also adversely affected the wages of the union and nonunion noncollege-educated workforce (Tables 3.34 to 3.38). The erosion of the real value of the minimum wage since 1979 has meant lower wages for at least 11% of the workforce (Table 3.41) and has perhaps undercut the wages of many more. The minimum wage is just one of the many elements of the "social wage" whose weakening has depressed wages: overtime standards, unemployment insurance, workers' compensation, and antidiscrimination protections.

Technological change has also diminished the demand for noncollege-educated workers and rewarded, in the form of wage premiums, those using new technologies. Finally, as discussed earlier, the economic problems in various white-collar intensive industries—finance, retail trade, banking, real estate—and employment "restructuring" in manufacturing and in services has diminished white-collar employment growth, thereby leading to lower wages for white-collar and college-educated workers.

The most common explanations of the poor wage performance for most workers are "slow productivity growth" and that technological change and international competition are placing an increased "premium" on education and skills. However, although slow productivity growth can explain *slow* wage growth, it cannot explain *falling* wages. Since 1979 there has been positive productivity *growth* at the same time that wages and compensation have dramatically *fallen* among noncollege-educated workers (1979-1991) and among college-educated workers (1987-1992). Only factors which affect the wage structure (lifting one group's wage and/or depressing another's) or cause average wages and compensation to fall can explain recent wage trends.

Similarly, attributing higher wage inequality solely to a rising "education wage premium" is misleading. The question is *why* the "education premium," the ratio of the wages of college graduates to those of high school graduates, has been increasing.

It is clear that a higher education premium is not the result of a benign "bidding up" of the wages of "more educated" workers. Rather, the greater wage gap between high school- and college-educated workers is almost entirely the result of a dramatic push *downward* of the wages of the

Although slow productivity growth can explain slow wage growth, it cannot explain falling wages.

noncollege-educated workforce, the result of deunionization, industry shifts, an eroded minimum wage, trade-induced wage reductions and other identifiable forces. Moreover, over the last twelve years the wages of college graduates (male and female) have hardly been bid upwards, growing only 0.3% from 1979 to 1991, and actually falling in the South and the Midwest.

It is also commonly asserted that wages are growing slower because fringe benefits are rising (or total compensation is growing even if wages are not). This is not supported by the evidence. Over the 1977 to 1989 period the value of fringe benefits fell, although not as much as wages (Table 3.2), and total compensation (wages and benefits) fell 7.9%.

Nor are adverse demographic trends—a rise in the number of college graduates or the entry of the baby-boomers—reducing wages. In the late 1980s the size of the college-educated workforce grew more *slowly* yet the wages of college graduates fell. The baby-boomers have entered the time in their careers when wages advance quickly and the baby-busters' short supply should be raising the relative wage of young workers, yet the opposite has happened.

Income Inequality

Income growth in the 1980s was modest by historical standards and even slower than the slow growth of the 1970s. Equally important, lower- and middle-income families either lost ground or struggled to stay even by working harder through longer hours and more family members working. In contrast, the top 1% of families had an extraordinary after-tax income growth of 75% from 1980 to 1989. One way of characterizing the income trends of the 1980s is that income growth for upper-income groups returned to the rates obtained in the more prosperous period from World War II to 1973, while the remainder of the population had stagnant or falling incomes. The result was a surge in inequality in the 1980s that reversed three decades of declining income inequality.

The rapid income growth of the top 1% is the result of both fast wage growth and the rapid growth in capital incomes from greater interest and dividend income and from more realized capital gains (their greater unrealized

> It is also commonly asserted that wages are growing slower because fringe benefits are rising. This is not supported by the evidence.

capital gains are reflected in the rapid growth of the net worth of the top 1%; see Chapter 5). The upper 1% received more capital income partly because there was an expansion of capital incomes relative to labor incomes and partly because capital incomes became more unequally distributed over the 1980s (see Chapter 1). The expansion of capital incomes is primarily due to the high real interest rates that prevailed in the 1980s. The reduced incomes at the bottom of the income scale reflect the erosion of wages as well as the reductions in government assistance, or transfer payments (see Chapter 6).

In our view, the growth in inequality has been generated by changes in the market economy and by government policies and not in any great measure, by changing "demographic trends": the smaller size of families, more female-headed households and more two-earner families. Analyses which take into account the smaller size of families (an indicator of how much income is "needed") show an even slower income growth in the 1980s relative to the 1970s (Table 1.2). Moreover, family size-adjusted income data show a *greater* polarization of income in the 1980s (Table 1.21). Any shift in the population to different family situations is at best a minimal explanation since there was a large growth in income inequality among each type of family, be it single parent or married couples (Table 1.8). Moreover, the pattern of increased wives' earnings prevented income declines among middle-class married couples and has meant *less* inequality among married-couple families (Tables 1.23 to 1.29). So, high-earning men marrying high-earning women did not cause greater inequality. However, wives working has contributed slightly to overall family income inequality since this engine of income growth among married couples was not available to single persons or single-parent families.

Arguments which explain income or poverty trends by the rise of female-headed households should be greeted with skepticism (Tables 6.13 and 6.14). At the broadest level, we wonder why it is a "demographic" phenomenon when a woman cannot support a family without access to a man's income. Is this not primarily a reflection of the lesser earnings opportunities available to women and inadequate access to child care?

It is also important to understand the demographic composition of female-headed families because it is too fre-

The growth in inequality has been generated by changes in the market economy and by government policies and not in any great measure, by changing "demographic trends".

21

quently assumed that the growth of female-headed families is an urban, black phenomenon of women with out-of-wedlock children. In fact, less than a fourth of female-headed families are headed by "never-married" women; the vast majority of female-family heads are divorced, separated or widowed (Table 6.17). Moreover, this is not primarily a black phenomenon, especially in the 1980s. White and black female-headed families accounted for, respectively, 59.1% and 33.8% of the growth of such families in the 1979-1989 period. It was in the 1970s and not in the 1980s that there was a major increase in black female-headed families.

The deterioration of incomes and the surge in income inequality in the 1980s could not have been driven by more female-headed families since the growth of female-headed families was actually slower in the 1980s than in the 1970s (Table 1.5).

It is true that any disproportionate growth of female-headed families does, given their higher poverty rates, raise the aggregate poverty rate. Nevertheless, the growth of female-headed families has been occurring for a long time and, as we have seen, has even slowed down. The growth in poverty, or the failure of poverty to fall in the 1980s recovery, is primarily due to the failure of economic growth in the 1980s to ameliorate poverty as it had in the prior twenty years (witness the higher poverty among married-couple families). In fact, economic forces led to *higher* poverty in the 1980s, a reversal of the trend in the prior two decades when economic growth was a force reducing poverty (Table 6.14). Finally, it is worth noting that the growth of poverty among female-headed families can mostly be attributed to an erosion of government support and not to any reduced work effort (Table 6.19).

The recent shifts in the tax structure were not responsible for the middle-class squeeze. Still, the large reductions in federal taxes were an important factor in the rapid growth of after-tax incomes among the top 1% of families: lower taxes allowed the top 1% to obtain a 75% gain in after-tax incomes on a 62.9% gain in pre-tax income (Tables 1.9 and 2.3). The remaining 99% of families paid only slightly higher federal taxes in 1989 than in 1980 (Table 2.6). Thus, changes in tax policy had a minimal effect on middle-class incomes, but a sizeable effect on the incomes of the very richest families. The slow and unequal income growth of the 1980s was primarily the product of

22

market outcomes as reflected in the pre-tax incomes of families and was not due to changes in tax policy.

What Has Greater Inequality Bought Us?

The recent surge in inequality of both incomes and wages might be viewed positively had greater inequality led to faster income or wage growth for most families or income groups. Clearly it has not. Neither productivity, nor investment, nor employment growth, nor wage growth, nor our international competitiveness was significantly better (and most fared worse) in the 1980s than the 1970s. For instance, employment growth over the 1979-1989 period or in the 1982-1989 recovery was not above average for the postwar period. The 1980s did have a long recovery (the second longest one of the postwar period), but it has been followed by a lengthy recession on the heels of several years of minimal growth. By now it is clear that the sources of consumption growth in the 1980s (debt, more family members working, longer hours of work) were unsustainable. It is also true that the groups with the greatest wage problems (noncollege-educated workers) *also* faced an erosion of employment prospects; for them, lower wages did not "buy" more jobs (Table 3.50).

The recent surge in inequality of both incomes and wages might be viewed positively had greater inequality led to faster income or wage growth for most families or income groups. Clearly it has not.

Conclusion

Policy discussions have increasingly, and usefully, characterized our options as whether we will follow a "high-wage" or a "low-wage" growth path. The panorama of indicators of economic performance and economic well-being that we present in this book suggests *that we have already taken the "low-wage path" without even becoming more competitive*. No one in government or business has explicitly announced a program of lowering American wages and working conditions in order to become "competitive"; nevertheless, the cumulative impact of both government policy and business strategies has achieved a lowering of wages and the standard of living of most Americans.

Recent wage problems sometimes are dismissed as the problems of "unskilled" or "less-educated" workers not fit-

23

ting into a world of new technologies and the "global marketplace." The problem, however, is not that a small group of workers are undergoing a painful adjustment to a new, more beneficial economic order. What has occurred is the lowering of wages, benefits and working conditions of the three-fourths of the workforce without a college degree and the consequent pressure on family incomes. Moreover, now that income problems have spread upwards to the white-collar and college-educated groups, it is harder to find beneficiaries of the new order.

It is obvious that the economy is not generating higher incomes for the vast majority of Americans. Therefore, the fundamental economic problem we face is to generate adequate income growth for the majority, based on jobs paying high hourly wages and benefits. Government policy and elected leaders must be judged on their ability to change the economic course of the country and leave the low-wage path for the higher-wage one.

The problem is not that a small group of workers are undergoing a painful adjustment to a new, more beneficial economic order. What has occurred is the lowering of wages, benefits and working conditions of the three-fourths of the workforce without a college degree. Income problems have spread upwards to the white-collar and college-educated groups.

Presentation and Methodology

Presentation

In this book we present a comprehensive portrait of changes in incomes, taxes, wages, employment, wealth, poverty and other indicators of economic performance and economic well-being. We rely almost exclusively on data in the tables and figures to describe the who, what, why, when and where of income changes in the post-war period. Consequently, the documentation of our analysis is essentially the documentation of the tables and figures in the book. This allows us to omit distracting footnotes or citations in the text or tables. All of the documentation is contained in the "Table Notes" section on pages 451–473 which provides the sources of the data we use and information about the calculations we made with the data. In some selective circumstances, however, we incorporate data in the discussion that is not in a table or figure.

Time Periods

Economic indicators fluctuate considerably with short-term swings in the business cycle. For example, incomes tend to fall in recessions and rise during expansions. Therefore, economists usually compare business cycle peaks with peaks and troughs with troughs, so as not to mix apples and oranges. In this book, we examine changes between business cycle peaks. The initial year for most tables is 1947 or, when using the National Income and Product Accounts,

1959 (the earliest year available). The intermediate years in the analysis are 1967, 1973, 1979, and 1989, all of which were business cycle peaks, at least in terms of having low unemployment. We also present the latest year for which data are available (usually 1990 or 1991) to show the effect of the early 1990s downturn. Some information was available only for other non-peak years. If this information was important enough, we included it.

Growth Rates and Rounding

Since business cycles differ in length, we usually present the annual growth rates in each period rather than the total growth. We present compound (log) annual growth rates rather than simple annual rates. Compound annual growth rates are just like compound interest on a bank loan: the rate is compounded continuously rather than yearly.

While annual growth rates may seem small, over time they can amount to a large change. For example, the median incomes of families headed by persons aged under 25 fell 2.5% per year between 1979 and 1989 (Table 1.3). Over the full period, incomes declined by a considerable 21.8%.

In presenting the data we "round" the numbers, usually to one decimal place. However, we use "unrounded" data to compute growth rates or percentage shares and so on. Therefore, it is not always possible to exactly replicate our calculations by using the data in the table. In some circumstances, this leads to an appearance of errors in the tables. For instance, we frequently present shares of the population (or families) at different points of time (i.e., an early and a later year) and compute changes in these shares. Because our computations are based on the "unrounded" data the change in shares presented in a table does not always match the difference in the actual shares presented in the table. Although our change in shares may appear to be in error because of rounding, in fact, our computations based on the "unrounded" data are more precise.

Adjusting for Inflation

In most popular discussions, the Consumer Price Index for All Urban Consumers (CPI-U), often called simply "the Consumer Price Index," is used to adjust dollar values for inflation. However, some analysts hold that the CPI-U overstated inflation in the late 1970s and early 1980s by measuring housing costs inappropriately. The methodology for the CPI-U from 1983 onward was revised to address these objections. Not all agree that it should have been revised. We chose not to use the CPI-U so as to avoid any impression that this report overstates the decline in wages and understates the growth in family incomes over the last few decades.

Instead of the CPI-U, we adjusted dollar values for inflation using the CPI-U-X1 index, an index which uses the new methodology for housing inflation over the entire 1967-1991 period. The CPI-U-X1 however is based on small sample, experimental indices for the 1970s and there is some slight variation in methods over the entire period. Nevertheless, the use of the CPI-U-X1 is becoming standard and we employ it. Because the CPI-U-X1 is not available for years before 1967 we extrapolate the CPI-U-X1 back to earlier years based on inflation as measured by the CPI-U.

The original data on which we draw were calculated with a variety of price indices. Whenever possible, we readjusted the figures using the CPI-U-X1. In our analysis of poverty in Chapter 6, however, we used the CPI-U rather than the CPI-U-X1. This is because Chapter 6 is based almost entirely on publications of the Census Bureau that use the CPI-U. Moreover, the net effect of all of the criticisms of the measurement of poverty is that current methods *understate* poverty. Simply switching to the CPI-U-X1 without incorporating other revisions (i.e., revising the actual poverty standard) would lead to an even greater understatement and would be a very selective intervention to improve poverty measurement. A fuller discussion of these issues appears in Chapter 6.

Household Heads

We often categorize families by the age or the race/ethnic group of the "household head." This is the person in whose name the home is owned or rented. If the home is owned jointly be a married couple, either spouse may be designated the household head. Every family has a single household head.

Hispanics

Unless we specify otherwise, we follow the Census Bureau's designation of Hispanic persons. That is, Hispanics are included in racial counts (e.g., with blacks and whites), as well as in their own separate category. For instance, in government analysis a white person of Hispanic origin is included both in counts of whites *and* in counts of Hispanics. In some tables (primarily in Chapter 3 on wages) we remove Hispanic persons from other racial (white or black) categories. Using this technique, the person described above would appear only in counts of Hispanics. When this technique is applied, it is noted in the table.

Acknowledgements

The preparation of this publication required the intensive work effort of many people on the EPI staff. Jessica Burton, Miranda Martin and Stephanie Scott diligently word processed the text and tables. Daphne Clones prepared all of the graphs and provided research assistance, especially on the regional analysis. Lory Camba provided computer assistance, including analyses of wage data on computer tapes. Edie Rasell provided advice on health and education matters. Max Sawicky carefully reviewed our tax analysis and Robert Blecker and Todd Schafer provided comments on international comparisons. Bill Spriggs provided advice on a wide variety of areas, but especially on the minimum wage and our cohort income growth analyses. Ruth Polk reviewed every word we wrote and effectively edited, checked, made consistent and substantially improved the text and the presentation. Carol Pott guided the production and design of the book as well as assisting with editing. Typesetting by Mid-Atlantic/Type 2000. Nan Gibson and Roger Hickey worked to provide a large audience for the book.

This third version of *The State of Working America* obviously owes much to the efforts, ideas and spreadsheets of the previous co-authors, David Frankel and Jacqueline Simon.

A number of experts were helpful in providing data for our use. Ed Wolff was especially kind in providing his analysis of wealth data. Others include: Frank Sammartino of the Congressional Budget Office; Wendell Primus of the House of Ways and Means Committee; Isaac Shapiro of the Center on Budget and Policy Priorities; Albert Schwenk, Bill Gullickson and Joseph Meisenheimer of the Bureau of Labor Statistics; Kevin Murphy; Rebecca Blank; Alan Krueger; Robert Moffitt; Eugene Steuerle; Michael Stone; Lee R. Jones of the National Assessment of Educational Progress and Lee Price of the Joint Economic Committee. We also drew heavily on the published works of Sheldon Danziger, Richard Freeman, Larry Katz, Timothy Smeeding, Bob Costrell and Chris Tilly. Our intention is to thank, not implicate, any of these researchers.

Chapter 1

Family Income: Slow and Unequal Growth

Introduction

A person's economic well-being depends upon his/her access to economic resources. Since most Americans live in families in which income is shared, family income is the best single measure of how Americans are doing economically. This chapter examines how the performance of the economy in generating jobs, wages and income from capital assets has affected the growth of family income and the recent surge in income inequality.

During the recession of the early 1990s, from 1989 to 1991, there was a 4.4%, or $1,640, fall in the median family's inflation-adjusted income. The character of the recessionary income decline was unusual in that the incomes of the wealthier families fell the most. Part of the income decline during the recession reflects adverse trends that developed in the late 1980s preceding the onset of the recession, factors such as the decline in wages for white-collar and college-educated workers and in higher-income regions such as the Northeast.

The post-1989 income decline, however, comes on the heels of a period from 1979 to 1989 (both years of relatively low unemployment) when family income grew even more slowly than it did in the 1970s and far more slowly than it did in the period between the end of World War II and 1973. The income growth slowdown in the 1979-1989 period did not affect all families equally. Upper-income groups, particularly the upper 1%, experienced significant

The income growth slowdown in the 1979-1989 period did not affect all families equally. Upper-income groups, particularly the upper 1%, experienced significant income growth while the bottom 60% of families actually experienced a decline in income.

31

income growth while the bottom 60% of families actually experienced a decline in income. This resulted in a dramatic rise in the income gap between high- and low-income families, reversing the entire postwar progress in lessening inequality. The incomes of the top 1% grew 62.9% from 1980 to 1989, capturing 53.2% of the total income growth among all families.

From 1979 to 1989 the income of every type of family fell except for married-couple families. Among married couples with children, however, there would have been no income growth had there not been an increase in the wives' earnings and hours of work. In fact, the bottom 80% of married-couple families with children would have had stagnant or falling incomes from 1979 to 1989 without the increased earnings of wives. Income growth over the 1979-1989 period was driven primarily by more work at lower hourly wages.

A major factor fueling the growing inequality was the acceleration of capital income growth in the 1980s due to high real interest rates and the stock market boom, both of which primarily benefitted the richest families. In contrast, hourly wages and fringe benefits, which provide support for most families, grew slower than inflation. Inequality among wage-earners also rose as real wages among high-income groups rose and wages among the broad middle class and lower income groups fell.

The pattern of increases in wives' hours and earnings lessened income inequality among married couples, but slightly increased inequality among all families.

Income growth has not only been slow, there has also been a decline in income for younger families. A cohort, or inter-generational, analysis of income growth shows that the recent groups of young families have started out at lower incomes and obtained slower income gains as they approach middle age. Consequently, those families headed by someone born after 1945 may not achieve the same incomes in middle age as the preceding generation achieved.

In the first few sections of this chapter we examine the changes in the level of income in recent years relative to other periods since 1947. This analysis focuses on changes in median family income (the income which is more than but also less than that of half the families) for families overall as well as for families differentiated by the age or race/

Those families headed by someone born after 1945 may not achieve the same incomes in middle age as the preceding generation achieved.

32

ethnicity of the household head and by family type (married couples, single parents and so on). In the final sections of this chapter we turn our attention to the growth of inequality and its causes.

Sluggish Income Growth

Income growth in recent years has been slow and the gains unequally distributed. **Tables 1.1 and 1.2** show changes in family income, adjusted for changes in consumer prices, in various cyclical peak (or low unemployment) years since World War II. As explained in the introductory section on presentation and methodology, examining income changes from business cycle peak to business cycle peak eliminates the distortion caused by the fact that incomes fall drastically in a recession and then recover in the upswing (**Figure 1A**).

Income growth in recent years has been slow and the gains unequally distributed.

TABLE 1.1
Median Family Income, 1947-1991*
(1991 dollars)

Year	Median Family Income
1947	$17,059
1967	29,765
1973	34,774
1979	36,051
1989	37,579
1991	35,939
Total Increases:	
1947-67	$12,706
1967-73	5,009
1973-79	1,276
1979-89	1,528
1989-91	1,640

*Income includes all wage and salary, self-employment, pension, interest, rent, government cash assistance and other money incomes.

33

TABLE 1.2
Annual Growth of Median Family Income, 1947-1991
(1991 Dollars)

| Period | Median Family Income Growth | | Median Family Income (Size-Adjusted)* |
	Percent	Dollars	Percent
1947-67	2.8	$635	n.a.
1967-73	2.6	835	n.a.
1973-79	0.6	213	1.3
1979-89	0.4	153	0.6
1989-91	−2.2	−820	−3.1

*Family income adjusted for changes in the size of families. 1989-91 data is based on 1989-90 income change.

FIGURE 1A
Median Family Income,
1967-1991

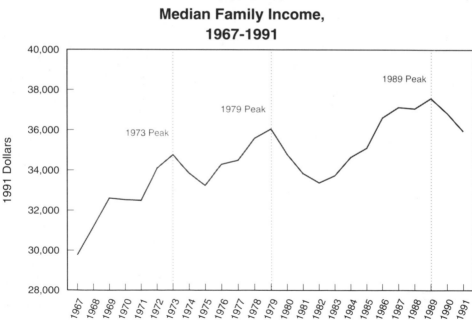

34

There was a substantial increase in family income in the two decades (1947-1967) immediately following World War II, when the median family income increased by $12,706 for an annual rate of growth of 2.8% (Table 1.2). Family incomes continued to grow into the early 1970s, but since 1973 have risen very slowly. In 1989, the median family's income was $1,528 greater than it was in 1979. This translates into a growth of just $153, or 0.4%, per year from 1979 to 1989, a rate of growth just two-thirds the sluggish 0.6% annual growth of the 1973-1979 period and only one-seventh the rate of income growth of the postwar years prior to 1973 (see Figure 1B). In fact, the $1,528 income growth over the *10 years* after 1979 equals the amount that incomes rose every *twenty-two months* (1.8 years) in the 1967-1973 period.

It is common practice to also examine measures of family income growth which adjust for changes in family size, on the basis that if the same total family income is shared by fewer family members then the economic well-being of each family member has improved. Another advantage of family size-adjusted income measures is that they incorporate income trends of individuals not living in families in addition to income trends among families. Because the average family size has been falling over the last several decades, family income growth is being shared with fewer family members and the change in economic well-being of family members exceeds the growth portrayed by a simple analysis of income that ignores changes in family size.

However, trends in incomes "adjusted for family size" can be misleading, since the recent decline in the average family's size (or growth of single-person households) is partially due to lower incomes, i.e., some families feel they cannot afford as many children (or individuals feel they cannot get married as early) as they could have, had incomes continued to rise at postwar rates. Yet a family deciding to have fewer children or a person putting off starting a family because incomes are down appears "better off" in size-adjusted family income measures. It also seems selective to adjust family incomes for changes in family size—yielding a greater growth rate of economic well-being in recent years—and not adjust family income trends for other demographic trends that are lowering economic well-being such as more hours of work and the loss of leisure.

The $1,528 income growth over the 10 years after 1979 equals the amount that incomes rose every twenty-two months (1.8 years) in the 1967-1973 period.

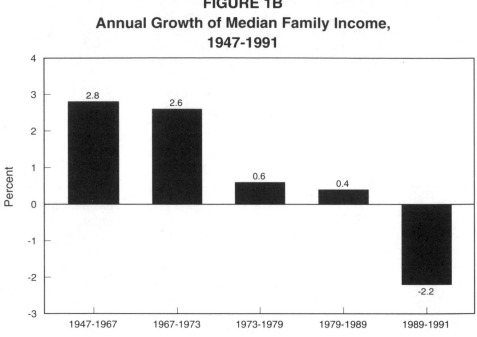

FIGURE 1B
Annual Growth of Median Family Income,
1947-1991

TABLE 1.3
Growth of Median Family Income by Age of Householder, 1967-1990
(1991 Dollars)

| Year | By Age of Household Head | | | | | |
	Under 25	25-34	35-44	45-54	55-64	Over 65
Median Family Income						
1967	$21,927	$30,373	$34,665	$36,305	$30,174	$14,738
1973	23,125	35,222	41,284	43,927	36,881	18,543
1979	23,956	35,626	42,257	46,660	40,457	20,817
1989	18,743	33,911	44,157	50,637	41,347	25,354
1991	16,848	31,539	41,859	46,606	40,014	24,805
Annual Growth Rate						
1967-73	1.0%	2.6%	3.0%	3.3%	3.5%	3.9%
1973-79	0.9	0.5	0.7	1.3	1.8	2.2
1979-89	−2.5	−0.5	0.4	0.8	0.2	2.0
1989-91	−5.3	−3.6	−2.7	−1.0	−1.6	−1.1

Nevertheless, even when income growth is adjusted for the shift towards smaller families (as in Table 1.2), the income growth from 1979 to 1989 is only slightly more than an "unadjusted" measure (0.6% versus 0.4%). It is noteworthy that the size-adjusted family income measure shows a far greater slowdown in income growth between the 1979-1989 period and the 1973-1979 period (0.6% versus 1.3%), reflecting the slower decline in family size in the 1980's than in the 1970s.

The recent downturn starting in 1989 has significantly reduced incomes. For instance, the 4.4% fall from 1989 to 1991 meant a loss of $1,640 in income for the median family, a reversal of income growth over the entire 1979-1989 period (Table 1.1). The 1989-1991 income decline appears to reflect more than a normal business cycle downturn. For example, this is a large income fall for a less than average recessionary increase in unemployment, up 1.4% from 5.3% to 6.7%. In addition, the large income decline reflects several ongoing and new structural shifts in income growth, such as the fall off in wages among white-collar and college-educated workers that preceded the recession (see Chapter 3), the continuing reductions in blue-collar wages, and a slowdown in labor force growth (see Chapter 4).

The largest drop in incomes has occurred among the youngest families. The incomes of families headed by someone between the ages of 25 and 34 fell 0.5% annually from 1979 to 1989.

Young Families Hurt Most

Table 1.3 shows that the largest drop in incomes has occurred among the youngest families. The average income of families headed by someone under age 25 declined at an annual rate of 2.5% from 1979 to 1989. Theirs is also the only age group for which median family income is lower today than it was in 1967; such young families in 1989 had $3,184 less income to spend in real dollars than their 1967 counterparts had when they were starting out.

Families headed by someone between the ages of 25 and 34 years have also fared poorly relative to earlier years. The incomes of this type of family eroded 0.5% per year from 1979 to 1989. This is in stark contrast to the six years between 1967 and 1973, when income for this group increased at a 2.6% annual rate, or even to the six years between 1973 and 1979 when income grew at a 0.5% pace. Many families in this age group are likely to be bring-

TABLE 1.4
Growth of Median Family Income by Race/Ethnic Group, 1947-1991
(1991 Dollars)

Year	Race or Hispanic Origin of Household Head			Ratio to White Family Income of:	
	White	Black	Hispanic	Black	Hispanic
Median Family Income					
1947	$17,768	n.a.	n.a.	n.a.	n.a.
1967	30,895	$18,291	n.a.	59.2%	n.a.
1973	36,344	20,975	$25,148	57.7	69.2%
1979	37,619	21,302	26,079	56.6	69.3
1989	39,514	22,197	25,753	56.2	65.2
1991	37,783	21,548	23,895	57.0	63.2
Annual Growth Rate					
1947-67	2.8%	2.3%	n.a.		
1967-73	2.7	2.3	n.a.		
1973-79	0.6	0.3	0.6%		
1979-89	0.5	0.4	− 0.1		
1989-91	− 2.2	− 1.5	− 3.7		

ing up young children and trying to buy a home of their own. The income problems of these young families thus represent income problems for the nation's children. Families with household heads aged 25 to 34 in 1989 had incomes $1,715 less than their counterparts did 10 years earlier in 1979. The deterioration of incomes for these young families is one of the most significant income developments over the last two decades.

The incomes of the 35 to 44 and 45 to 54 age groups have grown modestly—roughly one-half of 1% per year—since 1979. In contrast, family income for these age groups grew by more than 3.0% per year between 1967 and 1973. Incomes of families headed by someone over 65 increased at a 2% pace from 1979 to 1989, a healthy growth, but only half as fast as that of the 1967-1973 period.

From 1989 to 1991 there was significant slippage in income among nearly every age group, with families headed by someone under age 45 losing at least 5% and the youngest families losing 10.2%.

Income Growth Among Racial/Ethnic Groups

Sluggish income growth has affected all racial groups, as **Table 1.4** illustrates. White families, who fared the best from 1947 to 1973, experienced on average very modest 0.4% annual growth in real income from 1979 to 1989. Black families, with a median income more than 40% lower than that of whites, experienced slightly slower income growth than whites in the 1973-1979 period (0.3% versus 0.6%) and had slow income growth in the 1979-1989 period comparable to that of whites (0.4% versus 0.5%). The median income of families of Hispanic origin declined 0.1% per year between 1979 and 1989.

The ratio between white and black median family income fell from 1967 to 1973 but has remained fairly constant since 1973, reflecting comparably slow income growth among both groups. The decline in Hispanic family incomes, however, has led to a *larger* gap between white and Hispanic families. The ratio of Hispanic to white median income fell from 69.3% in 1979 to just 65.2% in 1989.

Sluggish income growth has affected all racial groups.

TABLE 1.5
Income Growth by Type of Family, 1947-1991

| | | Married Couples | | No Spouse Present | | |
Year	Total	Wife in Paid Labor Force	Wife Not in Paid Labor Force	Male-Headed	Female-Headed	All Families
Median Family Income						
1947	$17,498	n.a.	n.a.	$16,524	$12,224	$17,059
1967	31,671	$37,356	$28,557	25,567	16,111	29,765
1973	37,594	43,968	32,948	30,997	16,728	34,774
1979	39,441	45,758	32,589	30,936	18,185	36,051
1989	42,340	49,720	31,575	30,587	18,060	37,579
1990-91	40,995	48,169	30,075	28,351	16,692	35,939
Annual Growth Rate						
1947-67	3.0%	n.a.	n.a.	n.a.	n.a.	2.8%
1967-73	2.9	2.7%	2.4%	3.2%	0.6%	2.6
1973-79	0.8	0.7	−0.2	0.0	1.4	0.6
1979-89	0.7	0.8	−0.3	−0.1	−0.1	0.4
1989-91	−1.6	−1.6	−2.4	−3.8	−3.9	−2.2
Distribution of Families						
1951*	87.0%	19.9%	67.1%	3.0%	10.0%	100.0%
1967	86.9	31.8	55.1	2.4	10.7	100.0
1973	85.0	33.5	49.7	2.6	12.4	100.0
1979	82.5	40.6	41.9	2.9	14.6	100.0
1989	79.2	45.7	33.5	4.4	16.5	100.0

*Earliest year available.

40

There were sizeable income losses for every racial/ethnic category during the 1989-1991 downturn. That white family income fell more than black family income in a recession is unusual and further reinforces that this recession has a different character than prior recessions.

Only Married Couples Gain

The only type of family which experienced income growth from 1979 to 1989 was married couples with a wife in the paid labor force. Incomes among married couples where the wife was not in the labor force and among single-parent families, whether headed by a man or a woman, declined from 1979 to 1989. This was an especially dramatic turnaround for female-headed families since their incomes grew 1.4% per year in the 1973-1979 period, but fell thereafter.

This pattern of income growth suggests that it was only among families with two adult earners that incomes grew in the 1979 to 1989 period. The data in **Table 1.5** also show a sizeable growth in the importance of working wives. In 1979, there were more married couples without a wife in the labor force than those with a wife in the labor force (41.9% of all families versus 40.6% of all families). By 1989, married couples with two earners (assuming the husband worked) comprised 45.7% of all families, while one-earner married couples were proportionately fewer in number, just 33.5% of the total. This shift towards two-earner families has been a major factor in recent income growth.

Married-couple families, although still predominant—representing 79.2% of the total in 1989—comprise a smaller share of families than they did in the 1950s and 1960s. There has been a continuing rise in the importance of female-headed families who, in 1989, represented 16.5% of the total. Although this phenomenon has been the focus of increased attention in recent years, there was a much faster growth of female-headed families in the period from 1967 to 1979 than in the period since 1979 (Chapter 6 provides a further analysis of this issue).

The downturn from 1989-1991 caused income losses for every type of family. However, incomes fell most among

This pattern of income growth suggests that it was only among families with two adult earners that incomes grew in the 1979 to 1989 period.

41

TABLE 1.6
Shares of Family Income Going to Various Fifths,
and to Top 5%, 1947-1991

	Income Share Going to:						Breakdown of Top Fifth	
Year	Lowest Fifth	Second Fifth	Middle Fifth	Fourth Fifth	Top Fifth	Total	Top 5%	Next 15%
1947	5.0%	11.9%	17.0%	23.1%	43.0%	100.0%	17.5%	25.5%
1967	5.5	12.4	17.9	23.9	40.4	100.0	15.2	25.2
1973	5.5	11.9	17.5	24.0	41.1	100.0	15.5	25.6
1979	5.2	11.6	17.5	24.1	41.7	100.0	15.8	25.9
1989	4.6	10.6	16.5	23.7	44.6	100.0	17.9	26.7
1991	4.5	10.7	16.6	24.1	44.2	100.0	17.1	27.0
Point Change:								
1979-89	−0.6	−1.0	−1.0	−0.4	2.9	0	2.1	0.8
1989-91	−0.1	0.1	0.1	0.4	−0.4	0	−0.8	0.4

single-parent families and for married couples with the wife not in the labor force.

Growing Inequality of Family Income

The vast majority of American families have experienced either very modest income growth or an actual erosion in their standard of living in recent years. The small minority of upper-income families, however, had substantial income growth. The result has been an increase in inequality. The rich have gotten richer; the poor are more numerous and are poorer than they have been in decades. This section examines the income trends of families at different income levels and the dramatic growth of income inequality in the 1980s.

Table 1.6 presents the percentage distribution of income among the various fifths (or "quintiles") of the population, and the top 5%. For an analysis of income fifths the incomes of families are ordered from lowest to highest and the 20% of families with the lowest incomes are considered the "lowest fifth," the next best-off 20% of families are said to be the "second fifth" and so forth until the remaining fifth, the "top fifth," are the 20% of families with the highest incomes. Because the size of families differ, the bottom 20% of families does not necessarily include 20% of the population living in families. This is why some analysts categorize fifths by the number of people so that, for example, the lowest fifth contains the lowest income families comprising 20% of the population living in families.

The upper 20% received 44.6% of all income in 1989. The upper 5% received more of total income, 17.9%, than the families in the bottom 40%, who received just 15.2% in 1989. As we will see in a later chapter providing international comparisons (Chapter 9), income in the U.S. is distributed far more unequally than in other industrialized countries.

Income distribution has grown even more unequal since 1979, reversing the trend towards less income inequality over the postwar period into the 1970s. Since 1979, the

Income distribution has grown more unequal since 1979, reversing the trend towards less income inequality over the postwar period into the 1970s.

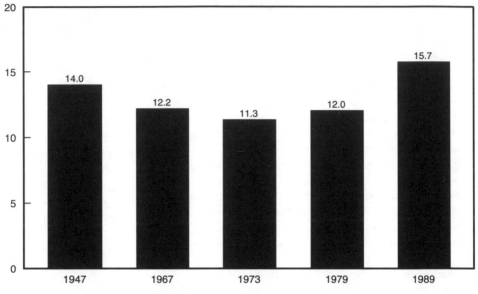

FIGURE 1C
Ratio of Family Income of Top 5% to Lowest 20%,
1947-1989

TABLE 1.7
Real Family Income Growth by Fifth, 1947-1991
(1991 Dollars)

Year	Lowest Fifth	Second Fifth	Middle Fifth	Fourth Fifth	Top Fifth	Top 5%
1947	$ 4,989	$11,875	$16,964	$23,051	$ 42,908	$ 69,850
1967	9,107	20,606	29,619	39,723	70,141	110,974
1973	10,746	23,451	34,456	47,090	80,794	121,931
1979	10,766	23,750	35,871	49,395	85,589	129,585
1989	10,359	24,185	37,571	54,055	101,780	163,042
1991	9,734	23,105	35,851	51,997	95,530	147,817
Annual Change						
1947-67	3.0%	2.8%	2.8%	2.7%	2.5%	2.3%
1967-73	2.8	2.2	2.5	2.8	2.4	1.6
1973-79	0.0	0.2	0.7	0.8	1.0	1.0
1979-89	− 0.4	0.2	0.5	0.9	1.7	2.3
1989-91	− 3.1	− 2.3	− 2.3	− 1.9	− 3.2	− 4.9

44

bottom 80% has lost income share, and only the top 20% gained. Moreover, the 1989 income share of the upper fifth, 44.6%, was far greater than the share it received during the entire postwar period and even higher than the 43% received in 1947. Even among the rich, the growth in income was skewed to the very top, as the highest 5% saw its income share rise by 2.1 percentage points (from 15.8% to 17.9%) between 1979 and 1989, which makes up the bulk of the 2.9 percentage point total rise in the income share of the upper fifth. At the other end of the income spectrum, the 1989 share of total income in each of the three lowest income fifths (i.e, the bottom 60% of families) was even smaller than in 1947.

The increase in the income gap between upper- and lower-income groups is illustrated in **Figure 1C**, which shows the ratio of the incomes of the top 5% to the incomes of the bottom 20% from 1947 to 1989. As Figure 1C shows, the gap between the top and the bottom incomes fell from 1947 to 1979, but grew to a historic ratio of 15.7 by 1989, reversing three decades of lessening inequality.

Another way of viewing this recent surge in income inequality is to compare the income growth of families by income fifth, or quintile, as in **Table 1.7**. Over the early postwar period from 1947 to 1973 there was strong income growth across the income spectrum. From 1947 to 1967, for instance, income growth ranged from the 2.5% annual pace obtained by the top fifth to the 3.0% annual pace obtained by the lowest fifth. Because incomes grew more quickly for lower- and middle-income families than upper-income families (the top fifth or 5%) from 1947 through 1973, there was a general decline in income inequality.

The pattern of income growth since 1973 was far more uneven and far slower than in the earlier period. From 1973 to 1979 the fastest income growth was the 1% annual growth among the top fifth and top 5% of families which, modest as it was, far exceeded the 0.2% annual income growth among the second fifth and the absence of growth among the families with the lowest incomes. Incomes continued to grow slowly in the 1979-1989 period, but the pattern of growth was even more unequal. The families with the lowest incomes actually lost ground from 1979 to 1989 (incomes fell 0.4% annually) while at the same time

Even among the rich, the growth in income was skewed to the very top, as the highest 5% saw its income share rise by 2.1 percentage points between 1979 and 1989, the bulk of the 2.9 percentage point total rise in the income share of the upper fifth.

do lower incomes necessarily lower living conditions?

45

TABLE 1.8
Income Growth by Fifth and Family Type, 1979-1989

Fifth	All Families	Families With Children			Childless Families	
		All	Married Couples	Single Mothers	Non-Elderly	Elderly
Highest	13.9%	12.3%	15.2%	7.5%	18.5%	29.5%
Fourth	4.4	5.1	9.2	−2.4	13.0	20.7
Middle	0.8	−0.8	5.3	−10.1	8.1	18.4
Second	−1.3	−7.6	1.3	−17.1	4.0	15.4
Lowest	−2.1	−17.7	−3.6	−23.2	−1.2	13.7

TABLE 1.9
Income Growth Among Top Fifth and by Fifth, 1977-1990
(1992 Dollars)

Income Group	Average Family Income in:			Percent Change	
	1977	1980	1989	1977-89	1980-89
All	$ 40,065	$ 39,433	$ 43,495	8.6%	10.3%
Top Fifth:	$ 87,268	$ 89,031	$109,424	25.4%	22.9%
Top 1%	314,526	343,610	559,795	78.0	62.9
Next 4%	107,945	109,551	132,036	22.3	20.5
Next 5%	76,525	75,876	87,711	14.6	15.6
Next 10%	60,073	60,428	65,900	9.7	9.1
Bottom Four Fifths:	$ 27,789	$ 26,886	$ 27,251	−1.9%	1.4%
Fourth	$ 46,772	$ 45,827	$ 47,913	2.4%	4.6%
Middle	34,505	32,948	32,681	−5.3	−0.8
Second	22,333	21,009	20,140	−9.8	−4.1
Lowest	9,368	8,791	8,391	−10.4	−4.6

the top 5% of families were able to obtain the same 2.3% rate of income growth as they had in the earlier 1947-1967 period.

This uneven pattern of income growth from 1973 to 1989 left the best-off families with their greatest share of income in the entire postwar period (Table 1.6) and the bottom 60% of families with their lowest income shares.

In contrast to the pattern over the 1970s and 1980s, the downturn from 1989 to 1991 affected the highest incomes the most. The top 5% lost 9.3% while the top fifth lost 6.1%. The income losses from 1989 to 1991 among the broad class—the middle three quintiles—were half as large as those of the upper 5%. Nevertheless, by 1991 the incomes of the bottom 60% of families were less than they were in 1979.

Inequality has widened among each type of family in much the same pattern as has occurred overall—income declines for families at the very bottom and rapid income growth for the best-off families (**Table 1.8**). For instance, the incomes of the bottom fifth declined for each family type, except elderly families. The greatest income decline was among the bottom 40% of single-mother families, a group whose income decline ranged from 17.1% to 23.2% from 1979 to 1989. In fact, the incomes of the bottom four-fifths of single-mother families have all fallen in recent years. On the other end, elderly families in each income fifth obtained significant income growth, although the highest income elderly had more than double the income growth of the lowest fifth of elderly families (29.5% versus 13.7%). This pattern of income growth among the elderly reflects growing social security benefits at all income levels.

Table 1.9 and **Figure 1D** examine changes among various income groups using a more comprehensive pre-tax measure of income (it includes capital gains). The data also provide finer detail on upper-income groups, but unfortunately are only available for 1977 and 1980—not for the last business cycle peak in 1979. Table 1.9 shows the bottom 60% losing income over the 1980s. These trends began prior to 1980, as shown by the income declines of the bottom 80% of families from 1977 to 1980.

Inequality has widened among each type of family in much the same pattern as has occurred overall.

FIGURE 1D
Income Growth Among Top Fifth and by Fifth,
1980-1989

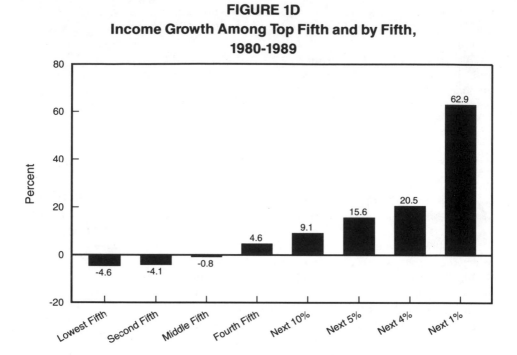

At the other end of the income scale, however, there was considerable income growth (see Figure 1D). The highest income fifth of families saw their incomes rise by 22.9% in the 1980s, five times the 4.6% income gain of the next richest fifth. In fact, the income *gain* of the average family in the upper 20% over the 1980s, $20,393, is more than the average income *level* of families in the bottom two fifths.

The most spectacular income growth was among the upper 1%, whose incomes grew by 62.9% over the 1980s. The $216,185 average income *gain* of the richest 1% of families in the 1980s is nearly double the average income *level* of the next best-off 4% of families and is roughly five times what the average family income was in 1989 ($43,495).

Income growth within the upper fifth was very unequal over the 1980s. Families with income in the 80th to 90th percentile range (the "next 10%" group, Table 1.9) experienced only a 9.1% income gain, far better than any group in the bottom 80% but only one-seventh of the income growth of the upper 1%.

The rapid income growth of the top fifth relative to the bottom four-fifths of the population led to a substantial increase in the share of total income accruing to the rich (**Table 1.10**). By 1989, the upper 20% of families received more than half (51.8%) of all income, increasing their share of income by 4.4 percentage points since 1980 and 5.3 percentage points from 1977. However, within the upper fifth, the top 5% gained a greater share of income while the remaining 15% saw their share of total income decline. The unbalanced income growth of the 1980s thus caused the bottom 95% of the population to lose income share to the upper 5%. Reflecting their spectacular income growth, the upper 1% of families increased their share of income from 9.4% in 1980 to 13.0% in 1989. As a result, the income share of the upper 1% (13.0%) in 1989 was equal to that of the bottom 40% (13.0%).

Table 1.11 uses an additional source of information—data on adjusted gross income from personal tax returns—to examine the pattern of income growth since 1979. Tax return data have a bias, it should be noted, because they necessarily exclude the poorest families who do not file tax returns (perhaps as many as 20% of all families), the result of which is to portray greater income

The most spectacular income growth was among the upper 1%, whose incomes grew by 62.9% over the 1980s. The $216,185 average income gain of the richest 1% of families in the 1980s is nearly double the average income level of the next best-off 4% of families.

TABLE 1.10
Changes in Family Income Shares, 1977-1989

Income Group	Maximum Income**	Family Income Shares in:			Share Change	
		1977	1980	1989	1977-89	1980-89
All*		100.0%	100.0%	100.0%	0.0	0.0
Top Fifth:		46.5%	47.4%	51.8%	5.3	4.4
Top 1%		8.7	9.4	13.0	4.3	3.6
Next 4%	$330,107	11.8	12.0	12.9	1.1	0.9
Next 5%	149,103	10.1	10.3	10.3	0.2	0.0
Next 10%	112,847	15.8	15.7	15.5	−0.3	−0.2
Bottom Four Fifths:		53.8%	52.9%	49.0%	−4.8	−3.9
Fourth	$ 83,437	22.6	22.5	21.4	−1.2	−1.1
Middle	55,109	15.7	15.5	14.6	−1.1	−0.9
Second	37,228	10.6	10.4	9.3	−1.3	−1.1
Lowest	20,496	4.9	4.5	3.7	−1.2	−0.8

*Shares of income add to more than one hundred because those with negative incomes were excluded from lowest fifth.

**Highest income in the group. Income of family of four in 1993 dollars.

TABLE 1.11
Change in Family Income by Income Level Using Tax Return Data, 1979-1988
(1989 Dollars)

Income Percentile	Family Income		Change 1979-88	
	1979	1988	Dollars	Percent
20th	$ 7,811	$ 6,681	$−1,130	−14.5%
40th	15,825	14,593	−1,232	−7.8
60th	26,723	25,041	−1,682	−6.3
80th	42,105	42,192	87	0.2
90th	55,522	58,109	2,587	4.7
95th	70,040	76,511	6,471	9.2
99th	134,998	168,725	33,727	25.0

growth than actually occurred (assuming the lowest income families fared worst). Remarkably then, the data in Table 1.11 show that incomes fell among the bottom sixty percent of tax-filing families, with a 6.3% income decline for a family at the 60th percentile (whose income is above 60%, but lower than 40% of other families). There was essentially no income growth, a rise of just 0.2%, for a family at the 80th percentile. As we have seen with other data, the income growth of the best-off families—here the 25% gain of the family at the 99th percentile—far exceeded the income gains of the rest of the population. Again, the income gain of the richest families, $33,727 over nine years, exceeded the total incomes of more than 60% of the families.

Some economists express doubts about analyses of income because the incomes of families fluctuate from year to year in response to special circumstances—a layoff, a one-time sale of an asset and so on. As a result, a family's income reflects transient events and does not indicate its economic well-being over the long term. A preferable item to study, in this view, is the *consumption* levels of families because families typically gear their consumption to their expected incomes over the long term.

Table 1.12, which presents the trend in the distribution of consumption, permits a view of this final dimension of growing inequality. The distribution of consumption appears to be more equal than that of income (compare Table 1.12 to Table 1.6) in any one year. However, the trend towards equality in the 1960s and towards inequality over the 1970s and 1980s is apparent in both income and consumption measures of well-being. Moreover, using both income and consumption data one sees rapid growth among the best-off while the relative well-being of the bottom 60% was reduced over the 1980s.

Another way of characterizing the unequal income growth of recent years is to calculate the increase in total family income (omitting income growth simply due to a greater number of families) that went to the various income groups, as shown in **Table 1.13** and **Figure 1E**. The income gains of the top 1% of families were so great relative to the rest of the population that their income growth accounted for 71.5% of total income growth from 1977 to 1989. Over the more recent time period, 1980 to 1989, the top 1% received over half (53.2%) of all of the

The trend towards equality in the 1960s and towards inequality over the 1970s and 1980s is apparent in both income and consumption measures of well-being.

TABLE 1.12
Shares of Consumption, 1960-1988

Year	Share of Total Consumption*				
	Lowest Fifth	Second Fifth	Middle Fifth	Fourth Fifth	Top Fifth
1960-61	8.2%	14.0%	18.3%	23.3%	36.2%
1972-73	9.3	14.5	18.5	23.0	34.7
1980	8.4	14.0	18.5	23.2	35.9
1988	7.5	13.5	18.2	23.6	37.2
Change, 1980-88	−0.9	−0.5	−0.3	0.4	1.3

*Adjusted for family size.

TABLE 1.13
Shares of Aggregate Income Growth, 1977-1989

Income Group	Shares of Aggregate Income Growth*	
	1977-89	1980-89
Top Fifth:		
Top 1%	71.5%	53.2%
Next 4%	28.1	22.1
Next 5%	16.3	14.6
Next 10%	17.0	13.5
Bottom Four-Fifths:		
Fourth	6.7%	10.3%
Middle	−10.6	−1.3
Second	−12.8	−4.3
Lowest	−5.7	−2.0

*Shares sum to more than one hundred because negative incomes have been excluded from the lowest fifth.

income growth. This can be contrasted to the much smaller 9.4% of total income growth (equal to their 1980 share of income) that the top 1% of families would have enjoyed from 1980 to 1989 if income inequality had not grown. Other income groups within the top fifth of families also obtained sizeable shares of the total income growth.

Reflecting the fall in their average incomes, the bottom 60% of families received none of (a negative share of) the income growth generated from 1977 or 1980 to 1989.

Other dimensions of the recent growth in inequality are examined in later chapters. Chapter 2 focuses on the effect of changes in tax levels and the distribution of the tax burden on after-tax income inequality and growth. Chapter 3 examines and explains trends in wage levels and inequality. Chapter 5 looks at growing wealth inequality while Chapter 6 examines the growth in poverty. We now turn to some explanations of the growth in income inequality we just documented.

From 1980 to 1989, the top 1% received over half (53.2%) of all of the income growth.

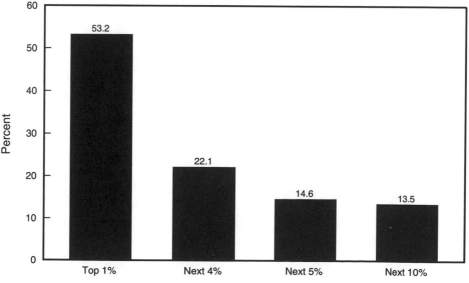

FIGURE 1E
Shares of Aggregate Income Growth Among Top Fifth, 1980-1989

TABLE 1.14
Source of Family Income for Each Fifth of Families, 1989

Income Group	Source of Family Income				
	Labor	Capital*	Gov't Transfer	Other	Total
All	70.7%	15.3%	7.0%	5.0%	100.0
Top Fifth:	72.7	22.9	2.3	4.1	100.0
Top 1%	51.4	46.4	0.6	1.6	100.0
Next 4%	70.9	22.2	2.0	4.9	100.0
Next 5%	79.6	13.3	2.5	4.6	100.0
Next 10%	81.0	9.9	4.0	5.1	100.0
Bottom Four Fifths:					
Fourth	80.4	8.3	5.8	5.5	100.0
Middle	76.4	7.4	9.9	6.4	100.0
Second	69.8	5.7	17.7	6.8	100.0
Lowest	50.9	3.6	39.1	6.4	100.0

Year	Shares of Market-Based Incomes**			
	Labor	Capital*	Total	
1977	86.1%	13.9%	100.0%	
1980	84.5	15.5	100.0	
1989	82.6	17.4	100.0	

*Includes rent, dividend, interest income and realized capital gains.
**Incomes from wages (wages and salaries, self-employment earnings) and capital, excluding transfer incomes (AFDC, social security, pensions, alimony, etc.)

Greater Capital Incomes, Lower Labor Incomes

In the 1980s, the fortunes of individual families depended on the *sources* of their incomes: labor income, capital income, or government assistance. One significant reason for the unequal growth in family incomes is that, in recent years, a greater share of our total income has been in the form of capital incomes (such as rent, dividends, interest payments, capital gains) and a smaller share has been earned as wages and salaries. Since most families receive little or no capital income, this shift has had a substantial impact on income distribution. There has also been a growing inequality in the distribution of both wages and capital income.

Table 1.14 presents data which show the sources of income for families in each income group. The top fifth gets a far larger percentage of its income from financial assets, i.e., capital, compared to the other 80% of the population. The top 1% receives nearly half its income from financial assets. Besides the top 1%, only the next richest 4% of families receives at least 20% of its income from capital incomes, with the bottom 90% of families relying on capital incomes for less than 10% of its income.

Those without access to capital income depend either on wages (the broad middle) or on government transfers (the bottom) as their primary source of income. As a result, the cutback in government cash assistance primarily affects the income prospects of the lowest 40% of the population, but particularly the bottom fifth (see Chapter 6). The income prospects of families in the 20th to 99th percentile, on the other hand, depend primarily on the level and distribution of wages and salaries.

Table 1.15 shows that income accruing to owners of capital has been growing far faster than labor income. In the 10 years between 1979 and 1989, those who owned income-producing property such as real estate, corporate stock, bonds, and other interest-bearing assets saw their incomes from these sources increase by 65.3%. The fast growth in capital income is primarily due to strong growth in interest payments of 78.9% which was caused by the high real (inflation-adjusted) interest rates of the 1980s.

Income accruing to owners of capital has been growing far faster than labor income primarily due to strong growth in interest payments of 78.9% which was caused by the high real (inflation-adjusted) interest rates of the 1980s.

TABLE 1.15
Real Income Growth by Type of Personal Income, 1979-1989

Income Type	Total Growth, 1979-89
1) Total Capital Income	65.3%
a) Rent	− 156.1
b) Dividends	41.9
c) Interest	78.9
2) Total Labor Income	22.8%
a) Wages & Salaries	22.9
b) Other Labor Income	21.8
3) Proprietor's Income*	13.9%
Total Market-Based Personal Income**	28.4%

*Business and farm owners' income.
**Total of listed income types.

TABLE 1.16
Shares of Market-Based Personal Income by Type, 1959-1991

Income Type*	1959	1967	1973	1979	1989	1991
1) Total Capital Income	10.7%	14.9%	13.7%	15.3%	19.7%	19.3%
a) Rent	3.9	3.2	1.7	0.5	− 0.2	0.3
b) Dividends	3.4	3.6	2.7	2.7	3.0	3.0
c) Interest	6.1	8.1	9.3	12.1	16.9	16.7
2) Total Labor Income	72.6%	73.6%	74.8%	74.8%	71.6%	71.9%
a) Wages & Salaries	69.8	70.0	69.9	68.1	65.2	65.1
b) Fringe Benefits	2.8	3.5	4.9	6.7	6.4	6.7
3) Proprietor's Income*	13.9%	11.6%	11.5%	9.9%	8.7%	8.8%
Total Personal Market − Based Income*	100.0%	100.0%	100.0%	100.0%	100.0%	100.0%

*See definitions in Table 1.15.

Dividend income grew by less, but by a still substantial 41.9%. The growth in capital, or property-based, income is actually somewhat understated in Table 1.15 since the data do not account for the appreciated value of assets in this period. As Chapter 5 shows over the 1979-1989 period there was a rapid gain in the value of financial assets (bonds, stocks) and real estate and businesses. This increased value of assets yields both realized capital gains when the assets are sold or unrealized capital gains that can generate income at a future time. The analysis in Table 1.15 ignores both realized and unrealized capital gains and therefore understates the increased returns to capital.

During the same period, total labor income, which includes the pay of executives and professionals as well as hourly workers, rose by 22.8%, just one third as much as capital income. (This rise in labor income primarily reflects a larger employed population working longer hours and is consistent with flat or declining real hourly wages.) Farmer and small business owners' incomes, called proprietor's income, rose 13.9%.

The post-1973 shift away from labor income and toward capital income is unique in the postwar period (**Table 1.16**) and is partly responsible for the recent surge in inequality. Since the rich are the owners of income-producing property, the fact that the assets they own have commanded an increasing share of total income automatically leads to income growth which is concentrated at the top. This is especially the case since, as we discuss below, there was also a growth in the inequality of the distribution of capital incomes among families.

Capital income was 19.7% of total income in 1989, nearly double the 10.7% share in 1959 (the earliest year for which there are data). Half of the increase in capital income's share of total income occurred since 1979, driven by high real interest rates. Labor income's share of total income declined from 1979 to 1989, reversing the pre-1979 trend in which labor income's share rose or held its own over the prior three decades. The share of wage and salary income in 1989 was the lowest in the postwar period. There was also a shrinkage of the share of fringe benefits in the 1980s, the first shrinkage over the last four decades.

Since the rich are the owners of income-producing property, the fact that the assets they own have commanded an increasing share of total income automatically leads to income growth which is concentrated at the top.

57

TABLE 1.17
Shares of Income by Type, by Sector, 1959-1989

Income Type	1959	1967	1973	1979	1989
National Income, All Sectors					
Labor	68.6%	69.9%	72.6%	73.4%	73.1%
Capital	18.6	19.2	16.0	16.3	16.5
Prop. Profit	12.5	10.4	10.4	8.9	8.1
Total	100.0	100.0	100.0	100.0	100.0
(a) Corporate and Business Sector					
Labor	44.3%	45.8%	48.2%	50.5%	49.4%
Capital	18.6	19.2	16.0	16.3	16.5
Total	63.0	64.9	64.3	66.8	65.9
(b) Proprietor's Sector					
Labor	9.0%	6.5%	5.2%	4.7%	4.4%
Capital	0.3	0.5	1.0	1.4	2.3
Prop. Profit	12.5	10.4	10.4	8.9	8.1
Total	21.9	17.4	16.6	15.0	14.8
(c) Government/Nonprofit Sector					
Labor	15.2%	17.6%	19.2%	18.2%	19.2%
Capital	0.0	0.0	0.0	0.0	0.0
Total	15.2	17.6	19.2	18.2	19.2

Addendum:

Shares of Corporate Sector Income*

	1959	1967	1973	1979	1989
Labor	78.5%	78.0%	82.4%	83.2%	82.1%
Capital	21.5	22.0	17.6	16.8	18.0
Total	100.0	100.0	100.0	100.0	100.0

*Does not include sole proprietorships, partnerships and other private noncorporate businesses. The corporate sector, which includes both financial and nonfinancial corporations, accounted for 58% of national income and 71.6% of private sector income in 1989.

It is difficult to interpret changes in proprietor's income because it is a mixture of both labor and capital income. That is, the income that an owner of a business (or farmer) receives results from his or her work effort (labor income) and his or her ownership (capital income) of the business or farm. To the extent that the shrinkage of proprietor's income results from a shift of people out of the proprietary sector (i.e., leaving farming) and into wage and salary employment there will be a concomitant increase in labor's share of income (i.e., as farm income is replaced by wage income). This shift out of proprietor's income thus helps to explain a rising labor share in some time periods. It is interesting to note, therefore, that labor's share of income fell from 1979 to 1989 despite an erosion of proprietor's income from 9.9% to 8.7% of total income.

The data in the bottom panel of Table 1.14 confirm a shift towards capital income among families. The share of capital income in all market-based income (i.e., excluding government and other transfers of income) rose from 13.9% in 1977 to 17.4% in 1989.

From the point of view of national income (incomes generated by the corporate, proprietor and government sectors) there does not appear to be a significant shift away from labor income towards capital income (**Table 1.17**). For instance, labor's share of national income fell only slightly from 73.4% in 1979 to 73.1% in 1989. A closer look at the underlying data, however, suggests a significant shift away from labor income. First, note that labor's share of national income had steadily risen from 1959 to 1979. One reason for the expanding share of labor income was the steady expansion of the government/nonprofit sector. When the government/nonprofit sector grows, there is a tendency for labor's share of income to grow because this sector generates *only* labor income and no capital income. For example, the growth of the government/nonprofit sector from 18.2% to 19.2% of national income between 1979 and 1989 necessarily added 1% to labor's share of national income (other things remaining equal).

Labor's share of national income also grows as the proprietary sector (farm and non-farm unincorporated businesses) shrinks, as it did from 1959 to 1979, because labor's share of income in that sector is relatively low (less than one-third of it in 1979). When resources shift from a sector with a low labor share of income, such as the propri-

The failure of labor's share to grow stems primarily from the unique decline in labor's share of the corporate and business sector between 1979 and 1989, reversing the tendency towards more labor income from the 1960s to the 1970s.

etor's sector, to sectors with a higher labor share (all of the other sectors) the share of labor income in the economy necessarily rises. Thus, the changing composition of income across organizational sectors (expanding government, shrinking proprietors) provides momentum for an increase in labor's share of national income.

Why then did labor's share of national income not continue to rise in the 1979-1989 period as it had earlier? Given the continued, albeit slow, expansion of the government/nonprofit sector one would have expected a continued expansion of labor's share of national income. The failure of labor's share to grow stems primarily from the unique decline in labor's share of the corporate and business sector between 1979 and 1989, reversing the tendency towards more labor income from the 1960s to the 1970s. This is most clearly seen in the bottom panel of Table 1.17 which shows the division of incomes in the corporate sector—labor's share fell from 83.2% in 1979 to 82.1% in 1989. These data suggest that there has been a shift away from labor income in the private sector (both corporate and proprietor) that does not show up in national income because of the growth of the labor-intensive government/nonprofit sector.

The data in Table 1.17 confirm the expansion of capital income's share of total income seen in other tables. For instance, there was an increase in the capital income share of national income between 1973 and 1979 and an even larger growth between 1979 and 1989.

Nevertheless, there was a larger shift away from labor towards capital income in our analysis of personal income in Tables 1.15 and 1.16. One reason is that capital income is defined differently in these tables. At the "personal level," capital income includes interest, dividends and rent while at the "national income" level capital income includes rents, profits, interest and dividends. The difference is that corporate generated capital income received by persons takes the form of dividends and interest paid by firms. Individuals also benefit from higher corporate retained profits (the after-tax profits not paid out in dividends), which are linked to realized, and unrealized, capital gains. The personal income data used in Table 1.15 and 1.16, however, do not include any capital gains. Capital income in "national income" is primarily based on corporate profits and interest income.

There was an increase in the capital income share of national income between 1973 and 1979 and an even larger growth between 1979 and 1989.

60

One possible explanation for a faster rise in capital income among persons than in national income is that increased corporate indebtedness has forced a change in the *composition*, or form, of capital income—more interest income and less capital gains based on corporate retained earnings—but not the total *amount* of capital income. The increased debt on corporate balance sheets over the 1980s, for instance, meant that corporations paid out more in interest to persons. These greater interest payments, however, reduce corporate profits and thus retained earnings (roughly defined as profits after dividend payments), slowing the appreciation of net worth in the corporate sector.

To the extent that greater interest payments to persons were the result of more corporate debt one could argue that households were just receiving their capital income in a different form—interest payments—rather than capital gains (from higher stock prices) based on higher retained corporate profits (if companies had not paid out so much interest they would have "plowed back" that much more in profits). In this view, since capital gains are not measured as part of personal income (in the relevant government data) what is actually a change in the form of capital income (more interest, less capital gains) appears as an expansion of capital income.

This dynamic, however, can provide only a partial explanation for the rising share of capital income in personal income. One reason is that interest income has risen not only because of increased corporate (and government) leverage, but also because interest rates in the 1980s, were historically high in real (inflation-adjusted) terms. Moreover, capital gains expanded over the 1980s, so it seems that households managed to receive both more interest (partially at the expense of retained earnings) and more capital gains. The increase in realized capital gains is discussed below. There was also an increase in unrealized capital gains, reflected in the rapid growth of real financial assets and wealth, which we discuss in Chapter 5. Thus, owners of capital in the 1980s were able to expand both their current flow of capital income (i.e., receive more dividends and interest income) and to augment their wealth holdings (i.e., their stocks and other assets appreciated in value).

Owners of capital in the 1980s were able to expand both their current flow of capital income (i.e., receive more dividends and interest income) and to augment their wealth holdings (i.e., their stocks and other assets appreciated in value).

TABLE 1.18
Distribution of Labor and Capital Incomes, 1977-1989

Income Group	Shares of Capital Income			Shares of Labor Income		
	1977	1980	1989	1977	1980	1989
All	100.0%	100.0%	100.0%	100.0%	100.0%	100.0%
Top Fifth:	72.6%	74.7%	77.5%	46.0%	46.4	50.3%
Top 1%	33.1	34.9	39.7	5.8	5.9	9.2
Next 4%	20.0	19.7	18.8	11.5	11.6	12.6
Next 5%	9.2	9.7	8.9	11.1	11.1	11.2
Next 10%	10.3	10.5	10.1	17.6	17.8	17.2
Bottom Four-Fifths:						
Fourth	12.3%	12.3%	11.6%	24.8%	25.1%	23.7%
Middle	7.9	6.9	7.1	16.8	16.6	15.3
Second	5.1	4.2	3.5	10.0	9.8	8.9
Lowest	1.8	1.5	0.9	2.8	2.6	2.6

FIGURE 1F
Distribution of Labor and Capital Incomes, Top 20%, 1980-1989

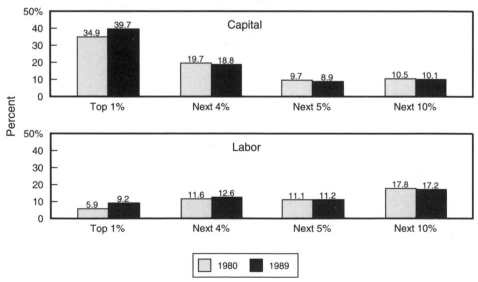

There was not only an increase in the share of total income accruing to owners of capital in the 1980s, there was also a growing inequality of the receipt of capital incomes (**Table 1.18** and **Figure 1F**). Between 1980 and 1989, for instance, the top 1% of families increased their share of capital income from 34.9% to 39.7%. All of the other income groups (except the middle fifth) had a lesser share of capital income in 1989 than in 1980, including a decline in the shares of the remaining groups within the top fifth.

There has also been a growing inequality of labor incomes. Between 1980 and 1989, for instance, the top 10% of families expanded their shares of labor income while the bottom 90% saw their share of labor income decline (Table 1.18). Because labor income roughly comprises a 71% share of total income (Table 1.14), any increased inequality of labor incomes will have a major impact on overall income inequality. In Chapter 3 we analyze the growth of wage inequality.

When we examine the growth of incomes of the top-fifth between 1980 and 1989 by type of income (**Table 1.19**), it is evident that the increased inequality of both labor and capital income and the shift towards greater capital income has benefitted upper-income groups. The top 1% had a spectacular 62.9% growth in their incomes between 1980 and 1989 because of fast growth (47.6%) in their capital income and an even faster growth (78.5%) in their labor incomes. As **Table 1.20** shows, the growth in capital income explains 38.8% of the total growth of the top 1%'s income from 1980 to 1989. The growth in realized capital gains alone account for 15.2% of the total income growth among the top 1%, providing $32,874 more in income in 1989 than in 1980—an amount greater than the total income growth among the next richest 4% from 1980 to 1989 an increase of $22,485. The fast growth of labor income fueled 58.6% of the total income growth of the top 1%. Any explanation of the rising income level and share of the top 1% must then account for the growth in both capital and labor incomes.

The remaining segments of the top fifth had much more modest income gains. For the "next 4%" and "next 5%"

> *There was not only an increase in the share of total income accruing to owners of capital in the 1980s, there was also a growing inequality of the receipt of capital incomes.*

[handwritten note: effects of stock market crash '87 lost over ten year period]

TABLE 1.19
Sources of Income Growth of Top Fifth, 1980-1989

Income Group	Wages and Salaries	Self-Employ-ment	All Labor	Rent, Dividends & Interest	Realized Capital Gains	All Capital	Total
Top 1%							
1980	$121,294	$ 39,859	$161,153	$ 84,528	$ 91,400	$175,928	$343,601
1989	209,363	78,371	287,735	134,911	124,274	259,745	559,795
Change							
Dollar	$ 88,069	$ 38,513	$126,582	$ 50,383	$ 32,874	$ 83,817	$216,185
Percent	72.6%	96.6%	78.5%	59.6%	36.0%	47.6%	62.9%
Next 4%							
1980	$ 68,360	$ 10,736	$ 79,205	$ 17,419	$ 7,340	$ 24,759	$109,551
1989	81,334	12,279	93,614	21,654	7,658	29,312	132,036
Change							
Dollar	$ 12,974	$ 1,543	$ 14,408	$ 4,235	$ 318	$ 4,553	$ 22,485
Percent	19.0%	14.4%	18.2%	24.3%	4.3%	18.4%	20.5%
Next 5%							
1980	$ 57,514	$ 4,097	$ 61,611	$ 7,588	$ 2,276	$ 9,864	$ 75,876
1989	65,432	4,386	69,818	9,279	2,368	11,666	87,711
Change							
Dollar	$ 7,918	$ 288	$ 8,207	$ 1,710	$ 92	$ 1,802	$ 11,835
Percent	13.8%	7.0%	13.3%	22.5%	4.0%	18.3%	15.6%
Next 10%							
1980	$ 49,068	$ 2,055	$ 51,183	$ 4,532	$ 1,088	$ 5,559	$ 60,428
1989	51,007	2,372	53,379	5,536	989	6,524	65,900
Change							
Dollar	$ 1,939	$ 318	$ 2,196	$ 1,004	$ −99	$ 965	$ 5,472
Percent	4.0%	15.5%	4.3%	22.1%	−9.1%	17.4%	−9.1%

(the remainder of the upper 10% of families) income growth was based on both increased capital incomes and labor incomes, but the importance of higher labor incomes was more important to these groups than for the top 1% (Table 1.20).

The Shrinking Middle Class?

Another dimension of income growth is the proportion of the population that has low, middle and high incomes. There are two factors which determine the distribution of the population at various income levels—the rate of growth of average income and changes in income equality. As average, or median, income grows there will be a greater proportion of the population at higher-income levels. However, if inequality grows such that the low-income population receives an historically low proportion of the income growth and the high-income population obtains an usually large proportion of the income growth then a rise in average income may not translate into a general upward movement of the population to higher-income levels. That is, it is possible for incomes to grow on average and have segments of the population with declining incomes.

Another dimension of income growth is the proportion of the population that has low, middle and high incomes.

TABLE 1.20
Shares of Income Growth by Type of Income for Top Fifth, 1980-1989

			Percent of Income Growth Due to:				
Income Group	Wages and Salaries	Self-Employ-ment	All Labor	Rent, Dividends & Interest	Realized Capital Gains	All Capital	Total*
Top 1%	40.7%	17.8%	58.6%	23.3%	15.2%	38.8%	100.0%
Next 4%	57.7	6.9	64.1	18.8	1.4	20.3	100.0
Next 5%	66.9	2.4	69.3	14.4	0.8	15.2	100.0
Next 10%	35.4	5.8	40.1	18.3	−1.8	17.6	100.0

*Includes transfer and other incomes not shown.

65

TABLE 1.21
Distributions of Persons, Households, and
Families by Income Level, 1969-1980

Income Level	Percent of Persons at Relative Income Levels			Percentage Point Change	
	1969	1979	1989	1969-79	1979-89
Families (Income)*					
Under $15,000	17.7%	16.3%	17.0%	−1.4	0.7
$15,000 to 50,000	63.9	57.3	51.4	−6.6	−5.9
Over $50,000	18.6	26.2	31.6	7.6	5.4
Households (Income)*					
Under $15,000	25.8%	25.0%	24.1%	−0.8	−0.9
$15,000 to 50,000	58.2	53.8	50.2	−4.4	−3.6
Over $50,000	16.1	21.1	25.7	5.0	4.6
Persons (Income Relative to Median)**					
Less than 50%	17.9%	20.0%	22.1%	2.1	2.1
From 50% to 200%	71.1	68.1	63.3	−3.0	−4.8
More than 200%	10.9	11.9	14.7	1.0	2.8

*1990 Dollars.
**Each person assigned his or her family's per capita (size-adjusted) income.

Table 1.21 shows the proportion of families, households and persons with low, middle and high incomes in 1969, 1979 and 1989. For households and families, the definition of middle income has been arbitrarily set as a range from $15,000 to 50,000. Among persons, a middle income is one which is from 50% to 200% of median family (size-adjusted) income.

Over the 1969-1989 period, there was a decline in the proportion of families with middle incomes, as more families attained incomes beyond $50,000. The shift upward was smaller over the 1979-1989 period than in the 1969-1979 period (5.4% versus 7.6%). The later period also saw a shifting of 0.7% of families out of middle incomes and into the low-income category.

When one looks at households—which includes single persons in addition to families—there does not appear to be any shift downward in the 1979-1989 period, although the upward shift is still somewhat smaller in the more recent than the earlier period.

The analysis of persons examines the incomes of people—single and in families—according to the per capita incomes in their family (size-adjusted), with a single person given an individual income. In this analysis, there has been a shift out of middle incomes since 1969, but the shift is into the lower- as well as into the higher-income group. However, there is a stronger shift upward in the most recent, 1979-1989, period than in the earlier, 1969-1979, period (2.8% versus 1.0%).

Table 1.22 repeats the analysis of persons from Table 1.21, but categorizes families and persons by the education level of their household head and is limited to people in their prime earnings years (25 to 64 years old). Over the 1969-1989 period, there has been a shrinkage in the proportion of families headed by a high school graduate (or a high school dropout) who had either a middle-class or high income, especially since 1979. Even among the "some college" category there has been a general shift to a smaller middle-income population and a greater low-income population, with a stronger shift downward from 1969 to 1979 (and a slight uptick of high-income families since 1979). The families with college graduates as their household head were shifting downward in income from 1969 to

In this analysis, there has been a shift out of middle incomes since 1969, but the shift is into the lower- as well as into the higher-income group.

more rich, but also more poor (less middle ground)

67

TABLE 1.22
Distribution of Prime Age Adults
by Relative Income Level, 1969-1984

Income Relative to Median*	Percent of Persons at Relative Income Levels			Percentage Point Change	
	1969	1979	1989	1969-79	1979-89
Less than High School					
Less than 50%	21.7%	29.0%	38.4%	7.3	9.4
From 50 to 200%	71.5	65.4	57.0	−6.1	−8.4
More than 200%	6.8	5.6	4.5	−1.2	−1.1
High School Graduate					
Less than 50%	7.5%	11.0%	15.7%	3.5	4.7
From 50 to 200%	77.8	75.6	71.4	−2.2	−4.2
More than 200%	14.6	13.4	12.9	−1.2	−0.5
Some College					
Less than 50%	5.9%	8.6%	10.2%	2.7	1.6
From 50 to 200%	71.1	71.7	69.5	0.6	−2.2
More than 200%	23.0	19.7	20.2	−3.3	0.5
College Graduate					
Less than 50%	3.8%	5.1%	4.6%	1.3	−0.5
From 50 to 200%	58.8	61.0	55.0	2.2	−6.0
More than 200%	37.4	33.9	40.4	−3.5	6.5

*Persons from 25 to 64 years old, based on a person's per capita (size-adjusted) family income.

1979, but upwards after 1979. These changes in the income levels of families and persons by the educational attainment of the household head reflects the trends in wages for the various educational groups, with college graduates faring well in the 1980s, but poorly in the 1970s (due to a surplus of them) and falling wages among the noncollege-educated workforce between 1979 and 1989 (see Chapter 3 for an analysis of these trends).

Increased Work by Wives Cushions Income Fall

Family earnings growth has not only been slow and unequal, it has also increasingly come from greater work effort—from a rise in the number of earners per family and in the average weeks and weekly hours worked per earner. The primary source of the increased work effort has been women, including many with children. As will be detailed in Chapter 3, this increased work effort has occurred simultaneously with a fall in real wages for men and for many women in the 1980s. The result has been increases in annual earnings primarily through more work rather than through higher hourly wages.

This is troublesome for several reasons. This type of earnings growth is "self-limiting," meaning it can only go on until all adult (or even teen) family members are full-time, full-year workers. The slowdown in the growth in women's labor force participation in recent years may even, in fact, signal the near exhaustion of this type of income growth (see Chapter 4). Moreover, there are significant costs and problems associated with this type of growth, one of the most significant being the lack of afford- ✗ able, adequate child care (see Chapter 8).

The problem is not that more women or mothers are working, but that they are doing so because it is the only way to maintain family income in the face of lower real wages. It is a sign of poor performance of the economy when increased work is elicited through falling real wages. In addition, it is clearly second-best for families to obtain higher incomes by working more hours and having more members in the paid labor force than by earning higher family wages.

Family earnings growth has not only been slow and unequal, it has also increasingly come from greater work effort—from a rise in the number of earners per family and in the average weeks and weekly hours worked per earner.

69

TABLE 1.23
Changes in Incomes of Married-Couple Families
with Children by Source, 1979-1989
(1989 Dollars)

Year	Lowest Fifth	Second Fifth	Middle Fifth	Fourth Fifth	Top Fifth	Average
Family Income						
1979	$16,071	$29,594	$38,903	$49,826	$77,692	$42,417
1989	15,448	29,639	40,626	54,144	89,471	45,866
Percent						
Change	−3.9	0.2	4.4	8.7	15.2	8.1
Dollar Change by Source						
Total	$−623	$45	$ 1,723	$ 4,318	$11,779	$ 3,449
Wives'						
Earnings	851	2,070	3,268	4,218	6,987	3,450
Husbands'						
Earnings	−1,438	−1,952	−1,374	284	5,563	124
Other Income	−36	−73	−171	−184	−771	−125

It is primarily married-couple families (79.2% of all families in 1989, Table 1.5) who are able to increase income through greater work effort because there are two potential adult workers. Single-parent families and individuals, however, can only increase work effort by having the adult work more weekly hours and/or more weeks in a year. It is for this reason that we initially focus on the greater work hours of married couples.

Table 1.23 shows the income growth in total and by type of income among married-couple families with children. Among the bottom two-fifths there was either stagnant or falling incomes, while the middle fifth achieved modest growth (4.4% over ten years or 0.43% annually). In contrast, the best-off married couples with children had a far faster (15.2%) income growth.

The data in Table 1.23 also show that among the bottom 60% there was a fall-off in the earnings of husbands and other incomes (capital incomes and transfers) while the earnings of wives grew in each income fifth. It is apparent that the rapid income growth among the top fifth was the result of a growth in *both* husbands' and wives' earnings and that the stagnant or falling incomes in the bottom two-fifths resulted from the fact that the higher earnings of wives could at best offset (as in the second fifth) the fall in husbands' earnings. On average (see the last column), all of the growth in the incomes of married-couple families with children can be attributed to the higher earnings of the wives in these families.

Table 1.24 presents the growth in annual hours worked by husbands and wives and shows that it is more work, rather than higher hourly wages, that has been fueling income growth. The data on the growth in the hours of "All husbands" and "All Wives" reflect changes in the hours of "Employed Husbands" and "Employed Wives" as well as changes in the proportion of husbands and wives employed in the year. As the data show, the drop in husbands' annual earnings from 1979 to 1989 (Table 1.23) occurred *despite* the fact that husbands were working more, not less, hours (except for a slight drop in the bottom fifth). In 1989, the average husband (including some not employed) in the second- to top- fifths worked at least full-time and year-round (40 hours for 52 weeks is 2080 hours).

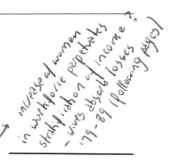

in increase of women in workforce perpetrates
stratification of income ?
- wives absorb losses
'79-89 (following pages)

On average all of the growth in the incomes of married-couple families with children can be attributed to the higher earnings of the wives in these families.

TABLE 1.24
Husbands' and Wives' Hours of Work, 1979-1989

Family Member*	Lowest Fifth	Second Fifth	Middle Fifth	Fourth Fifth	Top Fifth	Average
Annual Hours, All Husbands*						
1979	1,693	2,115	2,189	2,249	2,349	2,122
1989	1,682	2,138	2,211	2,274	2,411	2,143
Percent Change	−0.6%	1.1%	1.0%	1.1%	2.6%	1.0%
Absolute Change	−11	23	22	25	62	21
Annual Hours, Employed Husbands						
1979	1,996	2,180	2,224	2,273	2,372	2,211
1989	1,958	2,207	2,239	2,299	2,428	2,234
Percent Change	−1.9%	1.2%	0.7%	1.1%	2.4%	1.0%
Absolute Change	−38	27	15	26	56	23
Annual Hours, All Wives						
1979	450	708	852	1,078	1,068	831
1989	651	996	1,193	1,311	1,341	1,099
Percent Change	44.7%	40.7%	40.0%	21.6%	25.6%	32.3%
Absolute Change	201	288	431	233	273	268
Annual Hours, Employed Wives						
1979	1,001	1,226	1,314	1,478	1,567	1,347
1989	1,181	1,414	1,554	1,624	1,694	1,516
Percent Change	18%	15%	18%	10%	8%	13%
Absolute Change	180	188	240	146	127	169

*In married-couple families with children.

The reason that husbands' annual earnings fell in the bottom 60% of these families is the erosion of their hourly wages, which fell 5.5% for husbands in the middle fifth and 11.8% for husbands in the lowest fifth (**Table 1.25**). There was a growth in hourly wages only for husbands in the best-off fifth of families, a rise of 7.8% from 1979 to 1989. The reduction in the hourly wages of husbands, the general trend in the 1979-1989 period, led to their having lower annual earnings *despite* an increase in annual work hours.

As we have discussed, it was the greater earnings of the wives in these families which either moderated or counterbalanced the impact of the falling wages of husbands. The average wife in a married-couple family with children was employed 32.3% more hours in 1989 than in 1979, a growth of 268 hours annually or the equivalent of nearly

The reduction in the hourly wages of husbands, the general trend in the 1979-1989 period, led to their having lower annual earnings despite an increase in work hours.

TABLE 1.25
Change in Hourly Wages of Husbands and Wives, 1979-1989
(1991 Dollars)

Family Member*	Lowest Fifth	Second Fifth	Middle Fifth	Fourth Fifth	Top Fifth	Average
Husbands' Hourly Wage						
1979	$6.84	$10.95	$13.66	$15.98	$22.24	$14.38
1989	6.03	9.91	12.91	15.93	23.98	14.30
Percent Change	−11.8%	−9.5%	−5.5%	−0.3%	7.8%	−0.6%
Dollar Change	$−0.81	$−1.03	$−0.76	$−0.05	$1.74	$−0.08
Wives' Hourly Wage						
1979	$4.56	$6.01	$7.25	$8.41	$10.83	$7.97
1989	4.46	6.35	7.92	10.13	13.84	9.17
Percent Change	−2.2%	5.7%	9.2%	20.5%	27.8%	15.0%
Absolute Change	$−0.10	$0.34	$0.67	$1.72	$3.01	$1.20

*In married-couple families with children.

Wife's wages catching up to husband's wages

73

FIGURE 1G
Growth in Annual Hours Worked by All Wives, 1979-1989

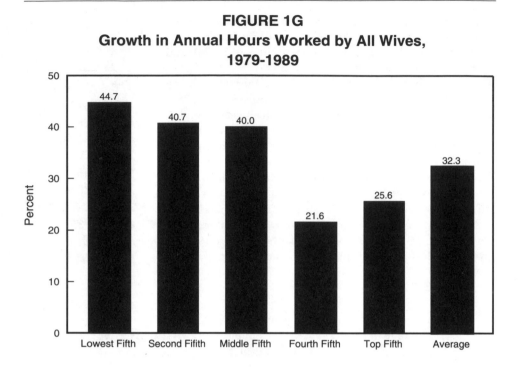

seven weeks of full-time work (see **Figure 1G**). There was at least a 40% growth in work hours among women in the bottom 60% of these families, nearly double the increase among the wives in the better-off families. Thus, the modest or falling incomes among families in the bottom three-fifths occurred despite significantly more work effort by these families and, in particular, by the wives in these families. These greater working hours were the result both of a higher proportion of wives being employed and of employed wives working more hours (up from 15% to 18% in the bottom three-fifths). In fact, 43% of the 268 hours growth in the average wives' work year was the result of employed wives increasing their hours by 169.

It is useful to note the degree to which an increase in the hours of wives is necessary to offset the fall in the wages of husbands given that the men earn significantly higher hourly wages. For example, the $0.76 drop in the hourly wage of husbands in the middle fifth from 1979 to 1989 (working 2,221 annual hours) created an annual loss of $1,688. Replacing this income would require an average wife in the middle fifth (earning $7.92 hourly) to work 213 additional hours annually, or more than five extra full-time weeks.

Table 1.26 brings together the information from the prior tables to identify the role of increased earnings of wives' and hours on family income growth. The essential point is that without the increase in the earnings of wives there would have been lower incomes in each of the lowest three-fifths in 1989 than in 1979 and a trivial $100 income growth for the fourth-fifth (see **Figure 1H**). In other words, only the top fifth did not depend on increased earnings from wives to obtain income growth or stem an income decline. The entire 8.1% growth in the average income of married-couple families with children from 1979 to 1989 can be attributed to the increased earnings of wives (see the 0.0% growth in the last column of the second panel of numbers).

Most of the contribution to the increased earnings of wives came from greater hours of work. If the average wife in the bottom three-fifths had not worked more hours there would have been a fall in income between 1979 and 1989 (or a greater fall for the lowest fifth).

The average wife in a married-couple family with children was employed 32.3% more hours in 1989 than in 1979, a growth of 268 hours annually or the equivalent of nearly seven weeks of full-time work.

TABLE 1.26
Role of Higher Wives' Earnings and Hours on Family Income Growth, 1979-1989*

	Lowest Fifth	Second Fifth	Middle Fifth	Fourth Fifth	Top Fifth	Average
Change in Family Income						
Percent	−3.9%	0.2%	4.4%	8.7%	15.2%	8.1%
Dollar	$−623	$45	$1,723	$4,318	$11,779	$3,449
Change in Family Income Without Higher Wives' Earnings						
Percent	−9.2%	−6.8%	−4.0%	0.2%	6.2%	0.0%
Dollar	$−1,474	$−2,025	$−1,545	$100	$4,812	$−1
Change in Family Income Without Higher Wives' Hours						
Percent	−9.5%	−6.0%	−2.5%	3.9%	10.3%	2.3%
Dollar	$−1,520	$−1,784	$−978	$1,958	$8,001	$992
Effect on Family Income of Higher:						
(a) Wives' Earnings						
Percent	5.3%	7.0%	8.4%	8.5%	9.0%	8.1%
Dollar	$851	$2,070	$3,268	$4,218	$6,967	$3,450
(b) Wives' Hours						
Percent	5.6%	6.2%	6.9%	4.7%	4.9%	5.8%
Dollar	$897	$1,829	$2,701	$2,360	$3,778	$2,457

*Married Couples with Children.

Has the growing earnings of wives contributed to the growth of income inequality? The notion that the growth of "two-earner" families has contributed to growing inequality is intuitively plausible if one thinks that there has been a growth of high-wage employed women marrying high-wage men, a trend that would increase the monetary gap between high- and middle- or low-income families. It is true, in fact, that the wives in higher income families do earn more than those in other families and that their hourly wages have grown the quickest (Table 1.25). However, the fastest growth in work hours has been among the wives in the bottom three-fifths (Table 1.24) and the effect of wives' earnings on family income growth has been fairly even, with a somewhat lower effect on the lowest two-fifths (Table 1.26). The data discussed so far, however, only indirectly relate to whether the pattern of growth of wives' earnings led to greater inequality and do not address whether inequality would be higher or lower without any earnings from wives.

If the average wife in the bottom three-fifths had not worked more hours there would have been a fall in income between 1979 and 1989.

FIGURE 1H
Growth in Family Income, by Wives' Higher Earnings, 1979-1989

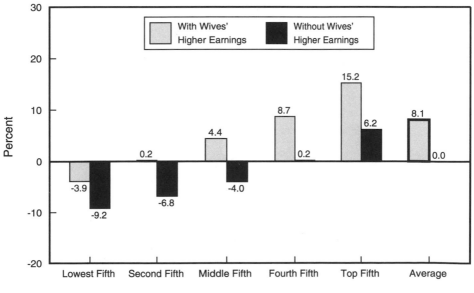

TABLE 1.27
Effect of Wives' Earnings on Income Shares
Among Married Couples with Children, 1979-1989

	Shares of Income					
	Lowest Fifth	Second Fifth	Middle Fifth	Fourth Fifth	Top Fifth	Total
Family Income, 1979						
Actual	7.6%	14.0%	18.3%	23.5%	36.6%	100.0%
Without Wives' Earnings	6.9	13.3	18.0	23.4	38.5	100.0
Effect of Wives' Earnings	0.7	0.7	0.3	0.1	−1.9	0.0
Family Income, 1989						
Actual	6.7%	12.9%	17.7%	23.6%	39.0%	100.0%
Without Wives' Earnings	5.8	12.0	17.0	23.2	41.8	100.0
Effect of Wives' Earnings	0.9	0.9	0.7	0.4	−2.8	0.0
Change in Income Shares, 1979-89						
Actual	−0.9	−1.1%	−0.6%	0.1%	2.4%	0.0%
Without Wives' Earnings	−1.1	−1.3	−1.0	−0.2	3.3	0.0
Effect of Wives' Earnings	0.2	0.2	0.4	0.3	−0.9	0.0

The data in **Table 1.27** do allow a direct examination of the effect of wives' earnings on income inequality in particular years (1979 and 1989) and on the growth of inequality over that time period. In 1979, the presence of wives' earnings led to a more equal distribution of income. For instance, without wives' earnings the lowest fifth would have had a 6.9% share of total income, but actually had a 7.6% share of income. The presence of employed wives positively increased the income shares of the bottom four-fifths in 1979 and decreased the share (although not the level) of income of the top fifth by 1.9 percentage points (because increased wives' earnings did not raise the incomes in the top fifth proportionately as much as in the bottom four-fifths). By 1989, the presence of wives' earnings had a larger effect on raising the income shares of the lowest 80% of these families and on lessening the income share of the top fifth.

Thus, the earnings of wives disproportionately augmented the incomes of the broad middle class and the lowest income families in 1979 and even more so by 1989. As a result, the increased earnings of wives had a positive effect on the relative income growth of the bottom 80% of families and a negative effect on the income share of the top fifth. That is, the pattern of growth of wives' earnings from 1979 to 1989 created a tendency for incomes of the bottom 80% to grow faster than the incomes of the top fifth.

Although egalitarian in nature, the effect of increased incomes from the earnings of wives was not sufficient to forestall the overall growth of inequality and the loss of income shares by the lowest three-fifths. Nevertheless, instead of a 1.0 percentage point drop in income share for the middle-fifth between 1979 and 1989, more wives' earnings meant a lesser 0.6% drop in income share. Greater wives' earnings, however, did enable the fourth-fifth to avoid a 0.2 percentage point loss in income share. The pattern of earnings growth among wives, therefore, ameliorated rather than exacerbated the growth in inequality among married-couple families with children from 1979 to 1989, at least as reflected by the lesser loss of shares of income of the bottom 80%.

The growth in work hours in the 1979-1989 period took place on average *in all families* and not just in married-couple families with children to whom all of the data previ-

marginal gain for upper income family is less

Although egalitarian in nature, the effect of increased incomes from the earnings of wives was not sufficient to forestall the overall growth of inequality and the loss of income shares by the lowest three-fifths.

TABLE 1.28
Changes in Hours Worked in All Families
and in Married-Couple Families, 1979-1989

Family Type	Annual Hours of Work*					
	Lowest Fifth	Second Fifth	Middle Fifth	Fourth Fifth	Top Fifth	Total
All Families						
1979	820	1,800	2,480	3,010	3,440	2,280
1989	850	1,840	2,550	3,020	3,510	2,330
Percentage Change	4.6%	2.4%	2.6%	0.5%	2.0%	2.3%
Married Couples with Children						
1979	2,240	2,950	3,270	3,600	3,990	3,250
1989	2,350	3,250	3,580	3,860	4,090	3,460
Percentage Change	4.6%	10.0%	9.6%	7.2%	2.5%	6.6%
Nonelderly Childless Married Couples						
1979	1,980	3,110	3,590	3,910	4,140	3,330
1989	2,150	3,390	3,890	4,270	4,410	3,610
Change	8.7%	8.9%	8.3%	9.3%	6.6%	8.5%
Nonelderly Individuals						
1979	590	1,350	1,820	2,030	2,160	1,590
1989	640	1,540	1,940	2,090	2,240	1,690
Change	7.0%	14.2%	6.5%	2.8%	4.0%	6.2%

*Rounded to nearest ten, with percent changes calculated from actual numbers.

ously presented applied. As **Table 1.28** shows, there were greater hours of work in 1989 than in 1979 among families in each income fifth and 2.3% greater hours overall. The largest growth in hours was among non-elderly married-couple families, especially those without children. This makes sense since families with two adults present (compared to single-parent families, for instance) have more potential labor-time to offer employers. Regardless, there was also a significant growth in hours by non-elderly single people from 1979 to 1989.

Because greater earnings from wives can contribute to greater income growth for married-couple families but not for single-parent families or individuals, it is possible that greater wives' earnings may have contributed to growing inequality among all families (the earlier discussion was of inequality among married couples with children). For instance, if increased wives' earnings raised the incomes of married couples, as it did, and increased work effort did not raise the incomes of single-parent families or of individuals in the same degree, then overall income inequality would grow.

Table 1.29 uses two measures of income inequality (the Gini coefficient and the squared coefficient of variation—higher numbers indicate more inequality) to examine the effect of wives' earnings on inequality among married-couple families and all families in particular years (1968, 1978, 1988) and on the growth of inequality over the 1968-1988 period. These data confirm our earlier analysis that wives' earnings do lead to lesser income inequality in any particular year and that the effect of greater wives' earnings has been to ameliorate the growth of inequality among married couples. For instance, income inequality in 1968 was, according to the two measures, either 17.4% or 6.2% less than if there had been no wives' earnings. Greater wives' earnings had a strong egalitarian impact on married couples' incomes from 1968 to 1978 (reducing inequality by 20.0% in 1978 rather than 17.4% in 1968 using the squared CV and by 8.5% in 1978 rather than 6.2% in 1968 using the Gini coefficient). Between 1978 and 1988, however the pattern of growth of wives' earnings only led to a slight decrease of inequality.

Although greater wives' earnings have created more equal incomes among married couples they have made a slight contribution to overall family inequality since 1968.

The growth in work hours in the 1979-1989 period took place on average in all families and not just in married-couple families with children.

81

TABLE 1.29
Effect of Wives' Earnings on Income Inequality
Among All Families and Married Couples, 1968-1988

By Family Type and Inequality Measure*	Inequality Among Families and Married Couples			Percent Change	
	1968	1978	1988	1968-88	1978-88
All Families					
(a) Squared CV of:					
Total Family Income	0.51	0.51	0.66	29.4%	29.4%
Less Wives' Earnings	0.56	0.55	0.69	23.2	25.5
Percent Change	−8.9%	−7.3%	−4.3%		
(b) Gini Coefficient of:					
Total Family Income	0.359	0.381	0.422	17.5%	10.8%
Less Wives' Earnings	0.366	0.384	0.420	14.8	9.8
Percent Change	−1.9%	−0.8%	0.5%		
Married Couples					
(a) Squared CV of:					
Total Family Income	0.38	0.32	0.41	7.9%	28.1%
Less Wives' Earnings	0.46	0.40	0.52	13.0	30.0
Percent Change	−17.4%	−20.0%	−21.2%		
(b) Gini Coefficient of:					
Total Family Income	0.305	0.300	0.336	10.2%	12.0%
Less Wives' Earnings	0.325	0.328	0.368	13.2	12.2
Percent Change	−6.2%	−8.5%	−8.7%		

*The squared coefficient of variation (CV) and the Gini coefficient are measures of inequality for which higher values indicate greater inequality.

By both measures the presence of wives' earnings lessened overall family income inequality in 1968, although only slightly according to the Gini coefficient. However, the egalitarian effect of wives' earnings lessened from 1968 to 1988, particularly in the 1980s. In fact, the Gini coefficient measure shows a slight inegalitarian effect of wives' earnings on all families in 1988.

Nevertheless, the changing pattern of wives' earnings played a very small role in the overall growth of family income inequality in the 1980s. This can be seen by comparing the increase in income inequality that actually occurred and that which would have occurred if there were no earnings from wives (the last column of Table 1.29). Total family income inequality grew a great deal from 1978 to 1988 according to both measures after growing more slowly (in the Gini measure) or not all in the prior ten years. The growth in inequality between all families from 1978 to 1988 would have been only slightly smaller (9.8% versus 10.8% or 25.5% versus 29.4%) without the presence of wives' earnings. Another way of assessing the effect of the changing pattern of wives' earnings on income inequality is to compute the hypothetical level of inequality that would have prevailed in 1988 if wives' earnings had as egalitarian an impact as in 1978. For instance, if wives' earnings had still reduced inequality by 7.3% in 1988 as in 1978 (using the squared CV) then the level of inequality would have been 0.64 and inequality between 1978 and 1988 would have grown by 25.4% from 0.51 to 0.64 rather than by the actual 29.4% growth from 0.51 to 0.66. According to the Gini coefficient, if wives' earnings had had as egalitarian an effect on incomes in 1988 as in 1978 then inequality would have grown 9.4% rather than the actual 10.8% growth in inequality.

Although greater wives' earnings have created more equal incomes among married couples they have made a slight contribution to overall family inequality since 1968.

The Downside of Increased Labor Market Work

As we have shown, the increased earnings of wives in married-couple families with children have been responsible for nearly all of the income growth in these families, especially for middle-income families. More than half of the increase in earnings by wives is due to more wives working and to more weekly hours and weeks per year worked by employed wives. The earnings from this

TABLE 1.30
Effect of Second Earner on Household Expenditures
(1990 Dollars)

Income Level*	Average Income and Expenditures		Difference Between 2-Earner and 1-Earner Families	
	1-Earner Families	2-Earner Families	Dollars	Percent
Low-Income Families				
Income				
Income	$12,952	$21,990	$9,038	70%
Annual Wage	10,576	18,996	8,420	80
Expenditures				
Work-Related	$4,802	$7,128	$2,326	48%
Transportation	3,775	5,225	1,450	38
Child Care	63	525	462	733
Food Away from Home	574	825	251	44
Other Expenditures	$13,136	$15,494	$2,358	18%
Middle-Income Families				
Income				
Income	$27,876	$38,475	$10,598	38%
Annual Wage	26,192	36,399	10,207	39
Expenditures				
Work-Related	$5,933	$9,139	$3,206	54%
Transportation	4,503	6,435	1,932	43
Child Care	81	677	596	736
Food Away from Home	817	1,210	392	48
Other Expenditures	$17,014	$19,403	$2,390	14%

*Married Couples with Children.

84

increased work effort is a positive financial gain but, as we have discussed, it comes with associated costs: increased work-related spending, child-care costs and problems, the loss of leisure time, and added stress. The downside of the increased work effort is delineated in the next few tables.

A two-earner family has considerably more expenses than a one-earner family with a comparable income. Each earner in a family requires transportation to work and frequently needs appropriate clothes. With two-earners there are many household tasks that must be completed for the family by purchasing services previously performed by a family member. A major example is the cost of child care. Other examples would be home repair and some meal preparation.

Table 1.30 shows the differences in expenditures between one- and two-earner families. Among low-income families, the work-related expenses of two-earner families are 48% more than those of one-earner families. In contrast, non-work related expenditures, "other expenditures," were only 18% greater in two-earner families. The major additional expenses for two-earner families are transportation and child care. Among middle-income families, two-earner families spend 54% more on work-related items than one-earner families. One interpretation of these higher expenditures is that the average two-earner family has more income than the average one-earner family. This explanation fails, however, because the growth of non-work related expenditures only rise by far less, 14%.

These added financial costs to two-earner families are large enough so as to significantly reduce the net gain from increased earners. Among middle-income families, for instance, the added work-related financial costs of $3,206 absorb 31% of the added $10,207 of annual wages associated with the second earner.

These expenses are averages among families which do and those which do not have to purchase child care. Many families do not have to pay for child care because their children are in school or because they can rely on unpaid relatives for assistance. For instance, only 32% of families with employed mothers pay for child care (**Table 1.31**). A much higher percentage (from 54.7% to 61.3%) of families with young children (ages 0 to 4) must pay for child care. For these families, the financial cost of child care absorbs from 6.4% to 7.4% of their incomes.

These added financial costs to two-earner families are large enough so as to significantly reduce the net gain from increased earners.

85

TABLE 1.31
Child-Care Expenditures and Family Income
for Employed Women with Children
(1990 Dollars)

	Number of Women (000)	Number Paying for Child Care (000)	Percent Paying for Child Care	Average Weekly Child-Care Expenses*	Average Monthly Family Income*	Percent of Income Spent on Child Care Per Month**
Total	18,244	5,831	32.0%	$53.18	$3,586	6.4%
Age of Youngest Child:						
Less Than 1 Year	1,473	806	54.7%	$62.00	$4,218	6.4%
1 & 2 Years	3,451	2,114	61.3	61.29	3,584	7.4
3 & 4 Years	2,602	1,509	58.0	51.76	3,375	6.6
5 Years & Older	10,718	1,401	13.1	37.18	3,454	4.7
Number of Children Less Than 5 Years Old:						
1 Child	6,030	3,510	58.2%	$54.00	$3,526	6.6%
2 or More Children	1,496	919	61.4	74.12	4,019	8.0

*Refers only to women making child-care payments.
**Average weekly child-care expenditures converted to a monthly average.

TABLE 1.32
Hours Worked by Employed Parents
by Gender, 1969 and 1989

Family Member*	Market Hours			Non-Market Hours			Total Hours		
	1969	1989	Change	1969	1989	Change	1969	1989	Change
All Parents	1,916	1,988	72	1,034	1,101	67	2,950	3,089	139
Mothers	1,281	1,627	346	1,583	1,402	−181	2,864	3,029	165
Fathers	2,316	2,330	14	688	816	128	3,004	3,146	142

*Limited to parents without involuntary leisure due to unemployment or short hours (involuntary part-time work).

86

Another cost of having family members spend more time in the paid labor force is that there is an erosion of leisure time. The trends in parents' annual hours of work, broken down into paid labor market work and unpaid household "non-market" (shopping, child care, cooking, repairs, laundry, etc.) work, from 1969 to 1989 are presented in **Table 1.32**. The total amount of work has increased in this time period, and has not been offset by a decline in non-market hours. This suggests that parents have less leisure time.

For instance, the average parent was employed for 72 more hours in 1989 than in 1969, but also had 67 more hours of non-market work. The average parents' work year thus rose by 139 hours over this time period, equivalent to three and a half full-time weeks of work. There was a rise in total hours for both mothers and fathers. The increase in the average mother's market hours was only partially offset by lesser non-market hours while the average father did not increase his market hours by much (he was already a full-time, year-round worker with over 2,300 annual market hours) but did put in 128 more non-market hours annually in 1989 than in 1969.

Falling Behind the Earlier Generations

Until this point we have exclusively focused on cross-section comparisons, e.g., comparing the incomes of high-income, older, or married-couple families in one year to those of another. Although these comparisons accurately portray changes in various dimensions of the income distribution over time, they do not trace the incomes of particular families or individuals over time. For instance, consider comparisons of income growth by income fifth over a ten-year period. A person or family may be in the middle fifth in the first year, but in a higher or lower fifth ten years later. Thus, a comparison of middle-income families over time actually compares one set of families in the first year to a different set of families in the later year.

It is especially important to note that the incomes of individuals and families generally follow a life-cycle pattern. Typically, a person, after completing schooling, starts earning income in a relatively low-paying entry level job; sees fast income growth as job changes, accumulated experience and seniority occur over the next two decades; and then, obtains slower income growth in his or her later

Another cost of having family members spend more time in the paid labor force is that there is an erosion of leisure time. The average parents' work year thus rose by 139 hours over this time period, equivalent to three and a half full-time weeks of work.

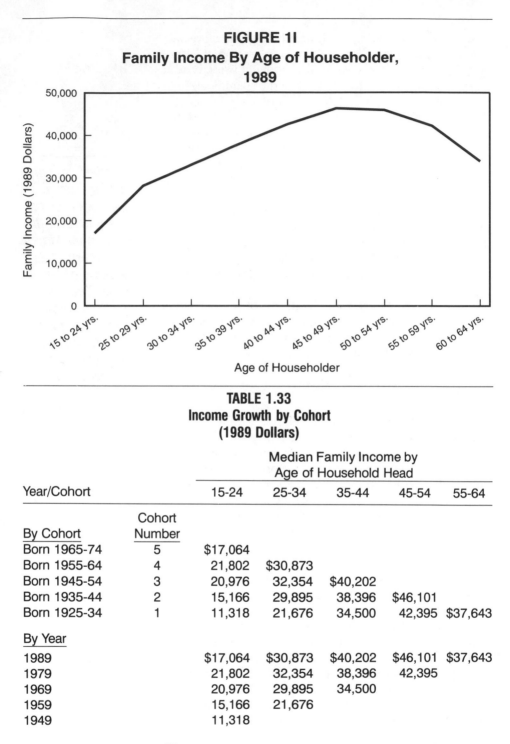

FIGURE 1I
Family Income By Age of Householder,
1989

Family Income (1989 Dollars)

Age of Householder

TABLE 1.33
Income Growth by Cohort
(1989 Dollars)

Year/Cohort	Cohort Number	Median Family Income by Age of Household Head				
		15-24	25-34	35-44	45-54	55-64
By Cohort						
Born 1965-74	5	$17,064				
Born 1955-64	4	21,802	$30,873			
Born 1945-54	3	20,976	32,354	$40,202		
Born 1935-44	2	15,166	29,895	38,396	$46,101	
Born 1925-34	1	11,318	21,676	34,500	42,395	$37,643
By Year						
1989		$17,064	$30,873	$40,202	$46,101	$37,643
1979		21,802	32,354	38,396	42,395	
1969		20,976	29,895	34,500		
1959		15,166	21,676			
1949		11,318				

88

working years. As **Figure 1I** shows, young families (headed by someone in his or her twenties) in 1989 had much lower incomes than families headed by a middle-aged person (in his or her forties or fifties). Plus, Figure 1I shows that incomes grow relatively rapidly as the household head proceeds through his or her thirties and forties and that income growth slackens and then declines as the household head approaches retirement years.

Viewed this way, the income growth of families as a whole over a ten-year period depends both on how high incomes are for young families when they start out and on how fast incomes grow as families progress through their life cycle pattern. In fact, the slow growth of median family incomes in recent years is most accurately portrayed as young families starting off with lower incomes than their predecessors and other families proceeding to higher incomes at an historically slow pace. Note that it is even possible for average family income to fall over a ten-year period even though each family may have achieved higher incomes over the period—the mechanism of income decline could be much lower starting incomes for the youngest families and very slow growth of incomes for families.

There are no data available which can trace the income growth of particular people or families over their life cycle. However, it is possible to examine the income trajectories of "birth cohorts" (a group of similarly aged persons or families) over time as in **Table 1.33** and **Figure 1J**. For ease of presentation, we number each postwar birth cohort with number one being the earliest cohort, the families headed by someone born between 1925 and 1934 and whom we first observe in 1949 as families with a household head 24-years-old or less. The latest cohort, number five, consists of families headed by someone born between 1965 and 1974. We can only observe the incomes of this youngest cohort in 1989 when the family head is 24-years-old or less.

The bottom line of Figure 1J shows the income trajectory of cohort number one. These families had a median income of just $11,318 in 1949 as they started out, but saw their incomes rise by 59.2% to $21,676 by 1959, to $34,500 by 1969 and to $42,395 by 1979.

The second cohort (born between 1935 and 1944) started out with a higher income than cohort number one

The slow growth of median family incomes in recent years is most accurately portrayed as young families starting off with lower incomes than their predecessors and other families proceeding to higher incomes at an historically slow pace.

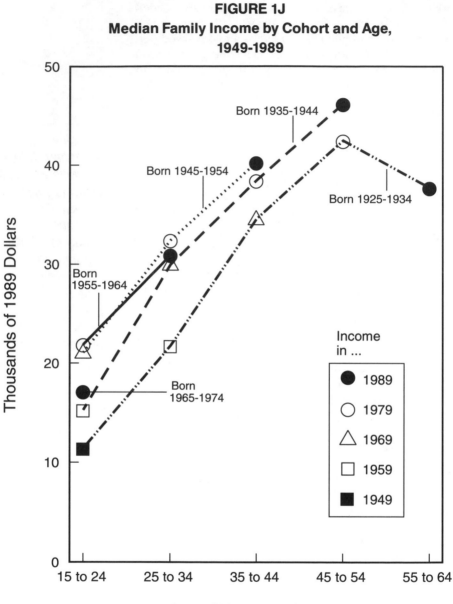

FIGURE 1J
Median Family Income by Cohort and Age,
1949-1989

Thousands of 1989 Dollars

Born 1935-1944

Born 1945-1954

Born 1925-1934

Born
1955-1964

Born
1965-1974

Income
in ...

● 1989

○ 1979

△ 1969

□ 1959

■ 1949

Age of Household Head

($15,166 versus $11,318) and achieved higher incomes at each age level than cohort number one. The same pattern holds for cohort number three which we first observe in 1969 with incomes of $20,976, a significantly higher income than that of the two earlier cohorts when they started out. Cohort number three, headed by someone aged 35-44 years old in 1989, earned $40,202 and was still ahead of the prior cohorts when they were similarly aged ($38,396 and $34,500).

The postwar pattern of upward income mobility was broken for the fourth cohort. This cohort, which was born between 1955 and 1964, did start out in 1979 with higher incomes than the earlier cohorts had at that age. However, ten years later when the fourth cohort was in their late twenties and early thirties their incomes were less than that attained by the earlier cohort (number 3) at similar ages ($30,873 versus $32,354). Matters have worsened for the most recent cohort, number five, which started out in 1989 with a median income of $17,064, significantly behind the starting incomes of the prior two cohorts. It is also possible that slow income growth could lead the third cohort to fail to achieve the incomes of the second cohort at ages 45 to 54 years old ($46,101).

The break in upward income mobility across cohorts raises the issue of whether the two, and maybe the three, most recent cohorts (those born after 1945 or 1955) will ever achieve incomes equal to that of the earlier postwar cohorts. Given continued slow income growth and falling real wages (see Chapter 3) in the 1990s it is very possible that the recent (and some future) cohorts will have lifetime incomes inferior to those of their parents' generation.

Given continued slow income growth and falling real wages in the 1990s it is very possible that the recent (and some future) cohorts will have lifetime incomes inferior to those of their parents' generation.

Income Mobility

The previous section examined the growth in the median family income of the various postwar age cohorts and found that the recent sets of younger families were starting out with lower incomes and achieving a slower growth in incomes over their twenties and thirties. This section examines the income growth of families over a recent ten-year period using "panel" data which tracks the same set of families over time. These panel data provide information on the degree of family income mobility in certain periods as reflected in the ability of particular families

91

TABLE 1.34
Distribution of Individuals in Final Year by Family Income
Fifth in Starting Year

Family Income Fifth in 1967*	Family Income Fifth in 1976					
	Lowest	Second	Middle	Fourth	Top	All
Bottom	11.2%	5.2%	2.0%	1.3%	0.3%	20.0%
Second	4.1	6.0	5.0	3.0	1.7	19.8
Third	2.5	4.2	6.0	4.9	2.4	20.1
Fourth	1.3	2.9	4.7	5.9	5.2	20.0
Top	0.9	1.8	2.1	4.8	10.4	20.0
All	20.0	20.0	19.9	20.0	20.0	100.0

Family Income Fifth in 1977*	Family Income Fifth in 1986					
	Lowest	Second	Middle	Fourth	Top	All
Bottom	10.6%	5.0%	2.2%	1.3%	0.8%	20.0%
Second	4.3	6.0	5.1	2.9	1.7	20.1
Third	2.9	3.8	5.9	4.8	2.6	20.0
Fourth	1.0	2.9	4.3	6.8	5.0	20.0
Top	1.2	2.2	2.5	4.1	10.0	20.0
All	20.0	20.0	20.0	20.0	20.0	100.0

*Sample limited to adults, ages 25 to 54 in starting year.

to start with low incomes and end with high incomes, or vice versa.

Table 1.34 uses panel data in two time periods (1967-1976 and 1977-1986) to examine the ten-year relative income growth of individuals who were from 25 to 54 years old in the starting year. Specifically, the table presents the fraction of the individuals in each income fifth in the starting year by the income fifth achieved in the final year. For instance, the top row of the top panel shows the percent of persons that were in the lowest income fifth in 1967, delineated by the income fifth they had achieved in 1976. For example, 5.2% of the people in the sample had incomes in the lowest fifth in 1967 but in the second fifth in 1976.

The data reflect two different dimensions of income growth—"within-cohort" and "across-cohort." Because the group examined includes relatively young persons (ages 25 to 34 years old) as well as people already in their peak earning years (ages 45 to 54 years old) some of the observed income mobility is due to the different income growth rates of the earlier versus later cohorts, i.e., the life-cycle pattern of the various cohorts. Thus, some of the upward income mobility simply reflects the younger individuals experiencing faster income growth than older individuals (55 to 64 years old). This is the "across-cohort" dimension.

The "within-cohort" dimension is that within any age group individuals or families may have relatively better or worse income growth than their peers. That is, someone may have a lower (greater) than average income in the starting year and a greater (lower) than average income at the ending year. The degree to which individuals change their income position relative to their peers, either up or down, can be considered to be the degree of "income mobility."

There are several reasons for interest in income mobility. One is that an individual's ability to achieve a relatively higher income, or move up the relative income ladder, reflects a more fluid and open society and greater opportunities for advancement. Moreover, if upward mobility is more possible there may be a lesser concern about the growing inequality of what jobs pay, since there may be a greater income gap between those in well-paid and poorly paid jobs because an individual's chance of getting a well-

Some of the upward income mobility simply reflects the younger individuals experiencing faster income growth than older individuals.

93

TABLE 1.35
Transitions Into or Out of Middle Income
for Families with Children

Transition*	1967-80	1980-89
Out of middle income:		
Fraction of middle-income families falling to low-income status	8.5%	9.8%
Fraction of middle-income families attaining high-income status	5.8	6.8
Into middle income:		
Fraction of low-income families attaining middle-income status	35.1%	24.6%
Fraction of high-income families falling into middle-income status	30.8	27.6

*Income transition of men and women over consecutive five-year periods for those aged 25-50 in the first year. Income is defined as after-tax incomes including the value of food stamps. Middle incomes are defined as between $18,500 and $55,000 in 1987 dollars.

94

paid job has improved. Last, it is important to note that incomes fluctuate both up and down for particular people and families year by year, a dimension of income change that can not be captured in the usual cross-section comparisons.

What does Table 1.34 tell us about income mobility? First, the minority of families do not stay in the same income fifth over a ten-year period. For instance, only 30% of the families in the middle fifth (6.0% divided by 20.1%) in 1967 were still in the middle fifth nine years later in 1976. Second, a large portion of the low-income families seem to remain low-income over a long period of time— more than half of the lowest fifth remained in the lowest fifth over each time period, 1967-1976 and 1977-1986. Likewise, many of the upper-income families remain upper income. This rigidity at the top and bottom of the income ladder, it should be noted, partly reflects the statistical fact that poor families can only move up and not down and well-off families can only move down and not up.

Perhaps the most important point to draw from Table 1.34 is that there has not been much change in income mobility from the first period to the second period. Thus, a greater inequality of income "positions" has not been off-set by a greater chance of obtaining a better "position." The implication is that the widening inequality of incomes discussed in earlier sections has led to a widening inequality of the *lifetime* incomes of people and families.

Panel data—tracking the same families over time—can also be used to examine the mobility of families into and out of particular absolute income ranges. In **Table 1.35**, for instance, panel data are used to show the percentage of families moving into and out of the "middle class." These transitions are categorized by whether there was downward mobility (from high to middle income or from middle to low income) or upward mobility (from low to middle income or middle to high income).

The starting point of the analysis is to note, as we did in an earlier section, that there has been a shrinkage in the proportion of families with middle-class incomes over the last two decades. The data in Table 1.35 allow us to see the flows of families into and out of the middle class so we can determine what underlying income trends are driving the middle-class shrinkage, e.g., are more people moving up or down the income scale?

Perhaps the most important point to draw from the data is that there has not been much change in income mobility from 1967-1976 to 1977-1986.

95

Looking at the transitions out of the middle (the top panel of Table 1.35) we see that in the post-1980 period families were both more likely to fall out of the middle class (9.8% of them did versus 8.5% in the earlier period) and more likely to "climb out" of the middle-class (6.8% versus 5.8%). The middle class also declined in the recent period because far fewer low-income families were able to attain middle-class incomes (24.6% versus 35.1%) and a lesser fraction of high-income families fell into the middle class.

These data amplify the earlier findings of widening inequality and income polarization. The positive trends are that in the post-1980 period middle-income families were better able to attain high incomes and more high-income families were able to sustain their high incomes. The downside, however, is that more middle-income families fell into lower incomes and fewer low-income families were able to rise into the middle class.

The positive trends are that in the post-1980 period middle-income families were better able to attain high incomes and more high-income families were able to sustain their high incomes. The downside, however, is that more middle-income families fell into lower incomes and fewer low-income families were able to rise into the middle class.

Conclusion

There was historically slow income growth over the 1979-1989 period and an historically large surge in income inequality. These trends can also be viewed as there having been rapid income growth among upper-income families, particularly the 62.9% income growth of the top 1%, and stagnant or falling incomes for the bottom 80% of families.

The remainder of the book elaborates on the themes established in this chapter. In the next chapter we focus on changes in the level and distribution of taxes to examine the extent to which our tax system has exacerbated or ameliorated the slow and unequal income growth of the 1980s. The third and fourth chapters examine the labor market trends (wages and employment) which are at the heart of the growth in inequality and our sluggish income growth. Chapter 5 and 6 broaden our income analysis by examining trends in wealth and poverty. Chapter 7 examines income trends by geographic location (region/states, urban/rural), while Chapter 9 compares trends in the U.S. to those in other advanced countries.

Chapter 2.

Taxes: A Further Cause of Worsening Inequality

In Chapter 1, we showed that the pre-tax incomes of most families have stagnated, while the incomes of wealthy families have grown significantly. This chapter broadens our analysis by examining the role played by the tax system in these developments. The major finding of this chapter is that federal, state, and local taxes have not ameliorated the economic problems documented in Chapter 1. In fact, recent tax changes have worsened the distribution of after-tax income by taxing the middle class and the poor more heavily and giving large tax cuts to the richest 1%. Since 1977, federal tax changes alone amounted to an average tax break of $49,262 in 1989 for the richest families. The causes of this shift include a less progressive personal income tax, higher payroll taxes, and lower corporate taxes. There has also been a steadily increasing reliance on state and local taxes, which tend to be regressive.

Recent tax changes have worsened the distribution of after-tax income by taxing the middle class and the poor and giving large tax cuts to the richest 1%.

The Tax Burden: Still Light by Comparison

In comparative terms, taxes have increased little and the overall U.S. tax burden remains one of the lightest among the Western industrialized countries. **Table 2.1** shows the total tax burden in the U.S. as a percent of Gross Domestic Product (GDP) from 1959 to 1991, broken out by federal and state/local contributions. The overall burden has gradually edged up during the postwar period, but has held rela-

97

TABLE 2.1
Federal vs. State and Local Tax Burdens, 1959–1991

	Revenue as Percent of GDP*		
	Federal	State/Local	Total
1959	18.3%	7.7%	26.0%
1967	18.7	9.6	28.4
1973	19.5	11.6	31.1
1979	20.3	11.0	31.3
1989	20.1	11.9	32.0
1991	19.7	12.2	32.0

*Gross Domestic Product

tively constant since 1973, staying between 31% and 32% of GDP. However, the state and local burden grew by 4.5% of GDP over the total period while the federal burden grew by only 1.4% of GDP. Since 1979, the federal burden has been stable or slightly in decline (although the 1991 data may reflect the recession), while the state and local burden grew. As we show below, the effect of shifting the tax burden to state and local governments is to widen inequality.

Table 2.2 puts the U.S. tax burden in an international context by showing government revenues as a percent of GDP over time for the countries in the Organisation for Economic Co-operation and Development (OECD), the group of advanced industrial countries. The percentage point changes in the last column show that since 1967 every country other than the U.S. has had a greater increase in the ratio of tax revenues to GDP. As a result, the total U.S. tax burden in 1988 (the latest year of available data) was lower than in any other OECD country save Turkey.

Every country other than the U.S. has had a greater increase in the ratio of tax revenues to GDP. As a result, the total U.S. tax burden in 1988 was lower than in any other OECD country save Turkey.

TABLE 2.2
Tax Revenues in OECD Countries, 1967–1988
As Percent of GDP

| Country | Tax Revenues as % of GDP* | | | Percentage Point Change |
	1967	1979	1988	1967-88
Sweden	37.1%	49.5%	55.3%	18.2
Denmark	33.1	44.5	52.1	19.0
Norway	36.6	45.7	46.9	10.3
Netherlands	35.7	45.0	48.2	12.5
Belgium	33.5	44.5	45.1	11.6
France	34.7	40.2	44.4	9.7
Luxembourg	30.8	40.2	42.8	12.0
Austria	35.3	41.0	41.9	6.6
Ireland	28.7	31.2	41.5	12.8
New Zealand	25.4	32.9	37.9	12.5
Germany	32.2	37.7	37.4	5.2
U.K.	32.9	32.8	37.3	4.4
Greece	23.3	30.1	35.9	12.6
Italy	26.2	26.6	37.1	10.9
Finland	31.6	33.3	37.9	6.3
Canada	28.2	30.6	34.0	5.8
Spain	16.8	23.4	32.8	16.0
Switzerland	21.6	31.1	32.5	10.9
Portugal	19.7	26.0	34.6	14.9
Australia	23.4	27.9	30.8	7.4
Japan	18.3	24.4	31.3	13.0
U.S.	**27.3**	**29.0**	**29.8**	**2.5**
Turkey	16.2	20.8	22.9	6.7

*Social Security Included. United States numbers differ from those in Table 2.1 because the tables come from different sources.

Recent Federal Tax Changes Have Favored the Very Rich

Within the context of the relatively low U.S. tax burden, there have been important changes in the *distribution* of taxes. These changes have combined with changes in pre-tax income to enrich the highest income families—primarily the top 1%—at the expense of almost everyone else. The redistributive effects of the changes in the tax system constitute the primary focus of this chapter.

Family income inequality *after* federal taxes has increased just as it has *before* federal taxes. **Table 2.3** examines this trend by looking at the changes in after-tax income (the years chosen for the federal tax analysis in this section are dictated by the data source; therefore, non-peak years appear in some of these tables). The average after-tax income of the top fifth of families grew by 28.1% from 1977 to 1989. But the most dramatic growth occurred among the most wealthy families of all: the top 1% of the income distribution. After taxes, their average income grew by 102.2% over the period in question. Note that this level of income growth exceeds their pre-tax rate of growth (final column) by 24.2 percentage points, showing that reduced taxation significantly boosted their after-tax incomes. Moreover, comparisons of pre- and after-tax growth in incomes of each group show the top 1% to be the only group whose after-tax growth significantly exceeded its pre-tax growth.

It is particularly striking, in terms of equity, that it was the poorest members of society who posted the biggest percentage declines in after-tax incomes.

TABLE 2.3
Average After-tax Family Income*

Income Group	1977	1980	1989	Percent Change in After-tax Income — Percent Change 1980-89	Percent Change in After-tax Income — Percent Change 1977-89	Percent Change in Pre-tax Income 1977-89
All	$30,948	$30,269	$33,663	11.2%	8.8%	8.6%
Top Fifth:	63,546	64,583	81,399	26.0	28.1	25.4
Top 1%	202,809	234,516	410,148	74.9	102.2	78.0
Next 4%	78,820	78,937	98,058	24.2	24.4	23.1
Next 5%	57,218	55,884	65,250	16.8	14.0	14.6
Next 10%	45,660	45,170	49,959	10.6	9.4	9.7
Bottom Four-Fifths:	22,582	21,694	22,061	1.7	-2.3	-2.8
Fourth	36,563	35,320	37,379	5.8	2.2	2.4
Middle	27,788	26,417	26,350	-0.3	-5.2	-5.3
Second	18,885	17,740	16,987	-4.2	-10.1	-9.8
Lowest	8,495	8,079	7,608	-5.8	-10.4	-10.4

*Federal Taxes Only

TABLE 2.4
Shares of After-tax Income for All Families, 1977–1989

Income Group	Shares of After-tax Income 1977	Shares of After-tax Income 1980	Shares of After-tax Income 1985	Shares of After-tax Income 1989	Percentage Point Changes 1980-89	Percentage Point Changes 1977-89
All	100.0%	100.0%	100.0%	100.0%	0.0	0.0
Top Fifth:	44.0	44.9	49.0	49.7	4.8	5.7
Top 1%	7.3	8.4	11.2	12.4	4.0	5.1
Next 4%	11.3	11.3	12.3	12.3	1.0	1.0
Next 5%	9.9	9.9	10.2	9.9	0.0	0.0
Next 10%	15.6	15.3	15.4	15.2	-0.1	-0.4
Bottom Four-Fifths:	56.3	55.6	51.8	51.2	-4.4	-5.1
Fourth	22.7	22.6	22.0	21.6	-1.0	-1.1
Middle	16.3	16.2	15.3	15.2	-1.0	-1.1
Second	11.6	11.4	10.1	10.1	-1.3	-1.5
Lowest	5.7	5.4	4.4	4.3	-1.1	-1.4

After-tax income trends were different at the other end of the income distribution, as the income of the average family in the bottom 80% of the distribution fell by 2.8% before federal taxes and 2.3% after federal taxes (Table 2.3). It is particularly striking, in terms of equity, that it was the poorest members of society who posted the biggest percentage declines in after-tax incomes.

The disparity in after-tax income growth implies substantial changes in the distribution of after-tax incomes. **Table 2.4** shows that between 1977 and 1989, the after-tax income growth of the most wealthy occurred at the expense of the bottom 90% of the income distribution, all of whom lost income shares to the top 10%. By 1989, the top 20% of families held almost 50% of total after-tax income, up from 44% in 1977 and 44.9% in 1980. Again, most of the gain to the upper quintile was generated by those in the top percentile, who gained 5.1 percentage points in their share of after-tax income over the 1977-1989 period, with most of the shift occurring in the period between 1980 and 1985. On the other hand, the shares received by each of the bottom four-fifths and the second-richest tenth of families (i.e., the bottom 90%) declined steadily over the period.

The distributional findings shown in the previous tables pose an important question regarding the impact of federal tax changes: did the major income shifts occur before or after taxes? **Table 2.5** examines this question by comparing pre- and after-tax income shares, 1977 and 1989.

The after-tax income growth of the most wealthy occurred at the expense of the bottom 90% of the income distribution, all of whom lost income shares to the top 10%.

TABLE 2.5

TABLE 2.5
The Effects of Tax and Income Changes
on After-tax Income Shares, 1977–1989*

	Pre-tax Shares		After-tax Shares		Change in After-tax Shares	Change in Shares Due to:	
						Pre-tax Income Shifts	Lesser Tax Progressivity
	(1)	(2)	(3)	(4)	(5)	(6)	(7)
Income Group	1977	1989	1977	1989	1977-89	1977-89	1977-89
All	100.0%	100.0%	100.0%	100.0%	0.0	0.0	0.0
Top Fifth:	46.6	51.1	43.9	49.0	5.1	4.5	0.6
Top 1%	8.7	12.6	7.3	11.9	4.6	3.9	0.7
Next 4%	12.0	12.8	11.3	12.2	0.9	0.8	0.1
Next 5%	10.1	10.3	9.8	9.8	0.0	0.1	−0.1
Next 10%	15.7	15.4	15.5	15.1	−0.4	−0.3	−0.1
Bottom Four Fifths:	53.4	48.9	56.1	51.0	−5.1	−4.5	−0.6
Fourth	22.4	21.4	22.6	21.5	−1.1	−1.0	−0.1
Middle	15.6	14.6	16.3	15.1	−1.2	−1.1	−0.1
Second	10.5	9.3	11.5	10.1	−1.4	−1.2	−0.2
Lowest	4.9	3.7	5.7	4.3	−1.4	−1.2	−0.2

*Based on recalculation of the underlying data in Table 2.4 which force the sum of shares to be exactly 100%; due to rounding error, this is not the case in the original data.

Column five of Table 2.5 shows the difference in after-tax income shares that developed over the period in question. Columns six and seven "decompose" these differences into pre-tax shifts (generated prior to the imposition of tax liabilities) and into differences caused by the less progressive tax system (the remainder of the change, after accounting for pre-tax shifts). The effect of changes in the tax code are derived by comparing 1989 after-tax incomes and shares under 1989 and 1977 effective tax rates.

Column five shows that the bottom 90% of families had a lower after-tax income share in 1989 than in 1977 (as noted in Table 2.4), with the bottom 80% of families losing 5.1% of total after-tax income over the period. These losses primarily reflect a lower share of pre-tax incomes. In fact, 4.5 of the 5.1 percentage point decline in the after-tax income share of the bottom 80% was due to a relative loss of pre-tax income, attributable to a more unequal distribution of wages and other incomes. Thus, shifts in the tax burden, though significant, were not the primary mechanism of the overall redistribution of income in recent years.

Nevertheless, as shown in column seven, the less progressive tax structure did provide a significant 0.7% increase in the after-tax income share of the top 1%. As the next section shows, a modest increase in the effective tax rates among most families permitted a sizable tax reduction for the top 1%. However, as noted above, the largest part of the income gains made by the most wealthy occurred before taxes, from greater wages and capital incomes, as seen in Chapter 1.

The average effective tax rate on the top percentile fell by 8.8 percentage points between 1977 and 1989.

Table 2.6
Efective Average Federal Tax Rates in 1977, 1980, and 1989

Income Group	Effective Federal Tax Rates			Change in Tax Rates
	1977	1980	1989	1977-89
All	22.8%	23.3%	22.7%	− 0.1
Top Fifth:	27.3	27.5	25.6	− 1.7
Top 1%	35.6	31.7	26.8	− 8.8
Next 4%	26.9	27.9	26.2	− 0.7
Next 5%	25.3	26.3	25.6	0.3
Next 10%	23.9	25.3	24.1	0.2
Bottom Four-Fifths:	16.3	16.5	16.6	0.3
Fourth	21.9	22.9	22.0	0.1
Middle	19.5	19.8	19.3	− 0.2
Second	15.4	15.6	15.6	0.2
Lowest	9.3	8.1	9.3	0.0

FIGURE 2A
Federal Tax Burden, 1977 and 1989

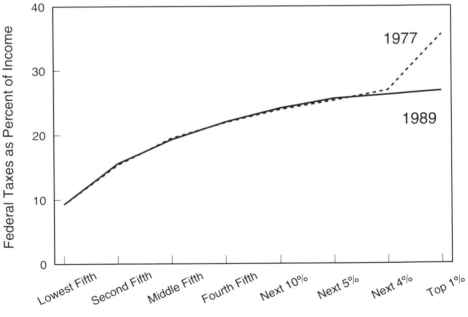

The Diminished Progressivity of Federal Tax Rates

Even while most of the income shifting between 1977 and 1989 occurred before taxes, regressive changes in federal taxes since 1977 have contributed to the increased inequality of after-tax family incomes. **Table 2.6** lists the effective federal tax rates (effective, or average, tax rates are the ratio of taxes paid to pre-tax income) by family income group. The average effective tax rate changed little over the time period, from 22.8% to 22.7%. What has changed is the tax rate on different income groups. For example, the rate on the top percentile fell by 8.8 percentage points, from 35.6% to 26.8%. Conversely, the effective rates on the bottom 95% of families grew slightly or remained unchanged (with the exception of the middle quintile). Thus it appears that slightly higher taxes on the bottom 95% paid for a substantial reduction in the tax rate for the top 1%. **Figure 2A** portrays the decreased progressivity, 1977-1989, in terms of average tax rates, at the top of the income distribution of the 1989 federal tax system.

The structure of marginal rates on income taxes (the tax rate on the last dollar of income) has also become less progressive at the top of the income distribution. **Figure 2B** shows the percent of returns taxed at or below the various marginal rates in 1979 and 1988 (base years are slightly different than other figures due to data availability). Note that in 1979, the top (approximately) 16% of income tax payers had higher marginal rates than in 1988. Due to the highly progressive structure of the 1979 top marginal rates (part of which resulted from inflation), the 1979-1988 rate differential grew rapidly at the very top of the distribution.

Due to the highly progressive structure of the 1979 top marginal rates the 1979-1988 rate differential grew rapidly at the very top of the distribution.

FIGURE 2B
Federal Income Tax: Cumulative Returns by Marginal Rates,
1979 and 1988

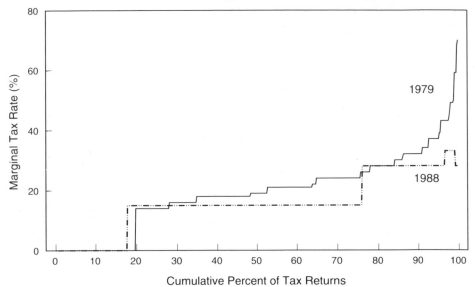

What Federal Tax Changes Mean in Dollars

The effect of any change in a group's tax rate on their actual, after-tax income depends on both the size of the change in the tax rate and on their level of income. **Table 2.7** shows the average pre-tax family income in 1989 for each income group (column one, in constant 1992 dollars). Columns two through four show the changes in the average amount of taxes paid by each income group due to federal tax changes enacted in different periods between 1977 and 1989, assuming that incomes were maintained at their 1989 levels. The final column shows the cumulative effect of changes in the tax code between 1977 and 1989 on 1989 federal tax payments.

Because of federal tax changes since 1977, the top 1% of families each received an average tax cut of $49,262 in 1989. The next richest 4% of families received tax cuts that averaged $924 per family in 1989—considerably smaller than the gains of the richest 1%. Since their effective rates changed little over the period, the bottom 95% of families either lost or gained marginally. The poorest families gained income from tax changes in the late 1980s, but these gains were 'washed out' by regressive changes over the total period. Clearly, the distributional impact of the rate changes was primarily driven by the gains made by the most wealthy. Their tax cuts came mainly from steps taken between 1980 and 1985, though changes in the late 1970s also contributed. Tax changes since 1985, including the Tax Reform Act of 1986, reduced the tax cut somewhat.

The poorest families gained income from tax changes in the late 1980s, but these gains were 'washed out' over the total period.

109

TABLE 2.7
Effect of Federal Tax Changes on Family
Tax Payments, 1977–1989

Income Group	Average 1989 Pre-tax Family Income	The Effect of Federal Tax Changes, 1977-89 on the Amount of Tax Payments, Assuming 1989 Income Levels			
		1977-80	1980-85	1985-89	Total 1977-89
All	$43,495*	$217	$ - 652	$391	$ - 43
Top Fifth:	109,424	219	- 3,611	1,532	- 1,860
Top 1%	559,795	- 21,272	- 38,626	10,636	- 49,262
Next 4%	132,036	1,452	- 4,885	2,509	- 924
Next 5%	87,711	965	- 1,842	1,140	263
Next 10%	65,900	857	- 1,120	395	132
Bottom Four-Fifths:	26,841	54	54	- 27	81
Fourth	47,913	479	- 575	144	48
Middle	32,681	98	- 229	65	- 65
Second	20,140	40	20	- 20	40
Lowest	8,391	- 101	185	- 84	0

*Constant 1992 Dollars.

110

The Causes of Changes in the Federal Tax Burden

In order to understand the causes of the regressive changes in the federal tax system, **Table 2.8** decomposes the federal effective rates into their main components: the personal income tax, payroll taxes, the corporate income tax, and the excise tax.

The personal income tax is progressive; the effective rates go up consistently as income rises. However, it has become less progressive, a point taken up in the next table.

Since 1977, the overall payroll tax rate has risen from 6.5% to 8.5% (Table 2.8). The bottom 99% have borne the brunt of increased payroll taxes; the top 1% has been virtually unaffected. This is partly because the rich earn much of their income from their investments (Chapter 1), which are not subject to payroll taxes. Another reason is that payroll taxes are 'capped': they apply only to the first $55,500 (1992 dollars) of earnings in 1992. The payroll tax was the largest federal tax paid by the bottom 80% of the distribution in 1989. As we discuss below, the growth of payroll taxes has led to greater inequality.

In this analysis, the tax incidence (i.e., who ultimately bears the burden of the tax) of the payroll tax falls totally on employees: the employer portion is shifted to employees in the form of lower wages. While this is a common and valid assumption of payroll tax incidence, it does not speak to the redistributive effects of the social security system. In the current context, retirement benefits are redistributed in a progressive manner: less wealthy retirees receive more benefits than they contributed over their lifetime, while the most wealthy receive fewer benefits then they put in. This redistributive effect counteracts the regressive nature of the tax documented in the text.

Since 1977, the overall payroll tax rate has risen from 6.5% to 8.5%. The bottom 99% have borne the brunt of increased payroll taxes; the top 1% has been virtually unaffected.

111

TABLE 2.8
Effective Tax Rates for Selected Federal Taxes, 1977–1989

| | Effective Tax Rates | | | | | | | |
| | Personal Income Tax | | Payroll Tax | | Corporate Income Tax | | Excise Tax | |
Income Group	1977	1989	1977	1989	1977	1989	1977	1989
All	11.1%	11.0%	6.5%	8.5%	3.9%	2.3%	1.3%	0.9%
Top Fifth:	16.1	15.3	5.3	7.0	5.0	2.8	0.9	0.5
Top 1%	25.2	20.7	1.3	1.6	8.8	4.2	0.3	0.3
Next 4%	16.6	16.2	4.4	6.8	5.1	2.8	0.8	0.4
Next 5%	13.9	13.1	6.5	9.6	3.9	2.2	1.0	0.7
Next 10%	12.0	11.3	7.4	10.0	3.4	2.0	1.1	0.8
Bottom Four-Fifths:	4.7	4.2	7.1	9.3	2.7	1.6	1.9	1.5
Fourth	9.6	8.9	7.8	10.3	3.2	1.9	1.3	0.9
Middle	6.9	6.4	8.1	10.0	3.0	1.8	1.5	1.1
Second	3.4	3.2	7.5	9.4	2.7	1.5	1.8	1.5
Lowest	−0.6	−1.8	5.1	7.6	1.9	1.1	2.9	2.4

However, the age structure of the population is such that the worker/beneficiary ratio will fall in the future. This demographic phenomenon will severely strain the social insurance system's ability to maintain its progressive distributive structure. Without this distributive component, the burden of the tax falls on wage earners in the present, and the regressive nature of the tax is not mitigated for future generations. Therefore, the rise in payroll taxes is considered a regressive change.

Corporate income taxes, which have a progressive structure, have declined considerably. For example, the average effective rate for the richest fifth of families fell from 5.0% in 1977 to 2.8% in 1989 (Table 2.8). Since corporations are owned by households through shares of stock, households also bear the burden of corporate taxes. The burden can be transferred to households in a variety of ways. In this analysis, it is assumed that half of corporate taxes are borne by stockholders in the form of lower dividends and slower stock appreciation, and half are paid by consumers in the form of higher prices.

Excise taxes have fallen since 1977 while maintaining their regressive structure. These are taxes levied on alcohol, gasoline, cigarettes, etc.; they are the most regressive federal taxes (Table 2.8, **Figure 2C**). In 1989, the poorest families paid 2.4% of their income in excise taxes while the richest fifth paid 0.5%. This is because families with higher incomes spend smaller proportions of their incomes on gasoline, cigarettes, alcohol, and other goods subject to excise taxes.

The burden of the tax falls on wage earners in the present, and the regressive nature of the tax is not mitigated for future generations.

113

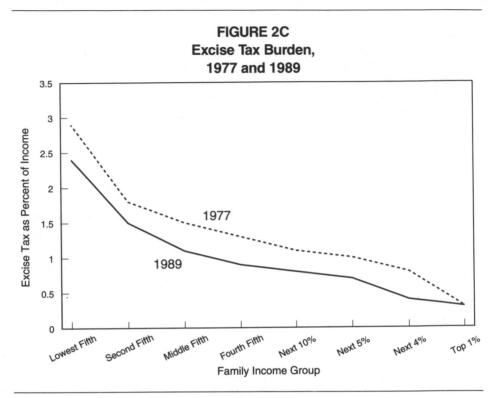

FIGURE 2C
Excise Tax Burden,
1977 and 1989

TABLE 2.9
Changes in Effective Federal Taxes, 1977–1989

	Point Change, 1977-89				
Income Group	Personal Income Tax	Payroll Tax	Corporate Income Tax	Excise Tax	Total
All	−0.1	2.0	−1.6	−0.4	−0.1
Top Fifth:	−0.8	1.7	−2.2	−0.4	−1.7
Top 1%	−4.5	0.3	−4.6	0.0	−8.8
Next 4%	−0.4	2.4	−2.3	−0.4	−0.7
Next 5%	−0.8	3.1	−1.7	−0.3	0.3
Next 10%	−0.7	2.6	−1.4	−0.3	0.2
Bottom Four-Fifths:	−0.5	2.2	−1.1	−0.4	0.3
Fourth	−0.7	2.5	−1.3	−0.4	0.1
Middle	−0.5	1.9	−1.2	−0.4	−0.2
Second	−0.2	1.9	−1.2	−0.3	0.2
Lowest	−1.2	2.5	−0.8	−0.5	0.0

Although the personal income tax is still the most progressive federal tax, it has become less so over time (**Table 2.9, Figure 2D**). Since 1977, the average personal income tax for the richest families (the top 1%) has fallen by 4.5 points. In contrast, reductions in personal income taxes for groups in the bottom 99% have been much smaller.

Except for the top 1%, the reductions in income taxation have been more than offset by higher payroll taxes. For instance, the effective income tax rate for the middle fifth fell 0.5 percentage points between 1977 and 1989, but the payroll tax grew by 1.9 percentage points over the same period.

Between 1977 and 1989, federal corporate taxes declined by 1.6 percentage points (Table 2.9). According to our burden assumptions, corporate taxes are progressive; thus, lower corporate taxes have benefitted the rich more than other groups. In particular, the top 1% of families saw their corporate tax burdens reduced by 4.6 percentage points, which accounts for more than half the overall 8.8 percentage point decline in the effective tax rate for the top 1%.

The 0.4 percentage point decline in federal excise taxes, from 1.3% of family incomes in 1977 to 0.9% in 1989, has reduced the tax burden somewhat on the bottom 99% of families, with slightly greater tax cuts going to low-income families. Nevertheless, the average family in the bottom 80% saw their total tax burden increase by 0.3 percentage points.

Although the personal income tax is still the most progressive federal tax, it has become less so over time. Since 1977, the average personal income tax for the richest families has fallen by 4.5 points.

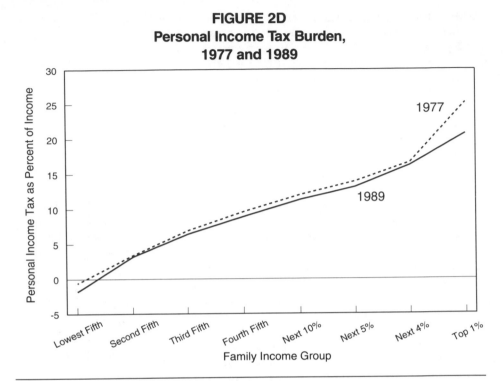

FIGURE 2D
Personal Income Tax Burden, 1977 and 1989

Personal Income Tax as Percent of Income

1977

1989

Family Income Group

Lowest Fifth · Second Fifth · Third Fifth · Fourth Fifth · Next 10% · Next 5% · Next 4% · Top 1%

TABLE 2.10
Taxed and Untaxed Corporate Profits, 1977–1991
(Nonfinancial Corporations Only)

| | As Percent of GDP in: | | | | |
	1977	1980	1986	1989	1991
All Profits, Taxed and Untaxed	8.2%	6.6%	7.1%	7.7%	7.8%
Taxed profits	8.0	6.7	3.5	4.8	3.6
Untaxed profits	0.2	−0.1	3.6	2.9	2.6
Net Interest	1.6	2.1	2.3	2.7	2.6
Depreciation Allowances	−0.5	−0.7	1.1	0.5	0.0
Other Deductions	−0.8	−1.6	0.2	−0.3	0.1
Corporate Profits Taxes*	3.0	2.5	1.8	1.9	1.5
Profits After Taxes					
Taxable Profits Only	5.0	4.2	1.7	2.9	2.1
All Profits	5.2	4.1	5.3	5.8	6.3

*Federal, state and local combined.

116

Changes in Corporate Taxation: The Shift to Untaxed Profits

Though corporate rates have dropped, this does not necessarily lead to lower corporate tax liability, since the lower rates could be applied to greater absolute profits (i.e., an expanded tax base). In fact, this was a goal of the 1986 tax reform. However, contrary to the goal of the reform, corporate tax revenue *did* decline through the period due to the growth of *untaxed* corporate income.

Since 1980, corporate profits as a percent of GDP have consistently risen, from 6.6% to 7.8% in 1991 (**Table 2.10**). However, taxed profits fell significantly from 1980 to 1986 (6.7% to 3.5%) and from 1989 to 1991 (4.8% to 3.6%). This phenomenon of rising total profits and falling taxed profits is due to the rise in untaxed corporate profits, which rose from 0.2% of GDP in 1977 to 2.9% in 1989 (Table 2.10, **Figure 2E**). Over the full period (1977 to 1989), corporate taxed profits have been cut virtually in half, from 8.0% of GNP to 4.8%.

There are two main reasons for the shift from taxed to untaxed profits: increased indebtedness (along with higher real interest rates) and a more favorable tax treatment of depreciation. Since 1977, corporations have increasingly raised money by selling bonds (i.e., they have borrowed) rather than by selling stocks to raise money. As a result, corporations have been paying out more and more of their gross profits as interest payments (on bonds) rather than as dividend payments (on stocks). This is reflected in Table 2.10 in the steady increase in net interest payments, from 1.6% of GDP in 1977 to 2.7% in 1989.

Since interest payments are treated more favorably than dividends by the federal tax system (they are considered an expense for non-financial corporations and deducted from taxable profits), and since interest rates have been high relative to inflation, the corporate emphasis on debt over equity has lowered the corporate tax burden. Corporate liability is lowered, as corporations deduct interest payments from their tax base.

The phenomenon of rising total profits and falling taxed profits in the corporate sector is due to the rise in untaxed corporate profits, which rose from 0.2% of GDP in 1977 to 2.9% in 1989.

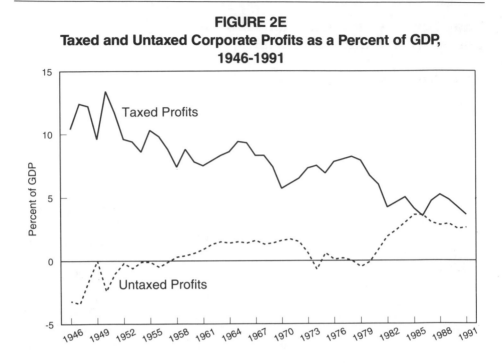

FIGURE 2E
Taxed and Untaxed Corporate Profits as a Percent of GDP, 1946-1991

TABLE 2.11
Corporate Profits Tax Rates, 1947–1991
(Nonfinancial Corporations Only)

	Corporate Taxes* as Percent of:	
	Taxable Profits	Actual Profits
1947	37.1%	50.9%
1957	48.0	48.6
1967	41.2	34.5
1977	37.8	36.8
1980	36.9	37.4
1985	42.2	22.4
1989	39.4	24.6
1991	41.1	24.0

*Federal, state, and local combined.

118

The second reason for lower corporate taxes is the federal tax system's relatively favorable treatment of capital depreciation. With the introduction of the Accelerated Cost Recovery System in 1981, corporations were able to take tax deductions on purchases of new equipment and other investments sooner. Since this allowed them to defer some of their taxes for several years, accelerated depreciation amounted to an interest-free loan. The main tax break of this type came between 1980 and 1986, when untaxed profits due to depreciation allowances went from -0.7% of GDP to 1.1% (Table 2.10). Since 1986, Congress has taken back part of this tax cut, reducing untaxed profits in this category to 0.5% of GDP in 1989.

Table 2.11 shows the results of these changes. Since 1977, corporate taxes have declined from 36.8% of actual profits (defined as the sum of taxable profits, net interest, and the difference between allowable depreciation and true depreciation) to 24.6% in 1989, while generally *increasing* as a percent of taxed profits. Moreover, the 1989 effective tax rate, 24.6%, is barely over half of what corporate taxes were in 1957 (Table 2.11; **Figure 2F**). The beneficiaries of this fall in corporate tax liability relative to true economic profits are by and large those who own and lend to corporations: the wealthy.

The 1989 effective corporate tax rate, 24.6%, is barely over half of what corporate taxes were in 1957.

119

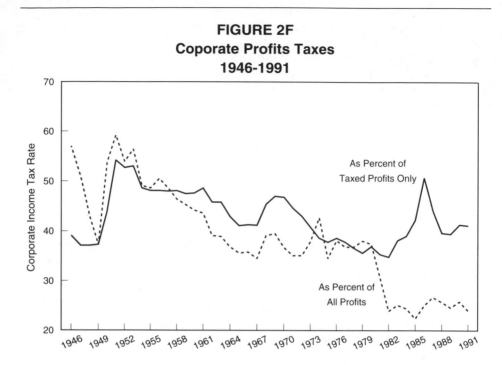

FIGURE 2F
Coporate Profits Taxes
1946-1991

As Percent of
Taxed Profits Only

As Percent of
All Profits

Corporate Income Tax Rate

The Shift to State and Local Taxes

As noted in the beginning of this chapter, the proportion of total tax receipts contributed by state and local taxpayers has grown over time, relative to the federal tax burden (see Table 2.1). **Figure 2G,** total tax receipts as a percentage of GNP, by different components, makes this point graphically. The figure shows that, starting in the post-war period, the growth of tax receipts has been led by state and local taxes (as well as federal payroll taxes), while the federal income tax shows a relatively flat trend. Since state and local taxes are less progressive than federal taxes, the distribution of the overall tax burden is considerably, and increasingly, less progressive than the distribution of federal taxes alone.

State and local governments rely predominantly on regressive taxes for their revenues: sales taxes, property taxes (here regressivity is sensitive to incidence assumptions, discussed below), and nontax revenues (regressive when they apply to consumption) such as fines and fees. **Table 2.12** gives the effective rates for state and local taxes by family income group for a family of four. The regressive structure of the state and local burden is shown in the table's final column: the proportion of income that a family of four paid in state and local taxes fell as their income increased.

Since state and local taxes are less progressive than federal taxes, the distribution of the overall tax burden is less progressive than the distribution of federal taxes.

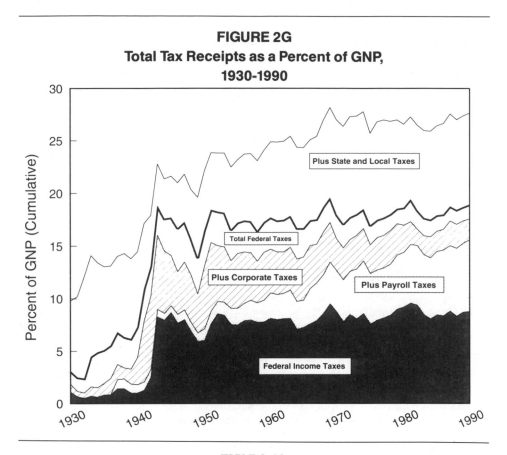

FIGURE 2G
Total Tax Receipts as a Percent of GNP,
1930-1990

Percent of GNP (Cumulative)

Plus State and Local Taxes

Total Federal Taxes

Plus Corporate Taxes

Plus Payroll Taxes

Federal Income Taxes

TABLE 2.12
Total State and Local Taxes in 1991 (Effective Rates)
as Shares of Income for Families of Four

Income Group	Personal Income Tax	Corporate Income Tax	Property Tax	Sales Tax	Excise Tax	Total Tax	Total After Federal Deductions
Top Fifth:							
Top 1%	4.6%	0.4%	1.3%	1.2%	0.1%	7.6%	6.0%
Next 4%	4.1	0.2	2.3	1.8	0.3	8.7	6.9
Next 15%	3.5	0.1	2.7	2.4	0.5	9.2	7.7
Bottom Four-Fifths:							
Fourth	3.0	0.1	2.9	2.9	0.7	9.5	8.4
Middle	2.6	0.1	3.2	3.3	0.8	10.0	9.5
Second	2.0	0.1	3.7	4.0	1.1	10.9	10.7
Lowest	0.7	0.1	5.4	5.7	1.9	13.8	13.8

However, as with federal income and corporate taxes (Table 2.8), state and local income and corporate taxes are progressive. Table 2.12 shows that the average family at the bottom of the income distribution paid 0.7% of its income in state and local personal income taxes, while the wealthiest 1% of families paid 4.6%. The state corporate tax is flat throughout most of the distribution, then slightly progressive at the top.

Conversely, property, sales, and excise taxes are regressive. In the case of sales and excise taxes, their regressivity results from the fact that the percentage of income consumed falls as income increases. This burden was exacerbated in 1986 when federal deductibility of state sales taxes was removed. In 1991, the poorest families in the average state paid 5.7% of their income in sales taxes and 1.9% in excise taxes. This proportion fell as income increased, until the wealthiest families paid a combined 1.3%.

The calculation of property tax incidence is particularly sensitive to the assumptions upon which the analysis is based. To the degree that owners of land and structures are able to shift the property tax burden onto tenants, the tax is regressive. Conversely, since ownership of land and capital generally rises with income, the property tax is progressive to the extent that the owners of these factors are unable to shift the tax forward onto property users.

The property tax column in Table 2.12 assumes that homeowners bear the full burden of their property taxes. For residential renters, half of the property tax is allocated to renters and half to owners. These two assumptions lead to the regressive structure reflected in the table, since poorer homeowners and renters devote a larger proportion of income to housing than the wealthy. The property tax liability on business is assumed to be that part of state property tax revenue *not* accounted for by residential renters and homeowners.

> *In 1991, the poorest families in the average state paid 5.7% of their income in sales taxes and 1.9% in excise taxes. This proportion fell as income increased, until the wealthiest families paid a combined 1.3%.*

TABLE 2.13
Federal vs. State & Local Taxes, 1991
as Percent of Revenue at Each Level

Type of Tax	Federal	State & Local
Progressive	51.1%	19.1%
Personal Income Tax	40.9	16.0
Corporate Income Tax	9.2	3.1
Estate/Gift Taxes	1.0	0.0
Regressive	47.5	67.8
Excise/Customs/Sales/Other*	5.7	35.8
Contributions for Social Insurance	41.8	23.4
Property	0.0	8.6
Nontaxes**	1.5	13.1
Total	100.0	100.0

---

* Other taxes include vehicle licenses, severance taxes, etc.
**Fines, certain fees, rents, royalties, tuition, hospital fees, etc.

The shift to state and local governments' revenues as seen in Figure 2G is of particular concern from a distributional perspective because state and local taxes are more regressive than federal taxes. In spite of increases in social insurance taxes, in 1991, 51.1% of federal revenues still came from progressive taxes, but only 19.1% of state/local revenues were raised progressively (**Table 2.13, Figures 2H and 2I**). (Payroll taxes at the state level are not strictly comparable with the federal version, since these contributions at the state level are mostly for pension funds for state and local employees. As such, they are more like personal assets than federal payroll taxes which are distributed under a pay-as-you-go system. In this regard, they are less regressive than federal payroll taxes.) Over 67% of state/local revenues are raised from regressive taxes, compared with less than half (47.5%) of federal revenues.

Over 67% of state/local revenues are raised from regressive taxes, compared with less than half (47.5%) of federal revenues.

FIGURE 2H
Federal Revenue Sources,
1991

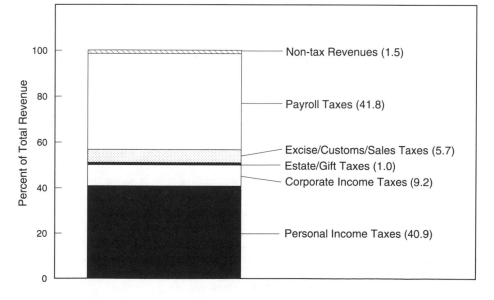

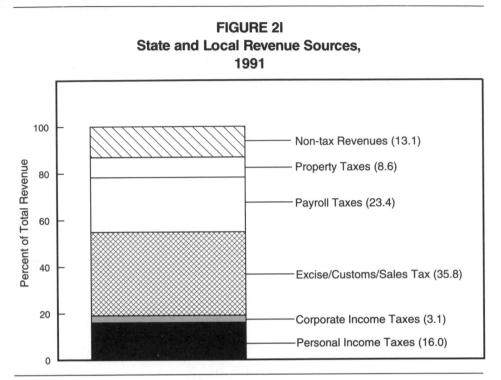

FIGURE 2I
State and Local Revenue Sources,
1991

- Non-tax Revenues (13.1)
- Property Taxes (8.6)
- Payroll Taxes (23.4)
- Excise/Customs/Sales Tax (35.8)
- Corporate Income Taxes (3.1)
- Personal Income Taxes (16.0)

Percent of Total Revenue

TABLE 2.14
The Composition of Taxes, 1959–1991
As Percent of GDP

Type of Tax	1959	1967	1973	1979	1989	1991
Progressive*	13.3%	13.0%	13.5%	14.3%	13.3%	12.4%
Federal	12.6	11.9	11.7	12.2	10.9	10.1
State and Local	0.7	1.1	1.8	2.1	2.4	2.3
Regressive**	12.6	14.5	16.5	15.7	17.0	17.6
Federal	5.6	6.6	7.8	7.9	9.0	9.4
State and Local	6.9	7.9	8.8	7.8	8.0	8.3
Nontaxes***	0.2	0.8	1.1	1.3	1.7	1.9
Federal	0.1	0.2	0.1	0.2	0.2	0.3
State and Local	0.1	0.7	1.0	1.1	1.5	1.6

*   Personal and corporate income taxes; estate and gift taxes.
** Customs, excise, sales, and other taxes; property taxes; contributions for social insurance. Other taxes include vehicle licenses, severance taxes, etc.
*** Fines, certain fees, rents, royalties, tuition, hospital fees, etc.

Table 2.14 shows the percent of GDP taxed by progressive and regressive taxes, together with nontax revenues, at peaks of business cycles since 1959. While progressive taxes varied slightly since 1959, regressive taxes have increased their share of GDP substantially—from 12.6% to 17.0% in 1989. This has resulted from increases at both the federal and state/local levels. Nontax revenues have risen but remain low, at only 1.7% of GDP in 1989.

Conclusion

The growth of income inequality documented in Chapter 1 has not been ameliorated by either federal or state taxes. In fact, during the 1980s the tax system has generally worked to the advantage of the wealthy, who received large tax cuts at the expense of the poor and middle class. The causes of these tax changes were a less progressive tax rate structure, a rise in untaxed corporate profits, and a shift to greater dependence on regressive state and local taxes.

During the 1980s the tax system has generally worked to the advantage of the wealthy, who received large tax cuts at the expense of the poor and middle class.

Chapter 3

Wages: Working Longer for Less

Introduction

Wage trends have been the primary determinant of the slow growth in income and the greater inequality of income we have experienced in recent years. This should not be surprising since wages and salaries comprise roughly three-fourths of total family income and an even higher percentage of the incomes of the broad middle class.

From 1979 to 1991, the real hourly wage of most workers severely eroded. This is true whether we examine wages or total compensation (= both wages and benefits). The groups experiencing the greatest fall in wages include the three-fourths of the workforce with less than a college degree, the bottom eighty percent of men, low-wage women workers, younger workers and blue-collar workers. The result of this widespread wage erosion was a sizeable growth in the 1980s in the proportion of the workforce earning less than poverty level wages and proportionately fewer workers earning mid-level wages.

Starting in the final stages of the 1980s recovery, wages began falling for groups that had previously escaped the downward pressure on wages, including white-collar and college-educated workers and middle- and high-wage women. Meanwhile, the wages of those who lost the most in the 1980s (high school graduates, blue-collar workers and men) have continued to fall. By the end of the 1980s the only group seemingly exempt from falling real wages was the 8% of the workforce with advanced or professional degrees.

Starting in the final stages of the 1980s recovery, wages began falling for groups that had previously escaped the downward pressure on wages, including white-collar and college-educated workers and middle- and high-wage women.

129

The recent fall-off in the wages of white-collar and college-educated workers occurred prior to the early 1990's recession and can be expected to continue even after the economy recovers, especially given the expected slow rate of future growth. The wage decline among college-educated workers is due to a slower growth in employer demand, as reflected in the historically high levels of white-collar unemployment and the historically slow growth in white-collar employment in recent years (see Chapter 4). Projected employment trends for the 1990s suggest continued slow growth in white-collar employment and sluggish demand for college-educated workers (see Chapter 4).

The most severe wage reductions, however, have been for entry-level jobs for young, high school graduates, a group comprising two-thirds to three-fourths of all young workers. In 1991, the wages paid to young male and female high school graduates were, respectively, 26.5% and 15.4% less than the wages their counterparts received in 1979. Over the 1973-1991 period, the wages of entry-level college graduates fell by 9.8% while the wages of entry-level high school graduates dropped 25.4% (29.3% among men and 20.4% among women). Thus, young workers face a job market providing considerably lower wages than comparably educated young people faced two decades ago.

There have been several consequences of falling wages. The most significant is that in order to maintain or improve their standard of living, workers are putting in more hours per week as well as working more weeks per year and having more members of the family employed.

Why have these changes in the wage structure occurred? Wage growth would have been stronger had productivity growth been robust, but slow productivity growth cannot wholly explain stagnant or falling real hourly pay (either wages or compensation), nor the widening of the gap between high- and low-wage workers and college-educated and high school-educated workers. Part of the explanation is the effect of technological change and other factors which are expanding the relative demand for more educated workers. Yet, despite this expanding demand, the wages of college-educated workers grew only a modest 1.8% from 1979 to 1989 and fell from 1987 to 1991. We find that the forces depressing the wages of the vast majority of workers include a lower minimum wage, increased import competition, fewer and weaker unions and the employment shift to low-wage industries.

More Hours and Stagnant Wages

To understand changes in wage trends it is important to clearly distinguish between trends in annual, weekly and hourly wages. Trends in annual wages, for instance, are driven by changes in both hourly wages and the amount of time spent working (weeks worked per year and hours worked per week). Likewise, weekly wage trends reflect changes in hourly pay and weekly hours. In this chapter we focus on the hourly pay levels of the workforce and its subgroups. We do this to be able to distinguish changes in earnings as a result of more (or less) work rather than more (or less) pay. Chapter 4 addresses employment, unemployment, underemployment, and other issues related to changes in work time and opportunities.

Table 3.1 illustrates the importance of distinguishing between annual, weekly and hourly wage trends. The annual wage and salary of the average worker in inflation-adjusted terms was 8.2% greater in 1989 than in 1979. However, much of this growth in annual wages was due to longer working hours. For instance, the average worker worked 1,785 hours in 1989, or 78 hours more than the 1,707 hours worked in 1979. This increase is equivalent to each worker working roughly two additional full-time weeks in 1989 than in 1979. The end result was that the average worker in 1989 worked 4.6% *additional* hours at an hourly wage that was only 3.7% *more* than in 1979. Any "wage" analysis which focuses on annual wages would miss the fact that more than half the growth in annual wages from 1979 to 1989 was due to more work rather than higher hourly wages.

The wage and hour trends in the 1980s—more hours and stagnant hourly wages—represent a continuation of the trends in the 1973-1979 period, when hourly wages were essentially flat (falling 0.1% annually) while work hours and the number of weeks worked per year were increasing. In contrast, real hourly wages rose 2.9% annually (and annual hours declined 0.4% annually) between 1967 and 1973. Thus, the post-1973 trend of greater work effort with modestly rising or falling wages replaced a

We focus on the hourly pay levels of the workforce and its subgroups to be able to distinguish changes in earnings as a result of more (or less) work rather than more (or less) pay.

131

TABLE 3.1
Trends in Average Wages and Average Hours, 1967-1990

Year	Produc-tivity Per Hour (1987=100)	Real Wage Indices (1987=100)			Hours Worked Trends		
		Annual Wages	Weekly Wages	Hourly Wages	Annual Hours	Weeks Per Year	Hours Per Week
1967	78.9	81.5	84.2	83.5	1,720	42.8	40.2
1973	88.9	94.8	98.2	99.3	1,683	42.7	39.5
1979	92.2	95.5	98.0	98.5	1,707	43.1	39.7
1989	99.9	103.3	102.1	102.1	1,785	44.8	39.9
1990	100.1	100.1	99.1	99.1	1,781	44.7	39.9
Change		(Annual Growth Rates)					
1967-73	2.0%	2.5%	2.6%	2.9%	−0.4%	−0.1%	−0.3%
1973-79	0.6	0.1	−0.0	−0.1	0.2	0.2	0.1
1979-89	0.8	0.8	0.4	0.3	0.4	0.4	0.1
1989-90	0.2	−3.1	−2.9	−2.9	−0.2	−0.2	−0.1

TABLE 3.2
Changes in Hourly Wages, Benefits and Compensation, 1966-1992
(1991 Dollars)

Year	Private Sector Employer Cost Per Hour			
	Wages & Salaries	Health & Pension	Payroll Taxes	Total Compensation
Pay Level				
1966	$11.83	$0.61	$0.73	$13.17
1972	13.94	1.03	0.91	15.88
1977	14.50	1.43	1.22	17.15
1987	13.41	1.45	1.36	16.21
1989	12.98	1.40	1.40	15.79
1992	12.70	1.53	1.43	15.67
Percent Change				
1966-72	17.8%	68.5%	25.2%	20.5%
1972-77	4.1	38.4	33.5	8.0
1977-89	−10.5	−1.7	15.5	−7.9
1989-92	−2.2	9.3	1.7	−0.7

*Based on available data since peak year data are not available. Data for 1987, 1989 and 1992 are for March.

132

trend of strong real annual wage growth based on higher real hourly wages which allowed for reductions in work time.

Other measures of wage trends presented below suggest that hourly wages were falling over the 1979-1989 period, especially in the latter part of the 1980s. Thus, the picture presented by Table 3.1 may be somewhat optimistic for the 1979-1989 period.

The onset of rising unemployment in 1989 led to a reduction in both working time and real hourly wages by 1990, resulting in a 3.1% drop in real annual wages. As we will show below, the decline in hourly wages evident in the early 1990s recession reflects both the cyclical downturn and a long-term drop in wage growth that began several years before the onset of the recession.

Productivity growth between recent cyclical peaks has been less than that of the pre-1973 economy (Table 3.1). However, lower productivity growth is not sufficient to explain the modest growth in real wages from 1979-1989. After all, hourly productivity actually *increased* by 0.8% annually between 1979 and 1989 while real hourly wages grew by only 0.3%. We will examine explanations for recent wage trends below.

The data in **Table 3.2** provide a more comprehensive portrait of hourly pay trends showing more up-to-date information on trends in hourly wages, benefits and total compensation. Unfortunately, there are no data available between the years of 1977 and 1987, so our analysis must necessarily deviate from an examination of peak-to-peak trends (although one would expect more favorable wage trends between 1979 and 1989 than between 1977 and 1989).

Between 1977 and 1989 there was a 10.5% erosion in hourly wages and a 7.9% drop in hourly compensation. Both hourly wages and compensation continued to fall in the recession years from 1989 to 1992 dropping 2.2% and 0.7% respectively. It is important to note that hourly wages and benefits began falling before the onset of the recession, so the recent decline cannot be ascribed to a cyclical weakness in the labor market. In fact, hourly wages and compensation fell faster in the two years before unemployment started rising in 1989. Between 1987 and 1989, hourly wages and compensation fell 3.2% and 2.5%, respectively. This suggests that the post-1989 erosion of

Between 1977 and 1989 there was a 10.5% erosion in hourly wages and a 7.9% drop in hourly compensation.

133

TABLE 3.3
Hourly and Weekly Earnings of
Production and Non-supervisory Workers, 1947-1991*
(1991 Dollars)

Year	Average Hourly Earnings	Average Weekly Earnings
1947	$ 6.37	$256.53
1967	10.06	382.11
1973	11.37	419.54
1979	11.34	404.75
1982	10.94	380.76
1989	10.61	367.12
1991	10.34	354.66

Changes (Annual Rates of Growth)

Peak to Peak

1947-67	2.3%	2.0%
1967-73	2.0	1.6
1973-79	0.0	−0.6
1979-89	−0.7	−1.0

Contractions

1979-82	−1.2	−2.0
1989-91	−1.3	−1.7

Recovery

1982-89	−0.4	−0.5

*Production and non-supervisory workers comprise more than 80% of wage and salary employment.

compensation reflects long-term rather than cyclical trends.

The erosion of real hourly wages and compensation since 1977 represents a dramatic reversal of their strong growth between 1966 and 1977. From 1966 to 1972 there was a 17.8% growth in real wages, a 2.7% annual rate of growth. Because health and pension benefits grew by 68.5% in this period, hourly compensation grew even faster than wages. Both wages and benefits grew more slowly between 1972 and 1977, but still a respectable 4.1% and 8.0% increase.

Some analysts have presumed that fringe benefit growth in recent years has balanced declining wages, leaving overall compensation growing slowly. This reasoning seems plausible since it is well-known that health-care costs have been rising rapidly (see Chapter 8) and it is believed that fringe benefits comprise a large share of total compensation, perhaps as high as 40 to 45%.

In actuality, benefits are not as important in the overall compensation package as many people believe, nor have the benefits been rising rapidly in recent years. The data in Table 3.2 indicate that over the 1977 to 1989 period the cost of fringe benefits, measured as employer pension and insurance costs per hour, did not grow, and that they comprised less than 10% of the total compensation package in 1989.

Over the 1977 to 1989 period the cost of fringe benefits, measured as employer pension and insurance costs per hour, did not grow.

It is certainly true that health insurance costs have risen quickly. Apparently the rapid growth of jobs with little or no employer-provided health benefits and the increased shift of employer health-care costs onto employees has meant that average fringe benefit costs did not rise over the 1977 to 1989 period. In fact, fringe benefits declined modestly (-1.7%) over this period.

Part of the confusion about the role of fringe benefits is definitional. In surveys of employers by trade associations and by the Bureau of Labor Studies, fringe benefits are broadly defined (following standard corporate accounting procedures) to include paid leave (holidays and vacations), supplemental pay (overtime and shift premiums), and payroll taxes (employer social security and unemployment taxes). Under this broad definition, benefits do comprise about 28% of total compensation costs. However, wage-related items that are received by workers in their regular paychecks, such as paid leave and supplemental pay, are

FIGURE 3A
Real Hourly Earnings of Production and Nonsupervisory Workers, 1967-1991

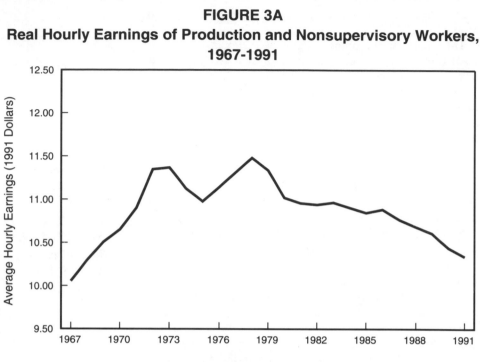

FIGURE 3B
Real Weekly Earnings of Production and Nonsupervisory Workers, 1967-1991

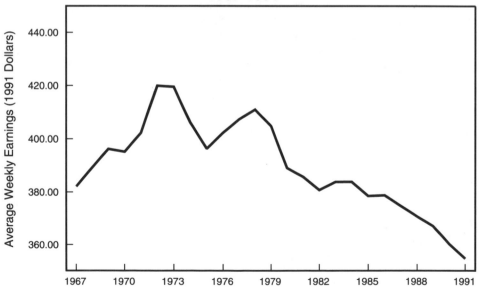

defined as wages by workers when they report their wages in government surveys.

Although studies of labor market trends should examine both wage and benefit trends, those that focus on wage trends alone (usually because of a lack of benefit data) are not misleading. That is, taking account of pension and insurance costs (including both health and life insurance), given their small size and slow growth, would not substantively alter the picture emerging from an analysis of government wage data frequently used to track labor market trends. It should be kept in mind that the erosion of wages is somewhat larger than the erosion of overall compensation. Plus, the years since 1989 have seen a 9.3% expansion of health and pension costs, an increase of $0.13 per hour worked, which partially offset the $0.28 drop in hourly wages.

Further, it should be noted that the data in Table 3.2 show an even larger drop in real hourly wages than the data in Table 3.1. Since the data in Table 3.2 are drawn from a survey of employers rather than one of households, they are probably more accurate.

Low-Paid Occupations Fared Worse

We now turn our attention to the various segments of the workforce and how they managed during the 1980s. In general, the workers who experienced the greatest fall in real wages were those who initially had lower wages, were without a college degree, were in blue-collar or service occupations, or were in the younger age brackets. Since 1987, however, the wages of white-collar and college-educated workers have also eroded in inflation-adjusted terms.

The data in **Table 3.3** and **Figures 3A** and **3B** show wage trends for the 80% of the workforce who are "production and non-supervisory workers." This category includes factory workers, construction workers, and a wide variety of service sector workers, ranging from restaurant and clerical workers to nurses and teachers. For all of these workers, average hourly earnings fell $0.73 from 1979 to 1989, a decline of 0.7% each year. In contrast, hourly earnings were flat in the 1973-1979 period and grew 2.0% to 2.3% per year from 1947 to 1973.

Because of reductions in weekly hours since 1979 as well as in hourly earnings, weekly earnings fell at a rate of 1.0% each year until 1989. The earnings of production and

For the 80% of the workforce who are "production and non-supervisory workers" hourly earnings fell $0.73 from 1979 to 1989, a decline of 0.7% each year.

TABLE 3.4
Changes in Wages and Compensation, 1987-1992
(1991 Dollars)

Year*	Real Wages and Salaries Per Hour		Real Compensation Per Hour	
	Blue-Collar	White-Collar	Blue-Collar	White-Collar
Pay Level				
1987	$12.91	$15.82	$16.22	$18.79
1988	12.74	15.56	16.10	18.54
1989	12.53	15.37	15.87	18.32
1990	12.05	15.46	15.33	18.51
1991	11.83	15.12	15.15	18.15
1992	11.93	15.27	15.42	18.40
Percent Change				
1987-89	−2.8%	−2.8%	−2.2%	−2.5%
1989-92	−4.9	−0.7	−2.8	0.4
1987-92	−7.6	−3.5	−4.9	−2.1

*Data are for March. Consistent data for earlier years not available.

non-supervisory workers in 1989 were $367.12 per week (in 1991 dollars), less than what they were earning in 1967.

Because of cutbacks in hours worked, the weekly wages of production and non-supervisory workers fell 1.7% annually between 1989 and 1991, even faster than the 1.3% annual fall of hourly earnings.

Table 3.4 presents wage and compensation trends between 1987 and 1992 for the blue- and white-collar workforces. Unfortunately, there are no consistent data available for earlier years.

Blue-collar workers have experienced a severe, 7.6% reduction in hourly wages over the 1987-1992 period. White-collar wages also fell in this time period, declining 3.5%. Among both blue- and white-collar workers, wages were falling in the final two years of the 1980s recovery, from 1987 to 1989, suggesting that the forces leading to lower pay were present before the onset of the early 1990s recession. Both groups also saw their total compensation per hour decline between 1987 and 1992, with a 4.9% loss among blue-collar workers and a 2.1% loss among white-collar workers.

Wage Trends by Wage Level

For any given trend in average wages, there will be different outcomes for particular groups of workers if wage inequality rises (or falls), as it has in recent years. **Table 3.5** provides data on wage trends for workers at different points (or levels) in the wage distribution, thus allowing us to characterize wage growth for low-, middle-, and high-wage earners. The data are presented for the cyclical peak years of 1973, 1979, 1989, and for the most recent year, 1991.

These data (and **Figure 3C**) show that the deterioration in real wages since 1979 was both broad and uneven. The breadth of falling real wages is clear from the fact that over the 1979 to 1989 period wages fell for the bottom 80% of the workforce. The overall pattern of wage growth showed that a group's wages fell *more* the lower the group's wage, with wages falling by 11.8% at the 20th percentile and by just 0.4% at the 80th percentile. The wage of the median worker, who earned more than half the workforce but also less than half the workforce, fell 4.9% from 1979 to 1989.

Blue-collar workers have experienced a severe, 7.6% reduction in hourly wages over the 1987-1992 period. White-collar wages also fell in this time period, declining 3.5%.

TABLE 3.5
Wages for All Workers by Wage Percentile, 1973-1991
(1991 Dollars)

Year	Wage by Percentile				
	20	40	Median	60	80
Real Hourly Wages					
1973	$6.49	$8.97	$10.30	$11.60	$15.70
1979	6.44	8.85	10.10	11.50	15.82
1989	5.68	8.23	9.61	10.98	15.76
1991	5.75	8.00	9.48	10.99	15.45
Percent Change					
1973-79	−0.8%	−1.3%	−1.9%	−0.8%	0.8%
1979-89	−11.8	−7.1	−4.9	−4.5	−0.4
1989-91	1.3	−2.8	−1.3	−0.1	−2.0
1973-91	−11.4	−10.8	−8.0	−5.3	−1.6
Dollar Change					
1973-79	−$0.05	−$0.12	−$0.20	−$0.10	$0.12
1979-89	− 0.76	− 0.63	− 0.50	− 0.52	−0.06
1989-91	− 0.07	− 0.23	− 0.13	− 0.01	−0.31
1973-91	− 0.74	− 0.97	− 0.82	− 0.61	−0.25

'Over '89-91 income distribution
reversed trend of stratification

Only those people at the very top of the earnings scale were exempt from wage decline (e.g., wages at the 90th percentile—not shown in the table—did rise 2.5% from 1979 to 1989).

During the recession years from 1989 to 1991 some of the largest wage declines were among the highest wage workers: the hourly wage at the 80th percentile fell 2.0% in these two years, far greater than the 0.4% decline in the prior ten years. These data, along with the findings of falling white-collar wages, show that in recent years high-wage workers had been experiencing the wage declines that blue-collar and low- and middle-wage workers experienced over the entire 1980s.

Over the entire 1973-1991 period the hourly wage of the median worker fell $0.82 from $10.30 to $9.48, an 8.0% decline. There were also wage declines among high-wage workers at the 80th percentile (1.6%) and among low-wage workers at the 20th percentile (11.4%), with the largest wage reductions experienced by the workers with the lowest wages.

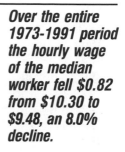

Over the entire 1973-1991 period the hourly wage of the median worker fell $0.82 from $10.30 to $9.48, an 8.0% decline.

just a blip or real trend?

FIGURE 3C
Real Wage Growth by Wage Percentile, 1979-1991

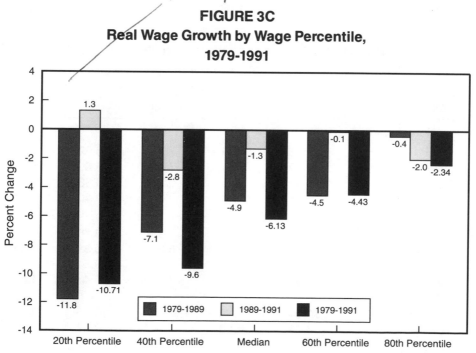

TABLE 3.6
Wages for Male Workers by Wage Percentile, 1973-1991
(1991 Dollars)

Year	Wage by Percentile				
	20	40	Median	60	80
Real Hourly Wages					
1973	$8.08	$10.82	$12.29	$14.09	$18.02
1979	7.84	11.02	12.43	13.80	18.37
1989	6.59	9.61	10.98	13.17	17.64
1991	6.42	9.25	10.83	12.50	17.49
Percent Change					
1973-79	−3.0%	1.9%	1.2%	−2.0%	1.9%
1979-89	−15.9	−12.9	−11.7	−4.6	−4.0
1989-91	−2.6	−3.7	−1.4	−5.1	−0.8
1973-91	−20.6	−14.5	−11.9	−11.3	−3.0
Dollar Change					
1973-79	−$0.24	$0.20	$0.14	−$0.29	$0.34
1979-89	−1.25	−1.42	−1.45	−0.63	−0.73
1989-91	−0.17	−0.36	−0.15	−0.67	−0.15
1973-91	−1.66	−1.57	−1.46	−1.59	−0.53

TABLE 3.7
Wages for Female Workers by Wage Percentile, 1973-1991
(1991 Dollars)

Year	Wage by Percentile				
	20	40	Median	60	80
Real Hourly Wages					
1973	$5.74	$7.19	$7.91	$8.92	$11.54
1979	5.70	6.99	7.81	8.85	11.49
1989	5.32	7.06	8.23	9.33	13.17
1991	5.15	7.00	8.00	9.40	13.00
Percent Change					
1973-79	− 0.7%	−2.8%	−1.3%	−0.7%	−0.4%
1979-89	− 6.8	1.1	5.3	5.3	14.6
1989-91	− 3.1	−0.9	−2.8	−0.8	−1.3
1973-91	− 10.3	−2.6	−1.1	−5.4	12.6
Dollar Change					
1973-79	−$0.04	−$0.20	−$0.10	−$0.06	−$0.05
1979-89	− 0.38	0.08	0.41	0.47	1.68
1989-91	− 0.17	− 0.06	− 0.23	− 0.07	− 0.17
1973-91	− 0.59	− 0.19	− 0.09	0.48	1.46

142

This overall picture, however, masks somewhat different outcomes for men and women. Among men, wages have fallen more, and at all parts of the wage distribution (**Table 3.6**). In the middle, the median male hourly wage fell 11.7% between 1979 and 1989 with an additional 1.4% fall between 1989 and 1991 for a total fall of 12.9%. Even high-wage men (those at the 80th percentile) experienced a significant 4.8% wage decline over the twelve-year period, with the 1979-1989 rate of decline continuing after 1989. Wages among low-wage men fell the most (18.1%) from 1979 to 1991. These data show significant wage deterioration for nearly all men, with the bottom 60% of men suffering more than a 10% wage reduction since 1979. Some groups had experienced falling wages in the 1973-1979 period as well.

These data show significant wage deterioration for nearly all men, with the bottom 60% of men suffering more than a 10% wage reduction since 1979.

The only significant wage growth between 1979 and 1989 appears to have been among higher-wage women (**Table 3.7**). For instance, wages at the 80th percentile grew 14.6%. Even at the median, wages grew by 5.3%. Among women in the bottom 40%, however, wage growth was either minimal or negative.

One of the surprising stories emerging from these data is that women's wages fell across the board during the recession years from 1989 to 1991, with wage reductions at both the 80th and 20th percentiles. At the middle, the hourly wage of the median female worker fell 2.8% from 1989 to 1991, reversing half the 5.3% wage expansion over the prior ten years.

TABLE 3.8
Changes in the Gender Wage Differential, 1979-1991
(1991 Dollars)

Year	Median Hourly Wage		
	Male	Female	Ratio
1979	$12.59	$7.91	62.8%
1989	11.12	8.33	74.9
1991	10.83	8.00	73.9
1989 Alt.*	12.59	8.33	66.2
1991 Alt.*	12.59	8.00	63.5
Change, 1979-1989	$−1.47	$0.42	12.1% pts.

Contribution to Narrower Wage Gap of Changes in:**

	Male Wage Decline	Female Wage Growth	Total
1979-1989	72%	28%	100%

---

*Scenario if male wages had not declined in real terms between 1979 and 1989 or 1991.

**The contribution of "female wage growth" is the growth of the gender differential assuming male real wages had not fallen, relative to the actual change in the differential.

The Male-Female Wage Gap

From 1979 to 1989, the median hourly wage for men fell $1.47 or 11.7% while the median hourly wage for women rose $0.42, or 5.3% (**Table 3.8**). This led to a reduction in the hourly wage gap between men and women by 12.1 percentage points, from 62.8% in 1979 to 74.9% in 1989. This represents a sizeable reduction in wage inequality given that there was a 12.1 percentage point reduction in the initial 37.2 percentage point wage gap (100% less 62.8%). Even after this progress, however, women still earned one-fourth less than men in 1989.

This narrowing of the male/female wage gap is the result of both improvements in real hourly wages for women and real wage reductions for men. Table 3.8 provides an assessment of how much the narrowing of the male-female wage differential is due to rising real wages for women, and how much is due to the real wage loss for men. If real wages among men had not fallen by 1989 but had remained at their 1979 level, the wage gap would have been 66.2% and the wage gap would have closed by 3.4 rather than by the actual 12.1 percentage points. Thus, falling real wages among men can explain 72% of the closing of the gender wage gap between 1979 and 1989. Only 28% of the narrowing of the gender wage gap was due to rising women's real wages (3.4% divided by 12.1%). Unfortunately, the even greater fall in women's than men's median wages from 1989 to 1991 (4.0% versus 2.6%) meant that both genders had falling wages and that gender inequality grew (Table 3.6 and 3.7).

Falling real wages among men can explain 72% of the closing of the gender wage gap between 1979 and 1989.

— but not at 40th or 60th percentile
— interesting to track numbers today

TABLE 3.9
Distribution of Total Employment by Wage Level, 1973-1991

Hourly Wage Relative to Poverty Level*	Percent Distribution of Employment:				Percentage Point Change		
	1973	1979	1989	1991	1973-79	1979-89	1989-91
Total							
Below 75% Pov.	5.8%	4.1%	13.2%	12.7%	−1.7	9.1	−0.6
To below 100%	15.6	21.0	14.8	18.5	5.4	−6.2	3.7
To below 125%	13.5	14.7	14.7	14.3	1.0	0.2	−0.4
To below 200%	35.9	33.1	29.8	29.4	−2.8	−3.4	−0.4
To below 300%	20.5	20.1	18.9	16.4	−0.4	−1.2	−2.5
Above 300%	8.8	7.3	8.6	8.7	−1.5	1.4	0.1
All	100.0	100.0	100.0	100.0			
Men							
Below 75% Pov.	3.3%	2.7%	9.6%	9.5%	−0.6	6.9	−0.1
To below 100%	9.7	13.7	12.7	16.3	4.1	−1.1	3.7
To below 125%	10.3	10.9	13.2	13.1	0.6	2.3	−0.1
To below 200%	36.9	34.2	30.5	30.3	−2.8	−3.7	−0.2
To below 300%	27.3	27.4	22.4	19.4	0.1	−5.0	−3.0
Above 300%	12.5	11.1	11.7	11.5	−1.4	0.7	−0.3
All	100.0	100.0	100.0	100.0			
Women							
Below 75% Pov.	9.4%	6.1%	17.5%	16.3%	−3.4	11.4	−1.2
To below 100%	24.4	30.7	17.3	20.9	6.4	−13.5	3.7
To below 125%	18.3	19.3	16.4	15.7	1.1	−3.0	−0.7
To below 200%	34.4	31.7	28.9	28.4	−2.7	−2.8	−0.5
To below 300%	10.4	10.1	14.9	13.1	−0.3	4.8	−1.8
Above 300%	3.1	2.1	5.0	5.6	−1.1	3.0	0.6
All	100.0	100.0	100.0	100.0			

*The wage ranges are equivalent in 1991 dollars to: Low - $4.88, $4.89 - $6.52, $6.53 - $8.13, $8.14 - $13.02, $13.03 - $19.54, and $19.55 and more.

The Expansion of Low-Wage Jobs

Another useful way of characterizing changes in the wage structure is to examine the trend in the proportion of workers earning low, middle or high wages. These trends are presented in **Table 3.9** for all workers and for men and women. The workforce is divided into six wage groups based on multiples of the "poverty wage level," or the hourly wage a full-time, year-round worker must earn to sustain a family of four at the poverty threshold—which was $6.52 in 1991. Thus, workers are assigned to a wage group according to the degree to which they earned more (or less) than poverty level wages.

The data in Table 3.9 show that there was a significant expansion of workers earning less than poverty level wages between 1979 and 1989. In 1979, only 4.1% of the workforce earned wages at least 25% below poverty level wages. By 1989, 13.2% of the workforce earned such low wages, a shift of 9.1% of the workforce into this low-wage group. Likewise, in 1989, 28% of the workforce earned poverty level wages (adding the two lowest paying categories together), a rise from 25.1% in 1979 and just 21.4% in 1973.

Over the 1979 to 1989 period there was a general downward shift in the entire wage structure as there were proportionately fewer workers in the middle- and high-wage groups. The only exception is that there was a modest expansion of the share of the workforce at the very highest earning level (exceeding three times the poverty level wage). There was a further downward shift in the wage structure from 1989 to 1991, such that 31.2% of the workforce in 1991 earned poverty level wages or less.

Women are much more likely to earn low wages than men. In 1979, 36.8% of women (adding the two bottom groups) earned poverty level wages or less, more than double the 16.4% of men earning such low wages. Women are also much less likely to earn very high wages. In 1979, only 2.1% of women, but 11.1% of men, earned at least three times the poverty wage level.

Among women over the 1979-1989 period there was a larger shift downward—an additional 11.4% earned very low wages—and a larger shift upwards—the two highest wage groups grew by 7.8%. The shift downwards among

Over the 1979 to 1989 period there was a general downward shift in the entire wage structure as there were proportionately fewer workers in the middle- and high-wage groups.

TABLE 3.10
Distribution of White Employment by Wage Level, 1973-1991

Hourly Wage Relative to Poverty Level*	Percent Distribution of Employment:				Percentage Point Change		
	1973	1979	1989	1991	1973-79	1979-89	1989-91
Total Whites**							
Below 75% Pov.	5.4%	4.0%	12.0%	11.3%	−1.5	8.0	−0.6
To below 100%	14.7	19.6	13.4	16.8	4.9	−6.2	3.4
To below 125%	13.0	14.1	14.2	13.8	1.1	0.1	−0.4
To below 200%	35.8	33.5	30.3	30.2	−2.3	−3.1	−0.1
To below 300%	21.5	21.0	20.3	17.9	−0.6	−0.6	−2.4
Above 300%	9.6	8.0	9.8	9.9	−1.6	1.8	0.1
All	100.0	100.0	100.0	100.0			
White Men							
Below 75% Pov.	2.9%	2.4%	8.1%	7.8%	−0.4	5.6	−0.2
To below 100%	8.9	12.3	10.8	14.1	3.5	−1.5	3.2
To below 125%	9.6	10.3	12.4	12.3	0.7	2.2	−0.2
To below 200%	36.4	34.2	30.9	31.4	−2.2	−3.2	0.4
To below 300%	28.5	28.7	24.2	21.2	0.1	−4.5	−3.0
Above 300%	13.7	12.1	13.5	13.3	−1.6	1.4	−0.3
All	100.0	100.0	100.0	100.0			
White Women							
Below 75% Pov.	9.3%	6.1%	16.5%	15.2%	−3.3	10.4	−1.2
To below 100%	23.7	29.7	16.5	19.9	6.0	−13.2	3.4
To below 125%	18.1	19.3	16.2	15.6	1.2	−3.1	−0.6
To below 200%	34.9	32.5	29.6	29.0	−2.4	−2.9	−0.6
To below 300%	10.8	10.2	15.8	14.1	−0.5	5.6	−1.7
Above 300%	3.1	2.1	5.4	6.2	−1.0	3.3	0.8
All	100.0	100.0	100.0	100.0			

*The wage ranges are equivalent in 1991 dollars to: Low-$4.88, $4.89 - $6.52, $6.53 - $8.13, $8.14 - $13.02, $13.03 - $19.54, and $19.55 and more.
**Defined as white non-Hispanic.

women appears to be a shifting down of the workforce earning just below poverty level wages (the second group) to the very lowest wage category. The shift upwards was largely a shift from the middle-wage levels. During the recession years from 1989 to 1991, however, structure of women's wages generally shifted downward.

Among men, the overall changes in the wage structure between 1979 and 1989 meant proportionately fewer high-wage and more low-wage male workers. For instance, there was an increased proportion of men earning less than 125% of the poverty level wage and a shrinking proportion of men in the second and third highest wage groups. In addition, there was only a modest growth in the highest wage group.

Tables 3.10, 3.11 and **3.12** (and **Figure** 3D) present an analysis similar to Table 3.9 for, respectively, white, black and Hispanic employment. For instance, Table 3.10 shows that there was a modest shift downward in the wage structure for whites in the 1970s, followed by a larger downward shift in the 1979-1989 period, and during the early 1990s recession. As with the total workforce, there was a modest growth of high-wage employment among white men and a much larger shift to high-wage employment among white women. Over the entire period from 1973 to 1991, however, there was a slight shift toward proportionately fewer men in the middle and higher wage groups and proportionately more men in the lowest wage groups, which nearly doubled in size (from 11.8% in 1973 to 21.9% in 1991). Among white women, there was a simultaneous shift towards very low-wage work and an expansion of women at the highest wage levels.

Among blacks, there was a general shift out of high-wage employment into low-wage employment from 1979 to 1989 without any significant growth at the highest wage levels. By 1989, 37.4% of black workers were in jobs paying less than poverty level wages, with 33.7% of black men and 41% of black women earning such low wages. The shift towards the very lowest paying jobs—an additional 11.2% of black men and 16.5% of black women—was much larger than among whites. The early 1990s recession only added to the downward shift of the wage structure among both black men and black women.

> *Among blacks, there was a general shift out of high-wage employment into low-wage employment from 1979 to 1989 without any significant growth at the highest wage levels.*

middle class whites being squeezed from above, below

149

TABLE 3.11
Distribution of Black Employment by Wage Level, 1973-1991

Hourly Wage Relative to Poverty Level*	Percent Distribution of Employment:				Percentage Point Change		
	1973	1979	1989	1991	1973-79	1979-89	1989-91
Total Blacks**							
Below 75% Pov.	7.7%	4.7%	18.6%	17.1%	−2.9	13.8	−1.5
To below 100%	19.6	26.8	18.8	24.0	7.2	−8.0	5.2
To below 125%	16.3	17.0	16.9	16.3	0.7	−0.1	−0.6
To below 200%	36.9	31.5	27.8	27.3	−5.4	−3.7	−0.5
To below 300%	15.5	16.2	14.0	11.6	0.7	−2.2	−2.4
Above 300%	4.1	3.9	4.0	3.7	−0.3	0.1	−0.2
All	100.0	100.0	100.0	100.0			
Black Men							
Below 75% Pov.	5.6%	4.2%	15.4%	14.9%	−1.4	11.2	−0.5
To below 100%	14.2	20.9	18.3	23.7	6.7	−2.6	5.4
To below 125%	14.5	14.5	17.1	16.0	0.0	2.6	−1.1
To below 200%	40.7	33.4	29.1	28.0	−7.3	−4.2	−1.2
To below 300%	20.4	21.3	15.8	13.3	0.8	−5.4	−2.5
Above 300%	4.6	5.7	4.3	4.2	1.2	−1.4	0.0
All	100.0	100.0	100.0	100.0			
Black Women							
Below 75% Pov.	10.0%	5.2%	21.7%	19.3%	−4.8	16.5	−2.4
To below 100%	25.7	33.1	19.3	24.3	7.3	−13.8	5.0
To below 125%	18.3	19.6	16.7	16.6	1.3	−2.9	−0.1
To below 200%	32.5	29.5	26.5	26.6	−3.0	−3.0	0.1
To below 300%	9.8	10.7	12.2	10.0	0.9	1.4	−2.2
Above 300%	3.7	1.9	3.6	3.3	−1.8	1.7	−0.4
All	100.0	100.0	100.0	100.0			

*The wage ranges are equivalent in 1991 dollars to: Low-$4.88, $4.89 - $6.52, $6.53 - $8.13, $8.14 - $13.02, $13.03 - $19.54, and $19.55 and more.
**Defined as black non-Hispanic.

There has been a general downshifting of the Hispanic wage structure, for men and for both men and women combined, throughout the 1973-1991 period, coupled with a very modest growth in the highest wage jobs. Among Hispanic women, however, between 1979 and 1989 there was a large shift into the lowest wage jobs, but also a significant (4.6 percentage point) growth in employment paying twice the poverty wage level. Much of this growth in high wage jobs for Hispanic women was reversed in the 1989-1991 downturn.

There has been a general downshifting of the Hispanic wage structure.

TABLE 3.12
Distribution of Hispanic Employment by Wage Level, 1973-1991

Hourly Wage Relative to Poverty Level*	Percent Distribution of Employment:				Percentage Point Change		
	1973	1979	1989	1991	1973-79	1979-89	1989-91
Total Hispanics							
Below 75% Pov.	7.8%	5.3%	18.3%	19.2%	−2.5	12.9	1.0
To below 100%	21.9	30.2	22.5	26.7	8.3	−7.7	4.2
To below 125%	17.1	16.3	16.2	16.1	−0.8	−0.1	−0.1
To below 200%	36.1	30.9	27.0	24.5	−5.2	−3.9	−2.5
To below 300%	13.4	14.3	12.1	9.4	1.0	−2.2	−2.7
Above 300%	3.8	3.0	3.9	4.1	−0.9	0.9	0.2
All	100.0	100.0	100.0	100.0			
Hispanic Men							
Below 75% Pov.	6.8%	3.7%	15.9%	16.8%	−3.2	12.2	0.9
To below 100%	15.6	22.9	22.3	26.9	7.3	−0.6	4.6
To below 125%	14.9	15.1	15.3	16.6	0.2	0.1	1.3
To below 200%	39.7	35.1	28.1	24.3	−4.6	−7.0	−3.7
To below 300%	17.9	19.0	13.9	10.9	1.1	−5.1	−3.0
Above 300%	5.0	4.2	4.6	4.5	−0.8	0.4	−0.1
All	100.0	100.0	100.0	100.0			
Hispanic Women							
Below 75% Pov.	9.3%	7.8%	21.9%	22.9%	−1.5	14.1	1.0
To below 100%	32.2	41.2	22.8	26.5	9.0	−18.4	3.7
To below 125%	20.6	18.1	17.7	15.4	−2.5	−0.4	−2.3
To below 200%	30.2	24.6	25.4	24.7	−5.6	0.8	−0.7
To below 300%	5.9	7.4	9.5	7.2	1.4	2.1	−2.3
Above 300%	1.8	1.0	2.8	3.4	−0.8	1.7	0.6
All	100.0	100.0	100.0	100.0			

*The wage ranges are equivalent in 1991 dollars to: Low-$4.88, $4.89 - $6.52, $6.53 - $8.13, $8.14 - $13.02, $13.03 - $19.54, and $19.55 and more.

151

Figure 3D
Employment at or Below Poverty Level Wages, by Race,
1973-1991

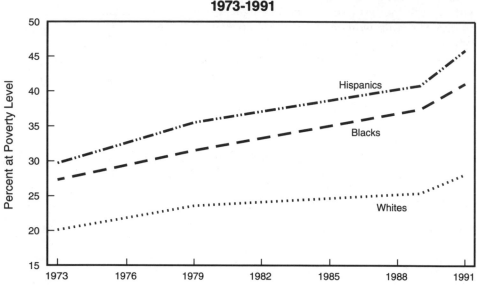

Benefit Reduction

This section examines the trends in the provision of fringe benefits. As we saw earlier in Table 3.2, the real value of both wages and fringe benefits has fallen in recent years. In the 1980s, employers reduced pension and health coverage and provided fewer days off with pay. These benefit reductions have affected workers across the wage scale, but, again, low-wage workers have experienced the greatest fall-off in health and pension coverage.

Table 3.13 examines the trend in employers' provision of the major benefit plans, pensions, and health insurance, between 1966 (the earliest available data) and 1992. Over this time period, the average employer contribution for pension and savings plans more than doubled between 1966 and 1977, but has been falling in each period thereafter. Between 1977 and 1989 the costs of retirement benefits fell nearly 40% from $0.75 to $0.46 an hour. Measured by average inflation (the "All Goods and Services" column), employer provided health insurance benefits rose rapidly over the late 1960s until 1977. Health insurance benefits continued to grow into the 1980s and through 1992 but at a slower *annual* rate of growth. However, the overall rise in employer health insurance costs of $0.26 per hour worked, between 1977 and 1989, is far from exorbitant. Apparently, even though health insurance costs had indeed risen quite rapidly among some employers in this period, there was such large employment growth among employers who provided little or no health insurance benefits that the *average* costs grew only modestly.

However, the far faster inflation in medical services means that the real health insurance coverage provided per hour worked—the amount of real medical services purchasable by an employer's average benefit cost—remained relatively stable between 1977 and 1989. That is, employers increased their spending on health insurance only about as fast as medical service prices were rising, so the quantity and quality of health insurance provided by employers did not generally rise between 1977 and 1989. There was an uptick in health insurance spending between 1989 and 1992 no matter which inflation measure is used.

As the last column in Table 3.13 shows (repeated from Table 3.2) the increase in "voluntary" fringe benefits

> *Even though health insurance costs had indeed risen quite rapidly among some employers in this period, there was such large employment growth among employers who provided little or no health insurance benefits that the average costs grew only modestly.*

TABLE 3.13
Employer Hourly Benefit Costs, by Type, 1966-1992
(1991 Dollars)

| Year | Pension and Savings | Health Insurance Adjusted for Inflation in: | | Total Voluntary Benefits** |
		All Goods & Services*	Medical Services*	
Benefit Level				
1966	$0.34	$0.27	$0.52	$0.61
1972	0.55	0.49	0.79	1.03
1977	0.75	0.68	1.00	1.43
1987	0.58	0.87	0.98	1.45
1989	0.46	0.94	1.01	1.40
1992	0.45	1.09	1.07	1.53
Percent Change				
1966-72	58.6%	81.2%	52.2%	68.5%
1972-77	36.6	40.5	27.3	38.4
1977-89	−37.8	37.7	0.6	−1.7
1989-92	−3.8	15.7	5.6	9.3

*The two inflation-adjusted measures of real insurance costs per hour differ because medical service prices rose substantially faster than average prices.

**Benefits exclusive of payroll taxes, adjusted for overall inflation.

(excluding payroll taxes for social security, workers compensation, and unemployment insurance) was rapid over the 1966-1977 period, but then did not resume until after 1989.

Table 3.14 examines the decline in pension and health insurance coverage for different demographic groups between 1979 and 1989. The percentage of the private workforce covered by a pension plan dropped from 50.0% in 1979 to 42.9% in 1989. This drop in coverage is perhaps one of the reasons for the lessening of pensions costs for employers over this time period. Lower pension coverage appears to be occurring primarily among men, whose coverage fell 10.1 percentage points. Women workers, however, are still less likely than men to be covered by an employer's pension plan. Blacks and whites fared about

The percentage of the private workforce covered by a pension plan dropped from 50.0% in 1979 to 42.9% in 1989.

TABLE 3.14
Changes in Private Sector Benefit Coverage, 1979-1989

Group*	Pension Coverage**			Health Insurance Coverage***		
	1979	1989	Change 1979-89	1979	1989	Change 1979-89
All Workers	50.0%	42.9%	−7.1	68.5%	61.1%	−7.4
By Gender						
Men	55.9%	45.8%	−10.1	74.6%	66.3%	−8.3
Women	41.1	39.2	−1.9	59.1	54.4	−4.7
By Race						
White	51.5%	45.1%	−6.4	69.7%	63.4%	−6.3
Black	45.7	40.5	−5.2	63.0	56.2	−6.8
Hispanic	37.8	26.1	−11.7	60.3	46.0	−14.3
By Education						
High School Dropout	43.7%	27.5%	−16.2	61.0%	44.6%	−16.4
High School Graduate	49.9	41.6	−8.3	68.4	60.0	−8.4
Some College	49.6	43.5	−6.1	69.2	60.9	−8.3
College	59.2	53.4	−5.8	78.5	73.5	−5.0
More than College	60.9	59.6	−1.3	78.5	77.1	−1.4

*Wage and salary workers, ages 18-64, with at least 20 weekly hours and 26 weeks of work.
**Employee participates in employer's plan.
***Employer provides coverage plan and pays at least some of the costs.

TABLE 3.15
Changes in Private Sector Benefit Coverage
by Wage Fifth, 1979-1989

Benefit Coverage*	By Wage Fifth					
	Lowest Fifth	Second Fifth	Middle Fifth	Fourth Fifth	Top Fifth	All
Pension Coverage						
1979	18.3%	36.6%	51.9%	67.8%	76.2%	50.0%
1989	12.8	28.8	44.1	59.1	69.8	42.9
Change, 1979-89	−5.5	−7.8	−7.8	−8.7	−6.4	−7.1
Health Insurance Coverage						
1979	37.9%	60.3%	74.3%	83.1%	87.6%	68.5%
1989	26.4	51.5	67.1	77.4	83.1	61.1
Change, 1979-89	−11.5	−8.8	−7.2	−5.7	−4.5	−7.4

*See Table 3.14 for definitions.

TABLE 3.16
Trends in Days Off with Pay, 1947-1988

Year	Number of Days Off with Pay per Year*	
	Non-farm Business	Manufacturing
1947	n.a.	15.9 days
1966	15.1 days	17.9
1972	17.4	20.5
1977	19.8	22.6
1979	n.a.	23.1
1981	19.8	22.9
1989	16.1	20.8

*Assuming 2,080 hours paid per year. Days off would include, for instance, holiday, vacation, sick, and funeral leave. Years selected based on data availability.

equally well, experiencing a 5.2% and 6.4% drop in coverage, respectively. Hispanics, however, were the hardest hit, with an 11.7% decline in pension coverage from 1979 to 1989. When coverage is examined by education level, the data show declining pension coverage among college graduates and those with less than a college degree, and that coverage declined more among those with the lowest education levels.

Similar trends have occurred regarding health insurance coverage. The greatest loss of health insurance coverage was among men, Hispanics, and workers with less than a college degree. By 1989, more than a third of the workers without a college degree—even those with some education beyond high school—did not have employer provided health insurance.

Table 3.15 shows the erosion of pension and health insurance coverage at each wage level from 1979 to 1989. The general pattern is that the groups with the lowest wages experienced the greatest decline in benefit coverage. The primary exception is for pension coverage among the lowest wage group which had such low pension coverage in 1979—just 18.3%—that there was not much room for erosion.

Workers are also receiving less time off for vacations and holidays (**Table 3.16**). The longest historical comparison available is for manufacturing workers. For these employees, the number of paid days off rose from 15.9 per year in 1947 to 23.1 days in 1979. But this trend towards increased time off with pay was reversed in the 1980s. In 1989, the average manufacturing worker enjoyed only 20.8 days off with pay, 2.3 days less than in 1979. For the non-farm business workforce as a whole, there was a growth in paid time off from 15.1 days in 1966 to 19.8 days in 1981. By 1989, however, paid time off had declined to 16.1 days, a decline of 3.7 days for the average worker. In contrast, European workers have more paid time off and have been obtaining more, rather than less, paid time off since 1980.

By 1989, more than a third of the workers without a college degree—even those with some education beyond high school—did not have employer provided health insurance.

157

TABLE 3.17
The Joint Effect of Education
and Experience on Wages, 1973-1991

| | Effect of: | | |
Years	More (Less) Education and Experience	Other Wage Growth*	Total Changes in Wages
Total			
1973-79	3.5%	−6.4%	−3.6%
1979-89	5.2	−8.4	−2.2
1973-91	11.6	−17.7	−6.6
Men			
1973-79	3.5%	−6.1%	−3.2%
1979-89	4.5	−9.6	−4.6
1973-91	10.5	−19.7	−9.6
Women			
1973-79	4.2%	−5.8%	−2.7%
1979-89	6.0	−1.2	7.6
1973-91	13.5	−8.7	5.7

*Wage growth of workers holding education and experience constant. The effect of the interaction between more education and experience and within-group wage trends was part of the decomposition but is omitted in the table.

What Explains Wage Trends

In this section we shift the discussion from a presentation of wage and benefit trends overall, and for subgroups, to an examination of explanations for the pattern of recent wage growth. The items to be explained include declining average wages since 1973 and the dramatic growth in wage inequality in the 1980s. More specifically, it is important to understand both the average performance of wage growth and why particular groups fared well or poorly.

Table 3.17 (in the last column) shows the change in the hourly wage of the average worker over several time periods between 1973 and 1991. As we have seen earlier, average wages have been falling since 1973. Because of differences in measurement, data sources, and time periods, the drop in average wages in Table 3.17 differs from estimates presented earlier—being a somewhat larger drop than shown in Table 3.1, but a smaller drop than shown in Table 3.2.

Slow productivity growth provides only a partial explanation for average wage trends since productivity grew, but average wages fell.

The most commonly mentioned reason for these wage problems is slow productivity growth (i.e., changes in output per hour worked) since 1973. As the data in Table 3.1 show, productivity grew by only 0.6% annually from 1973 to 1979. Productivity did pick up in the 1979-1989 period, to a slightly higher 0.8% annual rate. The productivity growth record since 1973, however, does not come near the rapid growth in the earlier post-war period—productivity grew 2.4% annually from 1959 to 1973.

Slow productivity has been a major problem and it is important to raise our productivity growth. Notwithstanding this, it is also true that slow productivity growth provides only a partial explanation for average wage trends since productivity *grew,* but average wages *fell*. For example, productivity grew a total of 3.6% between 1973 and 1979 and another 8.3% from 1979 to 1989. It should also be noted that slow productivity growth cannot explain changes in the wage structure, or why some groups experienced wage growth and others experienced wage reductions (such as men's wages falling 9.6% and women's wages rising 5.7% from 1973 to 1991).

TABLE 3.18
The Separate Effects of Education
and Experience on Wages, 1973-1991

Years	Effect of: More (Less) Education*	More (Less) Experience*	Total Wage Growth
Total			
1973-79	3.0%	0.0%	−3.6%
1979-89	3.4	1.7	−2.2
1973-91	7.7	2.7	−6.6
Men			
1973-79	2.9%	−0.2%	−3.2%
1979-89	2.8	1.7	−4.6
1973-91	6.5	2.6	−9.6
Women			
1973-79	3.8%	0.4%	−2.7%
1979-89	4.5	1.3	7.6
1973-91	10.6	1.9	5.7

*Exclusive of any interaction between rising education and experience and wage growth of education/ experience categories.

It has been suggested that the exclusion of benefit trends from a table such as Table 3.17 yields a misleading characterization of pay trends since wages may be falling, but since benefits have risen, there has been an overall increase in total compensation (wages and benefits). However, as we saw earlier in Table 3.2, both compensation and wages have fallen since 1973. It is true, however, that compensation has not fallen as much as wages because, in various time periods, benefits declined less than wages or even grew slightly. So, fringe benefit trends do not solve the puzzle of falling pay and rising productivity.

Unfortunately, there has not been extensive research on this issue. One explanation is that prices for national output have grown more slowly than prices for consumer purchases. Therefore, the same growth in nominal, or current dollar, wages and output yield a faster growth in real (inflation adjusted) output (which is adjusted for changes in the prices of investment goods, exports, and consumer purchases) than in real wages (adjusted for changes in consumer purchases only). Another explanation is that a greater share of productivity growth is accruing to owners of capital via higher profits and interest rates, as shown in Chapter 1.

Economists have identified that greater education and more work experience (from accumulated knowledge and seniority) are associated with wage growth both for individuals and for the economy.

The Role of Education and Experience

Economists have identified that greater education and more work experience (from accumulated knowledge and seniority) are associated with wage growth both for individuals and for the economy. Changes in the economic benefits of having greater education and experience can also be an explanation for changes in the wage differences among educational and age groups and between high- and low-wage workers.

Since 1973 the workforce has been getting older (more experienced) and more educated, factors which lead to economy-wide wage increases. Table 3.17 identifies the effect of greater education and experience on average wage growth overall and by gender. As expected, the shift to a more educated and older workforce has meant higher wages, an increase of 11.6% over the 1973-1991 period.

161

TABLE 3.19
Change in Real Hourly Wage by Education, 1973-1991
(1991 Dollars)

Year	High School Drop-out	High School Graduate	Some College	College	College 2+ years
Real Hourly Wage					
1973	$9.87	$11.28	$12.41	$16.45	$20.13
1979	9.59	10.69	11.85	14.72	17.85
1987	8.24	9.92	11.32	15.24	19.04
1989	7.95	9.63	11.14	14.99	19.20
1991	7.62	9.43	11.03	14.77	19.24
Percent Change					
1973-79	−2.8%	−5.2%	−4.5%	−10.5%	−12.1%
1979-89	−17.1	−9.9	−6.0	1.8	7.6
1989-91	−4.2	−2.1	−1.0	−1.5	0.2
1973-91	−22.8	−16.4	−11.1	−10.2	−5.3
Share of Workforce*					
1973	24.8%	40.8%	18.0%	9.1%	4.5%
1979	21.9	41.8	18.0	10.9	4.9
1987	14.2	41.3	21.9	13.7	6.3
1989	13.7	40.5	22.3	14.0	6.9
1991	12.6	40.0	23.1	14.7	7.0

*Since the shares of those with one year of schooling beyond college are not shown, the presented shares do not sum to one hundred.

Wages received a similar wage boost from greater education and experience (on an annual basis) over both the 1973-1979 and the 1979-1989 periods.

It is also useful to examine the column in Table 3.17 labeled "Other Wage Growth," which tells us what the change in wages would have been had the workforce not become more educated and experienced. Or, in other words, this column tells us the average wage trends among workers with similar education and experience. The results show that economic forces dramatically reduced the wages paid for particular types of workers, yielding a 17.7% decline from 1973 to 1991. Therefore, the greater education and experience of the workforce in recent years was necessary to counter the strong wage reductions among groups of workers with similar education and experience.

The data also shed some light on the reasons for the closing of the gender wage gap. Men's wages received a lesser boost from greater education and experience than did women's wages, 10.5% versus 13.5%. Plus, the economic forces reducing wages for workers of similar education and experience ("Other Wage Growth") had twice the effect on men's wages as they did on women's wages, 19.7% versus 8.7%, over the entire 1973-1991 period. It was in the 1979-1989 period that the effect of economic forces particularly disadvantaged men relative to women. Other sections of this chapter detail some of the factors involved such as international trade, the shift to low-wage industries, and deunionization.

Table 3.18 separates out the wage effects of more education and more experience. These data show that it was educational upgrading rather than experience accumulation that generated the strong wage effects in Table 3.17. Educational upgrading—the shifting of the workforce to proportionately more high school and college graduates and fewer high school dropouts—raised men's and women's wages, respectively, by 6.5% and 10.6% between 1973 and 1991. These data also show that it was in the 1979-1989 period that the experience levels of the workforce grew and that educational upgrading was weaker (on an annual basis).

The greater education and experience of the workforce in recent years was necessary to counter the strong wage reductions among groups of workers with similar education and experience.

163

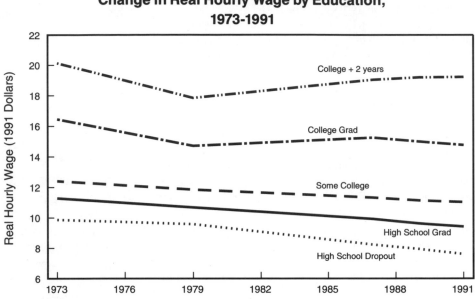

FIGURE 3E
Change in Real Hourly Wage by Education,
1973-1991

Rising Education Wage Differentials

As we have seen, the growth in education achievement affects the level of wages. Changes in the economic returns or payoff to greater education, however, affects the structure of wages by changing the wage gaps between different educational groupings. The growth in "education wage differentials" led to greater wage inequality in the 1980s and helps explain the faster wage growth among high-wage workers. This section examines wage trends among workers at different levels of education and begins the discussion of the causes of rising education wage differentials.

Table 3.19 presents the wage trends and employment shares (percentage of the workforce) for workers at various education levels over the 1973-1991 period. It is common to point out that the wages of "more-educated" workers grew faster than the wages of "less-educated" workers from 1979 to 1989, with the real wages of "less-educated" workers falling sharply. This pattern of wage growth is sometimes described in terms of a rising differential between the wages of the college-educated and high school-educated workforces. For instance, college-educated workers earned 37.7% more than high school graduates in 1979 ($14.72 versus $10.69), but 55.7% more in 1989 (**Figure 3E**).

The usual terminology of the "less-educated" and "more-educated" turns out to be somewhat misleading. Given that workers with some college education (from one to three years) also experienced falling real wages, it is apparent that the "less-educated" group with falling wages comprises more than three-fourths of the workforce. Moreover, the "college-educated" group that did well consists of those with just four years of college who enjoyed a minimal 1.8% wage gain from 1979 to 1989 as well as the more-educated (college plus at least two more years of schooling), but smaller, group that enjoyed better wage growth.

This increased differential between college-educated and other workers is frequently ascribed to an increased relative employer demand for workers with greater skills and education. This interpretation follows from the fact that the wages of college-educated workers increased relative to others despite a sizeable increase in their relative supply from 10.9% of the workforce in 1979 to 14.0% in 1989.

The usual terminology of the "less-educated" and "more-educated" turns out to be somewhat misleading. Given that workers with some college education also experienced falling real wages, it is apparent that the "less-educated" group with falling wages comprises more than three-fourths of the workforce.

165

TABLE 3.20
Change in Real Hourly Wage for Men by Education, 1973-1991
(1991 Dollars)

Year	High School Dropout	High School Graduate	Some College	College	College 2+ years
Real Hourly Wage					
1973	$11.48	$13.50	$14.08	$18.99	$21.09
1979	11.01	12.77	13.80	17.08	19.16
1987	9.35	11.55	13.01	17.55	20.85
1989	9.01	11.15	12.65	17.11	21.02
1991	8.45	10.72	12.49	16.69	21.11
Percent Change					
1973-79	−4.2%	−5.4%	−2.0%	−10.0%	−9.2%
1979-89	−18.2	−12.7	−8.3	0.2	9.7
1989-91	−6.2	−3.8	−1.3	−2.5	0.3
1973-91	−26.4	−20.6	−11.3	−12.1	0.4
Share of Workforce*					
1973	26.6%	37.1%	18.6%	9.4%	5.6%
1979	24.0	38.0	17.8	11.4	6.0
1987	16.4	39.0	20.7	14.1	7.3
1989	15.9	38.7	21.0	14.2	7.8
1991	14.7	38.5	21.8	14.7	7.8

*Since the shares of those with one year of schooling beyond college are not shown, the presented shares do not sum to one hundred.

That is, given the increased supply of educated workers, the fact that their wages were bid up implies a strong growth in employer demand for more-educated workers, presumably reflecting technological and other workplace trends.

An increased relative demand for educated workers is only a partial explanation, especially if ascribed to a benign process of technology or other factors leading to a higher value of education, thus bidding up the wages of more-educated workers. Note, for instance, that the primary reason for an increased wage gap between college-educated and other workers is the precipitous decline of wages among the non-college-educated workforce and not any strong growth of the college wage. Moreover, as discussed below, there are many other factors, such as the shift to low-wage industries, deunionization, and import competition that are important factors.

Perhaps the most important new development is that the real wages of college graduates have begun to fall. From 1989 to 1991 the wages of college graduates fell 1.5% and the wages of those with education beyond college rose a minimal 0.2%. It is critical to note that this trend pre-dates the recession. The college wage began falling in 1987, two years before unemployment started rising in 1989. This suggests that the fall-off in the college-wage reflects long-term rather than cyclical factors. Moreover, the fact that the share of college-educated workers in the workforce increased slowly from 1987 to 1989, and more slowly than from 1979 to 1987, suggests that it was a slowdown in the growth of demand for educated workers rather than any oversupply that was forcing wages down. This slowdown in demand for college-educated workers probably reflects the misfortunes of several white-collar intensive industries in the late-1980s (finance, banking, insurance, retail stores, and real estate) as well as the shrinking of middle-management in manufacturing.

American industries now picking up

The pattern of wage growth in the 1970s was far different. In that period it was the wages of college-educated workers that fell sharply—a drop of 10.5%. Given the sharp drop in the college wage from 1973 to 1979, the fact that the college wage grew only a modest 1.8% from 1979 to 1989 and fell during the 1989-1991 recession years has meant that the college-wage was a remarkable 10.2% less in 1991 than in 1973. In fact, the wages of every educational group fell over this time period. This finding rein-

Perhaps the most important new development is that the real wages of college graduates have begun to fall. The college wage began falling in 1987, two years before unemployment started rising in 1989.

167

TABLE 3.21
Change in Real Hourly Wage for Women by Education, 1973-1991
(1991 Dollars)

Year	High School Dropout	High School Graduate	Some College	College	College 2+ years
Real Hourly Wage					
1973	$7.10	$8.66	$9.78	$12.78	$18.01
1979	7.07	8.34	9.28	11.14	14.63
1987	6.44	8.25	9.59	12.41	16.14
1989	6.24	8.07	9.63	12.54	16.48
1991	6.29	8.10	9.60	12.65	16.57
Percent Change					
1973-79	−0.4%	−3.7%	−5.2%	−12.9%	−18.7%
1979-89	−11.7	−3.2	3.8	12.6	12.6
1989-91	0.8	0.4	−0.3	0.9	0.5
1973-91	−11.4	−6.4	−1.9	−1.0	−8.0
Share of Workforce*					
1973	22.2%	46.2%	17.2%	8.6%	2.9%
1979	19.0	46.6	18.4	10.2	3.4
1987	11.7	44.0	23.3	13.2	5.2
1989	11.2	42.6	23.9	13.8	5.8
1991	10.2	41.8	24.5	14.8	6.1

*Since the shares of those with one year of schooling beyond college are not shown, the presented shares do not sum to one hundred.

forces our earlier conclusion that had there not been a significant increase in education levels since 1973 there would have been a much more severe fall in average wages.

Table 3.20 and **Table 3.21** present wage and employment share trends for the various education groups for, respectively, men and women. Among men, the decline in wages among non-college-educated workers was stronger than that for women and the rise in the college wage was a trivial 0.2% (which was wiped out between 1989 and 1991). The wage of the average high school-educated man fell 12.7% from 1979 to 1989, with the wages of those with some college education falling somewhat less, 8.3%. Among men, the post-1987 drop in the college-wage was also stronger than among women, falling 4.9% from $17.55 to $16.69. The fact that the college-wage fell more among men than among women while there was a slower growth in the supply of college-educated men than of women once again suggests a significant slowdown in employer demand for college-educated men. The fact that the wage among college-educated women has continued to grow from 1987 to 1991 despite a continued fast growth in their supply implies a continued relative growth in the demand for more educated women.

Even though the wages of college-educated women grew rapidly since 1979, a woman college graduate in 1989 still earned less than a man with "some college" education ($12.54 versus $12.65) or than what a high school-educated man earned in 1979 ($12.77).

The wage of the average high school-educated man fell 12.7% from 1979 to 1989, with the wages of those with some college education falling somewhat less, 8.3%.

Young Workers Have Been Hurt Most

Since 1973, the wages of younger workers have been falling faster than the wages of older workers (**Table 3.22**). As a result, there have been significant changes in the wage differentials between younger and older workers. The real hourly wages of workers with from 1 to 15 years of experience fell at least 10% from 1973 to 1991. In contrast, the wages of workers with a minimum of 26 years of experience fell by less than 5% in the same time period. This wage shift against young workers was especially pronounced among men.

TABLE 3.22
Change in Real Hourly Wage by Work Experience, 1973-1991

Years of Work Experience

Years	1-5	6-10	11-15	16-20	21-25	26-30	31-35	35+
All								
1973-79	−4.7%	−6.6%	−3.6%	−7.7%	−4.7%	−1.0%	−0.5%	2.8%
1979-89	−9.2	−7.2	−5.5	−0.6	0.0	−2.4	−1.6	−3.6
1989-91	−3.1	−1.4	−2.0	−2.1	−0.7	0.5	−2.4	−1.7
1973-91	−16.2	−14.6	−10.7	−10.1	−5.4	−2.8	−4.4	−2.6
Men								
1973-79	−3.4%	−5.7%	−3.4%	−5.1%	−6.2%	−1.2%	−0.2%	2.6%
1979-89	−14.1	−10.4	−9.7	−4.5	−1.3	−2.3	−1.3	−2.3
1989-91	−3.7	−3.3	−2.6	−3.6	−3.0	−0.7	−3.5	−3.3
1973-91	−20.1	−18.3	−14.9	−12.6	−10.2	−4.2	−4.9	−3.0
Women								
1973-79	−5.9%	−5.9%	0.4%	−7.5%	−0.3%	−0.9%	−0.3%	1.4%
1979-89	−1.6	2.6	8.4	11.7	12.0	5.6	4.9	2.0
1989-91	−2.1	1.6	−1.1	1.4	1.7	3.7	0.8	1.4
1973-91	−9.5	−1.9	7.6	4.8	13.6	8.5	5.5	4.9

Since the wages of both younger and non-college-edu-cated workers have fallen most rapidly, it follows that the wages of workers who are both young and non-college edu-cated have dramatically fallen. These adverse wage trends were strongest among men. **Table 3.23** and **Figures 3F** and **3G** present trends in "entry-level" wages for high school and college graduates as reflected in the wages of workers with from one to five years of experience. The entry-level hourly wage of a young, male high school gradu-ate in 1989 was 22.4% less than that for the equivalent worker in 1979, a drop of $2.11 per hour. The accumulated

The entry-level hourly wage of a young, male high school graduate in 1989 was 22.4% less than that for the equivalent worker in 1979, a drop of $2.11 per hour.

TABLE 3.23
Entry-Level Wages and Employment Shares, 1973-1991
(1991 Dollars)

Year	High School Graduates			College Graduates		
	All	Men	Women	All	Men	Women
Entry-Level Hourly Wage*						
1973	$8.69	$9.75	$7.56	$12.52	$13.39	$11.54
1979	8.32	9.39	7.12	11.32	12.57	10.07
1987	6.91	7.46	6.32	11.70	12.54	10.96
1989	6.74	7.28	6.16	11.72	12.32	11.17
1991	6.48	6.90	6.02	11.30	11.93	10.75
Percent Changes						
1973-79	−4.2%	−3.8%	−5.8%	−9.6%	−6.1%	−12.8%
1979-89	−18.9	−22.4	−13.5	3.5	−2.0	11.0
1989-91	−3.9	−5.2	−2.3	−3.6	−3.2	−3.8
1973-91	−25.4	−29.3	−20.4	−9.8	−10.9	−6.9
Shares of Employment**						
1973	41.5%	38.5%	45.2%	14.1%	13.3%	15.2%
1979	42.4	41.2	43.9	14.9	13.7	16.3
1987	37.7	38.1	37.1	19.0	17.5	20.5
1989	35.7	36.4	35.1	19.1	17.3	21.1
1991	35.3	36.5	34.0	19.4	17.6	21.4

*Wage of workers with 1 to 5 years of work experience.
**Share of those with 1 to 5 years of work experience by education level within gender.

171

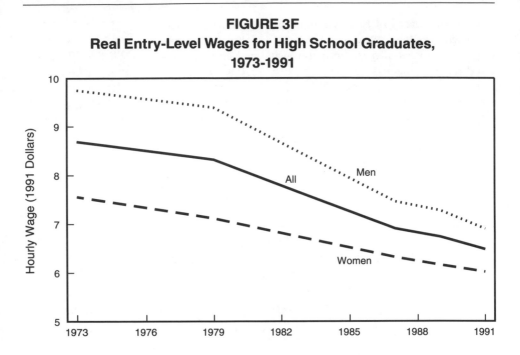

FIGURE 3F
Real Entry-Level Wages for High School Graduates,
1973-1991

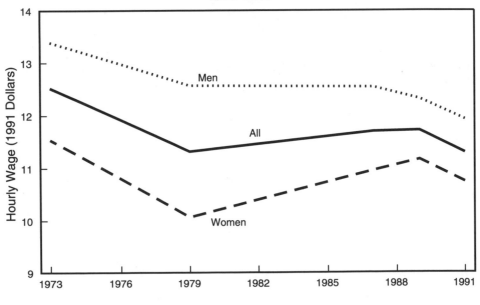

FIGURE 3G
Real Entry-Level Wages for College Graduates,
1973-1991

wage declines from 1973 forward, left entry-level wages for male high school graduates 29.3% lower in 1991 than in 1973. Among women, the entry-level high school wage fell a remarkable 20.4% from 1973 to 1991.

Entry-level wages among college graduates have fallen as well. Following the steep wage decline of the 1970s due to a surplus in college graduates, the entry-level college wage fell modestly over the 1980s and into the 1990s. By 1991, the entry-level college wage for men and women had fallen 10.9% and 6.9%, respectively, since 1973. The fact that entry-level wages for college graduates have fallen less than for high school graduates in recent years means that it still makes economic sense for individuals to complete college. Nevertheless, those who obtain a college degree will have a lower wage than that obtained by an earlier generation of college graduates.

By 1991, the entry-level college wage for men and women had fallen 10.9% and 6.9%, respectively, since 1973.

The Shift to Low-Paying Industries

There was a large employment shift to low-wage sectors in the 1980s that was a consequence of trade deficits and deindustrialization, as well as of stagnant or falling productivity growth in service sector industries. This section examines the significant erosion of wages and compensation that occurred as a result.

Recent employment growth by major industry sector is presented in **Table 3.24**. The 17.2 million (net) jobs created between 1979 and 1989 involved a loss of roughly 1.7 million manufacturing and mining jobs and an increase of 18.8 million jobs in the service sector. The largest amount of job growth (13.7 million) was in the two lowest paying industries—retail trade and services (business, personnel and health). In fact, these two industries accounted for 79.7% of all the (net) new jobs over the 1979-1989 period.

The extent of the shift to low-wage industries is more evident in an analysis of changes in the *shares* of the workforce in various sectors (**Table 3.25**). Several high-wage sectors such as construction, transportation, wholesale trade, communications, and government increased employment in the 1980s but still had a smaller or similar share of overall employment in 1989 as in 1979. A lower share of employment in these high-wage sectors caused the average wage to fall. Overall, the share of the workforce working in the low-wage services and retail trade indus-

173

TABLE 3.24
Employment Growth by Sector, 1979-1989

Industry Sector	Employment (000)			Industry Share of Job Growth	Median Weekly Earnings 1989
	1979	1989	Growth		
Goods Producing	26,461	24,815	−1,646	−9.6%	
Mining	958	678	−280	−1.6	$565
Construction	4,463	4,741	278	1.6	$431
Manufacturing	21,040	19,396	−1,644	−9.6	$415
Durable Goods	12,760	11,448	−1,312	−7.6	$445
Nondurable Goods	8,280	7,948	−332	−1.9	$373
Service Producing	63,363	82,211	18,848	109.6%	
Trans, Comm, Util	5,136	5,549	413	2.4	$502
Wholesale	5,204	6,195	991	5.8	$412
Retail	14,989	19,115	4,126	24.0	$276
Fin, Ins, Real Est	4,975	6,639	1,664	9.7	$406
Services	17,112	26,702	9,590	55.7	$357
Government	15,947	18,011	2,064	12.0	$472
Total	89,823	107,026	17,203		

TABLE 3.25
Changes in Employment Share by Sector, 1979-1989

Industry Sector	Share of Employment		Change in Employment Share
	1979	1989	1979-1989
Goods Producing	29.5%	23.2%	−6.3% pts
Mining	1.1	0.6	−0.4
Construction	5.0	4.4	−0.5
Manufacturing	23.4	18.1	−5.3
Durable Goods	14.2	10.7	−3.5
Nondurable Goods	9.2	7.4	−1.8
Service Producing	70.5%	76.8%	6.3% pts
Trans, Comm, Util	5.7	5.2	−0.5
Wholesale	5.8	5.8	0.0
Retail	16.7	17.9	1.2
Fin, Ins, Real Est	5.5	6.2	0.7
Services	19.1	24.9	5.9
Government	17.8	16.8	−0.9

tries was 7.1 percentage points higher in 1989 than in 1979. The parallel trend was the 7.6 percentage point drop in the share of the workforce in high-paying industries such as manufacturing, construction, mining, government, transportation, communications, and utilities.

The effect on pay levels of the employment shift towards lower paying sectors is illustrated in **Table 3.26**. The first column shows the level of pay that would have prevailed in 1989 if the workforce was in the same occupations and industries as in 1980 (the earliest available year for this analysis) but worked at 1989 wage levels in each occupation and industry. The second column shows the actual pay levels in 1989. The difference between the pay levels in the

The largest amount of job growth was in retail trade and services. These two industries accounted for 79.7% of (net) new jobs over 1979-1989.

TABLE 3.26
Effect of Structural Employment Shifts on Pay Levels, 1980-89

Occupation Group	1989 Pay Levels With Employment Composition of:		Effect of 1980-89 Employment Composition Shift	
	1980*	1989**	Dollars	Percent
All Workers				
Wages	$12.05	$11.72	$ − 0.33	− 2.7%
Benefits	1.42	1.29	− 0.13	− 8.8
Compensation	14.79	14.28	− 0.51	− 3.4
White Collar				
Wages	$13.76	$13.88	$0.12	0.8%
Benefits	1.47	1.42	− 0.05	− 3.1
Compensation	16.46	16.57	0.11	0.6
Blue Collar				
Wages	$12.10	$11.31	$ − 0.79	− 6.5%
Benefits	1.68	1.50	− 0.18	− 10.8
Compensation	15.41	14.35	− 1.06	− 6.9

*March 1989 pay levels using 1980 Census weights corrected for differences between household and employer surveys.
** March 1989 pay levels using current 1989 weights.

175

TABLE 3.27
Pay in Expanding and Shrinking Industries, 1948-1987
(1987 Dollars)

	1948-54	1954-62	1962-73	1973-81	1981-87
Annual Rate of Industry Job Shift*	0.91	0.78	0.78	0.80	1.09
Wages and Salaries					
Expanding Industries	$14,938	$13,648	$16,598	$19,144	$19,154
Shrinking Industries	14,204	18,609	16,765	19,058	26,194
Wage Gap**	734	−4,961	−167	86	−7,040
Benefits					
Expanding Industries	$817	$839	$1,603	$2,778	$2,829
Shrinking Industries	951	2,018	2,091	3,672	6,194
Benefits Gap**	−134	−1,179	−488	−894	−3,365
Compensation					
Expanding Industries	$15,753	$14,491	$18,206	$21,921	$21,983
Shrinking Industries	15,156	20,623	18,853	22,732	32,387
Compensation Gap**	597	−6,133	−647	−811	−10,404

*The annual percentage points that employment shares among industries are shifting.

**Dollar gap by which pay of expanding industries is higher or lower than pay in shrinking industries. Expanding (shrinking) industries are those whose share of total employment increased (decreased) over the particular time period.

Note: These are the only time intervals for which data are available.

first two columns thus reflects the change in the industrial and occupational composition of employment between 1980 and 1989. We use the percentage difference between the first two columns as a measure of the effect of changes in the composition of employment on wages, benefits and compensation. Since there was a shift towards higher-paying *occupations* in this time period this comparison understates the adverse effect of the shift to lower-paying *industries*.

The change in the composition of employment from 1980 to 1989 led to a 2.7% fall in wages, an 8.8% fall in benefits, and a 3.4% fall in total compensation. White-collar pay levels, except benefits, were only mildly affected by recent compositional shifts. Among blue-collar workers, however, the changing industrial composition of jobs lowered wages and compensation by more than 6%.

The degree to which the employment shift, from high- to low-paying industries, lowers average pay levels depends on two factors. One factor is the amount of shifting that occurs, i.e., the percentage of the workforce that is shifting out of high-paying sectors. The other factor is the size of the pay gap between *expanding* and *shrinking* industries. Both factors significantly increased in the 1980s (**Table 3.27**). For instance, a measure of the rate of structural shifting in each period shows that there was more rapid shifting in the 1981-1987 period than in any other period. The degree of shifting accelerated by 36%, from 0.80 to 1.09 percentage points per year, between the 1973-1981 and the 1981-1987 periods.

There was also an increase in the pay gap between the expanding and shrinking industries. In the 1981-1987 period, the industries where employment contracted paid $10,404, or 47%, more in annual compensation than the expanding industries (**Table 3.27, Figure 3H**). This was by far the largest compensation gap between expanding and shrinking industries in the post-war era. The biggest differential was in benefits, with shrinking industries offering more than twice as much in annual benefits.

The faster pace of job shifting and the larger pay gap between expanding and shrinking sectors in the 1980s led to a significant reduction in both wages and benefits

In the 1981-1987 period, the industries where employment contracted paid $10,404, or 47%, more in annual compensation than the expanding industries.

better salaries/benefits
, w/ shrinking industries

177

FIGURE 3H
Pay in Expanding and Shrinking Industries, 1948-1987

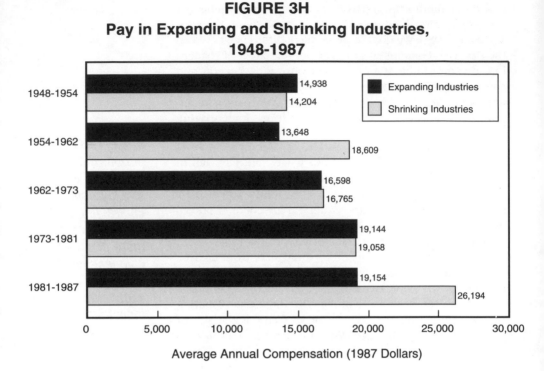

Average Annual Compensation (1987 Dollars)

TABLE 3.28
Effect of Industry Employment Shifts on Pay, 1948-1987

Pay	Effect of Industry Shifts on Annual Pay Growth				
	1948-54	1954-62	1962-73	1973-81	1981-87
Wages	.05%	−.22%	.01%	.00%	−.32%
Benefits	.01	−.05	−.02	−.03	−.15
Compensation	.04	−.28	−.02	−.03	−.48

Note: These are the only time intervals for which data are available.

178

(**Table 3.28**). Industry employment shifts reduced compensation growth by 0.48% a year from 1981 to 1987, far higher than in any other period. The compensation of the overall workforce was thus reduced by 3% from 1981 to 1987 because of the shift to lower paying sectors.

The expansion of low-wage industries reduced the wage growth of production and nonsupervisory workers by twice as much as for the average worker. As previously mentioned, production and nonsupervisory workers make up over 80% of all wage and salary employment. In the most recent period for which data are available, 1981-1986, the wages paid by expanding industries were $134.69 less per week than those paid by shrinking industries (**Table 3.29**). This pay gap, combined with an even faster rate of job shifting, lowered wage growth by 0.61% annually. This compares to the 0.32% wage reduction induced by industry shifting among all workers (Table 3.28).

The compensation of the overall workforce was thus reduced by 3% from 1981 to 1987 because of the shift to lower paying sectors.

TABLE 3.29
Industry Employment Shifts and Production Worker
Weekly Wages, 1972-1986
(1987 Dollars)

| Year | Rate of Industry Job Shift* | Weekly Wage | | | Shift Effect on Annual Wage Growth |
		Expanding Industries	Shrinking Industries	Gap	
1972-81	1.23	$295.65	$ 61.13	$ −65.48	−0.24%
1981-86	1.46	287.51	422.20	− 134.69	−0.61

*The annual percentage points that employment shares among industries are shifting.

Note: These are the only time intervals for which data are available.

TABLE 3.30
Trade Induced Changes in Labor Supply, 1967-1985*

Year	Implicit Labor Input Represented by:			
	As Percent of Total Work Hours			As Percent of Mfg. Hours
	Imports	Exports	Trade Balance	Trade Balance
1967-69	1.31%	1.57%	−0.26%	−0.87%
1970-72	1.64	1.69	−0.05	−0.18
1973-75	1.82	2.17	−0.35	−1.39
1976-78	2.06	2.26	−0.20	−0.80
1979-81	2.31	2.75	−0.44	−1.86
1985	3.49	2.15	1.34	6.36
Change, 1979-81 to 1985	1.18%	−0.60%	1.78%	8.22%

*Equivalently, these numbers can be viewed as increases or decreases in labor demand.

Trade and Wages

Increased international trade and the emergence of large trade deficits in the 1980s were important factors in slowing wage growth and in reducing the wages of non-college-educated workers. The mechanism by which international trade affects wages is that increased imports (or lower exports) cause certain types of jobs, e.g., manufacturing or blue-collar jobs, to be lost or to grow more slowly. Displaced workers, or those not hired in manufacturing because of trade pressures, then compete with similar workers in other sectors, and usually accept lower wages. The increased competition lowers the wages of many workers not directly affected by fewer exports or greater imports. International trade can also affect the wages of workers in the tradeable goods sector who are not displaced, by forcing wage "restraint" or concessions in order to maintain or improve exports or to deter imports.

This section examines the effect of international trade on the wage structure in recent years. Because all of the ways in which international trade affects wages have not been examined by economists, the discussion is necessarily incomplete and *understates* the effect that trade had on wages in the 1980s. We also consider the effect of greater immigration. Consider that imports and exports represent a certain amount of embodied labor. For instance, an imported car represents the hours worked by employees in the auto industry and its feeder industries. Likewise, an exported airplane represents the domestic workforce in the aerospace industry and its feeder industries. An increase (decrease) in imports (exports) can thus be represented by an increased supply of labor competing in the domestic labor market, a factor which can be expected to depress wages. Or, equivalently, greater imports can be considered to lower the demand for domestic labor and therefore depress wages.

Table 3.30 presents such an analysis by translating imports and exports into their equivalent supply of labor in various periods from 1967 to 1985. Because we had a trade surplus (exports exceeding imports), the net effect of trade flows until the 1980s was to lower the size of the workforce (measured in total hours), albeit slightly. For instance, the fact that the labor embodied in exports in the

Increased international trade and the emergence of large trade deficits in the 1980s were important factors in slowing wage growth and in reducing the wages of non-college-educated workers.

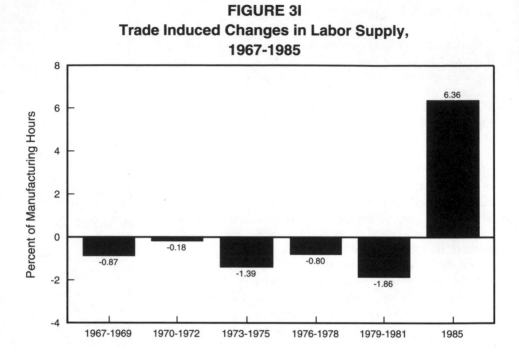

FIGURE 3I
Trade Induced Changes in Labor Supply,
1967-1985

1979-1981 period (2.75% of work hours) was greater than the labor embodied in imports (2.31% of work hours) had the effect of decreasing the overall labor supply by 0.44%. It is as if 0.44% of the workforce moved abroad to compete with foreign workers, and therefore no longer competed with U.S. workers for jobs. All things equal, a cut in domestic labor supply would be expected to raise wage levels.

The growth of imports and the decline in exports over the early 1980s (i.e., the rise of the trade deficit) meant the effect of our trade balance in 1985 was to raise the effective labor force by 1.34%. Our trade failures in the early 1980s thus can be characterized as augmenting the labor force by 1.78% (the shift from the 1979-1981 period to 1985).

Of course, trade developments do not fall on all sectors of the workforce equally but, in fact, impinge directly on the manufacturing workforce. When our trade balance is translated into the equivalent share of the manufacturing workforce (in the last column) we see that the deteriorating trade deficit was effectively equivalent to increasing the manufacturing workforce by 8.22% (**Table 3.30, Figure 3I**). These data indicate that changes in trade flows can have a sizeable effect on the domestic workforce. This is especially the case since these data only consider the direct effects of trade flows (the loss of steel jobs to steel imports), but not the indirect effects (the loss of iron ore and coal jobs when domestic steel production declines).

Table 3.31 examines the size of the immigrant labor force in total and by education level. Increased immigration in the 1980s increased the immigrant share of the male (female) labor force from 7.0% to 9.9% (6.8% to 8.6%) from 1980 to 1988. Immigrants accounted for twenty-five percent of the increase in the labor force over this time period (not shown in the Table).

Did the increase in immigration adversely affect particular segments of the native workforce? Table 3.31 shows the share of the immigrant and native workforces at particular education levels. Overall, the native and immigrant workforces had similar education levels, particularly in the percentage with a college degree. The only striking difference is that immigrants are much more likely to be high school dropouts, a disparity that grew stronger over the 1980s. This suggests that immigration may have adversely affected high school dropouts relative to college graduates.

Increased immigration in the 1980s increased the immigrant share of the male (female) labor force from 7.0% to 9.9% (6.8% to 8.6%) from 1980 to 1988. Immigrants accounted for twenty-five percent of the increase in the labor force over this time period.

TABLE 3.31
Immigration and Labor Supply, 1980-1988

	Distribution of Workers					Immigrant Share of Labor Force
	High School Dropout	High School Graduate	Some College	College or More	Total	
Immigrant Men						
1980	39.6%	22.4%	16.3%	21.7%	100.0%	7.0%
1988	36.0	22.6	16.2	25.1	100.0	9.9
Immigrant Women						
1980	35.7%	30.3%	17.9%	16.0%	100.0%	6.8%
1988	28.3	27.6	21.8	22.3	100.0	8.6
Native Men						
1980	22.7%	37.9%	19.2%	20.2%	100.0%	
1988	15.3	36.0	24.6	24.0	100.0	
Native Women						
1980	18.2%	44.9%	20.9%	16.0%	100.0%	
1988	11.0	40.6	27.6	20.7	100.0	

Table 3.32 carries forward the analysis of Table 3.30 by translating the overall effect of trade into the effects on the size of (or demand for) the high school and college-educated workforce. These data show that the deterioration of the trade deficit from 1980 to 1985/86 raised the size of the high school-educated workforce by 3.1% and the college-educated workforce by 0.5% (in effect, reducing it by 1.2% rather than 1.7%). This suggests that trade developments had a particularly adverse effect on high school-educated workers (who are about two-thirds of the entire workforce), absolutely, as well as relative to college graduates. With the decline of the trade deficit in the late 1980s the overall effect of trade lessened, but remained large.

Table 3.33 presents estimates of the effect of trade and immigration developments on the wage differential between college- and high school-educated workers. The impact on the wage differential depends on two factors. One is the impact of trade and immigration on raising the

Trade developments had a particularly adverse effect on high school-educated workers (who are about two-thirds of the entire workforce), absolutely, as well as relative to college graduates.

TABLE 3.32
Effect of Trade on Labor Supply of
High School and College Workers, 1980-1988

| Year | Trade Induced Increased (Decreased) Labor Supply* | |
	High School Equivalents**	College Equivalents**
Share of Workforce		
1980	0.4%	−1.7%
1985-86	3.5	−1.2
1987-88	2.5	−1.5
Change		
1980-85/86	3.1%	0.5%
1980-87/88	2.1	−0.2

*This analysis expresses a trade deficit as an increased supply of workers (i.e., as if those producing imports were augmenting domestic labor supply). Equivalently, these data could be interpreted as reduced demand (positive numbers) or increased demand (negative numbers).

**In this analysis the "high school dropout" and "some college" workforce has been assigned to be either a high school or college equivalent.

TABLE 3.33
Effect of Trade and Immigration on
Education Wage Differential, 1980-1988

Item	Time Period	
	1980-85	1980-88
Change in College/High School Wage Differential*	10.7% pts.	12.4% pts.
Change in Wage Differential Due to Trade and Immigration with Elasticity**:		
(a) 0.709	2.0% pts.	1.3% pts.
(b) 1.0	2.9	1.9
(c) 0.5	1.5	1.0
Contribution of Trade and Immigration to Change in Wage Differential with Elasticity**:		
(a) 0.709	19%	10%
(b) 1.0	27	15
(c) 0.5	14	8

*The differential and effects of trade and immigration are computed as changes in log wages, which approximates percentage or percentage point changes.

**The "elasticity" gives the percentage change in the college/high school wage differential resulting from a percentage change in the relative supply of college graduates.

labor supply of (or lowering the demand for) high school-relative to college-educated workers. The second factor is the degree to which a given increase in the relative supply of (or decrease in the demand for) high school workers translates into a change in the wage differential. The uncertainty about the size of this second factor—the "elasticity" of the wage differential with respect to relative supplies—motivates the need to examine the effect of trade and immigration using a range of estimates of the "elasticity."

As the first line of Table 3.33 shows, the wage gap between high school- and college-educated workers grew by 10.7 percentage points in the early 1980s and by 12.4 percentage points by 1988. The estimates of the effects of trade and immigration on the change in the wage differential through 1985 range from 1.5 to 2.9 percentage points. Over the longer period the effect is from 1.0 to 1.9 percentage points. Overall, trade and immigration can account for from 14% to 27% of the higher differential over the early 1980s or from 8% to 15% of the higher differential over the longer period through 1988.

Trade and immigration can account for from 14% to 27% of the higher differential over the early 1980s or from 8% to 15% of the higher differential over the longer period through 1988.

The Union Dimension

The percentage of the workforce represented by unions fell more rapidly in the 1980s than in the previous several decades. This falling rate of unionization has lowered wages, not only because some workers no longer receive the higher union wage, but also because there is less pressure on non-union employers to raise wages.

Table 3.34 and **Figure 3J** show the union wage premium—the degree to which union wages exceed non-union wages—by sector, by occupation, and by type of pay (benefits or wages). The union premium is larger for total compensation, 33.8%, than for wages alone, 25.7%. This reflects the fact that unionized workers are paid insurance and pension benefits which are more than double those of non-union workers. For blue-collar workers, the union premium in insurance and benefits is even larger, with union blue-collar workers receiving from 157.6% to 278.3% more than their non-union counterparts. The union wage differential is also much higher among blue-collar workers. The union premium is generally higher within the service- than the goods-producing sector.

187

TABLE 3.34
Comparison of Union and Non-Union Hourly Wages and Benefits, 1989
(1989 Dollars)

Occupation or Industry Group	Total Compensation	Wage	Insurance	Pension
All Workers				
Union	$16.47	$14.13	$1.52	$0.76
Nonunion	12.31	11.24	0.72	0.35
Union Premium*:				
Dollars	$4.16	$2.89	$0.80	$0.41
Percent	33.8%	25.7%	111.1%	117.1%
Collar				
Union	$17.46	$4.82	$1.70	$0.87
Nonunion	10.40	9.49	0.66	0.23
Union Premium*:				
Dollar	$7.06	$5.33	$1.04	$0.64
Percent	67.9%	56.2%	157.6%	278.3%
Goods-Producing				
Union	$17.84	$15.00	$1.85	$0.89
Nonunion	14.6	13.15	1.04	0.44
Union Premium*:				
Dollar	$3.18	$1.85	$0.81	$0.45
Percent	21.7%	14.1%	77.9%	102.3%
Service-Producing				
Union	$15.11	$13.25	$1.20	$0.64
Nonunion	11.57	10.62	.62	0.32
Union Premium*:				
Dollar	$3.54	$2.63	$0.58	$0.32
Percent	30.6%	24.8%	93.5%	100.0%

*The dollar and percent by which the pay of union workers exceeds that of nonunion workers.

The effect of the erosion of unionization on the wages of a segment of the workforce depends on the degree to which deunionization has taken place and the size of the union wage premium among that segment of the work-force. **Table 3.35** shows both the degree to which unionization declined and the union wage premium by occupation and education level. These data are used to calculate the effect of deunionization over the 1978-1988 period on the wages of particular groups and how deunionization affected occupation and education wage differentials.

Union representation fell dramatically among blue-collar and high school-educated workers from 1978 to 1988. Among the high- school graduate workforce 12% fewer were unionized in 1988 than in 1978, a more than 25% shrinkage of the unionization rate from 42% to 30%. Because unionized high school graduates earned 16% more than equivalent non-union workers, the loss of unionization lowered the average high school graduate's wage by 1.4%. The net effect of deunionization was to increase the college to high school wage differential by 1.5 percentage points.

Because unionized high school graduates earned 16% more than equivalent nonunion workers, the loss of unionization lowered the average high school graduate's wage by 1.4%.

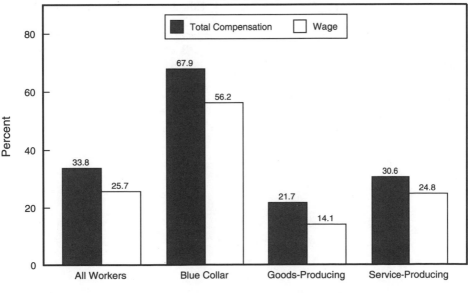

FIGURE 3J
Union Pay Premiums,
1989 Dollars

TABLE 3.35
Effect of Deunionization on Male Occupation and Education Differentials, 1978-1988

A. Effects of Union Decline on Wages*

Group	Union Wage Premium**	Percent Union			Effect of Union Decline On Wages
		1978	1988	Change 1978-88	
By Occupation					
White-Collar	1%	18%	13%	− 5	−0.1%
Blue-Collar	26	47	33	− 14	−3.6
Difference	3.5				
By Education					
College	− 2%	17%	14%	− 3	0.1%
High School	16	42	30	− 12	−1.4
Difference	1.5				

B. Contribution of Deunionization to Higher Wage Differentials*

	(1) Change in Wage Differential 1978-88*	(2) Union Decline Effect on Wage Differential	(3) Percent of Higher Differential Explained by Union Decline
White-Collar/Blue-Collar	7%	3.5%	50%
College/High School	6	1.5	25

*Differentials and change in differentials computed in natural log percentage points.
**Controlling for workforce characteristics.

190

Deunionization had a larger negative effect on blue-collar wages—lowering them 3.6%—and thus a larger effect on the occupational than the educational wage differential. Less unionization can account for 25% and 50% of, respectively, the higher educational and occupational wage differentials in 1988.

Table 3.36 presents a similar analysis for workforce groups by race, gender and education level. In 1979, unionization rates were higher among blacks than whites and

Deunionization had a larger negative effect on blue-collar wages—lowering them 3.6%.

TABLE 3.36
Impact of Deunionization on Changes in
Average Hourly Earnings, 1979-1989

Demographic/ Education Group*	Percent Union			Union Premium in 1979**	Effect of Union Decline On Wages
	1979	1989	Change 1979-89		
White Males					
High School Dropout	48%	24%	− 24	24%	− 6%
High School Graduate	47	32	− 15	10	− 1
College or More	24	17	− 7	− 1	0
Black Males					
High School Dropout	42%	29%	− 13	22%	− 3%
High School Graduate	56	30	− 26	18	− 5
College or More	41	42	1	− 12	0
White Females					
High School Dropout	27%	11%	− 16	14%	− 2%
High School Graduate	19	12	− 7	11	− 1
College or More	35	25	− 10	15	− 2
Black Females					
High School Dropout	32%	18%	− 14	17%	− 2%
High School Graduate	43	24	− 19	10	− 2
College or More	52	28	− 24	21	− 5

*Workers ages 25-64.
**Controlling for workforce characteristics.

191

TABLE 3.37
Effect of Unions on Wages, by Wage Fifth, 1973-1987

	Lowest Fifth	Second Fifth	Middle Fifth	Fourth Fifth	Top Fifth	Average
Percent Union						
1973	38.9%	43.7%	38.3%	33.5%	12.5%	33.7%
1987	23.5	30.3	33.1	24.7	17.7	26.4
Change, 1973-87	−15.4	−13.4	−5.2	−8.8	7.2	−7.3
Effect of Union on:						
Union Wage, 1987	27.9%	16.2%	18.0%	0.9%	10.5%	15.9%
Average Wage, 1987	6.6	4.9	6.0	0.2	2.1	4.2
Wage Effect of Deunionization						
1973-87	−4.3%	−2.2%	−0.9%	−0.1%	0.8%	−1.1%

TABLE 3.38
Effect of Unions on Male Wage Inequality

Item	Wage Inequality, 1973-87*	Wage Inequality, 1978-88*
Early Year	.227	.235
Later Year	.284	.269
Change in Inequality	.057	.034
Change Due to Lower Unionization	.012	.007
Deunionization Contribution to Total Rise in Inequality	21%	21%

*Change in variance of Ln earnings among men ages 25-64.
**Change in variance of Ln earnings among men ages 24-66.

among men than women. Among men of both races, the decline in unionization was greatest for high school dropouts and graduates. Because of the relatively high-unionization rates of black and white women college graduates in 1979, the extent of deunionization among women was sizeable for all educational groups. The effect of deunionization on wages was as high as 6% for white high school dropouts and 5% for black high school graduates. Among men, the pattern of deunionization's impact on wages led to a sizeable increase in the differential between less educated and more educated workers.

Table 3.37 examines the effect of lower unionization on workers at various wage levels. The data show that unions have their largest effect on the wages of lower-wage workers, as unions raise the wages of union members in the lowest and second lowest fifths by respectively, 27.9% and 16.2%. Because workers in the bottom three-fifths have higher unionization rates and higher union wage premiums, the effect of unions on average wages for these groups is largest—increasing the average wage from 4.9% to 6.6%. Thus, unionization is a force that moderates the wage gap between high-wage and middle- or low-wage workers.

Unionization declined more among low-wage workers than among high-wage workers from 1973 to 1987, with unionization actually increasing among the top fifth. The wage impact of this deunionization was to increase the wage gap between high- and low-wage workers.

Table 3.38 shows two studies of the effect of the drop in unionization on overall wage inequality. Both studies show that there was a sizeable growth in wage inequality between the 1970s and the late 1980s. Moreover, both studies show that lower unionization can account for 21% of the higher wage inequality.

Unionization is a force that moderates the wage gap between high-wage and middle- or low-wage workers.

193

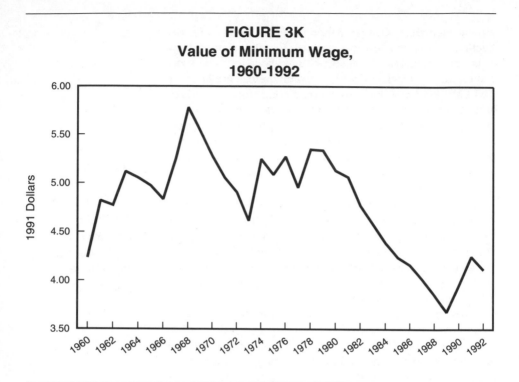

FIGURE 3K
Value of Minimum Wage,
1960-1992

TABLE 3.39
Value of Minimum Wage

Year	Minimum Wage, Current Dollars	Minimum Wage, 1991 Dollars
1967	$1.40	$5.25
1973	1.60	4.62
1979	2.90	5.34
1989	3.35	3.68
1990	3.80	3.96
1991	4.25	4.25
1992	4.25	4.11
Period Averages		
1960s	$1.29	$5.04
1970s	2.07	5.11
1980s	3.33	4.39
1990-91	4.25	4.11

194

An Eroded Minimum Wage

The real value of the minimum wage has fallen considerably since its high point in the late 1960s (**Figure 3K**). The decline was particularly steep and steady between 1979 and 1989, when inflation whittled the real minimum wage (in 1991 dollars) down from $5.34 to $3.68 (**Table 3.39**). The legislated increases in 1990 and 1991 raised the minimum wage, but still left it $1.09 less in 1991 than in 1979. The minimum wage's purchasing power in 1992 ($4.11) was 20% less than the value of the minimum wage in the 1960s or 1970s.

While a full-time, year-round job at the minimum wage kept a family of three above the poverty line in 1979, the same job would have placed such a family $2,300 *below* the poverty line in 1992 (**Table 3.40**). Even a two-person family dependent on a minimum wage worker would have been $606 below the poverty line in 1992.

It has been argued that the minimum wage primarily affects teenagers and others who do not have family responsibilities. **Table 3.41** examines the demographic composition of the workforce earning less than the minimum wage. In fact, 84.8% of minimum wage workers in

The minimum wage's purchasing power in 1992 ($4.11) was 20% less than the value of the minimum wage in the 1960s or 1970s.

TABLE 3.40
Amount by Which Earnings of a Full-Time, Full-Year Minimum Wage Worker are Above (Below) the Poverty Line (1991 Dollars)

Year	Dollar Difference Between Annual Minimum Wage Earnings and Poverty Line by Family Size		
	2-Person	3-Person	4-Person
1967	$2,711	$1,017	−$2,046
1973	1,045	−649	−3,712
1979	2,152	459	−2,605
1989	−1,510	−3,204	−6,268
1990	−927	−2,621	−5,685
1991	−324	−2,017	−5,081
1992	−606	−2,300	−5,364

TABLE 3.41
Minimum Wage Workforce Demographic Composition, 1991

Groups	At or Below Current Minimum Wage		At or Below Real Value of 1979 Minimum Wage	
	Number of Workers (000)	Percent of Minimum Wage Workforce	Number of Workers (000)	Percent of Minimum Wage Workforce
Gender				
Male	2,019	35.6%	6,487	39.2%
Female	3,630	64.3	10,063	60.8
Age				
Teenagers	859	15.2%	2,312	14.0%
Adults	4,796	84.8	14,237	86.0
Race/Ethnicity				
White	3,853	68.1%	11,229	67.9%
Black	878	15.5	2,523	15.2
Hispanic	729	12.9	2,220	13.4
Other	197	3.5	577	3.5
Hours				
Full-time	2,409	42.6%	8,199	49.5%
Part-time	3,248	57.4	8,351	50.5
Total	5,657	100.0%	16,550	100.0%
Minimum Wage Workforce as Share of Total	5.7%		16.8%	

1991 were adults, suggesting that many minimum wage workers do have economic responsibilities. Although the majority of minimum wage workers do work part-time (less than 35 hours weekly), there were 2.4 million full-time minimum wage workers in 1991, comprising 42.6% of the total. While minorities are disproportionately represented among minimum wage workers, more than two-thirds of the 5,657,000 minimum wage workers in 1991 were white. Minimum wage workers also tend to be women (64.3% of the total).

This analysis of the minimum wage workforce is narrow, however, as a higher minimum wage affects workers who earn more than, but close to the minimum—they receive increases when the minimum wage increases. Moreover, any legislated minimum wage increase would affect those earning below the *new* rate, as well as those somewhat above the *new* rate. For these reasons, Table 3.41 also presents the demographic breakdown of those workers who, in 1991, earned at or below, the minimum wage level that prevailed in 1979 ($5.34 in 1991 dollars). This more broadly defined minimum wage workforce included 16,550,000 workers, or 16.8% of the total workforce. Thus, any significant change in the minimum wage would affect a substantial portion of the workforce. The demographic breakdown of the minimum wage workforce under this broader definition is more inclusive of full-time workers and men but otherwise similar to the narrower definition.

Table 3.42 examines the degree to which minimum wage workers live in poor families. The analysis presents the percentage of low-wage workers living in poor families, under three definitions of poverty. One definition (the third in the Table) is the conventional definition where a family is considered poor if its total wages do not exceed the poverty threshold. This definition is inadequate since many families may have "earnings problems" but have above poverty incomes because there are multiple workers. The other two definitions of "poor" families identify those families with "earnings problems" because the family head has either a low hourly wage (the first section in the Table) or low annual wages (the middle section in the Table). The analysis separately examines the workforce at or below the 1989 minimum wage and those workers who would be affected by the 1990 and 1991 legislated increases.

Any legislated minimum wage increase would affect those earning below the new rate, as well as those somewhat above the new rate.

has lower minimum wage increased employment?

197

TABLE 3.42
Distribution of Wage Earners by Minimum Wage Status
and Family Income, 1989

Distribution by Definition of Poor Family	Percent of Workers in Wage Class in Poor Families*	
	Men	Women
1. Family Head Earns Poverty Level *Hourly* Wage		
Below 1989 Minimum Wage ($3.35)	62.7%	52.2%
Affected by 1990 Minimum Wage ($3.36-3.80)	54.4	40.8
Affected by 1991 Minimum Wage ($3.81-4.25)	50.7	38.1
Above 1991 Minimum	11.6	16.8
2. Family Head Earns Poverty Level *Annual* Wage		
Below 1989 Minimum Wage ($3.35)	64.4%	54.4%
Affected by 1990 Minimum Wage ($3.36-3.80)	56.1	49.6
Affected by 1991 Minimum Wage ($3.81-4.25)	56.2	46.8
Above 1991 Minimum	16.2	22.7
3. Total Family *Annual* Wages Below Poverty Level		
Below 1989 Minimum Wage ($3.35)	46.4%	45.1%
Affected by 1990 Minimum Wage ($3.36-3.80)	38.1	37.4
Affected by 1991 Minimum Wage ($3.81-4.25)	34.3	31.8
Above 1991 Minimum	6.2	9.1

*Shows percentage of workers in particular wage ranges living in poor families.

Using the conventional definition of poverty, the percentage of minimum wage workers in poor families was 46.4% among men and 45.1% among women. Among workers earning above the 1989 but below the 1991 minimum wage there were from 30% to 40% in poor families.

When the definition of poor is expanded to include families where the head earns poverty level wages (either hourly or annually) we see that nearly two-thirds of male and over half of female minimum wage workers in 1989 were "poor." Also, roughly half of the workforce in 1989 that would be affected by future minimum wage increases were poor in 1989. These data suggest that the majority of workers affected by the minimum wage live in either poor families or in families where the head has low earnings.

Table 3.43 shows the share of the workforce that was aided by the minimal increases in the minimum wage in 1990 and 1991. These increases lifted 3.6% of the workforce (and 3.1% of adults and 15.9% of teenagers) above the new minimum.

When the definition of poor is expanded to include families where the head earns poverty level wages we see that nearly two-thirds of male and over half of female minimum wage workers in 1989 were "poor."

TABLE 3.43
Distribution of Workers Before and After
Minimum Wage Increases 1990-1991

Shares of Workers Earning*	All		Teens (16-19)		Adults (20+)	
	First Qtr. 1990	Second to Fourth Qtr. 1991	First Qtr. 1990	Second to Fourth Qtr. 1991	First Qtr. 1990	Second to Fourth Qtr. 1991
Less than 1990 Minimum	5.1%	2.2%	21.1%	6.1%	4.5%	2.0%
to 1991 Minimum	5.1	4.4	22.9	22.0	4.4	3.8
to 1979 Minimum	11.1	10.2	30.8	38.2	10.3	9.2
Above	78.7	83.2	25.3	33.7	80.9	85.0
Total	100.0	100.0	100.0	100.0	100.0	100.0
Percent of workers shifted above new 1991 minimum**	3.6%		15.9%		3.1%	

*Measured in inflation adjusted wages so distribution changes because of minimum wage change or the (very unlikely) chance that low-wage worker wage gains exceeded inflation.
**Difference between share of workforce below new 1991 minimum in last nine months of 1991 versus first three months of 1990.

199

TABLE 3.44
Effect of Computer Usage on Wage Structure, 1984-1989

Education Group	Percent Using Computer on Job		Wage Premium for Computer Use*		Computer Use Average Wage Effect**		
	1984	1989	1984	1989	1984	1989	Change 1984-89
High School Dropout	5.0%	7.8%	15.4%	14.5%	0.8%	1.1%	0.4%
High School Grad.	19.3	29.3	17.0	17.5	3.3	5.1	1.8
Some College	30.6	45.3	18.6	20.6	5.7	9.3	3.6
College	41.6	58.2	20.3	23.7	8.5	13.8	5.4
Post-College	42.8	59.7	22.0	27.0	9.4	16.1	6.7
All	24.6	37.4					

*Wage differential received by workers using computer on the job.
**Effect of computer usage on average wage in educational group.

Technology

Technological change can affect the wage structure by displacing some types of workers and by increasing demand for other types of workers. Given the seemingly rapid diffusion of microelectronic technologies in recent years, many analysts have considered technological change as a major factor leading to the recent increase in wage inequality. Unfortunately, because it is difficult to measure the extent of technological change and its overall character (whether it is generally de-skilling or up-skilling) it is difficult to identify the role of technological change on recent wage trends. There is some information available on the spread of one leading type of technology—computer use— that does suggest that technological change has played a significant role in creating greater wage inequality.

Table 3.44 shows that there was a considerable rise in the use of computers at the workplace, with the percentage of the workforce using computers at work growing from 24.6% in 1984 to 37.4% in 1989. This increased use of computers has affected educational wage differentials because the most educated groups are more intensive users of computers on the job and receive a higher wage premium for doing so. For instance, in both 1984 and 1989 a college graduate was at least twice as likely as a high-school graduate to use a computer on the job (41.6% versus 19.3% and 58.2% versus 29.3%). Although high school graduates received about 17% extra pay for having computer skills in either 1984 or 1989, the wage premium for computer use among college graduates rose from 20.3% to 23.7%.

The result of differential payment for and differential use of computers on the job has been to widen pay differences between educational groups. This can be seen in the last three columns of Table 3.44 which present the effect of computer use on the average wage of each educational group (based on multiplying the intensity of computer use by the wage premium) in 1984 and 1989 and the change between 1984 and 1989. These data suggest that the spread of workplace computer technology widened the educational pay gap between 1984 and 1989 by 3.6% by increasing the pay of the average college graduate by 5.4% but increasing the pay of the average high school graduate by just 1.8%.

The result of differential payment for and differential use of computers on the job has been to widen pay differences between educational groups.

201

TABLE 3.45
Executive Pay Levels, 1979 and 1989
(1989 Dollars)

	United States		France		West Germany		Japan		United Kingdom	
	1979	1989	1979	1989	1979	1989	1979	1989	1979	1989

Annual CEO Pay (Thousands of Dollars)*

Pre-Tax Pay	$308.2	$612.8	$119.4	$181.7	$136.2	$206.7	$149.3	$371.1	$121.2	$194.9
After-Tax Pay	153.9	429.1	77.5	111.7	75.3	112.4	70.9	178.4	35.0	122.2

*Includes the salaries and capital distributions (such as equities and bonds) for CEOs of firms with sales exceeding $790 million.

TABLE 3.46
Real Growth in Executive Pay, 1979-1989

	Percent Change, 1979-1989	
	Pre-Tax Pay	After-Tax Pay
United States	19%	66%
France	13	7
West Germany	17	15
Japan	22	24
United Kingdom	3	123

*In national currencies adjusted for domestic consumer price increases. Same definition as Table 3.45.

Executive Pay Soars

Another cause of greater wage inequality has been the enormous pay increases received by top executives and the spill-over effects.

The 1980s was a very prosperous decade for top U.S. executives. In stark contrast to the declining real wages of average workers, the pay of chief executive officers (CEOs) of major U.S. companies grew by 19% from 1979 to 1989 (Tables 3.45 and 3.46). Given the poor performance of the U.S. economy relative to competitor nations in the 1980s, it may be surprising to find that the pay of the United States' CEOs has far outpaced that of the CEOs in other countries. The 19% growth in pre-tax pay for U.S. CEOs in the 10 years from 1979 to 1989 was greater than the growth of CEO pre-tax pay of 13%, 17%, and 3% respectively, in France, West Germany, and the United Kingdom (Table 3.46).

Since tax rates on high-income residents have been severely reduced in the U.S. and the United Kingdom over the last 10 years, changes in pre-tax and after-tax pay differ widely. In Britain, for instance, tax rates for the rich have been reduced so much that CEO after-tax pay increased 123% from 1979 to 1989, even though pre-tax pay increased by only 3% (Figure 3L). In the United States, after-tax pay of CEOs increased by 66%, more than three times as fast as their pre-tax pay increased. In the 10 years between 1979 and 1989, after-tax CEO pay increased far faster in the U.S. than in Japan, West Germany, or France.

CEOs in the U.S. are paid roughly twice as much as the CEOs of our major industrial competitors (Table 3.47). For instance, the average annual compensation of a CEO heading a U.S. firm with at least $100 million of sales was $508,000 in 1988. A comparable executive in Japan makes 62% as much while a CEO in West Germany makes 51% as much.

The 1980s was a very prosperous decade for top U.S. executives. In stark contrast to the declining real wages of average workers, the pay of chief executive officers grew by 19% from 1979 to 1989.

203

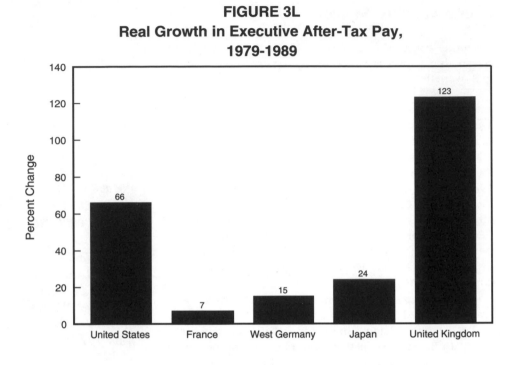

FIGURE 3L
Real Growth in Executive After-Tax Pay,
1979-1989

TABLE 3.47
Comparative Pay Levels of Workers and CEOs, 1988

Country	CEO Total Compensation*		Index, Manufacturing Production Worker Hourly Compensation (U.S. = 100)**
	Dollars	Index (U.S. = 100)**	
Canada	$267,000	53	96
France	255,000	50	99
Germany	260,000	51	136
Italy	216,000	43	97
Japan	317,000	62	98
United Kingdom	286,000	56	77
United States	**508,000**	**100**	**100**

*CEOs of firms with sales exceeding $100 million.
**Using April 1988 exchange rates.

In contrast, the pay of American manufacturing workers was more equal to that of our major competitors in Canada, France, Italy, and Japan in 1988. However, West German workers earn 36% *more* than American workers. Only British workers have significantly lower wages than U.S. workers (see Chapter 9 for further analysis).

The pay gap between CEOs and manufacturing production workers is far larger in the U.S. than in other industrialized countries (**Table 3.48**). In 1988, U.S. CEOs were paid 17.5 times as much as manufacturing production workers, a pay gap about twice as wide as in West Germany, Italy, and France and 50% greater than in Japan.

The pay gap between CEOs and manufacturing production workers is far larger in the U.S. than in other industrialized countries.

TABLE 3.48
The Pay Gap Between Executives and Production Workers, 1988

Country	Ratio of CEO Pay to Production Worker Pay*
Canada	9.5
France	8.9
Germany	6.5
Italy	7.6
Japan	11.6
United Kingdom	12.4
United States	**17.5**

*Assumes CEO works 52 40-hour weeks.

TABLE 3.49
Black-White Wage Differentials Among Young Workers

Year	Total	Education Level			Region***		
		High School Dropouts	High School Graduates	College Graduates	Midwest	North-East	South

Black-White Earnings Gap*

Year	Total	High School Dropouts	High School Graduates	College Graduates	Midwest	North-East	South
1973	−10.3%	−16.4%	−10.3%	− 3.7%	0.8%	− 0.4%	−13.9%
1979	−10.9	−17.4	−12.5	− 2.5	− 2.5	− 6.6	−15.8
1989	−16.4	−16.5	−16.7	−15.5	−18.9	−13.8	−16.7

Annual Growth in Earnings Gap

	Total	High School Dropouts	High School Graduates	College Graduates	Midwest	North-East	South
	−0.6%	−0.2%	−0.5%	−1.6%	−1.4%	−0.8%	−0.2%

Cause of Increased Racial Earnings Gap**

	Total	High School Dropouts	High School Graduates	College Graduates	Midwest	North-East	South
Region	−4%	−95%	−12%	7%	0%	31%	−13%
Urban	15	43	21	3	13	7	19
Industry	10	51	10	7	32	18	−26
Occup'n	19	−9	35	19	11	−5	44
Deunion-ization	5	23	10	2	9	14	24
Lower Min. Wage	17	98	27	3	7	4	75
Unexplained	38	0	9	59	28	22	0
Total	100	100	100	100	100	100	100

*Based on regression of log hourly earnings on race, schooling, education, region and metropolitan status (converted to percentage terms) of workers with less than nine years experience.

**Positive (negative) numbers imply the factor led to a larger (lower) earnings gap between black and white hourly earnings. Each causal factor can lead to a greater earnings gap if black workers become more concentrated in lower wage parts of the wage structure (e.g., occupations, regions, industries) or if the parts of the wage structure where blacks are concentrated see less wage growth.

***For high school graduates and dropouts only.

Increased Black-White Wage Inequality

One other dimension of increased wage inequality is that the pay of black workers fell relative to that of white workers. As the top panel (first column) in **Table 3.49** shows, a black worker in 1989 earned 16.4% less than an equivalent (in terms of education, experience, region and so on) white worker in 1989. This "black-white earnings gap" jumped up fifty percent from 1979 to 1989 from a 10.9% level in 1979 to its 16.4% level in 1989. Education-wise, the greatest increase in the black-white earnings gap was among college graduates, with a minimal 2.5% differential in 1979 exploding to 15.5% in 1989 (**Figure 3M**). Regionally, racial inequality rose the most in the Midwest and in the Northeast and increased only slightly in the South (where substantial racial pay differences persisted).

Table 3.49 also presents information (in the bottom panel) on what factors explain the growth in the overall racial wage gap (shown in the middle panel) as well as the

Education-wise, the greatest increase in the black-white earnings gap was among college graduates, with a minimal 2.5% differential in 1979 exploding to 15.5% in 1989.

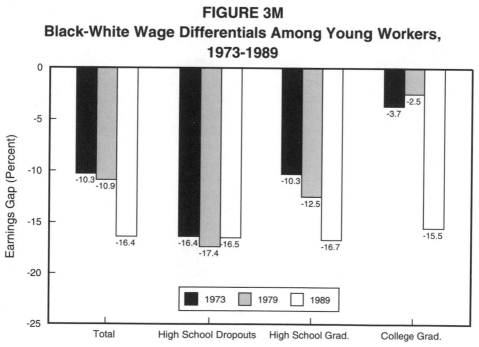

FIGURE 3M
Black-White Wage Differentials Among Young Workers, 1973-1989

TABLE 3.50
Employment Opportunity and Wage Growth, 1980-1989

Group*	Employment/Population Ratio			Real Wage Growth (Annual Rate)
	1980	1989	Change 1980-89	
White Males				
High School Dropout	75%	71%	−4	−1.8%
High School Graduate	88	86	−2	−1.1
College Graduate	94	93	−1	0.3
Black Males				
High School Dropout	64%	57%	−7	−0.3%
High School Graduate	84	76	−8	−1.2
College Graduate	90	86	−4	0.2
White Females				
High School Dropout	40%	42%	2	−0.3%
High School Graduate	58	65	7	0.3
College Graduate	71	79	8	1.4
Black Females				
High School Dropout	43%	41%	−2	−0.5%
High School Graduate	64	68	4	−0.2
College Graduate	85	86	1	0.5

*Workers ages 25-64.

gap among workers by education and region. Not surprisingly, the causes of rising racial wage inequality differ for the various workforce subgroups. Among the workforce as a whole, the increase in blacks' wage disadvantage arose from the fact that the occupations and cities in which blacks are concentrated had lower wage growth, that blacks became relatively more concentrated in low-wage industries and non-union settings, and that blacks were particularly disadvantaged by the failure of the minimum wage threshold to keep up with inflation.

The large increase in the racial gap among college graduates is largely unexplained, except for the concentration of blacks in occupations with low wage growth. The greater racial wage gap in the Midwest is primarily due to an increased concentration of blacks (relative to whites) in non-union low-wage industries and in occupations with below average wage growth.

That a sizeable portion of the growth in the racial pay gap remains unexplained suggests that greater, or more effective, discrimination as well as weaker government enforcement of anti-discrimination laws may have played an important role.

The greater racial wage gap in the Midwest is primarily due to an increased concentration of blacks (relative to whites) in non-union low-wage industries and in occupations with below average wage growth.

Did Lower Wages Buy More Employment?

This chapter has found that inequality rose between the college- and non-college-educated and the black and white workforces. Pay differences between men and women lessened, but primarily because men's wages fell. This analysis, however, can not tell us what happened to differences between groups in their total labor market experiences without addressing the various groups' employment and unemployment trends. The reason is that a group with falling relative wages (a growing wage gap between it and other groups) may have improved its relative opportunities for employment (or lower unemployment) independent of, or because of, its falling relative wage.

Table 3.50 shows what happened to various groups (by race, gender and education) between 1980 and 1989 in terms of wage growth and in changes in the employment-population ratio, a measure of employment opportunity (which falls because of higher unemployment and rises with greater labor force participation at steady unemploy-

TABLE 3.51
The Effect of Occupation and Industry Employment
Shifts on Skill and Education Requirements, 1970-2000

Education or Skill Requirement	1970-79	1980-88	BLS Projections 1988-2000
	(Ten-Year Rates of Change*)		
Skill Indices			
Handling Data	4.02%	4.28%	1.37%
Verbal Aptitude	2.31	2.05	0.80
Intellectual Aptitude	2.28	2.03	0.75
General Education Development (GED-L)	4.34	3.91	1.52
Handling People	2.19	1.85	0.69
Handling Things	− 1.36	− 2.13	− 0.37
Education			
Mean Years Required	1.41%	1.09%	0.49%
Shares of Employment Requiring: (Percentage Point Change*)			
Less than High School	− 1.44%	− 0.88%	− 0.42%
High School Graduate	− 1.33	− 1.88	− 0.67
Some College	0.56	0.63	0.33
College Graduate or More	2.22	2.00	0.83

*To facilitate comparisons of these time periods which are of different length the data have been converted to ten-year rates of change: the change if the annual rate of change in these time periods had continued for ten years.

ment rates). In general, the groups that fared most poorly on the wage front also fared poorly on the employment front. Among both black and white men, for instance, non-college-educated workers not only fell behind college-educated workers in wage growth, they also experienced a greater employment drop. Among white women, the groups with the fastest wage growth—high school and college graduates—also had a greater expansion of employment. Only among black women did high school graduates fare worse in wage growth but do better in terms of employment expansion. In general, that is, the groups that experienced wage difficulties also experienced employment difficulties. Among the demographic groups in the 1980s, lower wages did not "buy" more employment. The groups most adversely affected by wage trends were also adversely affected by reduced employment opportunities.

The groups that fared most poorly on the wage front also fared poorly on the employment front.

Jobs of the Future

The jobs of the future will not be markedly different than the jobs available today. Future jobs will have somewhat greater education and skill requirements, primarily the need for basic literacy and numeracy, but will not necessarily pay more than current jobs. Moreover, the skill and education requirements of jobs are expected to grow more slowly than in the 1970s and 1980s. Despite the widely held assumption that higher-paying white-collar jobs are the wave of the future, there is little evidence that the deterioration of job quality and wages that took place in the 1980s will be reversed in the 1990s, unless current trends change dramatically. One view of future jobs can be obtained by analyzing labor market trends anticipated by the Bureau of Labor Statistics (BLS) in its employment projections to the year 2000.

Key to this analysis is the examination of both the continued expansion of white-collar, high-paying *occupations* and the job shift from high-paying to low-paying *industries*. Analyses of future jobs which focus solely on occupational change, as many do, paint too optimistic a picture.

Tables 3.51 and 3.52 provide data which allow us to assess the combined effect of industry shifts (e.g., the rising importance of services) and occupation shifts (e.g., the rising importance of white-collar professional/technical jobs).

211

TABLE 3.52
The Effect of Occupation and Employment Shifts on Pay, 1970-2000

Pay	1970-79	1980-88	BLS Projections 1988-2000
	(Ten-Year Rates of Change*)		
Weekly			
Wages	2.76%	1.52%	0.20%
Compensation	2.20	0.64	−0.17
Hourly			
Wages	2.47%	1.49%	0.32%
Compensation	1.96	0.63	−0.03

*To facilitate comparisons of these time periods which are of different length the data have been converted to ten-year rates of change: the change if the annual rate of change in these time periods had continued for ten years.

FIGURE 3N
Growth in Skill and Education Requirements, 1970-2000

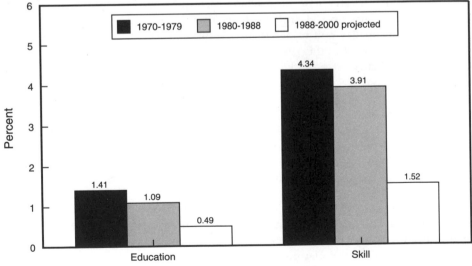

Ten-Year Rates of Change

Specifically, the data show the effect of changes in the distribution of jobs, among occupations and industries, on the education levels and skills (measured by six indices) required on the job, and on hourly compensation (wages and fringe benefits) levels in recent years, as well as the effects anticipated by Bureau of Labor Statistics employment projections.

Our analysis in Table 3.51 shows that job skill requirements have been increasing over the last two decades and are projected to increase over the 1990s. Rather than the skills explosion projected by some analysts, however, future growth in skill and education requirements will be historically slow. For instance, the new distribution of jobs across industries and occupations in 2000 will require workers' education levels to grow at a 0.49% (ten-year) rate over the 1988-2000 period, a rate less than half the 1.09% rate, and a third the 1.41% rate required by actual job shifts, respectively, in the 1980s and 1970s (**Figure 3N**).

The data in Table 3.52 confirm these trends by showing that expected shifts in the industry and occupation distribution of jobs will have a slight negative effect on hourly and weekly compensation. Over the 1970s and 1980s, in contrast, employment compositional shifts led to higher rates of pay.

These analyses corroborate one of our conclusions drawn from the recent declines in the pay of white-collar and college-educated workers—the expansion of demand for more "skilled" and more "educated" workers is slowing down. The ultimate conclusion to be drawn, therefore, is that wage trends and employment projections both suggest that only a modest skill and educational upgrading of jobs will occur in the 1990s, absent some change in government policies and employer strategies.

> *Rather than the skills explosion projected by some analysts, however, future growth in skill and education requirements will be historically slow.*

Conclusion

There have been dramatic changes in the wage structure over the last dozen years. The real hourly wages of most workers have fallen. The group experiencing the greatest wage decline was male, non-college-educated workers. Between 1973 and 1991, the wages paid on entry-level jobs for high school graduates have declined by 29.3% for young men and 20.4% for young women. Given that three-fourths of the workforce have not completed college, the recent drastic deterioration of the wages of high school graduates (whose wages fell somewhat more than high school dropouts, but somewhat less than those with "some college") means that the vast majority of men are working at far lower wages than their counterparts did a generation earlier.

The vast majority of men are working at far lower wages than their counterparts did a generation earlier.

There were, however, some bright spots in the wage trends of the 1980s. College graduates obtained a modest growth in wages; workers with advanced or professional degrees enjoyed substantial wage growth; and, middle- and high-wage women made significant wage advances. Unfortunately, most of the positive news of the 1980s turned negative in the later stages of the recovery (1987-1989) and/or during the early-1990s downturn. The wages of men and women have fallen across the board in recent years. Moreover, there are reasons to believe that wages will not improve as the economy rebounds.

Chapter 4

Jobs: Worsening Underemployment

There has been much attention focused on the length of the 1980s recovery—the second longest in the post-war period—and the length of the 1990s recession—the longest of the post-war period. However, it is the *character* rather than the duration of these phases of the business cycle that is important to note. As described in Chapter 3, the incidence of low-wage work grew over the 1980s and expanded further in the early 1990s. This chapter describes the growth of other types of labor market distress.

For instance, the recent recession was characterized by an unusually large rise in white-collar unemployment coupled with historic slow growth in white-collar employment. Although groups traditionally impacted heavily by recessions—manufacturing, construction, and blue-collar workers—experienced an even greater growth in their unemployment rate than white-collar workers, the rise in white-collar unemployment signaled important market shifts. For example, this sluggish growth of white-collar employment signifies the end of the service sector boom of the 1980s and helps explain the recent reductions in the real wages of white-collar and college-educated workers.

Further, since the 1970s, there has been a growth in part-time and temporary employment—situations where workers receive low pay, are economically insecure, and receive few benefits or opportunities for training and advancement. The increase in these and other types of "contingent" work reflects the types of jobs being created by

Sluggish white-collar employment growth signifies the end of the 1980s service sector boom . . . helps explain the recent reductions in the real wages of white-collar and college-educated workers.

215

TABLE 4.1
Unemployment Rates

Year	Total	Male	Female	White	Black	Hispanic
1947	3.9%	4.0%	3.7%	n.a.	n.a.	n.a.
1967	3.8	3.1	5.2	3.4%	n.a.	n.a.
1973	4.9	4.2	6.0	4.3	9.4%	7.5%
1979	5.8	5.1	6.8	5.1	12.3	8.3
1989	5.3	5.2	5.4	4.5	11.4	8.0
1991	6.7	7.0	6.3	6.0	12.4	9.9

TABLE 4.2
Rates of Underemployment*, 1973-1991

	1973 (000)	1979 (000)	1989 (000)	1991 (000)
Civilian Labor Force	89,429	104,962	123,869	125,303
Unemployed	4,365	6,137	6,528	8,426
Discouraged Workers	689	771	859	1,025
Involuntary Part-Time	2,343	3,373	4,894	5,767
Total Underemployed*	7,397	10,281	12,281	15,218
Rate of Underemployment**	8.2%	9.7%	9.8%	12.0%
Unemployment Rate	4.9	5.8	5.3	6.7

*Unemployed, discouraged, and involuntary part-time.
**Total underemployed workers divided by the sum of the labor force plus discouraged workers.

Many people work in temporary jobs because they cannot find permanent jobs.

employers rather than any increased preference of the workforce for these types of jobs. That is, many people are working in part-time or temporary jobs because they cannot find full-time or permanent jobs.

There has also been an expansion of low paying self-employment plus a growth of multiple jobholding primarily fueled by the fact that the wages received on one job are not sufficient to meet regular expenses. The character of

216

employment has decidedly shifted so that a much larger proportion of the workforce is either underemployed, overemployed, low paid, or trapped in unfavorable job situations.

Unemployment and Underemployment

Table 4.1 gives a broad view of unemployment rates by gender and race during various peak years in the business cycle since World War II and for 1991, the most recent year for which data are available. In peak years, the economy is at its strongest, and therefore unemployment is at its lowest. In 1989, the most recent cyclical peak year, unemployment in every category was less than or roughly equal to that in 1979, the prior cyclical peak. Relative to 1973 and earlier peak years, however, 1989 unemployment rates are generally above average. The recession caused unemployment to rise to 6.7% by 1991 and to 7.5% in the second quarter of 1992.

Unemployment among minority workers continues to be roughly double that of white workers, as has been the case throughout the post-war period. Moreover, even at the peak of the last business cycle in 1989, the 11.4% unemployment rate among black workers was higher than the average unemployment rate reached in any post-war *recession* (see Table 4.3 below). The major shift in the 1980s was a lowering of the unemployment rate for women relative to men.

A broader measure of the lack of employment success in the labor market is the rate of underemployment. This alternative measure includes unemployed workers but also includes people working part-time who want to work full-time ("involuntary" part-timers) and those who want to work but have been discouraged from searching for jobs by lack of previous success ("discouraged workers"). The rate of underemployment was essentially the same at the end of the 1980s recovery in 1989 as it was in 1979, 9.8% versus 9.7% respectively, despite a somewhat lower unemployment rate (**Table 4.2** and **Figure 4A**). The 1989 underemployment rate was substantially higher than the 5.3% unemployment rate primarily because of a high rate of involuntary part-time work, a phenomenon discussed below.

The character of employment has decidedly shifted so that a much larger proportion of the workforce is either underemployed, overemployed, low paid, or trapped in unfavorable job situations.

217

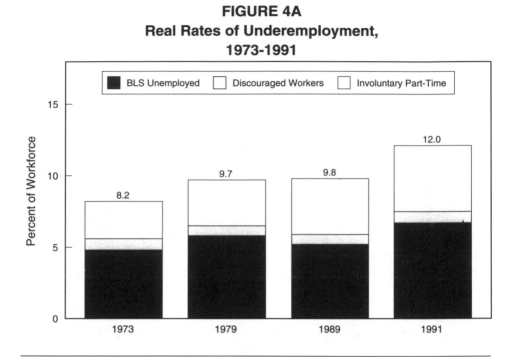

FIGURE 4A
Real Rates of Underemployment,
1973-1991

Legend: ■ BLS Unemployed □ Discouraged Workers □ Involuntary Part-Time

Y-axis: Percent of Workforce

Bars: 1973: 8.2; 1979: 9.7; 1989: 9.8; 1991: 12.0

TABLE 4.3
Changes in Unemployment in Postwar Recessions

Recessions: Beginning and Ending Quarter	Unemployment Rate		Changes in Unemployment by Cause:			Duration of Contraction
	Peak	Trough	All Unemployment	Permanent Job Loss	Other Reasons*	
1948:4-1949:4	3.8%	7.0%	3.2%	n.a.	n.a.	11 Months
1953:3-1954:2	2.7	5.8	3.1	n.a.	n.a.	10
1957:3-1958:2	4.2	7.4	3.2	n.a.	n.a.	8
1960:2-1961:1	5.2	6.8	1.6	n.a.	n.a.	10
1969:4-1970:4	3.6	5.8	2.2	0.9%	1.3%	11
1973:4-1975:1	4.8	8.2	3.4	1.3	2.1	16
1980:1-1980:3	6.3	7.7	1.4	0.6	0.8	6
1981:3-1982:4	7.4	10.7	3.3	1.7	1.6	16
Average of prior recessions	4.8	7.4	2.7	—	—	11
1990:2-1992:2	5.3	7.5	2.2	1.6	0.6	22

*Includes unemployment due to temporary layoff or quits and of new entrants or re-entrants who have not yet found work.

218

The 1989 underemployment rate, equivalent to the 1979 rate, 9.7%, was significantly higher than the underemployment rate of 8.2% in 1973. The data in Table 4.2 also show that in the recession year of 1991, underemployment has risen from 1989 not only because of higher unemployment but also because of nearly one million more involuntary part-time workers.

The Early 1990s Recession

The recent recession lasted at least 22 months, twice as long as the 11-month average length of earlier downturns.

The recession of the early 1990s differed from prior post-war recessions in several different ways (based on the assumption that the recession ended in the second quarter of 1992). For example, even though the recent recession was longer than other recessions, unemployment showed lesser gains. As **Table 4.3** shows, the recent recession lasted at least 22 months, twice as long as the 11-month average length of earlier downturns (**Figure 4B**). Unemployment, however, rose by 2.2%, far less than the 3% plus rise in the mid-1970s and mid-1980s recessions. Nevertheless, the

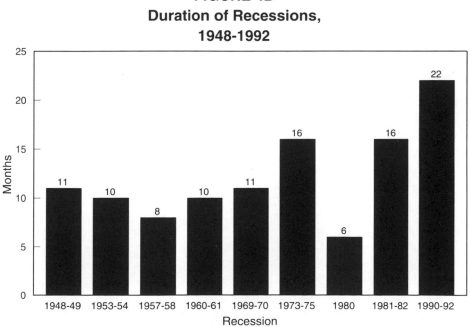

FIGURE 4B
Duration of Recessions, 1948-1992

219

TABLE 4.4
Changes in Labor Force Levels
and Participation in Recessions, 1969-1992

Recession	Labor Force Growth			Change in Labor Force Participation Rate*		
	Total	Men	Women	Total	Men	Women
	(Annual Growth)					
1969:4-1970:4	2.4%	2.2%	2.8%	0.1%	−0.3%	0.4%
1973:4-1975:1	2.2	1.2	3.6	0.1	−0.7	0.7
1980:1-1980:3	1.4	0.9	2.1	0.0	−0.4	0.2
1981:3-1982:4	1.7	1.2	2.4	0.2	−0.1	0.6
1990:2-1992:2	0.9	1.0	1.1	0.0	−0.1	0.1

*Percentage point change annualized.

recent recession involved roughly the same amount of permanent job loss—a rise of 1.6%—as in recent, heavier downturns.

What's the difference between permanent job loss and unemployment? In government statistics unemployed people are defined as those who are without a job and have looked for work in the last four weeks. Therefore, someone could be unemployed because of a job loss (either a permanent or a temporary layoff) or because she/he has been unsuccessfully looking for work after completing school (an "entrant") or after a spell out of the labor force (a "re-entrant") or after quitting a job (a "quit"). So, the relatively large 1.6% increase in the unemployment of those who permanently (rather than temporarily) lost their job suggests that the recent recession involved as much job loss as prior recessions.

Overall unemployment did not rise much in the recent recession due to slow labor force growth (fewer unsuccessful entrants and re-entrants). The growth in both the male and female labor force was far slower in the early 1990s than in the prior four downturns (**Table 4.4**). During the recent recession the labor force grew at a rate (0.9%) roughly half that (1.7%) during the prior recession and only forty percent of that (2.2%) during the mid-1970s recession. A major reason for this slow labor force growth is a more slowly growing adult population because of the lower birth rates in the 1960s.

However, the labor force also grew more slowly because the *proportion* of adults choosing to work (the labor force participation rate) did not grow during the recent recession, primarily reflecting an historically modest annual rise in women's labor force participation of 0.1%. Had the labor force grown as quickly in the recent recession as in the prior four recessions (at a 1.9% rather than an 0.9% rate, or by 1.0 percentage point more per year) the unemployment rate would have risen by roughly 2 percentage points more (1.0 percentage point for two years). Thus, if it had not been for slow population growth and the stall in the long-term rise of labor force participation, unemployment in the recent recession would have reached an historically high level—over 9% (7.5% plus 2%)—because of an historically high 4.2% rise in unemployment (2.2% plus 2.0%).

Had the labor force grown as quickly as in the prior four recessions the unemployment rate would have risen by roughly 2 percentage points more to over 9%.

221

TABLE 4.5
Change in Unemployment Rate by Occupation
Gender, Race, and Industry, 1990-1992

Group	1990:2	1992:2	Change in Unemployment
All	5.3%	7.5%	2.2%
Occupation			
Managers, Prof	2.1	3.2	1.1
Tech, Sales, Admin	4.0	5.7	1.7
Craft	5.3	8.8	3.5
Operatives & Laborers	8.4	11.2	2.8
Gender			
Adult Men	4.7	7.2	2.5
Adult Women	4.7	6.3	1.6
Race/Ethnic			
White	4.6	6.5	1.9
Black	10.6	14.5	3.9
Hispanic	7.6	11.2	3.6
Industry			
Construction	10.5	17.0	6.5
Manufacturing	5.5	7.9	2.4
Services	5.0	6.9	1.9

TABLE 4.6
Changes in Employment and Unemployment
in Recessions by Occupation

Recessions: Beginning and Ending Quarter	Change in Employment (000)		Change in Unemployment (000)		Peak Share of Employment	
	White-Collar	Blue-Collar	White-Collar	Blue-Collar	White-Collar	Blue-Collar
1960:2-1961:1	764	−1,142	210	592	43.0%	36.9%
1969:4-1970:4	695	−737	516	971	47.7	36.0
1973:4-1975:1	871	−2,004	765	1,903	48.1	35.1
1980:1-1980:3	721	−1,557	253	1,013	51.5	32.4
1981:3-1982:4	827	−2,583	826	2,124	52.7	31.3
1990:2-1992:2	643	−1,500	1,130	1,018	57.0	26.7

Was the demographic and occupational composition of unemployment different in the recent recession? There has been some discussion, for instance, of this being a "white-collar" recession. There is some truth to this characterization since the white-collar unemployment rate has risen by an above-average amount. Still, blue-collar workers have been more deeply hurt by the recession, with unemployment among blue-collar operatives and laborers rising by 2.8%, far more than the 1.7% rise in unemployment among technical, sales, and administrative workers (**Table 4.5**).

Moreover, recession levels (1992:2) of unemployment among white-collar workers are lower than the unemployment rates among blue-collar workers at the cyclical peak (1990:2). The same comparison could be made of workers by race/ethnicity—recession levels of white unemployment (6.5%) are still far below the unemployment among blacks (10.6%) or Hispanics (7.6%) at the prior cyclical peak. The absolute rise in unemployment from 1990 to 1992 was greater among white-collar (1,130,000) than among blue-collar workers (1,018,000), which is unusual given that blue-collar unemployment rose far more than white-collar unemployment in prior recessions (**Table 4.6**). The greater rise in white collar unemployment reflects the increased dominance of white-collar employment (57% of total in 1990), the above-average rise in the white-collar unemployment rate, and the fact that unemployment rose nearly as much in services as in manufacturing (Table 4.5).

The most unique aspect of the recession, however, was in the modest growth of white-collar employment. Over eight quarters, white-collar employment grew by only 643,000, far less than the 827,000 growth over just five quarters in the prior recession (Table 4.6). The slow growth in white-collar jobs signals the end of the service-sector boom of the 1980s and is likely responsible for the recent falloff in wages among white-collar and college-educated workers (see Chapter 3).

The rise in unemployment in the recent recession was greater among white-collar than among blue-collar workers . . . blue-collar unemployment rose far more than white-collar unemployment in prior recessions.

✗ , What exactly are 'service-sector' jobs?

223

TABLE 4.7
Proportion of the Unemployed Who Receive Some Unemployment Insurance Payment

Year	Percent of Unemployed Receiving Benefits	Unemployment Rate
1960	54%	5.5%
1967	43	4.9
1973	41	5.8
1975	76	8.5
1976	67	7.7
1979	42	5.8
1982	45	9.7
1983	44	9.6
1989	33	5.3
1990	37	5.5
1991	42	6.7

TABLE 4.8
Employment Growth in Expansions, 1949-1990

Expansion Trough	Peak	Length (Mo.'s)	Private Sector Employment Growth Total	Goods	Services
			(Annual Rate of Growth)		
Oct. 1949	July 1953	45	4.3%	5.9%	2.8%
May 1954	Aug. 1957	39	2.8	2.9	2.8
Apr. 1958	Apr. 1960	24	3.6	3.7	3.5
Feb. 1961	Dec. 1969	106	3.5	2.9	4.0
Nov. 1970	Nov. 1973	36	3.6	3.6	3.6
Mar. 1975	Jan. 1980	58	4.0	3.4	4.3
July 1980	July 1981	12	2.8	2.6	2.9
Nov. 1982	July 1990	92	3.0	1.0	3.8
Average		52	3.5	3.3	3.5

Being unemployed was a bigger financial hardship in the 1980s and 1990s than in the 1970s. As **Table 4.7** shows, in 1990 and 1991, only about 40% of the unemployed received unemployment insurance, a substantial drop from the financial protection available in the 1975 and 1976 recession years when 76% and 67%, respectively, of the unemployed received unemployment insurance. Unemployment insurance also provided less assistance in the 1980s downturn. Changes in the laws and administration of unemployment insurance at both the federal and state levels are primarily responsible for the lower coverage of unemployment insurance.

Job Creation: How Fast in the 1980s?

The fact that unemployment dropped after 1982 led to the impression that the 1980s were a time of exceptional job creation. Now that the 1980s recovery has ended, it is possible to directly compare it to other recoveries. As it turns out, the notion that the 1980s recovery was a time of rapid job creation is factually incorrect.

Table 4.8 provides the growth rates of private sector employment in each of the eight post-war recoveries. The 3% annual employment growth over the mid- and late-1980s exceeded two previous recoveries and was less than in five other recoveries. The recovery from 1982 to 1990 was the second longest recovery of the post-war period, lasting 92 months. The mid-1980s recovery is sometimes referred to as the longest post-war "peacetime" recovery, implicitly labeling the 1960s recovery as a "wartime" recovery. While the Vietnam buildup did occur during this period, it is also true that there was a major military buildup in the 1980s (and even larger in terms of economic output) so the distinction between "wartime" and "peacetime" recoveries seems manufactured and misleading.

In 1990 and 1991, only about 40% of the unemployed received unemployment insurance, a substantial drop from 1975 and 1976.

TABLE 4.9
Employment Growth, 1947-1991

| Period | Measures of Employment | | | Working Age Population | Labor Force Participation Rate |
	Civilian Employment	Hours of Work	Full-time Equivalent Employment		
	(Annual Rates of Growth)				(Percentage Point Annual Growth)
1947-67	1.3%	1.7%	1.8%	1.2%	0.07%
1967-73	2.2	1.6	1.9	2.1	0.20
1973-79	2.5	1.8	2.3	1.9	0.48
1979-89	1.7	1.6	1.8	1.2	0.28
1989-91	−0.2	n.a.	n.a.	0.9	−0.25

FIGURE 4C
Civilian Employment Growth, 1947-1991

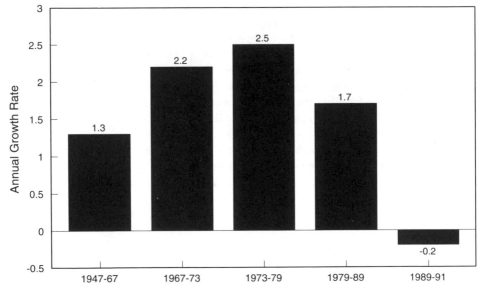

226

Table 4.9 looks at the employment growth over the last two business cycles (from peak to peak) relative to the earlier post-war period to see whether the long-term growth in employment has been faster in recent years. Three measures of employment growth are presented: civilian employment, total hours worked, and full-time equivalent employment (which combines part-time and full-time according to practices within each industry). The trend is unmistakable: each measure of employment grew far more slowly from 1979 to 1989 than between 1973 and 1979. For instance, the rate at which civilian employment rose from 1979 to 1989, 1.7% annually, was more than 30% slower than the 2.5% annual employment creation rate prevailing between 1973 and 1979 (**Figure 4C**).

The last two columns of Table 4.9 show two reasons why unemployment has fallen despite *a much slower growth in job creation since 1979*. First, the working-age population has grown more slowly than it did in the period from 1967 to 1979. For instance, there were fewer new potential young workers in 1989 than in 1979, even though the overall population grew by over 12% (1.2% annually for ten years). In 1989, there were 32.2 million 16- to 24-year-olds, a smaller number than the 37.0 million in 1979 or even the 33.5 million in 1973.

Second, the long-term rise in the proportion of the working-age population seeking work (the labor force participation rate) has also leveled off in recent years. As Table 4.9 shows, the annual percentage point increase in the labor force participation rate in the ten years between 1979 and 1989 was only sixty percent as much as in the six years between 1973 and 1979. This primarily reflects a slower increase in women's labor force participation since 1979.

These two trends, the smaller number of potential young workers and the slower labor force participation growth, have meant a slower growth in the number of people seeking work. Thus, the lower unemployment of the later part of the 1980s was *not* due to superior job creation. Despite the slower growth rate of new jobs, unemployment was reduced because of the historically slow growth of new workers seeking employment.

The lower unemployment of the later part of the 1980s was not due to superior job creation but to the historically slow growth of new workers seeking employment.

TABLE 4.10
Composition of Non-Agricultural Employment, 1973-1991

Year	Percent Part-Time			Percent Full-time	Total
	Total	Involuntary	Voluntary		
1973	16.6%	3.1%	13.5%	83.4%	100.0%
1979	17.6	3.8	13.8	82.4	100.0
1989	18.1	4.3	13.8	81.9	100.0
1991	18.9	5.4	13.5	81.1	100.0

FIGURE 4D
Part-Time Employment Rates,
1973-1991

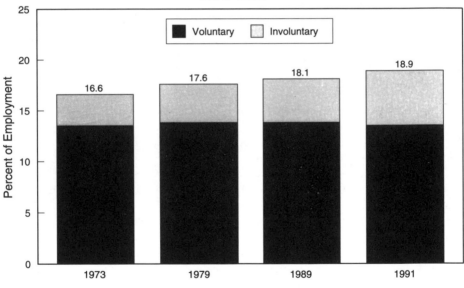

The Growth in Part-Timers

As we have seen earlier, there has been a growth in underemployment due to more people working part-time who want full-time jobs. This section examines the growth of part-time work and the associated problems in more detail.

The expansion of part-time work is not *necessarily* a problem. Many workers prefer a part-time schedule because it allows time to pursue education, leisure, or family responsibilities. But large numbers of part-timers would prefer to work full-time. Part-timers generally have lower pay, lower-skilled jobs, poor chances of promotion, less job security, inferior benefits (such as vacation, health insurance, and pension), and lower status overall within their places of employment.

Table 4.10 shows that the share of total employment made up by full-timers has declined steadily from 1973 to 1989. At the same time, the share of jobs which are part-time increased from 16.6% in 1973 to 18.1% in 1989, at the end of the business cycle (**Figure 4D**). This increase in the proportion of workers working part-time from 1973 to 1989 has been almost entirely due to the increased rate at which workers are working part-time *involuntarily*. It thus reflects the increased use of part-timers by employers and not the preferences of the workforce for shorter hours.

In 1989, involuntary part-time workers comprised 4.3% of the workforce, an increase of 0.5 and 1.2 percentage points of the workforce over, respectively, 1979 and 1973. Nearly five million workers (Table 4.2), on average, were involuntary part-timers in 1989, encompassing nearly one-fourth of all part-time workers.

This increase in the proportion of workers working part-time from 1973 to 1989 has been almost entirely due to the increased rate at which workers are working part-time involuntarily.

229

TABLE 4.11
Age and Gender Composition of the Labor Force
and Rate of Part-time Employment, 1969, 1979, and 1989

Gender & Ages	1969		1979		1989	
	Share of Employment	Percent part-time	Share of Employment	Percent part-time	Share of Employment	Percent part-time
All, 16-21	12.8%	40.6%	14.0%	41.7%	10.36%	46.3%
Women, 22-44	17.3	22.7	23.1	22.5	27.7	21.9
Women, 45-64	13.2	22.5	11.3	24.4	11.6	23.8
Men, 22-64	53.2	3.7	48.9	4.8	47.8	6.7
All, 65+	3.5	41.1	2.7	52.9	2.6	52.4
Total	100.0	15.5	100.0	17.6	100.0	18.1
Total, holding within-group rates at 1969 levels	—	15.5	—	16.4	—	15.9
Total, holding within-group rates at 1979 levels	—	—	—	17.6	—	17.0

Teenagers, persons of retirement age, and adult women are the groups most likely to work part-time (**Table 4.11**). In 1989, 46.3% of employed 16- to 21-year olds and 52.4% of workers 65 or older worked in part-time jobs. More than one in five employed adult women was a part-time worker in 1989.

These demographic groups—women, teenagers, and older workers—are the ones most willing to accept lower pay and status in order to obtain a reduced work schedule.

However, a demographic explanation for the expansion of part-time jobs—the growth of women and younger workers in the labor force raises the need for part-time work—is not consistent with the available data. As shown in Table 4.10, the rise of part-time work since 1973 is entirely due to the increased incidence of involuntary part-time work. Moreover, for adult men, the group with the least preference for part-time work, the rate of part-time work rose from 3.7% in 1969 to 6.7% in 1989.

In fact, the increase in part-time work over the last twenty years can be fully explained by a rise in part-time work within each demographic group rather than by any change in the age-gender composition of employment. Table 4.11 presents an analysis which allows us to assess the impact of demographic shifts on the rise in the overall rate of part-time employment between 1969 and 1979 and between 1979 and 1989. If the rates of part-time work within each group had remained at their 1969 levels while the mix of employment, such as more women in the workforce, changed as it did from 1969 to 1979, then the overall rate of part-time work would have risen from 15.5% in 1969 to 16.4% in 1979. Thus, demographic shifts can account for just 0.9 percentage point (16.4% less 15.5%) of the overall 2.1 percentage point rise (17.6% less 15.5%) in the rate of part-time employment between 1969 and 1979.

Surprisingly, demographic shifts between 1979 and 1989 were a force for *less* part-time work. Had demographic shifts been the only factor affecting the overall rate of part-time work then 0.6% less of the workforce (17.0% less 17.6%) would have been part-time workers. Yet, the rate of part-time work actually rose from 17.6% to 18.1%, indicating that non-demographic factors led to a 1.1 percentage point rise in the rate of part-time work (the difference between the demographically neutral 17.0% and the actual 18.1%).

Nearly five million workers were involuntary part-timers in 1989, encompassing nearly one-fourth of all part-time workers.

231

TABLE 4.12
Industry Composition of the Labor Force
and Rate of Part-time Employment, 1969, 1979, and 1989

Industry	1969 Share of Employment	1969 Percent part-time	1979 Share of Employment	1979 Percent part-time	1989 Share of Employment	1989 Percent part-time
Construction	6.0%	8.6%	6.0%	10.5%	5.9%	10.5%
Durable Mfg.	18.2	3.2	15.3	3.8	12.0	3.9
Nondurable Mfg.	12.3	7.8	9.9	8.6	8.3	8.1
Trans., Comm. Util.	7.3	7.8	7.0	9.0	7.3	8.7
Trade	18.5	26.3	20.7	30.0	21.4	29.7
Finance	5.1	10.5	6.2	11.9	7.1	11.5
Services	25.3	26.2	28.1	25.0	32.1	24.0
Public Admin.	6.5	6.2	5.9	6.6	5.3	5.8
Mining	0.7	5.0	1.0	4.0	0.6	4.8
All industries	100.0	15.1	100.0	17.1	100.0	17.6
All industries, holding within-industry rates at 1969 levels	—	15.1	—	16.2	—	17.2
All industries, holding within industry rates at 1979 levels	—	—	—	17.1	—	18.1

Over the entire 1969 to 1989 period, demographic shifts can account for only 0.4 percentage points (15.9% less 15.5%) of the 2.6 percentage point rise (18.1% less 15.5%) in the rate of part-time employment. This is because the overall rate of part-time work is rising because teens, older workers, and men are more likely to work part-time. Adult women, on the other hand, were more likely to work full-time in 1989 than in 1979.

The major reason for growing part-time work is that job growth has been concentrated in the service industries which intensively use part-timers. In 1989, for instance,

232   yet prediction of service decline

29.7% of the retail/wholesale trade workforce and 24% of the service industry workforce were employed part-time (**Table 4.12**). As we saw in Chapter 3, roughly three-fourths of the net new jobs created between 1979 and 1989 were in these two industries. This shift of employment towards industries which provide low-wage, part-time employment can explain 2.1 of the 2.5 percentage point rise (or 84% of the increase) in the rate of part-time employment among non-agricultural wage and salary workers between 1969 and 1989. Shifts in the industry composition of employment has led to an additional 1% of the workforce in part-time work in each of the last two decades.

The rate of voluntary part-time work in each industry sector generally rose between 1969 and 1979, but fell between 1979 and 1989 (**Table 4.13**). Involuntary part-time work, on the other hand, has generally risen over the entire post-1969 period, especially in the service and trade industries where the largest numbers of involuntary part-time workers are employed. This suggests that the rise in part-time work in particular sectors reflects employer strategies (using a low-wage, high-turnover workforce) rather than workforce preferences.

The major reason for growing part-time work is that job growth has been concentrated in the service industries which intensively use part-timers.

TABLE 4.13
Rates of Voluntary and Involuntary
Part-time Work by Industry, 1969, 1979, and 1989

Industry	Involuntary			Voluntary		
	1969	1979	1989	1969	1979	1989
Construction	4.4%	5.4%	6.1%	4.2%	5.0%	4.4%
Durable Mfg.	1.4	1.5	1.6	1.9	2.3	2.3
Nondurable Mfg.	3.4	3.8	3.4	4.4	4.8	4.7
Trans., Comm. Util.	1.8	2.6	2.7	6.0	6.4	6.0
Trade	2.9	5.4	6.3	23.4	24.5	23.4
Finance	1.0	1.7	1.8	9.5	10.2	9.6
Services	3.1	4.1	4.7	23.1	21.0	19.3
Public Admin.	0.8	1.3	0.9	5.4	5.3	4.9
Mining	1.6	2.3	2.5	3.4	1.7	2.3
All Industries	2.5	3.6	4.1	12.6	13.5	13.5

233

TABLE 4.14
Wage Differences Between Part-time and
Full-time Workers by Gender and Selected Occupations, 1989

| | Percent of Part-time Workers | Average Hourly Wage, 1989 (1989 Dollars) | | Wage Difference | |
		Part-time	Full-time	Dollars	Percent
Women					
All Workers	100.0%	$7.02	$9.20	−$2.18	−23.7%
Prof., Tech.	16.9	11.81	12.42	−0.61	−4.9
Sales	18.4	5.49	8.19	−2.70	−33.0
Admin.	24.7	7.10	8.50	−1.40	−16.5
Service	29.3	5.12	5.88	−0.76	−12.9
Men					
All Workers	100.0%	$7.24	$12.28	$5.04	−41.0%
Prof., Tech.	12.6	13.43	16.19	−2.76	−17.0
Sales	13.0	6.26	12.60	−6.34	−50.3
Admin.	10.4	6.33	10.91	−4.58	−42.0
Service	25.6	4.88	8.43	−3.55	−42.1
Laborers	15.4	5.84	8.13	−2.29	−28.2

A major problem associated with part-time employment is lower hourly wages and benefits received by part-time workers compared to equivalent full-time workers.

A major problem associated with part-time employment is lower hourly pay received by part-time workers compared to equivalent full-time workers (**Table 4.14**). Women who work part-time earn 23.7% less wages per hour than those working full-time. This wage differential is not simply due to the concentration of part-timers in low-wage occupations since part-timers are paid significantly less in each occupation. The part-time wage differential is even greater among men than among women.

The pay difference between part-time and full-time workers is even greater for benefits, however (**Table 4.15**). For instance, only 25.6% of part-time female family heads are included in their employers' health plans compared to 74.1% of full-time female family heads. Similarly, men working in part-time jobs are only about half as likely (37.1% versus 79%) to be included in their employers' health plans.

234

TABLE 4.15
Differences in Fringe Benefits,
for Full-time and Part-time Workers,
by Gender or Marital Status and Occupation, 1987

Gender or Marital Status and Occupation	Included in Health Plan		Included in Pension Plan	
	Part-time	Full-time	Part-time	Full-time
Female Family Heads				
All Workers	25.6%	74.1%	14.2%	50.2%
Professional, Managerial, and Technical	41.3	85.9	23.0	62.4
Sales	20.5	60.3	11.8	31.9
Clerical	36.8	82.1	20.6	55.9
Service	17.2	46.4	8.1	28.3
Craft, Operative and Labor	22.8	69.1	18.8	45.2
Wives				
All Workers	17.8	59.7	17.9	50.9
Professional, Managerial, and Technical	23.5	68.0	26.2	64.0
Sales	16.4	44.7	12.0	29.7
Clerical	18.4	63.1	18.6	55.0
Service	12.1	37.2	13.4	27.6
Craft, Operative and Labor	20.8	58.8	18.3	41.7
Husbands and Male Family Heads				
All Workers	37.1	79.0	18.3	58.5
Professional, Managerial, and Technical	43.6	86.1	24.5	67.6
Sales	38.7	75.3	18.5	44.2
Clerical	44.1	84.8	17.6	70.0
Service	27.8	71.8	12.9	55.6
Craft, Operative, and Labor	36.5	75.2	17.7	54.5

FIGURE 4E
Partially or Fully Paid Medical Benefits Offered
to Employees, by Full- or Part-time Status, 1991

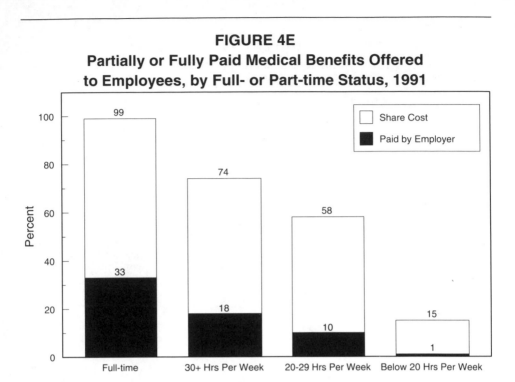

Even when part-time workers are covered by their employers' health insurance plan, they are much more likely to have to pay towards it—or less likely to receive insurance coverage paid by their employer.

As **Figure 4E** shows, the fewer the hours of work, the less likely an employee will have employer provided health insurance (99% of full-timers, but 58% of those working 20-29 hours per week) and the less likely the provided insurance will be paid for by the employer. More information on uninsured workers is provided in Chapter 9.

Pay differentials are even greater when it comes to pensions. In each occupation group, workers with part-time jobs are less likely than full-time workers to be enrolled in their employers' pension plans (Table 4.15).

The gap between part-time and full-time workers in the provision of health and pension benefits is almost as wide for women who are heads of households as it is for women in married couple families (Table 4.15). It is also just as wide among professional women as among women in clerical or service occupations.

The growth of multiple jobholding reflects the overemployment due to the deterioration of real wages since 1979.

More Than One Job

The growth of part-time work reflects growing underemployment and deteriorating pay and opportunity in the economy. The growth of multiple jobholding—people working in at least two jobs—reflects the overemployment due to the deterioration of real wages since 1979, which persisted even during the recovery years from 1985 through 1989. This increased incidence of multiple jobholding between 1979 and 1989 due to economic hardship reasons (adding one percentage point) was responsible for roughly 1.17 million additional multiple jobholders (if the multiple jobholder rate was 5.2% rather than 6.2% in 1989, there would have been 6.06 million rather than 7.23 million multiple jobholders).

TABLE 4.16
Growth of Multiple Jobholding, All Workers, 1973-1991

Year	Number of Multiple Jobholders (000)	Multiple Jobholding Rate	Percent of Workforce Who Hold Multiple Jobs Because of:	
			Economic Hardship*	Other Reasons**
1973	4,262	5.1%	n.a.	n.a.
1979	4,724	4.9	1.8%	3.1%
1985	5,730	5.4	2.2	3.2
1989	7,225	6.2	2.8	3.4
1991	7,183	6.2	2.5	3.7
Change				
1973-79	462	−0.2	n.a.	n.a.
1979-85	1,006	0.5	0.4	0.1
1985-89	1,495	0.8	0.6	0.2
1989-91	−42	0.0	−0.3	0.3

*To meet regular household expenses or pay off debts.

**Includes saving for the future, getting experience, helping a friend or relative, buying something special, enjoying the work, and so on.

In 1989, 7.2 million workers held at least two jobs (**Table 4.16**). The rate of multiple jobholding grew from 4.9% in 1979 to 6.2% in 1989, an increase of 1.3 percentage points (**Figure 4F**). It is especially noteworthy that most of the growth of multiple jobholding occurred in the recovery years from 1985 to 1989, when an additional 1.5 million workers began working more than one job. The multiple jobholding rate held steady at 6.2% even as total employment declined in the 1989-1991 downturn.

An analysis of the reasons for multiple jobholding shows that increased multiple jobholding over the 1979 to 1989 period reflects deteriorating economic performance, rather than enhanced opportunity. The growth of multiple jobholding has occurred primarily among workers who work at more than one job because of "economic hardship," the need to meet regular expenses or to pay off debts (Table 4.16). Multiple jobholding due to economic hardship increased by 1.0 percentage points from 1979 to 1989, accounting for more than three-fourths of the 1.3 percentage point rise in multiple jobholding. This same pattern holds even over the recovery years from 1985 to 1989,

Increased multiple jobholding over the 1979 to 1989 period reflects deteriorating economic performance, rather than enhanced opportunity.

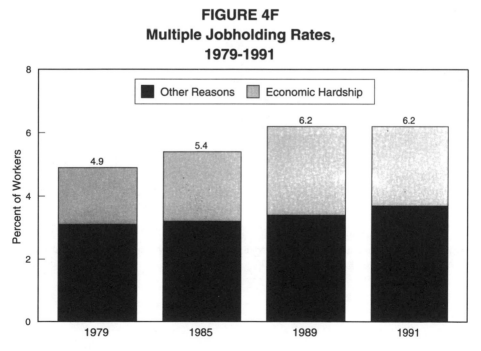

FIGURE 4F
Multiple Jobholding Rates,
1979-1991

TABLE 4.17
Growth of Multiple Jobholding by Gender, 1973-1991

Year	Number of Multiple Jobholders (000)	Multiple Jobholding Rate	Percent of Workforce Who Hold Multiple Jobs Because of: Economic Hardship*	Percent of Workforce Who Hold Multiple Jobs Because of: Other Reasons**
Women				
1973	869	2.7%	n.a.	n.a.
1979	1,407	3.5	1.5%	2.0%
1985	2,192	4.7	2.0	2.7
1989	3,109	5.9	2.9	3.0
1991	3,129	5.9	2.2	3.7
Change				
1973-79	538	0.8	n.a.	n.a.
1979-85	785	1.2	0.5	0.7
1985-89	917	1.2	0.9	0.3
1989-91	20	0.0	−0.7	0.7
Men				
1973	3,393	6.6	n.a.	n.a.
1979	3,317	5.9	2.1	3.8
1985	3,537	5.9	2.3	3.6
1989	4,115	6.4	2.6	3.8
1991	4,054	6.4	2.4	4.0
Change				
1973-79	−76	−0.7	n.a.	n.a.
1979-85	220	0.0	0.2	−0.2
1985-89	78	0.5	0.3	0.2
1989-91	−61	0.0	−0.2	0.2

*To meet regular household expenses or pay off debts.
**Includes saving for the future, getting experience, helping a friend or relative, buying something special, enjoying the work, and so on.

when increased economic hardship accounted for 0.6 percentage points of the 0.8 percentage point rise in the multiple jobholding rate. In contrast, the multiple jobholding rate for "other reasons" rose only 0.3 percentage points from 3.1% to 3.4% between 1979 to 1989 (with a rise of 0.2 percentage points between 1985 and 1989) and was responsible for about 350,000 more multiple jobholders (relative to a situation where the "other reasons" rate had held at 3.2%).

Many of those holding multiple jobs for "economic hardship" reasons may have lost their extra job (or jobs) in the 1989 to 1991 downturn, as their rate of multiple jobholding fell from 2.8% to 2.5%. It is curious that there was a growth in non-economic hardship multiple jobholding during a time of rising unemployment.

There was a rapid increase in the multiple jobholding rate among women between 1979 and 1989, rising from 3.5% to 5.9% **(Table 4.17)**. Economic hardship explains roughly 60% of this increase (1.4 percentage points of the 2.4 percentage point increase). Between 1985 and 1989, 75% of the rise in women's multiple jobholding is due to economic hardship. By 1989, a greater proportion of women (2.9%) than men (2.6%) worked more than one job in order to meet regular expenses or to pay off debts. The decline in multiple jobholding for "economic reasons" in the 1989 to 1991 downturn occurred primarily among women.

Many women unable to sustain two-jobs despite desire to

By 1989, a greater proportion of women (2.9%) than men (2.6%) worked more than one job in order to meet regular expenses or to pay off debts.

TABLE 4.18
Distribution of Multiple Jobholders Experiencing Economic Hardship, 1979-1989

Gender/Marital Status	Distribution of Multiple Jobholders Who Have Economic Hardship Reasons		
	1979	1985	1989
Total, 16 Years and Over	100.0%	100.0%	100.0%
Women	33.7	40.6	48.2
Married, Spouse Present	11.2	14.9	19.8
Other	22.5	25.7	28.5
Single	n.a.	10.8	13.1
Widowed, Divorced, or Separated	n.a.	14.9	15.5
Men	66.4	59.3	51.8
Married, Spouse Present	54.9	42.8	36.2
Other	11.6	16.5	15.6
Single	n.a.	10.2	11.4
Widowed, Divorced, or Separated	n.a.	6.4	4.2

*Workers who report they have multiple jobs in order to meet regular household expenses or pay off debts.

TABLE 4.19
Hours Worked by Multiple Jobholders, by Gender, 1989

Gender	Average Weekly Hours	Percent of Multiple Jobholders Working:				
		0-40 Hours	41-48 Hours	49-69 Hours	70+ Hours	Total
Total	52.0	17.6%	24.5%	43.9%	14.0%	100.0%
Male	55.8	9.3	23.9	48.4	18.5	100.0
Female	47.1	28.5	25.4	38.0	8.2	100.0

Table 4.18 provides a demographic breakdown of those working more than one job for economic hardship reasons. As suggested by Table 4.17, the share of women among those who worked more than one job because of economic hardship has rapidly increased so that by 1989 nearly half of these workers were women. In 1989, more than half of multiple jobholders were married (wives, 19.8%; husbands, 36.2%) and an additional fifth were widowed, divorced or separated men or women. These data thus show that the hardship associated with and reflected by multiple jobholding is concentrated in working families and among adult workers.

The majority of those working multiple jobs in 1989 worked at least 49 hours per week (**Table 4.19**). Two-thirds of men working more than one job worked at least 49 hours per week while about 46% of women multiple jobholders did the same. These data confirm that multiple jobholding does not simply reflect people combining two part-time jobs into the equivalent of one full-time job. Rather, multiple jobholders worked an average of 52 hours per week in 1989.

Surveys of major companies suggest that the use of contingent labor is widespread and rising.

The Contingent Workforce

A significant portion of people in today's workforce have become "contingent workers." Workers can be hired on a temporary or "contingent" basis in a variety of ways. Some firms put workers directly on their payroll but assign them to an internal temporary worker pool. Employers also use temporary help agencies to obtain workers on a temporary basis, sometimes for long periods. Some businesses hire independent contractors to perform work that would otherwise be done by employees. All three types of contingent workers are frequently denied health insurance and pension coverage and have little access to promotions and better jobs.

Data drawn from surveys of major companies suggest that the use of contingent labor is widespread and rising (**Table 4.20**).

In 1986, 36% of the surveyed firms had an internal temporary worker pool. A later survey (not of the same firms) shows that 49% of firms use their own temporary worker pool. The hiring of workers through temporary help agen-

TABLE 4.20
The Use of Various Types of Contingent Labor

| | Percent of Surveyed Firms That Use Contingent Labor, by Type of Labor | | |
Survey	Internal Temporary Worker Pool	Temporary Agencies Help	Independent Contracting
1986*	36%	77%	63%
1989**	49	97	78

*Survey of 477 major companies.
**Survey of 521 major companies.

TABLE 4.21
The Growth in Personnel Services Industry Employment, 1973-1991

| | Personnel Industry Employment* | | | |
| | Number (000) | | As Share of Total Employment | |
Year	Total	Women	Total	Women
1973	256	133	0.3%	0.2%
1979	527	309	0.6	0.3
1982	555	354	0.6	0.4
1989	1,351	782	1.2	0.7
1991	1,522	890	1.4	0.8

*This industry consists of temporary help agencies (75% of total employment) and employment agencies (25% of total employment).

cies is now nearly universal among large companies. In the 1989 survey, 97% of the firms used temporary help agencies. Independent contracting is also widespread, with 78% of the firms using this method in 1989. In the earlier survey, 63% of the firms hired independent contractors.

Unfortunately, these surveys do not have information on how many contingent workers these firms actually use. The only subgroup of contingent workers that is captured by government statistics is the workforce employed through temporary help agencies. Unfortunately, these data are not available for the years before 1982. For a longer perspective, however, it is possible to examine the growth of the entire personnel services industry, which consists primarily of workers hired through, or working for, temporary agencies (three-fourths of total) but also includes people working in employment agencies (**Table 4.21** and **Figure 4G**). There has been an explosive growth in personnel services employment from 1979 to 1989, but especially between 1982 and 1989. Industry employment rose by 824,000 from 1979 to 1989, with 796,000 jobs

The only subgroup of contingent workers that is captured by government statistics is the workforce employed through temporary help agencies.

FIGURE 4G
Temporary and Personnel Services Industry Employment, 1973-1991

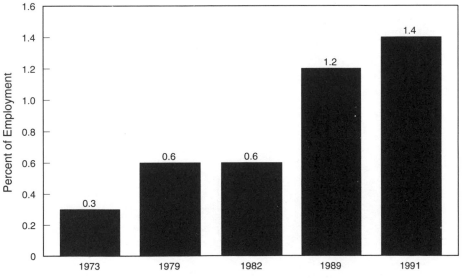

TABLE 4.22
Growth in Temporary Help Industry Employment, 1982-1991

	Temporary Help Industry Employment*			
	Number (000)		As Share of Total Employment	
Year	Total	Women	Total	Women
1982*	401	256	0.4%	0.3%
1989	1,032	618	0.9	0.7
1991	1,268	730	1.2	0.7

*Earlier data not available.

TABLE 4.23
Elements of the Marginal Workforce*

	Number of Workers (000)
Temporary Help Services**	944
Leased Workers**	120
At-home Workers***	2,243
8 hours/week or more	1,992
35 hours/week or more	1,067

*Data are from different sources and reflect the situation in the 1985-87 period.
**1987
***1985

added since 1982. As a result, the share of the workforce employed in the personnel services industry doubled, from 0.6% in 1982 to 1.2% in 1989. The industry share of total employment in 1989, 1.2%, was four times greater than its share in 1973, 0.3%. The increase in the proportion of the workforce in the personnel services industry from 1973 to 1989 (from 0.3% to 1.2%) meant an additional 1 million workers in the industry. Even as total employment fell between 1989 and 1991, the industry was able to add roughly 171,000 jobs.

Women are more likely to be employed as temporary workers, partly because such work provides flexible hours but also because there is a higher incidence of temporary work in occupations dominated by women, such as clerical work. Moreover, "temping" is sometimes the only option available. In 1989, 782,000, or 58%, of the 1,351,000 workers in the personnel services industry were women.

The available information on employment in the temporary help industry since 1982 is presented in **Table 4.22**. These data confirm that the growth in the overall personnel services industry is primarily due to more workers employed through temporary help agencies. An additional 0.5% of the workforce, or 631,000 more workers, were employed through temporary help agencies in 1989 compared to 1982. Most of the increase was among women. Temporary employment rose by more than 230,000 even during the recession years from 1989 to 1991.

Other types of marginal workers (**Table 4.23**) include "leased employees" who work for one firm but are leased to another, and workers employed at home (so employers can reduce their overhead and avoid labor regulations such as minimum wage, overtime, and safety protections). These workers, along with those employed by "temp" agencies, are the statistically visible portion of this new marginal workforce; many others—such as new immigrants—escape detection.

Women are more likely to be employed as temporary workers, partly because such work provides flexible hours but also because there is a higher incidence of temporary work in occupations dominated by women.

247

TABLE 4.24
The Growth of Self-Employment

Year	Self-Employment as Share of Total Employment* Among		
	All Workers	Men	Women
1948	12.1%	n.a.	n.a.
1967	7.3	8.8%	4.9%
1973	6.7	8.2	4.4
1979	7.1	8.8	4.9
1989	7.5	9.0	5.8
1991	7.8	9.4	6.0

*Nonagricultural industries.

TABLE 4.25
Self-Employment and Paid Employment Earnings

	Median Annualized Earnings of Full-time Year-Round Workers	
	($1983)	
	Men	Women
Self-Employed	$13,520	$3,767
Paid Employee	20,039	12,079
Self-Employed Relative to Paid Employee Earnings	67%	31%

Self-Employment

A significant portion of total employment consists of self-employed workers, those whose primary job is working in their own business, farm, craft, or profession. Individual independent contractors, discussed above, would be considered self-employed.

In 1989, self-employment represented 7.5% of total employment, up from 7.1% in 1979 (**Table 4.24**). The greatest growth in self-employment has been among women workers, who earn far less in self-employment than in regular paid employment. An additional 1.4% of women workers were considered self-employed in 1989 compared to 1973. The rate of self-employment among men is higher than among women but has risen more slowly.

Much of self-employment is disguised underemployment, as can be seen from the fact that self-employed workers earn far less than those on regular payrolls. Self-employed women earn only 31% as much as women wage and salary workers, the growth of self-employment means lower earnings for millions of women (**Table 4.25**). Self-employed men earn one-third less than men who are paid as wage and salary workers. So, the growth of male self-employment means depressed earnings for millions of men. The rise in self-employment between 1989 and 1991 probably suggests rising unemployment rather than rising entrepreneurialism.

Even in a year of relatively low unemployment such as 1989, an average of nearly ten percent of the labor force was either unemployed, working part-time but wanting full-time work, or too discouraged to look for work.

Conclusion

This chapter has reviewed recent trends in employment, underemployment, overemployment and unemployment. Even in a year of relatively low unemployment such as 1989, an average of nearly ten percent of the labor force were either unemployed, working part-time but wanting full-time work, or too discouraged to look for work. Millions more were holding at least two jobs to make ends meet, making do with much lower wages in some self-employed venture, or stuck in a temporary job. It is thus important to examine the character of employment, including wages and benefits, as well as the growth of unemployment and underemployment when analyzing employment trends.

Chapter 5

Wealth: Losses for Most, Gains for Few

Stagnant incomes and falling wages are only part of the decline in well-being of working Americans. A family's wealth also affects its ability to cope with financial emergencies as well as its standard of living. For example, financial assets, such as money in a bank account or stocks or bonds, can help a family make ends meet during periods of disability or unemployment. Tangible assets, such as a home or a car, can directly affect a family's quality of life and the ease with which it meets its needs for housing and transportation.

The distribution of wealth is even more concentrated at the top than the distribution of income. In 1983, for instance the richest 1% of families controlled 34% of household net worth, but received 12.8% of household income. During the 1983 to 1989 recovery the distribution of wealth became even more concentrated. In fact, the period 1983-1989 witnessed an accrual of accumulated household wealth almost exclusively among the very richest families, while wealth among the bottom 60% of families actually fell. There has also been a growth in the differences in wealth held by white and non-white families. The consequence of increased wealth inequality is a larger gap in overall financial security between the rich, on the one hand, and the middle class and the poor, on the other.

The rate of wealth creation in the 1980s was comparable to that of the 1970s, a growth rate of just under 2% annually. In the 1980s, however, there was only growth in the

The period 1983-1989 witnessed an accrual of accumulated household wealth almost exclusively among the very richest families, while wealth among the bottom 60% of families actually fell.

TABLE 5.1
Growth of Household Wealth, 1949-1991

Type of Wealth	Annual Growth of Household* Net Worth per Adult				
	1949-1967	1967-1973	1973-1979	1979-1989	1989-1991
Net Worth	3.6%	1.3%	1.9%	1.8%	−1.4%
Net Tangible Assets**	4.2	4.3	4.3	0.0	−5.3
Net Financial Assets	3.3	−0.1	0.5	2.9	0.5

*Includes all households, personal trusts, and nonprofit organizations.
**Consumer durables, housing and land assets less home mortgages.

FIGURE 5A
Growth of Household Wealth per Adult, 1949-1989

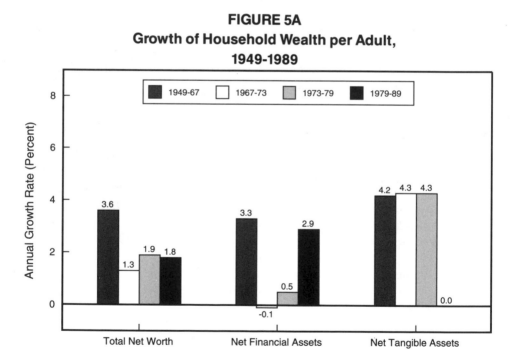

252

types of assets owned primarily by the wealthy—financial assets. On the other hand, there was no growth in tangible assets—homes and consumer durables—the type of wealth most likely to be held by middle-class families.

Aggregate Household Wealth: Financial Assets Boomed, Tangibles Failed to Grow

We have seen in Chapter 1 that income growth in recent years was slow by historical standards, increasingly unequal, and characterized by more work at lower wages. Has there been a similar trend regarding wealth creation and distribution? In this section we examine the change in the overall growth of wealth while trends in wealth inequality are examined in the next section.

A basic measure of aggregate wealth is *household net worth*—the total assets of all households minus their debts. **Table 5.1** traces the growth of household net worth over the post-war period between cyclical peak years. Household net worth per adult increased 1.8% per year between 1979 and 1989 slightly less than the 1.9% rate of 1973-1979 and well under the 3.6% annual growth rate of 1949-1967. Thus, the 1980s growth in household wealth as well as in income was slow by historical standards.

Not all household assets increased in value at the same rate. Financial assets boomed, but tangible assets grew much more slowly (Table 5.1 and **Figure 5A**). Since the wealthy own most of the financial assets in the country, these developments have benefitted them in particular. Growth of net financial assets per adult was 2.9% per year in the 1979-1989 period, close to the 3.3% growth rate of 1949-1967. The financial assets boom of the 1980s contrasts starkly with the modest 0.5% annual growth of 1973-1979 and the slight decline between 1967 and 1973.

On the other hand, the value per adult of tangible assets, such as housing and land, automobiles, appliances, and so on, did not grow at all in the 1979-1989 period. This lack of tangible asset growth from 1979 to 1989 is especially impressive because of strong tangible asset growth throughout the 1950s, 1960s, and 1970s. Since tangible assets are spread out more evenly than financial assets,

The financial assets boom of the 1980s contrasts starkly with the modest 0.5% annual growth of 1973-1979 . . . On the other hand, the value per adult of tangible assets did not grow at all in the 1979-1989 period.

253

TABLE 5.2
Distribution of Wealth, 1989

Wealth Class	Net Worth	Net Financial Assets	Distribution of Family Income
All	100.0%	100.0%	100.0%
Top 1%	38.3%	50.3%	14.7%
Next 9%	32.9	35.4	24.2
Bottom 90%	28.8	14.4	61.1

FIGURE 5B
Distribution of Income and Wealth, 1989

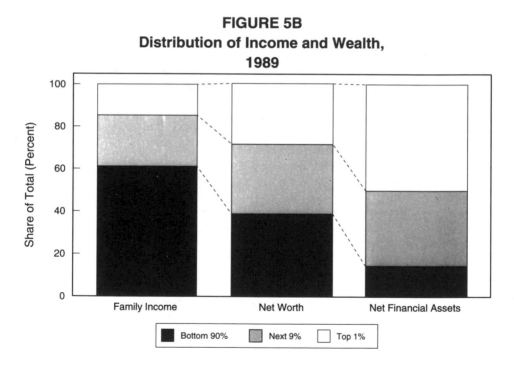

their stagnation affected mainly the bulk of the population who are not wealthy. The changing composition of wealth growth in Table 5.1 thus previews the growing wealth ine- quality shown in the next section.

Between 1989 and 1991, wealth creation suffered, as net financial assets grew at a modest 0.5% annual rate and the value of tangible assets fell rapidly.

Wealth Inequality Exceeds Income Gap

The distribution of wealth is less equal than the distribu- tion of income. The concentration of wealth among very high-income families is dramatic. **Table 5.2** and **Figure 5B** reveal that in 1989 (the most recent year for which such data are available), the top 1% of families earned 14.7% of total income, yet owned 38.3% of total net worth and a remarkable 50.3% of net financial assets. Net worth is the value of one's assets minus one's debts. For a typical family this might be the value of its house, car, other consumer goods, and bank accounts, less the amount owed on its mortgages and credit cards. Net financial assets are *finan- cial* assets minus debts. For the same family, this would be the bank account balance, minus mortgage and credit card debts. The value of pension plans are not included in this analysis.

There is no information on the holding of wealth among the bottom 90% of families in 1989. Earlier analyses for 1983, however, showed that at the bottom of the income distribution, 20% of families had a zero or negative net worth and fully 54% of families had zero or negative net financial assets. Though most of the latter are not poor, their lack of financial assets indicates that more than half of American families are living from paycheck to paycheck with little or nothing in the bank in case of a loss of job or other serious financial emergency.

The concentration of financial assets at the top implies that American businesses are owned and financed primar- ily by the richest families. In 1989, for example, the wealthiest top 0.5% owned 37.4% of all corporate stocks,

In 1989 the top 1% of families earned 14.7% of total income, yet owned 38.3% of total net worth and a remarkable 50.3% of net financial assets.

TABLE 5.3
Selected Holdings of Assets by
Family Wealth Level, 1989

(percent of total assets held by each group)

Asset Type	Super Rich (Top 0.5%)	Very Rich (Next 0.5%)	Rich (90-99%)	Rest (0-90%)	Total
A. Assets Held Primarily by the Wealthy					
Stocks	37.4%	9.3%	37.1%	16.1%	100.0%
Bonds	64.0	8.9	21.1	6.0	100.0
Trusts	33.3	19.3	37.5	9.9	100.0
Business	56.2	8.9	10.0	18.8	100.0
Non-Home Real Estate	33.8	10.0	37.4	18.8	100.0
B. Assets and Liabilities Held Primarily by the Non-Wealthy					
Principal Home	5.2%	3.3%	27.9%	63.6%	100.0%
Life Insurance	7.7	5.6	28.0	58.7	100.0
Liquid Assets*	12.3	6.8	38.7	42.2	100.0
Total Debt	11.8	2.7	22.9	62.6	100.0

*Includes demand deposits, savings and time deposits, money market funds, certificates of deposit, and IRA and Keogh accounts.

The share of wealth of the upper 0.5% grew by one percentage point between 1962 and 1983, but grew four times as much between 1983 and 1989.

while the bottom 90% owned only 16.1% (**Table 5.3**). The top 0.5% also owned 64% of bonds and 56.2% of private business assets, while the bottom 90% owned only 6.0% of bonds and 18.8% of business assets. Overall, Table 5.3 shows that the types of wealth which generate income, such as bonds, businesses, stocks, and other financial assets, tend to be held almost exclusively by the richest 10%, if not the top 1%, of families.

The types of wealth held by the bottom 90% of families are primarily homes and life insurance. Non-wealthy families also own liquid assets (primarily cash in checking, savings and money market accounts), which are used to meet regular expenses. Non-wealthy families, however, also "owe" 62.6% of the debt, primarily mortgages on their homes.

Growing Wealth Inequality

As we shall see, there was a dramatic growth in wealth inequality over the late 1980s. It is important to note, however, that the long-term trend prior to the 1980s was towards a lesser concentration of wealth. **Table 5.4** shows the share of total wealth (both excluding and including retirement wealth) over the 1922-1981 period for years in which data are available. In general, wealth was more concentrated in the 1920s and 1930s than in any period since World War II. The concentration of wealth (excluding retirement wealth) held by the upper 1% remained fairly steady over the 1940s, 1950s, and 1960s, ranging from a low of 25.7% in 1949 to a high of 31.9% in 1965 with no discernable trend up or down. The data for 1976 and 1981,

The types of wealth which generate income, such as bonds, businesses, stocks, and other financial assets, tend to be held almost exclusively by the richest 10%, if not the top 1%, of families.

TABLE 5.4
Share of Total Household Wealth Held
by Richest One Percent of Individuals, 1922-1981

Year	Excluding Retirement Wealth	Including Retirement Wealth
1922	38.3%	37.9%
1929	37.2	36.7
1933	28.9	28.2
1939	38.1	33.4
1945	28.9	22.4
1949	25.7	20.5
1953	28.1	21.6
1958	27.0	20.7
1962	30.1	22.5
1965	31.9	23.4
1969	29.0	21.0
1972	28.6	20.5
1976	18.9	13.8
1981	23.6	n.a.

TABLE 5.5
Composition of Aggregate Household Wealth,
1962, 1983, and 1989

Percent of Gross Assets Represented by:

Year	Gross House Value	Other Real Estate	Business Equity	Deposits	Bonds	Stocks	Trusts	Total Assets	Total Debt	Net Home Equity
1962	25.6%	6.2%	15.2%	19.3%	7.6%	19.5%	4.6%	100%	13.8%	18.5%
1983	29.8	14.7	18.6	18.7	4.1	8.9	2.6	100	13.0	22.3
1989	32.6	14.4	17.9	14.7	6.1	7.4	2.4	100	15.9	23.6

TABLE 5.6
Changes in Distribution of Net Worth
and Family Income, 1962-1989

Wealth Class	Percent of Net Worth				Percent of Family Income		
	1962	1983	1989	Change 1983-89	1983	1989	Change 1983-89
Top Fifth	81.7%	81.5%	84.3%	2.8%	51.9%	54.3%	2.4%
Richest 0.5%	25.2	26.2	30.3	4.1	9.1	11.5	2.4
Next 0.5%	8.2	7.8	8.0	0.2	3.7	3.2	− 0.5
Next 4%	21.6	22.1	21.6	− 0.5	13.3	13.8	0.5
Next 5%	12.4	12.1	11.3	− 0.8	8.3	10.4	2.1
Next 10%	14.3	13.3	13.1	− 0.2	17.5	15.4	− 2.1
Bottom							
Four-Fifths	18.3%	18.5%	15.7%	− 2.8%	48.1%	45.7%	− 2.4%
Fourth	12.9	12.5	13.0	0.5	21.7	22.2	0.5
Middle	5.2	5.2	2.7	− 2.5	14.1	12.6	− 1.5
Second	0.8	1.1	0.2	− 0.9	8.7	7.8	− 0.9
Lowest	− 0.5	− 0.3	− 0.2	0.1	3.7	3.0	− 0.7
Total	100.0	100.0	100.0	0.0	100.0	100.0	0.0

however, suggest that wealth became less concentrated during the 1970s. The backdrop for the recent surge in wealth inequality is a long-term drop in wealth concentration since the early 1920s including a falloff in wealth concentration in the 1970s.

Table 5.5 shows the changing composition of wealth from 1962 to 1983 and 1989, drawn from a consistent set of surveys. At first glance, it appears that housing represents a much larger percentage of household wealth, having risen from 25.6% of gross assets in 1962 to 32.6% in 1989. However, household mortgage debt also rose and, as the last column shows, the net value of people's homes (asset value less debt) rose a smaller amount.

In general, a lesser share of wealth is held in financial assets such as deposits, bonds, stocks, and trusts which in 1962 comprised 51% of all assets but fell to just 30.6% of all assets in 1989. Correspondingly, real estate and business ownership has increased in importance, growing from 21.4% of gross assets in 1962 to 32.3% in 1989. Since real estate and business ownerships as well as financial assets are disproportionately held by the very rich, the shift towards the former does not necessarily lead to greater or lesser inequality.

Fortunately, the 1962, 1983, and 1989 surveys allow a direct examination of changes in the distribution of wealth. Between 1962 and 1983 there were only minor changes in the distribution of wealth (**Table 5.6**). For instance, the percentage of total wealth held by each fifth of families remained comparable between 1962 and 1983, with the upper fifth having a slightly lower share—81.5% rather than 81.7%—in 1983 than in 1962. Although among the upper fifth, there was a modest redistribution towards the upper 5% and upper 0.5%.

Between 1983 and 1989, however, there was a major upward redistribution of wealth (**Figure 5C**). In 1989, the richest 0.5% of families owned 30.3% of household net worth, up 4.1% from the 26.2% share in 1983. The share of wealth of the upper 0.5% grew by one percentage point (from 25.2% to 26.2%) over the entire twenty-one-year period between 1962 and 1983, but grew four times as much in just six years between 1983 and 1989. The only other group to increase its share of wealth was the next richest 0.5% of families (and the fourth-fifth). The remainder of the population had a lesser share of wealth in 1989

The backdrop for the recent surge in wealth inequality is a long-term drop in wealth concentration since the early 1920s including a falloff in wealth concentration in the 1970s.

259

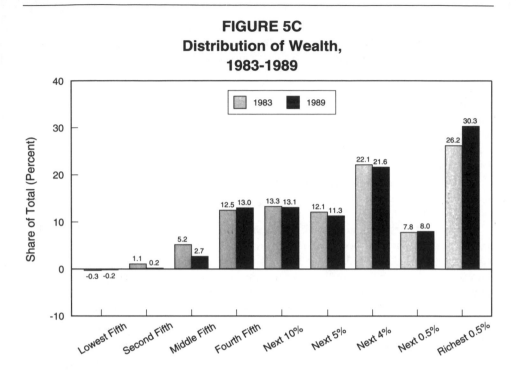

FIGURE 5C
Distribution of Wealth,
1983-1989

TABLE 5.7
Sources of Wealth Growth, 1962-1989

	Percentage of Wealth Growth Due to		
Years	Initial Wealth-holding Appreciating	Savings	Annual Growth of Wealth
1962-83	75%	25%	1.3%
1983-89	70	30	2.4

than in 1983, including the groups other than the upper 1% among the wealthiest fifth of families.

Most startling is the erosion of the wealth shares of the bottom sixty percent of families. The poorest fifth of families had more debt than assets in both 1983 and 1989, although slightly less so. The second fifth saw its share of wealth almost disappear, shrinking from a negligible 1.1% in 1983 to just 0.2% in 1989. The middle fifth saw its share of wealth essentially halved, falling from 5.2% in 1983 to 2.7% in 1989.

Aside from the modest gains of the fourth-fifth, the character of the wealth redistribution of the late 1980s was a much larger share of wealth for the upper 1% and a lower share of wealth for everybody else. The redistribution to the top was in fact spectacular—the upper 0.5% gained an additional 4.1% of household net worth, an amount greater than that held by the entire bottom sixty percent in 1989.

We have several clues as to why this occurred. As Table 5.6 also shows, there was a redistribution of family income during this same period. Given that, as the incomes of the well-off grew rapidly, it could be expected that their accumulation of wealth would also grow. In 1989, the upper fifth had an additional 2.4% of total family income relative to 1983. The bottom sixty percent of families, had a lower share of income in 1989 than in 1983, paralleling the trends in wealth.

The growth of income shares at the top, however, was less than what occurred for wealth—the upper 0.5% gained 2.4% of income but 4.1% of wealth. In addition, the growth of income shares was more widespread than that of wealth—the upper 10% gained income shares but only the upper 1% increased their share of wealth.

That income and wealth concentration should generally move together is not a surprise. Neither should it be surprising that there were differences in the extent of the growth of the concentration in income and wealth. As **Table 5.7** shows, most wealth growth arose from the appreciation (or capital gains) of pre-existing wealth and not from diligent savings out of income. Over the 1962 to 1989 period roughly three-fourths of new wealth was generated by increasing the value of initial wealth (much of it inherited). The somewhat more important role of savings in the 1983 to 1989 period reflects the unusually fast income growth of the very rich in that time period.

The redistribution to the top was in fact spectacular— the upper 0.5% gained an additional 4.1% of household net worth, an amount greater than that held by the entire bottom sixty percent in 1989.

TABLE 5.8
Change in Net Worth by Wealth Class, 1983-1989
(1989 Dollars)

Wealth Class	Net Worth (000)		Change 1983-89	Percent of Total Real Wealth Growth Accruing To:
	1983	1989		
Top Fifth	$596	$713	19.6%	94.2%
Richest 0.5%	7,491	10,248	36.8	46.9
Next 0.5%	2,457	2,706	10.1	6.6
Next 4%	1,445	1,856	28.5	19.1
Next 5%	519	552	6.4	13.1
Next 10%	211	222	5.2	8.5
Bottom Four-Fifths	$33.8	$33.2	−1.8%	5.8%
Fourth	91.4	109.8	20.1	14.8
Middle	38.0	22.8	−40.0	−6.1
Second	8.0	1.7	−78.8	−3.0
Bottom	−2.2	−1.7	n.a.	0.2
Total	146.3	169.1	15.6	100.0
Memo:				
Top 1%	$4,974	$6,477	30.2%	53.5%
Top 5%	1,647	2,026	23.0	72.6
Top 10%	982	1,204	22.6	85.7

262

The importance of the growth of pre-existing wealth in generating wealth accumulation suggests that the financial assets boom of the 1980s was responsible for the surge in wealth inequality (see Table 5.1). Since the richest 1% of families owns over half and the bottom 90% owns only 14.4% of the net financial assets (Table 5.2) rapid gains in financial assets such as stocks and bonds will generate wealth for the very rich and rising wealth inequality.

Table 5.8 and **Figure 5D** show another dimension of growing wealth inequality by presenting the pattern of percentage changes in wealth for the various wealth classes over the 1983 to 1989 period. On average, the bottom 60% of families not only had less wealth in 1989 than in 1983, but also experienced substantial losses in wealth. The middle fifth of families saw a 40% drop in average wealth from $38,000 per family to just $22,800 per family. The second fifth of families (wealthier than the poor but less wealthy than the middle) saw the modest wealth holdings of $8,000 in 1983 nearly wiped out by 1989, falling to just $1,700.

Since the richest 1% of families owns over half and the bottom 90% owns only 14.4% of the net financial assets, rapid gains in financial assets such as stocks and bonds will generate wealth for the very rich and rising wealth inequality.

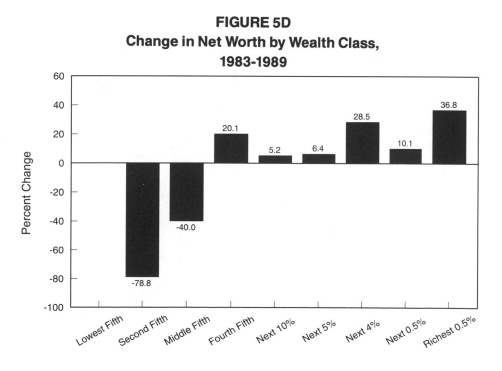

FIGURE 5D
Change in Net Worth by Wealth Class, 1983-1989

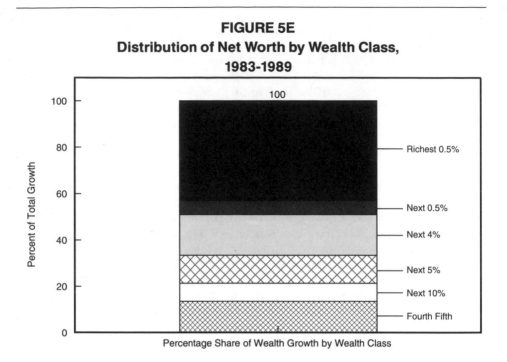

FIGURE 5E
Distribution of Net Worth by Wealth Class,
1983-1989

Percent of Total Growth

Percentage Share of Wealth Growth by Wealth Class

- Richest 0.5%
- Next 0.5%
- Next 4%
- Next 5%
- Next 10%
- Fourth Fifth

TABLE 5.9
Change in Wealth by Income Class, 1984-1988
(1988 Dollars)

| Income Fifth | Median Net Worth | | |
	1984	1988	Change 1984-88
Top	$98,411	$111,770	13.6%
Fourth	49,947	46,253	− 7.4
Middle	29,459	28,044	− 4.8
Second	21,248	19,694	− 7.3
Lowest	5,130	4,324	− 15.7
Total	37,012	35,752	− 3.4

264

It was only the fourth-fifth and groups in the upper 5% that experienced a faster than average growth in wealth. The richest 0.5% of families experienced an increase in wealth by more than a third (36.8%) in the six years after 1983, achieving an annual growth in wealth of 5.4%. Having started with nearly $7.5 million per family in 1983, the richest families were able to achieve an average net worth of $10.2 million by 1989.

This pattern of wealth growth yielded a highly skewed distribution of the share of real wealth growth accruing to the various wealth classes, as shown in the last column of Table 5.8 and in **Figure 5E**. As we have seen before, the bottom 60% of families did not participate in the wealth growth of the 1983 to 1989 period—the wealth of this group was falling or negative. On the other hand, fully 94.2% of the wealth created from 1983 to 1989 accrued to the wealthiest twenty percent of families. The richest 1% of families alone obtained 53.5% of the wealth created in this period.

The data in **Table 5.9** are taken from a different set of surveys and confirm the pattern of unequal wealth growth over the late 1980s shown in previous tables. Ranking families by income (rather than wealth), one sees that only the highest income families saw their wealth increase in the 1984 to 1988 period. The bottom eighty percent of families had less wealth in 1988 than in 1984. The startling truth is that during the 1980s recovery, the vast majority of families lost wealth as the economy grew, unemployment fell, and family income rose.

The bottom 60% of families did not participate in the wealth growth of the 1983 to 1989 period—the wealth of this group was falling or negative.

265

TABLE 5.10
Household Debt Burden, 1949-1991

| | Percent Debt as of: | |
Year	Personal Income	Total Assets*
1949	30.3%	6.9%
1967	61.7	12.5
1973	61.5	13.6
1979	66.6	14.1
1989	82.4	16.3
1991	86.7	17.2

*Financial assets (including pension funds and insurance), real estate, and consumer durables.

The gap in average wealth between minority and white households is even larger than the income gap with the average wealth in non-white families being just 19% of the average wealth in white families in 1989.

Soaring Debt

Household debt has skyrocketed in recent years. Two measures of the total debt burdens of households, debt as a percent of assets and as a percent of personal income, have each grown markedly in the 1980s after a long period of relative stability (**Table 5.10**). Household debt leapt from 66.6% of personal income in 1979 to 82.4% in 1989, and from 14.1% of household assets in 1979 to 16.3% in 1989.

These higher levels of debt have left families more vulnerable and the economy weaker. The recession of the early 1990s only worsened the situation, driving debt levels that much higher.

Increased Racial Wealth Gaps

We already know that blacks and other minorities tend to have lower incomes than whites. Yet, non-whites lag even further behind in the accumulation of wealth. As **Table 5.11** shows, the average income of a non-white household was 63% of that of an average white household in 1963, a ratio that prevailed in both 1983 and 1989 (looking at median incomes shows the same failure to close the racial income gap).

266

TABLE 5.11
Ratio of Household Income and Wealth
Between Non-White and White Families, 1940-1989

Ratio of Non-White to White:

Year	Means	Medians
A. Household Income		
1967	63%	58%
1983	62	57
1989	63	59
B. Net Worth		
1962	13%	4%
1983	24	9
1989	19	7
C. Homeownership Rates		
a. Census of Population		
1940	52%	
1950	61	
1960	60	
1970	64	
1980	65	
1985	64	
b. Federal Reserve Board Survey Data		
1983	62%	
1989	63	

TABLE 5.12
Net Worth by Race and Household Characteristics, 1989
(1989 Dollars)

Household Group	Average Net Worth ($000)		
	Whites	Non-Whites	Ratio
All	$210.9	$39.1	19%
A. Income Class			
Less than $10,000	$37.0	$5.6	15%
$10,000—$19,999	70.9	11.4	16
20,000-29,000	95.7	42.8	45
30,000-49,999	188.7	48.3	26
50,000 and more	664.1	236.6	36
B. Age Class			
Under 35 years	$117.5	$8.2	7%
35-44	159.0	53.4	34
45-54	211.5	75.8	36
55-64	425.6	37.3	9
65-74	331.9	69.5	21
75 and over	176.1	20.5	12
C. Household Type			
Married Couples	$276.5	$72.7	26%
Single, Male Head	114.9	22.8	20
Single, Female Head	147.3	18.2	12

The gap in average wealth between minority and white households is even larger than the income gap, with the average wealth in non-white families being just 19% of the average wealth in white families in 1989. There was, however, significant progress in lessening racial wealth inequality in the 1962 to 1983 period as non-white mean wealth grew from 13% to 24% of white mean wealth. In contrast, the racial wealth gap widened between 1983 and 1989.

The gap in racial wealth holding is pervasive. At every level of income a minority family holds far less wealth than a white family (**Table 5.12**). Likewise, a racial wealth gap is evident at every age level, but especially among the very oldest and youngest families. Racial wealth differences are also present in each type of family, whether in married couple families or those headed by single females.

Conclusion

Trends in the growth and distribution of wealth are comparable to those for income. Both the after-tax income and the wealth of the bottom 60% of families declined over the 1980s and the greatest share of both increased wealth and income accrued to the upper 1% of families. Thus, by 1989 the bulk of the families not only held a lower share of total wealth, they had less wealth to fall back on in case of a fiscal or medical emergency or to finance large expenditures such as a college education.

By 1989 the bulk of the families not only held a lower share of total wealth, they had less wealth to fall back on in case of emergency or to finance large expenditures such as a college education.

Chapter 6.

Poverty: High Rates of Poverty Unresponsive to Economic Expansion

The previous chapters have documented the winners and losers in the highly uneven economic expansion of the 1980s. This chapter focuses on the experience of the poorest members of society: those persons and families whose economic situations are the most precarious.

The rising tide lifted the yachts; the rowboats foundered.

The poor did not fare well in the 1980s, despite the economic growth economy from 1983 to 1989. The economic policy strategy of the period—a rising tide will lift all boats—proved ineffective. As one analyst noted, "Apparently, the rising tide lifted the yachts; the rowboats foundered."

This chapter examines in detail a number of the arguments proffered to explain the unresponsive poverty rates of the decade and finds that the facts do not support them. Specifically, some critics have claimed that poverty was mis-measured, and that the economic condition of the poor *did* improve over the decade. However, our analysis of both the government's official measurement and a series of more conceptually satisfying ways to measure poverty revealed that the general finding of high levels of poverty over the 1980s is valid no matter which form of measurement is used.

Others argue that the poor themselves are to blame, either because they formed families more likely to be poor regardless of the expansion (i.e., single-headed families), or because they failed to exploit the labor market opportunities that prevailed over the decade. To explore these issues, we analyze the perceived problem of female-headed family

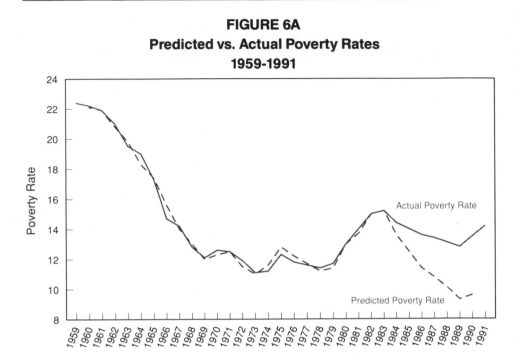

FIGURE 6A
Predicted vs. Actual Poverty Rates
1959-1991

formation, examine the question of whether welfare programs have created incentives that have increased poverty, and explore the issue of whether the poor chose not to work. Yet, the data do not support these explanations for the high and intractable poverty rates throughout the economic expansion of the 1980s.

In fact, the problems analyzed in previous chapters—the heightened inequality of the income distribution, lessened progressivity of the tax system, and in particular, falling wages—all conspired to keep poverty rates historically high throughout the decade. In addition, the "safety net" (the social provision of assistance to those in poverty) grew less effective at providing relief to the poor.

Background: The Failure of Economic Growth

The failed relationship between poverty and economic growth in the 1980s is portrayed graphically in **Figure 6A**. The dotted line in the figure represents a statistical model of changes in the poverty rate over time, based on economic variables historically correlated with poverty rates: unemployment, inflation, income, and government transfers. The bold line is actual poverty rates.

What is particularly notable about Figure 6A is the divergence of predicted and actual values in the 1980s. The model tracks poverty extremely well up until 1983 (the beginning of the expansion) when the model incorrectly predicts a fall in poverty rates. In other words, a major shift in the relationship between economic growth and poverty occurred in the decade such that the recent economic recovery failed to reduce poverty as much as occurred in earlier periods of growth. This chapter begins by exploring the extent of poverty in the 1980s, and then examines the reasons for the failure of economic growth to ameliorate poverty.

A major shift in the relationship between economic growth and poverty occurred in the decade such that the recent economic recovery failed to reduce poverty as much as occurred in earlier periods of growth.

273

TABLE 6.1
Percent and Number of Persons in Poverty, 1959-1991, with Averages Over Peak Years

Year	Actual Poverty Rate	Predicted Poverty Rate	Number in Poverty (000)
1959	22.4%	22.1%*	39,490
1967	14.2	14.0	27,769
1973	11.1	11.0	22,973
1975	12.3	12.8	25,877
1979	11.7	11.4	26,072
1983	15.2	15.2	35,303
1989	12.8	9.3	31,528
1991	14.2	n.a.	35,708

Averages Over Peak Years

1959-65	19.8%	19.4%	
1967-73	12.5	12.3	
1974-79	11.7	11.8	
1980-89	13.6	12.5	

*From 1960 due to data availability.

Measuring the Extent of Poverty

There are, of course, a variety of ways to measure poverty. The most commonly accepted measures are the official government poverty lines. These are pretax, post-transfer income thresholds, adjusted for family size and for price changes. That is, the Census Bureau categorizes as poor those families with cash incomes below the poverty line for that sized family. While there exist a number of conceptual problems with this definition of poverty (e.g., it ignores the value of non-cash benefits such as food and medical care), the official poverty measures have a long history and are a widely used measure of economic despair. Other, more conceptually satisfying measurements, are presented below. However, regardless of the choice of measure, the poverty trends they expose are similar.

Table 6.1 shows overall poverty rates at peaks in the business cycle since 1959 and for 1991, the last year of data availability. Poverty was exceptionally high in the late 1950s, but began falling in the 1960s in response to economic growth and more generous government transfers, dropping from 22.4% in 1959 to 14.2% in 1967. Poverty rates continued to fall during the early 1970s, hitting a low of 11.1% in 1973, before climbing again. On average, poverty rates were higher throughout the 1980s expansion at 13.6% over 1980-1989, than over the growth periods from 1967 onward, when they ranged from 12.5% (1967-1973) to 11.7% (1974-1979).

Table 6.1 also includes predicted poverty rates, generated by the model used for Figure 6A. Up to 1983, the model tracks poverty rates quite closely. For the years shown in Table 6.1, the predicted poverty rates never diverge more than 0.5 percentage points from the actual rates until 1989. These findings tell us that, based on the way economic growth has effected poverty in the past, the rates were expected to fall by 5.9 percentage points between 1983 and 1989, from 15.2% to 9.3%. However, the actual rates only fell 2.4 points over this period, from 15.2% to 12.8%. The causes of this divergence between the predicted and actual poverty rates, unique to the growth period of the 1980s, will be examined throughout the chapter.

On average, poverty rates were higher throughout the 1980s expansion at 13.6% over 1980-1989, than over the growth periods from 1967 onward, when they ranged from 12.5% to 11.7%.

TABLE 6.2
Consumption-Based Poverty Measures

Consumption Standard	Poverty Rate		Point Change 1977-1988
	1977	1988*	
Official Measure	11.6%	13.0%	1.4
Housing Consumption	20.7	23.0	2.3
Food Consumption	18.0	25.8	7.8

*Latest year of data availabilty.

TABLE 6.3
Poverty Rates when (Nonmedical) Non-cash Benefits are Included

Year	Official Measure	Plus Market Value of Food and Housing Benefits
1979	11.7	9.6%
1989	12.8	11.2
1990	13.5	11.8
Point Increase		
1979-89	1.1	1.6

Alternative Measurements of Poverty

In the analysis of poverty, the issue arises as to whether poverty is being appropriately defined and measured. The next few tables examine some of the ways the official Census Bureau's poverty measure both overstates and understates poverty. Other measures are presented, and each one stresses a different concept of what constitutes poverty. However, no matter which concept of poverty is used, the trend documented in Figure 6A and Table 6.1 is evident.

A common criticism of the official poverty lines is that they no longer reflect even minimal levels of consumption and thus understate the extent of poverty. The original consumption data were collected in 1955, when it was assumed that poor families spent one-third of their income on food (thus assuming that families could purchase all other necessities for twice what they spent on food). The poverty lines were then constructed by multiplying the Department of Agriculture's minimum food budgets for different sized families by three. However, patterns of consumption have changed a great deal since 1955. For example, the proportion of income spent on food has shifted over time, with the average family spending a smaller proportion of the family budget on this necessity (and, in turn, a larger proportion on other necessities). Therefore, if the poverty lines were recalculated today, they would be higher (as would poverty rates), since the food budget would be multiplied by a larger number than three.

Table 6.2 presents two alternative measures of poverty rates based on updated information on consumption of food and housing (housing consumption has also shifted over time, accounting for a larger percentage of family income than in the past). The available data are for 1977 and 1988. When the increased real cost of housing (see Chapter 8) is factored into the poverty thresholds, the poverty rate in 1988 rises from 13.0% to 23.0%, a full 10 points above the official measure. When considering the changing proportion of the family budget devoted to food expenditures, the rate is even higher (25.8%). Furthermore, the growth of poverty over the 1980s is even more dramatic when these consumption shifts are taken into account. Thus, changing consumption patterns imply that our official poverty measures severely understate the extent and growth of poverty.

As noted above, the official measure does not factor in the value of non-cash benefits, such as food stamps, housing

Changing consumption patterns imply that our official poverty measures severely understate the extent and growth of poverty.

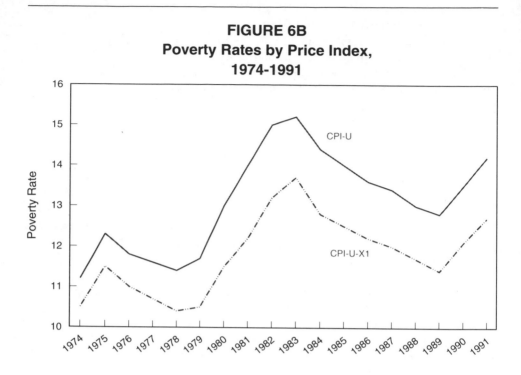

FIGURE 6B
Poverty Rates by Price Index,
1974-1991

CPI-U

CPI-U-X1

TABLE 6.4
Percent of Persons with Low Relative Income, 1964-1989
Adjusted for Family Size

	Relative Income Poverty Measures		
Year	Less than 1/4 the Median	1/4 to 1/2 of the Median	Less than 1/2 of the Median
1969	5.5%	12.4%	17.9%
1979	6.7	13.3	20.0
1989	8.3	13.7	22.0

assistance, and medical benefits, thus understating the extent of poverty. **Table 6.3** shows what poverty rates would be if the market value of food and housing benefits were included in recipients' income. Medical benefits are omitted since they are not a common part of everyday consumption like food and housing and their inclusion would have the perverse effect of making the ill appear less poor. Although the inclusion of food and housing benefits lowers the absolute rates in both 1979 and 1989, the increase in poverty over the period is even greater using the broader measure.

As noted above, the official poverty lines are indexed for inflation. However, some analysts claim that the price index used to adjust the poverty lines overstated inflation in the 1970s and early 1980s, and thereby overestimated real poverty rates. **Figure 6B** tracks poverty rates, 1974-1990, using an alternative price index, CPI-U-X1, which is considered a more conservative measure of inflation. As would be expected, the more conservative price index leads to lower measured poverty rates. However, Figure 6B shows that regardless of the price index chosen to adjust the poverty lines for price changes, there has been a rise in poverty since 1979 despite overall income growth.

Another important indicator of poverty is *relative* economic well-being. A conceptual shortcoming of the absolute poverty lines used in the above tables is that they are only adjusted for inflation; they do not reflect overall income growth. The poverty lines are fixed levels of income that represent a particular standard of living (level of consumption) at a point in time. However, as average income grows over time and standards of living rise, the economic "distance" between the officially poor and the rest of society expands. While the earliest poverty lines were close to 50% of the median family income for a given family size, they have fallen to about 35%.

Table 6.4 presents measures of poverty which adjust for economic growth by measuring poverty *relative* to the median family income (which changes yearly). As would be expected (since median family income has grown faster than prices), the poverty rates at one-half the median are substantially higher than the absolute rates in Table 6.1. For example, whereas 12.8% of the population was poor according to the official, or absolute, poverty measure in 1989, 22.0% of all persons were in families with incomes

Although the inclusion of food and housing benefits lowers the absolute rates in both 1979 and 1989, the increase in poverty over the period is even greater using the broader measure.

279

TABLE 6.5
Poverty Gap: Aggregates and Means, 1967-1991
(1990 Dollars)

Year	Families		Persons Not in Families	
	Aggregate Poverty Gap (Millions)	Mean Poverty Gap	Aggregate Poverty Gap (Millions)	Mean Poverty Gap
1967	$24,610	$4,342	$13,361	$2,672
1973	21,058	4,362	12,060	2,582
1979	26,010	4,762	15,153	2,638
1983	41,708	5,281	19,874	2,949
1989	36,966	5,237	20,225	2,989
1991	40,814	5,292	22,497	2,894
Percent Change				
1967-73	−14.4%	0.5%	−9.7%	−3.4%
1973-79	23.5	9.2	25.6	2.2
1979-89	42.1	10.0	33.5	13.3

TABLE 6.6
Persons Below 50% of the Poverty Level

Year	Percent of all Poor	Number of Persons (000)
1975	29.9%	7,733
1979	30.2	8,340
1983	38.5	13,590
1989	38.0	11,983
1990	39.4	14,059

below one-half of the median family income. Again, the trend of worsening poverty over the last two decades is evident.

The Poor Get Poorer

The depth of poverty at a point in time is another useful gauge of how the poor are faring. As **Table 6.5** shows, there has not only been a growth in poverty; the poor have also become poorer. This is evident in measures of the so-called "poverty gap," either the aggregate or the average dollar amount persons or families are from the poverty threshold. For instance, in 1989, the average poor family had an income $5,237 below the poverty line. The aggregate poverty gap, which was close to $37 billion in 1989, is the sum of every poor family's income deficit.

Looking again at trends, the aggregate gap grew by 42.1%, from approximately 26.0 to 37.0 billion dollars from 1979 to 1989. The average deficit for families has grown between 1979 and 1989 for both persons in families (by 10%) and not in families (by 13.3%). Such growth indicates that the poor have become poorer over time.

Table 6.6 shows another measure of the depth of poverty: the percentage of the poor below 50% of the poverty line. In 1979, slightly less than one-third (30.2%) of the poor were in "deep poverty." By 1983, this proportion had approached two-fifths (38.5%), where it essentially held throughout the decade. Thus, not only have poverty rates failed to fall in the context of the 1983-1989 recovery (as Figure 6A and Table 6.1 show), but more of the poor have fallen into deep poverty.

Poverty Spells: The Length of Time Spent in Poverty

All of the measures of poverty examined thus far have been "point-in-time" measures. That is, we have compared those in poverty (using different definitions) at one point in time, to those in poverty at a different point in time. This approach fails to answer important questions about the dynamics of poverty: how much mobility exists in the population of poor persons; are most poor persons in poverty for a short or a long period; what personal characteristics are associated with those experiencing short versus long spells of poverty?

The average poverty deficit for families has grown between 1979 and 1989 for both persons in families (by 10%) and not in families (by 13.3%) . . . indicating that the poor have become poorer over time.

281

TABLE 6.7
Distribution of Poverty Spells for
Nonelderly Persons Entering Poverty

Spell Length (Years)	Percent of Persons Completing Poverty Spells
1	44.5%
2	15.8
3	9.8
4	6.2
5	4.7
6	2.8
7	2.1
8	1.0
9	1.1
>9	12.0
Total	100.0

TABLE 6.8
Events Leading to Poverty Spells, and Average Spell Length

Primary Reason for Spell Beginning	Percent of Beginnings	Average Length of Completed Spell (Years)
Earnings of Head Fell	37.9%	3.3
Earnings of Wife Fell	3.7	3.1
Earnings of Others Fell	7.7	6.5
Transfer Income Fell	8.0	5.2
Rising Needs Standard*	8.2	5.3
Child Became Head or Wife	14.7	2.4
Wife Became Female Head	4.7	3.7
Child of Male Head Became Child of Female Head	6.4	4.0
Child Was Born Into Poverty	8.6	7.6
Total/Average	100.0	4.2

*The needs standard is a measure used in this research to reflect an increased burden on a family's economic situation, generally resulting from the addition of a new family member.

Researchers have analyzed these questions and found a good deal of turnover in the poverty population; chronic poverty is the exception, not the rule. Most poverty spells are relatively short, although there does exist a small group of long-term poor (a "poverty spell" is a continuous period wherein income is below the poverty line). Unfortunately, the most recent research of this type covers the time period from the late 1960s to the early 1980s.

Table 6.7 shows the distribution of poverty spells for the non-elderly population, and finds that for the vast majority, poverty spells last for less than three years (the data cover the years 1970-1982). Only a minority of spells last for eight or more years. The percentages in the table can be interpreted as answering the following question: "Of those persons just beginning a poverty spell, what percentage will leave poverty after a given time period?" For example, 44.5% of poverty spells ended within one year, and about 70% ended within three years. A relatively small percentage of poverty spells, 13.1%, lasted over eight years.

The high rates of turnover in the poverty population implied by Table 6.7 suggest that for most persons, being poor is a temporary condition. In fact, other research into poverty dynamics over the 1970s found that as much as one-quarter of the United States population was poor at some point within a ten-year period, usually for a short time. Recall also from Chapter 1 (Table 1.35) that the probability of falling out of the middle class to low-income status rose in the 1980s. Such findings debunk the notion that the majority of the poor are chronically impoverished and exhibit long-term dependency on government assistance (research on "welfare spells" shows similar findings to the above). Furthermore, as shown in the following table, the events that most commonly cause a poverty spell are phenomena common to most working persons (e.g., job or earnings' loss, child birth). Most persons experiencing such events will be poor for a relatively short time.

The events that cause a poverty spell to begin, and the average duration of such spells, are given in **Table 6.8**, covering the same period as the previous table. As noted, the most common spell-causing events are earnings' loss and family structure changes. By far the most common poverty spells (37.9%) began with a drop in earnings by the family head, and lasted an average 3.3 years. Spells beginning when a child (person 18 or under) becomes a family head

Researchers have found a good deal of turnover in the poverty population; chronic poverty is the exception, not the rule.

TABLE 6.9
Length of Poverty Spells for Children Age 1-10*, by Race, in Percent

Poverty Spell Length	White	Black	Other	Total
Never Poor	73%	22%	53%	65%
Poor 1-3 Years	19	22	28	20
Poor 4-6 Years	5	22	10	8
Poor 7-10 Years	3	34	8	8
Total	100	100	100	100

*Data are for children born around 1970.

FIGURE 6C
Persistent Poverty in Industrialized Countries: Households with Children, Mid-1980s

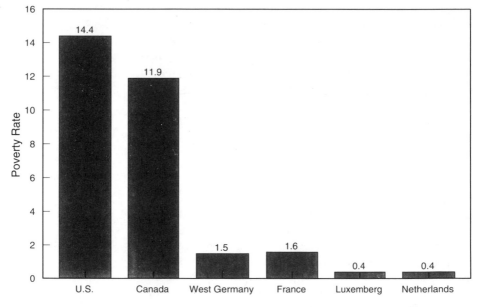

284

or a wife are also relatively common, accounting for 14.7% of spell beginnings. Such spells are the shortest in the table, lasting on average 2.4 years. The longest average spells (7.6 years) are caused by the birth of a child into a family already poor (the beginning spell refers to the new child). The phenomenon of persistent child poverty is examined next.

Table 6.9 examines the length of poverty spells for children between the ages of one and ten, by race (the data are for children born around 1970). The table shows that race is an important determinant of the duration of poverty: black children have the highest likelihood of spending their childhood in poverty. The last column shows that 65% of children experienced no poverty at all throughout the period. However, the results vary dramatically by race. Whereas 73% of white children spent no part of the period poor, the same could be said for only 22% of black children. Well over half (56%) of black children were poor for at least four of the first ten years of their lives—for white children, only 8% fell into this category. Finally, over a third (34%) of black children were poor from seven to ten years of their first decade; the analogous figure for white children was 3%.

A final measure of poverty dynamics shows that persistent poverty is more common in the U.S. than in other industrialized countries (this issue is examined at length in Chapter 9). **Figure 6C** shows the percentage of households with children that were poor in every year of a three year study in the mid-1980s (poverty here is measured in relative terms, as 50% of the median income). In the U.S., 14.4% of households with children were poor throughout the three-year study. Only Canada had a similarly high rate, at 11.9%. The other countries in the figure had rates well below that of the U.S.

Having examined a variety of alternative measures of poverty, we have shown that some measures—the inclusion of in-kind benefits and the alternate price index— make the official measure appear to overstate poverty. Other measures—consumption adjustments and relative measures—make the official measure appear to understate poverty. Furthermore, changes in the poverty gap, the incidence of deep poverty, and poverty dynamics are beyond the scope of the official measure. However, none of these alternative measures change the fundamental finding

Whereas 73% of white children spent no part of the period poor, the same could be said for only 22% of black children. Well over half (56%) of black children were poor for at least four of the first ten years of their lives.

285

TABLE 6.10
Poverty by Race/Ethnicity

Year	Poverty Rates		
	White	Black	Hispanic
1967	11.0%	39.3%	NA
1973	8.4	31.4	21.9%
1979	9.0	31.0	21.8
1989	10.0	30.7	26.2
1991	11.3	32.7	28.7

TABLE 6.11
Percent of Children in Poverty, by Race, 1979-1991

Year	Children under 18			
	Total	White	Black	Hispanic
1979	16.4%	11.8%	41.2%	28.0%
1989	19.6	14.8	43.7	36.2
1991	21.8	16.8	45.9	40.4
Point Change				
1979-89	3.2	3.0	2.5	8.2

Year	Children under 6			
	Total	White	Black	Hispanic
1979	18.1%	13.3%	43.6%	29.2%
1989	22.5	17.1	50.1	39.6
1991	24.6	19.2	51.7	44.6
Point Change				
1979-89	4.4	3.8	6.5	10.4

regarding the trend toward high poverty rates in the 1980s, despite the recovery. Given the wide use of the official measure, and the fact that it adequately captures poverty trends, we will use it throughout the rest of this chapter, except where noted.

The Poverty Status of Different Demographic Groups

Certain demographic groups are more vulnerable to poverty than others. Members of minority groups, families headed by an unmarried female, and children are at the highest risk of poverty. The poverty problem of the elderly, though historically significant, has been ameliorated to a degree by government transfers.

Table 6.10 shows the official poverty rate for different racial and ethnic categories. While both white and black poverty rates fell from 1967 to 1973, they have generally risen ever since. In all cases, black and Hispanic poverty is more extensive than that of whites. The black poverty rate has been about three times that of whites since 1979, while the Hispanic rate has climbed from 21.9% in 1973 to 28.7% in 1991.

Table 6.11 has poverty rates for children, by race/ethnicity. Child poverty grew in all racial categories between 1979 and 1991. Young Hispanic children (under six) experienced the highest growth in their poverty rate, up 10.4 percentage points between 1979 and 1989. By 1991, more than one out of every five children was poor. For children under six years old, the rate was even higher, reaching 24.6% in 1991. Perhaps the most alarming statistic in the table refers to young black children: in 1991 more than half of black children under six were poor.

As noted above, the poverty of the elderly has been greatly reduced by government transfers. **Table 6.12** and **Figure 6D** examine the reasons for this decrease by contrasting the "before-transfer" poverty rate, which is the rate that would prevail if there were no government cash assistance, with the actual or "after-transfer" poverty rate, which includes such assistance. The reduction in poverty among the elderly has come largely from expanded government transfer payments, particularly between 1967 and 1973. During this period, the before-transfer poverty rate dipped very slightly, from 58.3 to 58.0%, but higher Social Security

Perhaps the most alarming statistic refers to young black children: in 1991 more than half of black children under six were poor.

287

TABLE 6.12
Poverty among the Elderly and All Persons
Before and After Transfers, 1967-1990

| | Poverty Rate Among: | | | |
| | All Persons | | The Elderly | |
Year	Before Transfers	After Transfers	Before Transfers	After Transfers
1967	19.4%	14.3%	58.3%	29.7%
1973	19.0	11.1	58.0	16.1
1979	20.4	11.6	58.9	15.1
1989	20.9	12.8	51.9	11.4
1990	21.5	13.5	51.0	12.1

FIGURE 6D
Poverty Before and After Transfers: Elderly vs. All Persons, 1967-1990

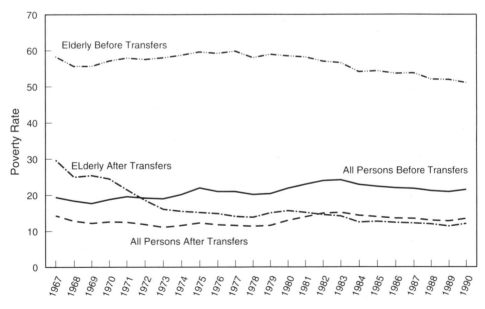

benefits virtually halved after-transfer poverty, from 29.7 to 16.1%. In 1989, more than half of the elderly would have been poor without government transfer programs. The effect of government benefits in 1989 was to dramatically reduce the poverty rate among the elderly from 51.9 to 11.4%.

Family Structure and Poverty

Family structure has historically been an important determinant of poverty status, as certain family types are more vulnerable to poverty than others. However, the important questions regarding family structure and poverty are as follows: to what extent are poverty rates and family structure changes *causally* related? To what degree are the high and intractable poverty rates documented above driven by individuals' choices to form vulnerable family types?

Table 6.13 takes a first look at these questions by showing the percentage of persons in female-headed families, married couple and male-headed families, and not in families from 1959 to 1991. The table also shows the poverty rates for each group in each time period, along with percentage point changes over time.

Persons in female-headed families and persons not in families are more likely to be poor than persons in married-couple or male-headed families. In 1991, 39.7% of persons in families headed by a woman were poor. For persons not in families in 1991, the poverty rate (21.1%) was also substantially higher than the rate for all persons. Those in married-couple and male-headed families are the least likely to be poor; since 1967 their poverty rates have stayed below 10%.

Over time, the distribution of family types has shifted toward family structures more vulnerable to poverty. The percentage of persons in married-couple and male-headed families, which have the lowest poverty rates, has consistently fallen, from 85.9% in 1959 to 71.5% in 1991. Conversely, there has been a consistent expansion of female-headed families and an even faster growth of singles.

Turning to the poverty trends of these different groups, all family types saw their poverty rates fall between 1967 and 1979, with single persons showing the largest drop

Over time, the distribution of family types has shifted toward family structures more vulnerable to poverty.

289

TABLE 6.13
Changing Family Structure and Poverty, 1959-1991

	Percent of Persons in:			
Year	Female-Headed Families	Married-Couple and Male-Headed Families*	Not Living in Families	Total
1959	8.0%	85.9%	6.1%	100.0%
1967	9.1	84.2	6.7	100.0
1973	10.5	80.7	8.8	100.0
1979	12.1	76.2	11.7	100.0
1989	13.2	72.5	14.3	100.0
1991	13.9	71.5	14.7	100.0
Point Changes				
1967-79	3.0	−8.0	5.0	
1979-89	1.1	−3.7	2.6	

	Poverty Rate of Persons in:			
Year				All Persons
1959	49.4%	18.2%	46.1%	22.4%
1967	38.8	9.6	38.1	14.2
1973	37.5	6.0	25.6	11.1
1979	34.9	6.4	21.9	11.7
1989	35.9	7.3	19.2	12.8
1991	39.7	7.9	21.1	14.2
Point Changes				
1967-79	−3.9	−3.2	−16.2	−2.5
1979-89	1.0	0.9	−2.7	1.1

*Including unrelated subfamilies since 1979.

(16.2 points). This trend was reversed in 1979-1989, when poverty grew slightly for persons in married-couple and female-headed families (0.9 and 1.0 percentage points, respectively), and fell much more slowly for individuals.

What does Table 6.13 reveal about the relationship between demographic shifts and changes in poverty rates? The *prima facie* evidence is mixed. On the one hand, it is clear that there has been a compositional shift to families more vulnerable to poverty. However, when the demographic shifts were occurring most rapidly, 1967-1979, the overall poverty rates declined from 14.2 to 11.7% and poverty fell among persons in female-headed families and singles. Conversely, when demographic forces slowed over the 1980s, the poverty trend reversed (as noted above), and persons in married couple families saw a similar increase in their poverty rate as did those in female-headed families (0.9 versus 1.0 percentage points). Thus, while demographic shifts to family types with elevated vulnerability to poverty have played a role in the high poverty rates of the 1980s, the extent of that role is unclear. It is to this issue we now turn.

Decomposing the Role of Demographics

One way to investigate the effect of demographic change on poverty rates is to assume that poverty rates are influenced by three factors: 1) changes in family structure, i.e., the proportion of persons living in the different family types shown in Table 6.13; 2) changes in economic factors, like lower wages and benefits, as well as changes in family size; 3) the combined effect of these two factors.

Table 6.14 is an example of this exercise. The first column shows the actual changes in poverty rates over peak years in the economy. Column two shows how poverty rates would have been expected to change over the period in question, given the changes that took place in family structure. For example, family structure changes occurring between 1959 and 1967 are predicted to have led to 0.5 percentage point growth in overall poverty. However, non-demographic factors had a powerful countervailing effect and poverty rates fell 8.2 points over the period. There was no interaction effect during this period (column four).

It is clear that there has been a compositional shift to families more vulnerable to poverty. However, when the demographic shifts were occurring most rapidly the overall poverty rates declined.

291

TABLE 6.14
Changing Family Structure and Poverty

Period	Change in Poverty Rate	Predicted Change Due to Family Structure*	Change Due to Other Factors**	Interaction of Family Structure and Other Factors***
	(1)	(2)	(3)	(4)
1959-67	-8.2	0.5	-8.7	0.0
1967-73	-3.1	1.0	-4.0	-0.2
1973-79	0.6	1.1	-0.3	-0.2
1979-89	1.1	0.7	0.5	-0.1
1989-91	1.4	0.2	1.2	0.0

*Effect on overall poverty rate due to the changes in proportion of persons in female-headed families, married-couple and male-headed families, and not in families.
**Effect on overall poverty rate due to the changes in poverty rates within these three main demographic groups.
***Effect on overall poverty rate due to the interaction of family structure changes and poverty rate changes.

TABLE 6.15
Poverty Rates for Female-Headed Families

Year	All	White	Black	Hispanic
1973	32.2%	24.56%	52.76%	51.4%
1979	30.4	22.3	49.4	49.2
1989	32.2	25.4	46.5	47.5
1991	35.6	28.4	51.2	49.7

The second column shows that the demographic shift over time into families more susceptible to poverty—the increase in the proportion of persons living alone or in female-headed households (Table 6.13), has in fact contributed to higher poverty rates. However, the post-1967 demographic pressure on poverty rates was at its lowest in the period from 1979-1989, with the exception of the two year period 1989-1991. This difference is a result of the relatively slow recent growth of female-headed families and single persons, and the falling poverty rates of these same demographic groups prior to 1979.

Column three in Table 6.13 shows that in previous periods, non-demographic factors worked to reduce poverty. Between 1959 and 1973, these countervailing factors were far more powerful than the demographic effects shown in column two, so that the poverty rate fell substantially. However, between 1979 and 1989, factors such as lower wages and a less effective transfer system actually added 0.5 points to the poverty rate. During this same period, demographic changes added 0.7 points, less than the demographic impact in the two previous periods.

The point of this decomposition exercise is that while the shift to more poverty-prone family types has continued to create upward pressure on poverty rates, that pressure has lessened throughout the 1980s. The shift over time to female-headed families and persons living alone has added to poverty rates, yet such shifts fail to fully explain the high poverty rates of the 1980s. Moreover, the most important factor in rising poverty appears to be the failure of economic forces to lessen poverty.

The shift over time to female-headed families and persons living alone has added to poverty rates, yet such shifts fail to fully explain the high poverty rates of the 1980s.

The Poverty of Female-Headed Families

Female-headed families were identified above as particularly vulnerable to poverty. These families are stereotypically thought to be mostly black women who have had children out-of-wedlock. The next few tables examine these myths and find that mother-only family poverty is not exclusively a minority problem, nor are most single mothers never-married women.

Table 6.15 examines the trend in poverty rates of female-headed families by race and Hispanic origin. Overall, their poverty rates have changed little since 1973. Furthermore, while minority female-headed families have the highest poverty rates, their rates declined between 1979

TABLE 6.16
Increase in Poverty in Female-Headed Families, by Race, 1973-1991

Year	White	Black	Other*	Total	Number(000)
Percent of Poor Female-Headed Families Who Are in Each Racial Group					
1973	54.3%	44.4%	1.3%	100.0%	2,193
1979	51.0	46.7	2.3	100.0	2,645
1989	53.0	43.5	3.5	100.0	3,504
1991	52.7	44.1	3.2	100.0	4,161
		Share of Total			
Increase					
1973-79	35.4%	57.5%	7.1%	100.0%	452
1979-89	59.1	33.8	7.1	100.0	859

*Includes Asians, Pacific Islanders, American Indians, Aleuts, and Eskimos.

TABLE 6.17
Marital Status of Female Family Heads, 1973-1989

Year	Marital Status of Female Family Heads:*					Total Number (000)
	Married, Husband Absent	Widowed	Divorced	Never Married	Total	
1973	23.9%	37.7%	25.9%	12.6%	100.0%	6,535
1979	21.0	29.8	33.0	16.2	100.0	8,220
1989	17.1	23.9	36.4	22.6	100.0	10,890
Percent Increase in Number of Families:						
1973-79	10.6%	-0.4%	60.2%	62.5%	25.8%	
1979-89	8.1	6.0	46.4	84.4	32.5	

*Women without dependents are not regarded as family heads.

and 1989, while those for whites rose. The percentage of black female-headed families in poverty fell from 49.4 to 46.5%; Hispanic, from 49.2 to 47.5%. The rate for whites during this same period increased from 22.3 to 25.4%.

When the population of female-headed families is examined as a whole, it is clear that white families comprise the largest share (**Table 6.16**). In 1989, white families accounted for 53.0% of the total; black families accounted for 43.5%. The bottom panel of Table 6.16 shows the share of the total increase in the number of poor female-headed families by race. While blacks accounted for the largest share of the increase between 1973 and 1979 (57.5%), whites were responsible for the largest share between 1979 and 1989 (59.1%).

The stereotypical female head of a family is thought to have never been married and to have had a number of out-of-wedlock births. In fact, as **Table 6.17** shows, never-married female heads comprise the second smallest category in 1989. In that year, 22.6% of female family heads were never married, while 36.4% were divorced. Even widowed female family heads accounted for a larger proportion of the total group than never-married mothers in 1989 (as they have since 1973). However, never-married mothers were the fastest growing group; in the 1979-1989 period they grew by 84.4%.

A great deal of controversy exists regarding the rise of out-of-wedlock births documented in the previous table. Conventional thinking suggests that a precipitous rise in female-headed families led by never-married mothers, particularly among blacks, has become a major poverty problem. This perception has grown out of the fact that the ratio of expected unmarried to married lifetime births (this way of measuring birth trends is explained below) has grown significantly, from 23.2% to 62.2% for blacks, between 1960 and 1987 (**Table 6.18**). However, the data show that while out-of-wedlock births have become more common for both blacks and whites, they have *not* increased dramatically. What is driving the rise in the ratio of unmarried to married births, particularly among blacks, is less an increase in out-of-wedlock births than a decrease in married births.

Table 6.18 and **Figure 6E** present the relevant data. The table and figure use the concept of expected lifetime births, i.e., the number of in- and out-of-wedlock children a

The stereotypical female head of a family is thought to have never been married and to have had a number of out-of-wedlock births. In fact, never-married female heads comprise the second smallest category in 1989.

295

TABLE 6.18
Expected Lifetime Births, by Marital Status and Race, 1960-1987

Fertility	1960	1965	1970	1975	1980	1987
Unmarried Births*						
White	0.08	0.11	0.14	0.12	0.18	0.29
Black	1.05	1.08	1.16	1.09	1.25	1.43
Married Births*						
White	3.45	2.67	2.25	1.56	1.57	1.47
Black	3.49	2.75	1.93	1.15	1.01	0.87
Total						
White	3.53	2.78	2.39	1.69	1.75	1.77
Black	4.54	3.83	3.10	2.24	2.27	2.29
Unmarried Births as Percent of Lifetime Births						
White	2.3%	4.0%	5.7%	7.3%	10.2%	16.7%
Black	23.2	28.2	37.6	48.8	55.5	62.2

*The numbers in the table refer to the expected number of lifetime births given prevailing birth rates.

FIGURE 6E
Expected Lifetime Births by Marital Status and Race, 1960-1987

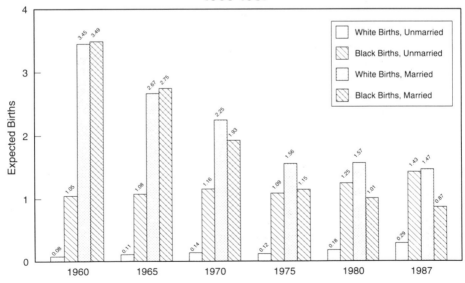

296

woman could expect to have throughout her life, derived from the birth rates in each time period. For example, based on prevailing birth rates at the time, a married white woman in 1960 would have been expected to have an average 3.45 children over her lifetime.

The first two bars for each year in Figure 6E show that while blacks have a higher level of expected unmarried births than whites, both groups show a slight upward trend. While a rise in the number of unmarried births is not a trivial development, it is hard to imagine that this development alone—a rise over the period in expected black unmarried births from 1.05 to 1.43—would have caused much controversy. The significant trend is the falling expected births to married women of both races, as the average white woman in 1960 went from having 3.45 children in her lifetime to having 1.47 children in 1987. The expected child-bearing behavior of her black counterpart changed even more dramatically, with her expected births falling from 3.49 to 0.87. The ensuing rise in the ratio of unmarried to all births (as shown in the last panel of Table 6.18) has been driven to a greater degree by the falling birth rates of married women than the rising rates of unmarried women.

When comparing child-bearing behavior of black and white women, Table 6.18 shows that in 1960, expected lifetime births were about equal for married women of both races (3.45 for whites; 3.49 for blacks). However, married women began a dramatic decline in their child bearing behavior, with lifetime births to married black women declining faster than married white women. By 1970, a typical married black woman was expected to have fewer children than her white counterpart, and by 1987 (the latest year of available data), the expected births between the two races diverged significantly. This trend had two effects. It lowered overall expected births (Table 6.18), and it led to the *appearance* of vastly accelerated out-of-wedlock birth rates, especially for black women.

In sum, family structure changes cannot be held accountable for the failure of economic growth to reduce poverty rates in the 1980s. Although a demographic shift to family types more vulnerable to poverty has contributed to high poverty rates over time, most of this shift occurred in earlier periods. As Table 6.14 (column two) shows, family structure created about the same degree of upward pressure on poverty rates from 1979-1989 as such changes did

While a rise in the number of unmarried births is not a trivial development, it is hard to imagine that this development alone—a rise over the period in expected black unmarried births from 1.05 to 1.43—would have caused much controversy.

TABLE 6.19
Poverty Rates* Using Different Income Definitions, 1979-1989

Family Relationship	Market Income Before Transfers	Plus Social Insurance (Including Social Security)	Plus Means-Tested Cash Transfers	Plus Food and Housing Benefits	Less Federal Taxes	Poverty Rate Reduction Due to Government Taxes and Benefits
	(1)	(2)	(3)	(4)	(5)	(1-5)
All Persons						
1979	19.1%	12.86%	11.6%	9.6%	9.9%	9.2
1989	19.9	13.8	12.8	11.2	11.8	8.1
Point change						
1979-89	0.8	1.0	1.2	1.6	1.9	−1.1
Persons in Single Parent Family with Related Children under 18						
1979	50.0%	45.1%	40.2%	30.0%	30.1%	19.9
1989	48.1	44.6	42.3	36.4	36.4	11.7
Point change						
1979-89	−1.9	−0.5	2.1	6.4	6.3	−8.2
Persons in Married Couple Family with Related Children under 18						
1979	9.4%	7.7%	7.1%	5.9%	6.3%	3.1
1989	10.5	9.1	8.5	7.4	8.0	2.5
Point change						
1979-89	1.1	1.4	1.4	1.5	1.7	−0.6

*Rates are based on adding benefits to income cumulatively, from left to right.

between 1959-1967, when poverty fell 8.2 points. The poverty of female-headed families, while high relative to overall poverty, has risen only slightly over the 1980s (Table 6.16). Furthermore, Tables 6.17 and 6.18 (and Figure 6E) show that the controversy surrounding out-of-wedlock births is overstated. Never-married mothers still comprise a minority of poor female family heads, and the rise in the ratio of out-of-wedlock births to married births for blacks is being driven by a dramatic fall in the latter rather than a substantial rise in the former.

The Changing Effects of Taxes and Transfers

Chapter 2 made the point that the decreased progressivity of the tax system over the 1980s favored the wealthy and hurt the poor. In tandem with this development, government transfers became less generous over the decade, particularly in the early Reagan years. Since the official poverty statistics are calculated prior to tax payments (or receipts), and are excluding the value of in-kind benefits, they shed little light on the effects of policy changes in these areas. Therefore, **Table 6.19** uses a more inclusive measure of poverty rates than the official rate—one that includes five separate income definitions.

Table 6.19 examines the effect of taxes and benefits on poverty rates, for all persons and for family types with children, 1979 and 1989. Column one shows the poverty rates generated by the market—these rates represent the degree of poverty that would exist in the absence of any government intervention. Moving left to right, the table introduces different transfers and taxes, and shows how poverty would be effected, showing in the first row, for example, that the poverty rate for all persons fell from 19.1 to 12.8% due to the receipt of social insurance benefits. The final column shows the extent to which government tax and transfer policies mitigated the poverty rates generated by market outcomes (here, negative signs mean less effective poverty reduction). For instance, taxes and transfers reduced the poverty rate by 9.2 percentage points in 1979; in 1989 they led to an 8.1 point reduction. Thus, the reduced effectiveness of taxes and transfers led to a 1.1 point increase in the poverty rate.

The reduced effectiveness of taxes and transfers led to a 1.1 point increase in the poverty rate.

299

FIGURE 6F
Poverty Before and After Transfers: Families with Children, 1967-1990

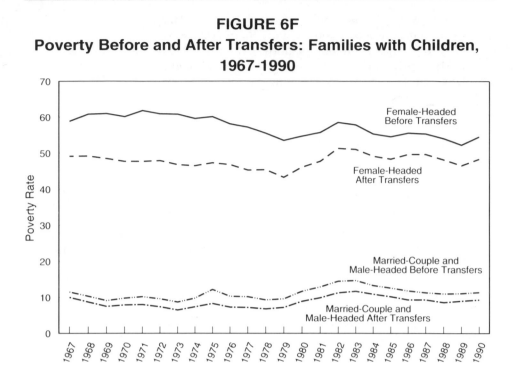

Almost every category of tax or transfer in the table shows either worse market outcomes or less effective poverty reduction in 1989 compared to 1979. Overall, tax and transfer policies reduced poverty rates by 9.2 percentage points in 1979, from 19.1% to 9.9%. In 1989, the market was 0.8 points less effective in reducing poverty before government intervention, and 1.1 points less effective after taxes and transfers. Single-parent families with children were the biggest losers in terms of reduced effectiveness against poverty. In 1979, through the receipt of various cash and in-kind benefits net of taxes, their poverty rates were reduced by 19.9 points; in 1989, taxes and transfers took only 11.7 points off of their market outcome poverty rates. The importance of the reduced effect for single-parents with children is particularly notable in light of the fact that their market outcome was slightly better in 1989 than in 1979 (48.1% in poverty versus 50.0%). The implication is that the primary distribution (market outcome) was somewhat more favorable to these persons in 1989 than in 1979; their entire increase in post-tax, post-transfer poverty is due to reduced government assistance.

Married couple families also had higher rates of poverty in 1989 than in 1979. The market was 1.1 points less effective at poverty reduction; each category of tax and transfer once again led to higher poverty rates in 1989 so that by the end of the period, poverty rate reduction fell by 0.6 points. Since the rates are based on adding the value of benefits cumulatively, we can take the ratio of the point change in column one to that in column five as an estimation of the proportion of reduced effectiveness due to market forces. For married couples, about two-thirds (1.1/1.7) is attributable to poverty-inducing market forces.

Figure 6F portrays the effect of transfers (taxes are ignored) on the poverty of non-elderly persons in families with children from 1967-1990, by comparing pre- and post-transfer poverty rates. The high poverty rates of female-headed families relative to married couple and male-headed families are evident in the figure. A subtler point is made by noting the distance between pre- and post-transfer poverty rates for both types of families. The two lines for male-headed and married couple families maintain a fairly consistent gap over time, suggesting that the effectiveness of transfers has not varied a great deal for these family types. However, the gap between the two lines for persons in female-headed

The gap between the two lines for persons in female-headed families begins to visibly narrow in the 1980s underscoring the reduced effectiveness of taxes and transfers.

301

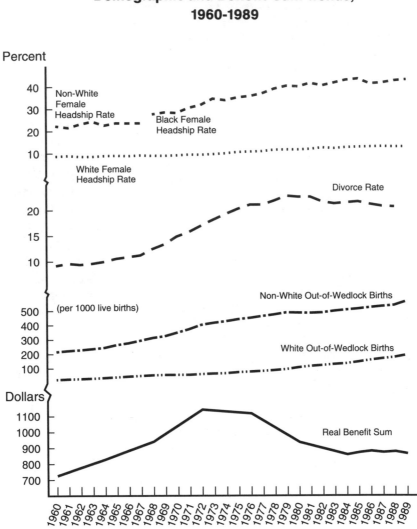

FIGURE 6G
Demographic and Benefit-Sum Trends, 1960-1989

Percent

40 — Non-White Female Headship Rate
30
20 — Black Female Headship Rate

10 ⋯⋯⋯⋯

White Female Headship Rate

Divorce Rate

20
15
10

Non-White Out-of-Wedlock Births

500 (per 1000 live births)
400
300
200
100

White Out-of-Wedlock Births

Dollars

1100
1000
900
800
700

Real Benefit Sum

1960 1961 1962 1963 1964 1965 1966 1967 1968 1969 1970 1971 1972 1973 1974 1975 1976 1977 1978 1979 1980 1981 1982 1983 1984 1985 1986 1987 1988 1989

families begins to visibly narrow in the 1980s, echoing the findings in Table 6.13.

Government Benefits and Family Structure

The previous sections examined the roles of family structure and benefit changes on poverty rates. This section looks at the interaction between these two issues and examines a question which has often been raised in the debate over government provision to the poor: to what extent have welfare programs caused poverty by creating incentives that heighten the probability that a family will remain poor? Specifically, welfare programs have been attacked as the primary cause of the increased proportion of female-headed families.

The argument regarding family structure has been developed as follows. Since the most valuable benefit package is available to single-headed families with children, there exists an incentive to form such families, either by delaying or avoiding marriage, dissolving existing unions, or having children out-of-wedlock. In fact, the evidence shows that the proportion of families with children headed by females has grown over-time, as has the benefit sum, at least up to the mid-1970s (the benefit sum includes the value of Aid to Families with Dependent Children [AFDC], Food Stamps, and Medicaid; see **Figure 6G**, bottom panel). Critics of the system of social provision have suggested that there exists a causal relationship between these two phenomena: family structure has been altered by the provision of benefits to female-headed families with children.

Yet the fact that both the benefit sum and the proportion of single-parent families with children has grown over time does not necessarily imply that the former causes the latter. Figure 6G challenges this causal connection. The figure shows that all the demographic indicators of growing female-headed families follow an upward trend since 1960. Throughout the initial part of the period, the benefit sum (bottom panel in the figure) also grew.

However, beginning around the mid-1970s the benefit sum began to fall, due primarily to the declining real value of AFDC benefits. Yet none of the demographic indicators follow the plunging benefit sum. The only series in the figure that reverses direction is the divorce rate, the one rate in the figure that is least relevant to the low-income population. While white female headship and non-white out-of-

The apparent independence of these demographic indicators and the benefit sum challenges the overly simplistic story that welfare causes the rising proportion of female-headed families.

303

TABLE 6.20
AFDC Participation Rates of Female-Headed Families
with Children, 1967-1987*

Year	Participation Rates
1967	36%
1973	63
1979	52
1983	45
1987	42

*Participation rate is the ratio of mother-only families on AFDC to mother-only families *not* participating in AFDC.

FIGURE 6H
AFDC Participation Rates,
1967-1987

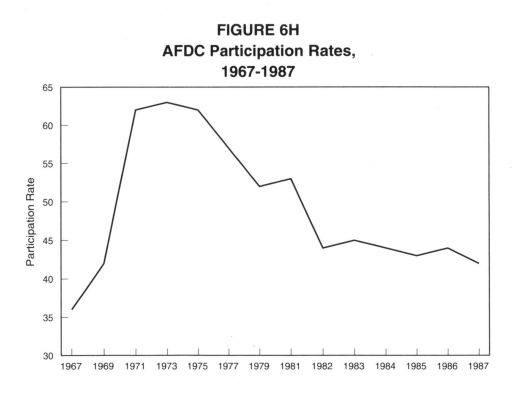

wedlock birth rates do appear to slightly decelerate by the end of the time period covered, the white out-of-wedlock birth rate does not appear to attenuate at all. The apparent independence of these demographic indicators and the benefit sum challenges the overly simplistic story that welfare causes the rising proportion of female-headed families.

Further evidence against the "welfare is the problem" argument comes from an analysis of AFDC participation rates, i.e., the proportion of the demographically eligible population (female-headed families with children) participating in the program. If single-mother families were forming specifically to take advantage of the eligibility for welfare, we would expect to see a greater proportion of female-headed families participating in AFDC over time (i.e., rising participation rates). In fact, as **Table 6.20** and **Figure 6H** show, participation rates peaked in the mid-1970s and fell thereafter, apparently stabilizing in the 1980s.

Female-headed families are forming for reasons other than to ensure AFDC eligibility.

How are falling participation rates to be explained in the context of the growing proportion of female-headed families with children? The explanation is quite simple: female-headed families are forming for reasons other than to ensure AFDC eligibility. The trend in Figure 6H suggests that it is a mistake to necessarily associate the rise in female-headed families with AFDC participation. In fact, common sense dictates the independence of these two events (family structure and AFDC eligibility). The decision to form a family of a particular structure is most likely to be based on a wide variety of factors, reflecting not only economic factors, but incorporating social influences such as society's changing mores regarding single-parent families and divorce.

Finally, the question of family structure and welfare has been extensively examined by economists who have modelled the family formation process, estimating the impact of a wide variety of variables thought to play a role in family structure decisions, including, of course, welfare benefits. A detailed discussion of this econometric work is beyond the scope of this text. However, the findings of this literature can be summarized as follows:

— the effect of the value of the benefit package has a small effect on family structure;
— this small effect is most apparent in lower rates of remarriage, and the decision of female-headed families

TABLE 6.21
Shares of Workers Earning Enough to Maintain a Family of Four at 0.75 of Poverty and up to the Poverty Line, by Gender and Race

Male Workers	Whites, Non-Hispanics			Blacks, Non-Hispanics			Hispanics, Any Race		
Share of Workers Earning:	1979	1989	Point Change 1979-89	1979	1989	Point Change 1979-89	1979	1989	Point Change 1979-89
Less Than 0.75 of the Poverty Line	2.4%	8.1%	5.7	4.2%	15.1%	10.9	3.7%	15.9%	12.2
Between 0.75 of Poverty and the Poverty Line	12.3	10.7	−1.6	20.9	18.2	−2.7	22.9	22.4	−0.5
Less Than the Poverty Line	14.8	18.8	4.1	25.2	33.3	8.1	26.6	38.3	11.7

Female Workers	Whites, Non-Hispanics			Blacks, Non-Hispanics			Hispanics, Any Race		
Share of Workers Earning:	1979	1989	Point Change 1979-89	1979	1989	Point Change 1979-89	1979	1989	Point Change 1979-89
Less Than 0.75 of the Poverty Line	6.1%	16.4%	10.3	5.26%	21.3%	16.1	7.8%	21.9%	4.2
Between 0.75 of Poverty and the Poverty Line	29.7	16.4	−13.4	33.1	19.3	−13.8	41.2	23.2	−17.9
Less Than the Poverty Line	35.8	32.7	−3.1	38.3	40.6	2.3	48.9	45.2	−3.8

to live independently (i.e., to form their own households instead of living with a relative);
— a review of the findings suggest that, over the period
covered in Figure 6G, the increase in the benefit sum
led to a 9 to 14 percent increase in the prevalence of
female-headed families with children.

Having examined the effect of the changes in taxes and
transfers over the 1980s, and the impact of benefits on family structure, we now turn to an explanation of the high
poverty rates over the decade.

Explaining the High Poverty Rates of the 1980s

As noted above (see also Chapter 2), the tax system grew
less progressive over the decade, and government benefits
grew less effective at reducing poverty (Table 6.19). However, when we consider these findings in the context of the
relatively long economic expansion of 1983-89, another
question is suggested: why were the poor unable to "cash
in" on the economic growth that prevailed throughout
most of the decade? That is, given the expansion, we would
expect those at the bottom of the income distribution (at
least those with some connection to the labor market) to
respond to the less generous transfers and more regressive
taxes documented above by turning to the labor market. In
the following section, we argue that such a reaction did in
fact occur, but that the wages of low-income workers
declined significantly over the decade (see Chapter 3), and
this development served to keep the poverty rates high
throughout the decade.

Falling Wages and Poverty in the 1980s
The problem of declining wages has already been presented in Chapter 3. The relevant part of that discussion in
the context of this chapter is the expansion of low-wage
employment and the declining wages of low-wage workers.
The following tables specifically examine earnings trends
as they affect the poor.
Table 6.21 answers the following question: given the
wage structure at a point in time, what percentage of workers, working full-time/full-year, fail to earn an hourly wage
that would lift a family of four out of poverty? The table

The data in Table 6.21 show that, the wage structure at the bottom of the earnings distribution shifted in such a way as to increase the percentage of workers earning poverty level wages.

TABLE 6.22
Wage Trends Relevant to the Poor and Near-Poor

Percent Changes by Tenths	Male Workers		Female Workers	
	1973-79	1979-89	1973-79	1979-89
Lowest Tenth	0.3%	− 17.5%	10.0%	− 17.8%
2nd Tenth	− 1.7	− 16.0	0.5	− 6.6
3rd Tenth	− 2.1	− 11.2	2.9	− 5.4
4th Tenth	6.1	− 12.8	− 1.7	1.8

TABLE 6.23
Work Experience of the Poor, 1979-1989

	1979	1989	Point Change 1979-89
Number of Poor Aged 15 + (thousands)	16,907	20,474	
Percent Not Employable*	35.1%	33.9%	− 1.2
Ill or Disabled	15.8	12.9	− 2.9
Going to School	10.0	9.7	− 0.3
Retired	9.2	11.2	2.0
Percent Employable	64.9	66.1	1.2
Worked	38.7	41.1	2.4
Did Not Work	26.2	25.0	− 1.2
Total	100.0	100.0	
Percent of Poor Workers Who Worked			
Year-Round**	29.9	34.1	4.2
Full-Time, Year-Round	20.9	22.4	1.6

*"Employable" poor are those who are neither retired, ill, disabled, nor in school. Those who are keeping house are in the employable group.
**At least 50 weeks.

answers this question for 1979 and 1989. In addition, the table breaks out the share of workers earning up to 0.75 of the poverty line.

The data in Table 6.21 show that, excepting white and Hispanic females, the wage structure at the bottom of the earnings distribution shifted in such a way as to increase the percentage of workers earning poverty level wages. For black men in 1979, 25.2% earned poverty level wages. By 1989, this percentage had increased to 33.3%, an increase of 8.1 points. For Hispanic men, the increase was even larger (11.7 points).

The deterioration in the wage has meant not only a growth in low-wage earners but also a growing proportion of workers with very low earnings. This can be seen in Table 6.21 in the increased share of workers who, even if they worked full-time and full-year would not be able to earn 75% of the poverty line. The proportion of these very low earners rose between 1979 and 1989 in every demographic category, with black females posting the largest increase (16.1 percentage points). However, also in all cases, the percentage of workers earning between 0.75 of poverty and the poverty line decreased, suggesting a strong downward shift at the very bottom of the earnings distribution for all men and women.

While Table 6.21 shows the proportion of low-wage workers, **Table 6.22** examines percentage changes in wage levels of males and females in the bottom four-tenths of the hourly earnings distribution. For low-wage men between 1973 and 1979, there was little change in the bottom three-tenths, and a 6.1% gain in the fourth. For low-wage women, this was a period of growth in the lowest tenth. However, this pattern of gains or small losses reversed over the period of 1979-1989. All groups, excepting women at the fourth tenth, experienced falling wages in recent years. In addition, the wage loss was greatest for the lowest earners, further evidence of a down shifting of the earnings distribution.

Work Effort

The increase in the prevalence of low wages clearly increases the likelihood of poverty. However, it is possible that employment possibilities—getting a job with sufficient hours of work—could have offset the effect of lower

All groups, excepting women at fourth tenth, experienced falling wages in recent years. In addition, the wage loss was greatest for the lowest earners, further evidence of a down shifting of the earnings distribution.

TABLE 6.24
Percentage of Half-Time and Full-Time "Worker Equivalents" in Poor Families with Children, 1979-1989

Families With Children	At Least 1 Half-Time Worker Equivalent*	At Least 1 Full-Time Worker Equivalent
All Families with Children		
1979	42.3%	26.4%
1989	44.0	28.1
Point Change		
1979-89	1.7	1.7
Female-Headed Families with Children		
1979	24.7%	10.0%
1989	27.8	12.7
Point Change		
1979-89	3.1	2.8
Married-Couple Families with Children		
1979	69.8%	52.4%
1989	72.7	55.2
Point Change		
1979-89	2.9	2.8

*A "full-time worker equivalent" is defined as family labor supply between 1,750 and 2,080 hours worked during the year.

wages. In this regard, it could be argued that the poor did not benefit from the expansion not because of low wages, but simply because they chose to work less. The following tables challenge that argument by showing that, with the exception of average annual hours worked by single mothers with children, the amount that poor (and near-poor) people worked grew over the decade. Poverty rose despite this extra work effort.

Table 6.23 begins the analysis of work effort by examining the work experience of poor in 1979 and 1989. A slightly larger percentage of the poor were employable in 1989 than in 1979 (66.1% versus 64.9%). But what is more central to the argument in question is the following: a larger percentage of the employable poor worked in 1989 than in 1979, and of those who worked, a larger percentage worked year-round and full-time.

The table considers only those poor persons age 15 and older, and examines the labor market participation of those who were employable (neither retired, ill, disabled, nor in school). In 1989, 41.1% of these poor persons worked, a 2.4 percentage point gain over the 38.7% of the employable poor who worked in 1979. There was also an increase in year-round work effort by the poor, as the percentage of poor workers working at least 50 weeks of the year increased by 4.2 points. The percentage of the poor working full-time/full-year also grew slightly (1.6 points).

In **Table 6.24**, the percentage of poor families with the equivalent of at least a half- or full-time worker is shown for 1979 and 1989. For example, when members of all poor families with children pooled their working hours in 1979, 42.3% of those families had the equivalent of at least one half-time worker (full-time labor supply is defined as between 1,750 and 2,080 hours of work per year). Once again, work effort is seen to have increased between 1979 and 1989 in each category.

Poor married couples with children have the highest percentage of half- or full-time worker equivalents in both years, a finding to be expected since they typically have the most potential workers per family. In 1989, close to three- quarters of these families had at least one half-time equivalent worker. Conversely, female-headed families with children have fewer potential workers (in addition to child

The amount of work performed by members of poor families with children increased slightly over the decade.

311

TABLE 6.25
Hours Worked by Family Type in the
Bottom Two Fifths*, 1979-1989

	Annual Hours Worked	
All Families	Lowest Fifth	Second Fifth
1979	820	1,800
1989	850	1,840
Percent change		
1979-89	3.7%	2.2%
Female-Headed Families With Children		
1979	280	570
1989	260	560
Percent change		
1979-89	−7.1%	−1.8%
Married Couples With Children		
1979	2,240	2,950
1989	2,350	3,250
Percent change		
1979-89	4.9%	10.2%
Unrelated Individuals (Non-Elderly)		
1979	590	1,350
1989	640	1,540
Percent change		
1979-89	8.5%	14.1%

*Fifths are defined separately for each family type.

care constraints, see Chapter 8); they have the smallest percentage of half- and full-time worker equivalents in both
years. However, with respect to the argument noted above,
the table shows that the amount of work performed by
members of poor families with children *increased* slightly
over the decade.

Table 6.25 looks at average annual hours of work among
low-income families within different family types: female-
headed families with children, married couples, and unrelated individuals. Whereas the previous table included only
the poor, Table 6.25 examines work effort by those in the
bottom two-fifths of the income distribution, which
includes both the poor and near-poor.

As with the previous table, the average hours of work in
Table 6.25 represent the pooled work effort of the family.
The table shows that, with the exception of female-headed
families with children, average annual hours of work grew
for all family types between 1979 and 1989. However, even
in light of extra work effort, the wage decline constrained
these families from realizing any economic gains. With the
exception of female family heads, they were running faster
yet losing ground.

The largest growth in percentage terms was for unrelated individuals. Those at the bottom of the income distribution increased their average hours of work by 8.5% over
the decade; those individuals in the second quintile
increased their average hours by 14.1%. Married couples
with children have by far the most hours of work; in each
year these families supplied an average of well over 2,000
hours of labor. By 1989, the average married-couple family
with children in the second quintile worked 3,250 hours,
10.2% more hours than in 1979. Mother-only families with
children consistently show a relatively small number of
hours of work, and their supply fell over the time period.
However, their annual change in hours was quite small (20
hours in the bottom fifth, 10 hours in the second fifth), and
their wages can be assumed to be low. Therefore, the magnitude of their annual income loss due to reduced hours
was negligible.

*Even in light of
extra work effort,
the wage decline
constrained these
families from
realizing any
economic gains
. . . they were
running faster yet
losing ground.*

Conclusion: What Does the Evidence Show?

This chapter began with the observation that, based on the movement of the economic variables usually correlated with poverty rates, poverty should have fallen after 1983. Yet a wide array of evidence shows that the expected fall in poverty did not materialize. Poverty rates stayed high throughout the decade, whether measured by the official thresholds or by alternative, more encompassing measures. Furthermore, demographic explanations (the increase of family types unresponsive to economic growth), while possibly relevant in earlier decades, are insufficient to explain the stubbornly high rates. Neither is lack of work effort a sufficient explanation; the work effort of the poor and near-poor increased over the 1980s.

Two simultaneous effects occurred which kept poverty rates high over the decade: (1) the wages of those at the bottom of the income distribution fell precipitously, and (2) the system of tax and transfers was less effective than in the past.

The conclusion we are left with is that two simultaneous effects occurred which kept poverty rates high over the decade: (1) the wages of those at the bottom of the income distribution fell precipitously, and (2) the system of tax and transfers designed to mitigate such a failure of the market was less effective than in the past. In other words, the primary distribution of market income was such that more families (as well as unrelated individuals) were unable to achieve incomes above the poverty level through the wages they earned over the 1980s. This development necessarily puts additional pressure on the secondary distribution, i.e., taxes and transfers, which must devote more resources to close a wider poverty gap (see Table 6.5). However, as shown in Table 6.19, the secondary distribution was in fact less effective at reducing poverty than in the past.

314

Chapter 7

Regional Analysis: The Differences in Growth by Region and Residence

In this chapter, we shift our focus from the national to the regional perspective, and examine differences in economic well-being at various state and urban/suburban/rural levels. Our analysis follows the Census Bureau's definitions of geographical areas, which divide the country into four regions, nine divisions, and, of course, fifty states and Washington, D.C. The last section of the chapter analyses urban/rural differences.

We find that economic growth was quite uneven on a regional basis over the 1980s. The Northeastern region, comprising New England and the Mid-Atlantic divisions, did comparatively well in terms of greater income and wage growth, and lower unemployment. However, the Northeast was the region most adversely effected by the economic downturn that began in 1989, as indicated by rises in both unemployment (2.8 percentage points, 1989-1991) and poverty rates (2.2 points, 1989-1991) that were the highest among all regions. Conversely, the 1980s' economy in the Midwestern and the Western regions was characterized by relatively flat or negative income growth over the 1980s, rising poverty, and significant wage loss. The South experienced somewhat more mixed results over the 1980s, but did sustain high unemployment and poverty rates, particularly for children.

Economic growth was quite uneven on a regional basis over the 1980s.

315

TABLE 7.1
Median Family Income by Region, 1973-1991
(1991 Dollars)

Median Family Income	Northeast	Midwest	South	West
1973	$37,080	$37,025	$30,665	$35,983
1979	37,956	37,862	32,301	38,079
1989	43,369	38,018	33,500	39,210
1991	40,265	36,759	31,940	37,171
Percent Change				
1973-1979	2.4%	2.3%	5.3%	5.8%
1979-1989	14.3	0.4	3.7	3.0
1973-1989	17.0	2.7	9.2	9.0
1989-1991	−7.2	−3.3	−4.7	−5.2

Income Inequality

Chapter 1 documents the dramatic rise in income inequality over the course of the 1980s. In that chapter we note that the share of total family income going to the top 20% of families grew by 5.3 percentage points between 1977 and 1989. Meanwhile the bottom 90% of families lost income shares. In this section, we present a state and regional analysis of growing income inequality. We find that inequality grew both within regions, as the distance between rich and poor expanded, and between regions, as the Northeast generally prospered more than the other regions.

We begin by examining changes in the levels of income by region and state. **Table 7.1** presents the income of the median family, 1973-1990 (1990 data is the most recent available), by region, and gives a first impression of the uneven nature of regional growth. The Northeast region had the highest levels of both income and economic growth throughout the period; the Midwest saw the least growth. Median income in the Northeast grew 14.3% between 1979 and 1989, from $37,956 to $43,369 (1991 dollars). In the Midwest, however, median income growth was flat over the 1980s; total growth was only 0.4%. The South and the West also experienced slow growth between 1979 and 1989, 3.7% and 3.0% respectively, compared to their levels of growth in the 1973-1979 period, when the median family income grew the fastest in those regions.

Although the Northeast experienced the most growth between 1979 and 1989, it was "hit" the hardest during the recent recession, a theme which resurfaces throughout this analysis. Between 1989 and 1991, median family income fell slightly in the Midwest (3.3%), and fell more steeply in the South and West (4.7% and 5.2%, respectively). Yet the median family in the Northeast saw a dramatic 7.2% drop in its income, the biggest regional loss. While the Northeast still had the highest median family income and the most growth over the full period, this two-year period (1989-1991) took $3,104 off the median income.

In **Table 7.2** we look more closely at the trend in median family income by state, for four-person families. (These data are only available for four-person families for the years 1974-1989.) Once again, the dramatic rise of the median family's income in the Northeast is evident.

Although the Northeast experienced the most growth between 1979 and 1989, it was "hit" the hardest during the recent recession.

317

TABLE 7.2
Median Income for Four-Person Families by State, 1974-1989
(1991 Dollars)

Region/ Division/State	Median Income for Four-Person Families			Annual Growth Rates	
	1974	1979	1989	1974-79	1979-89
Northeast					
New England					
Maine	$32,940	$33,266	$42,108	0.2%	2.4%
New Hampshire	36,703	41,108	52,704	2.3	2.5
Vermont	34,496	35,548	44,372	0.6	2.2
Massachusetts	41,017	43,779	56,895	1.3	2.6
Rhode Island	37,800	39,822	47,536	1.0	1.8
Connecticut	43,238	44,928	58,558	0.8	2.6
Mid-Atlantic					
New York	$39,808	$38,802	$47,992	−0.5%	2.1%
New Jersey	43,896	45,351	58,466	0.7	2.5
Pennsylvania	38,023	41,070	44,379	1.5	0.8
Midwest					
East North Central					
Ohio	$39,682	$41,464	$45,549	0.9%	0.9%
Indiana	37,994	41,622	41,959	1.8	0.1
Illinois	42,907	44,661	46,801	0.8	0.5
Michigan	42,445	44,950	47,038	1.1	0.5
Wisconsin	40,409	43,286	44,547	1.4	0.3
West North Central					
Minnesota	$41,443	$44,926	$46,533	1.6%	0.4%
Iowa	37,713	41,535	40,350	1.9	−0.3
Missouri	36,136	39,192	42,264	1.6	0.8
North Dakota	39,377	35,927	38,230	−1.8	0.6
South Dakota	33,654	35,355	36,059	1.0	0.2
Nebraska	35,071	38,189	41,631	1.7	0.9
Kansas	37,776	42,053	41,671	2.1	−0.1

TABLE 7.2 (continued)

Region/ Division/State	Median Income for Four-Person Families			Annual Growth Rates	
	1974	1979	1989	1974-79	1979-89
South					
South Atlantic					
Delaware	$39,970	$38,990	$47,000	−0.5%	1.9%
Maryland	43,694	45,436	55,079	0.8	1.9
District of					
Columbia	39,608	39,222	44,563	−0.2	1.3
Virginia	39,705	42,288	49,526	1.3	1.6
West Virginia	32,985	34,742	34,941	1.0	0.1
North Carolina	34,596	36,163	41,813	0.9	1.5
South Carolina	34,260	37,094	39,666	1.6	0.7
Georgia	35,863	39,715	43,956	2.0	1.0
Florida	38,808	38,204	41,079	−0.3	0.7
East South Central					
Kentucky	$32,840	$35,224	$37,774	1.4%	0.7%
Tennessee	33,559	35,775	38,314	1.3	0.7
Alabama	33,604	34,258	38,367	0.4	1.1
Mississippi	30,342	32,526	35,478	1.4	0.9
West South Central					
Arkansas	$31,203	$34,037	$34,987	1.7%	0.3%
Louisiana	33,066	37,116	37,791	2.3	0.2
Oklahoma	33,184	38,379	37,861	2.9	−0.1
Texas	36,540	43,098	38,419	3.3	−1.1
West					
Mountain					
Montana	$35,916	$36,905	$37,216	2.8%	0.8%
Idaho	36,937	37,600	36,942	1.8	−1.8
Wyoming	38,926	41,731	39,125	1.4	−0.6
Colorado	41,015	46,433	44,227	2.5	−0.5
New Mexico	31,867	38,710	34,221	3.9	−1.2
Arizona	39,968	42,332	42,120	1.1	−0.1
Utah	36,748	39,111	40,159	3.0	0.3
Nevada	40,301	46,855	43,647	1.0	−0.7
Pacific					
Washington	$40,416	$44,928	$45,833	2.1%	2.0%
Oregon	39,398	44,230	42,533	2.3	−0.4
California	41,807	46,214	47,025	2.0	0.2
Alaska	50,827	57,125	53,174	2.3	−0.7
Hawaii	44,794	45,244	49,414	0.2	0.9
Total U.S.	$38,700	$41,219	$44,774	1.3%	0.8%

319

TABLE 7.3
Percent of Families* with Low, Middle, and High Relative Income, by Region, 1969-1989

Region/ Income Group**	1969	1979	1989	Point Change 1969-1979	Point Change 1979-1989
Northeast					
Low	27.6%	31.8%	29.5%	4.2	−2.3
Middle	60.0	55.8	50.9	−4.2	−4.9
High	12.4	12.4	19.6	0.0	7.2
Total	100.0	100.0	100.0	0.0	0.0
Midwest					
Low	28.7%	30.7%	34.4%	2.0	3.7
Middle	60.3	57.0	52.6	−3.3	−4.4
High	11.0	12.3	13.0	1.3	0.7
Total	100.0	100.0	100.0	0.0	0.0
South					
Low	42.7%	40.4%	41.7%	−2.3	1.3
Middle	49.0	49.7	46.2	0.7	−3.5
High	8.3	9.9	12.1	1.6	2.2
Total	100.0	100.0	100.0	0.0	0.0
West					
Low	29.5%	32.6%	35.5%	3.1	2.9
Middle	57.1	53.0	48.7	−4.1	−4.3
High	13.4	14.4	15.8	1.0	1.4
Total	100.0	100.0	100.0	0.0	0.0

*Income adjusted for family size. Individuals are considered one-person families.

**Low-income group refers to 0-0.75 of the median; middle-income group refers to 0.75-2.00 of the median; high-income group refers to 2.00 and above times the median.

Between 1979 and 1989, the median income for a four-person family rose at an annual rate of 2.6% in Connecticut and Massachusetts, and 2.5% in New Jersey. Compare this annual level of growth to that of the same states for the period 1974 to 1979: 0.8%, 1.3%, and 0.7%, respectively.

Conversely, the median four-person family income in many Western states saw low or even negative growth in the 1980s, after sustaining relatively high rates of growth in the earlier period. California, for example, saw median income grow at an annual rate of 2.0%, 1974-1979; however, over the 1980s, income grew at a much slower 0.2%. Many other Western states (eight out of 13) saw negative growth. New Mexico, which had the highest annual growth rate between 1974 and 1979 (3.9%), had the second largest *negative* growth between 1979 and 1989 (-1.2%). Similarly, annual growth rates were relatively flat or negative in the Midwest, 1979-1989.

Table 7.3 sorts families into low-, middle-, or high-income classes based on their distance from the median (adjusted for family size). The findings show that the middle class contracted in all regions between 1969 and 1989 (with the one exception of the South, 1969-1979, where it grew slightly) and shrunk faster in the more recent decade (**Figure 7A**). With the reduction of the middle class we must examine whether middle-class families rose out of the middle class or fell into the lower-income class.

Families in the Northeast region appear to have made impressive gains over the 1980s, although as we show below, income inequality increased in all Northeastern states (in other words both low- and high-income families gained income shares, but the wealthy gained more). The middle class in the Northeast grew smaller in both periods (Figure 7A), but between 1969 and 1979 the shift was exclusively downward into the low-income class. Between 1979 and 1989, 7.2% of Northeastern families went from the low- or middle-income class to the high-income class, which contained 19.6% of Northeastern families in 1989. The Midwest did relatively poorly over the 1980s, both compared to the other regions and to its own performance over the prior decade. Of the 4.4% of Midwestern families that left the middle class between 1979 and 1989, most (3.7% out of 4.4%) fell into the lower class.

The middle class contracted in all regions between 1969 and 1989 and shrunk faster in the more recent decade.

321

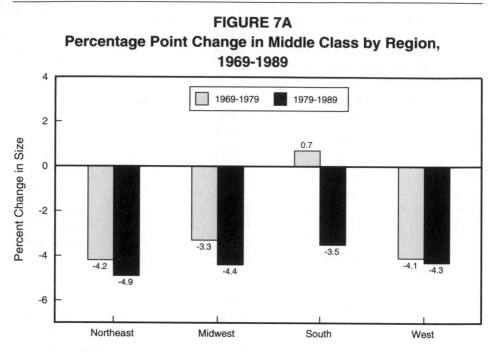

FIGURE 7A
Percentage Point Change in Middle Class by Region, 1969-1989

Note: Middle class refers to income 0.75-2.00 of the median.

In the South and West, both the lower- and higher-income classes grew at the expense of the middle class over the 1980s. In all three years, the South had the largest low-income class and the smallest middle- and high-income classes of the four regions. Of the 4.3% of Western families to leave the middle class, 1979-1989, most (2.9% of families) fell to the lower class.

Shifting our focus to the degree of income inequality within individual states, we find that income became more unequally distributed over the 1980s in 43 states. **Table 7.4** presents the ratio of the average income of families in the top fifth of the income distribution to the average income of families in the bottom fifth, by state. The growth of this ratio over time is an indicator of greater income inequality. The years of comparison are 1979 and 1987-1989 (data for the end period are pooled over three years to enhance their reliability; such pooled data are unavailable for the late 1970s).

In 1979, 34 out of 50 states had inequality ratios of between 6.0 and 8.0; only one state, Alaska, had a ratio greater than ten. However, the ratio grew over the 1980s in all but seven states (**Figure 7B**), as shown in the point change column of Table 7.4. In the Northeast region, New York saw a relatively large growth in inequality of 2.6 points. Furthermore, the ratio of average income of the top fifth to the bottom in New York was among the highest, at 10.7 at the end of the 1980s. Many Southern states also saw high and growing levels of inequality. Of the 16 states in the South, by the end of the 1980s, eight had inequality ratios of at least 10.0. In fact, outside of the South only New York and New Mexico had ratios greater than ten.

Income became more unequally distributed over the 1980s in 43 states. The ratio of average income of the top fifth to the bottom in New York was among the highest, at 10.7 at the end of the 1980s.

323

TABLE 7.4
Ratio of Average Income of the Top Fifth to
Average Income of Bottom Fifth, by State

Region/Division/State	1979	1987-89	Point Change
Northeast			
New England			
Maine	6.3	7.8	1.5
New Hampshire	5.7	6.2	0.5
Vermont	6.8	7.7	0.9
Massachusetts	7.2	8.6	1.4
Rhode Island	6.5	7.6	1.1
Connecticut	6.3	6.4	0.1
Mid-Atlantic			
New York	8.1	10.7	2.6
New Jersey	7.2	8.2	1.0
Pennsylvania	6.7	7.7	1.0
Midwest			
East North Central			
Ohio	6.8	8.5	1.7
Indiana	5.8	7.9	2.1
Illinois	7.6	9.8	2.2
Michigan	7.0	8.8	1.8
Wisconsin	6.4	7.0	0.6
West North Central			
Minnesota	7.0	7.7	0.7
Iowa	6.2	7.2	1.0
Missouri	7.5	8.5	1.0
North Dakota	8.4	8.0	−0.4
South Dakota	7.7	8.3	0.6
Nebraska	7.5	7.2	−0.3
Kansas	6.4	7.1	0.7

TABLE 7.4 (continued)

Region/Division/State	1979	1987-89	Point Change
South			
South Atlantic			
Delaware	6.9	6.8	−0.1
Maryland	7.2	7.5	0.3
Virginia	7.2	10.4	3.2
West Virginia	6.7	10.8	4.1
North Carolina	7.2	8.8	1.6
South Carolina	9.4	9.2	−0.2
Georgia	8.0	10.0	2.0
Florida	7.6	9.2	1.6
East South Central			
Kentucky	7.1	9.2	2.1
Tennessee	8.2	9.8	1.6
Alabama	9.4	10.7	1.3
Mississippi	9.5	11.1	1.6
West South Central			
Arkansas	9.7	9.9	0.2
Louisiana	8.7	14.5	5.8
Oklahoma	8.5	10.1	1.6
Texas	9.1	10.6	1.5
West			
Mountain			
Montana	8.8	8.0	−0.8
Idaho	7.2	7.4	0.2
Wyoming	6.1	7.0	0.9
Colorado	6.4	9.3	2.9
New Mexico	8.8	10.8	2.0
Arizona	7.2	9.1	1.9
Utah	6.2	6.3	0.1
Nevada	6.2	6.6	0.4
Pacific			
Washington	7.6	7.1	−0.5
Oregon	6.7	7.5	0.8
California	7.8	9.8	2.0
Alaska	10.1	9.4	−0.7
Hawaii	7.5	8.1	0.6

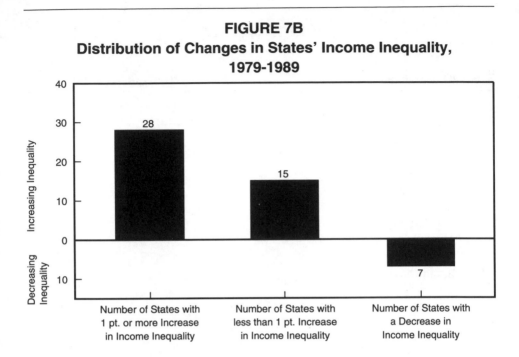

FIGURE 7B
Distribution of Changes in States' Income Inequality,
1979-1989

As shown in our analysis of national income trends (Chapter 1), the pattern of income growth over the 1980s led to income gains for some families but losses for the majority. **Table 7.5** shows what the changes over the 1980s have meant in terms of dollars for the average family in the bottom, middle, and top fifth by state. In 28 states, the average income of families in the lowest fifth fell over the 1980s. Low-income families in the Midwest, particularly the East North Central division, saw significant income losses, from $889 in Wisconsin to $2,519 in Indiana. Low-income Southern families also posted substantial losses; the average family in the bottom fifth in West Virginia had $3,381 less in the late 1980s than the average low-income family in that state in 1979.

On the other end of the income spectrum, certain regions experienced dramatic income gains over the 1980s. In fact, the average income of the top fifth fell in only six states over the period, and four of those six were in the West (Mountain division). In the Northeast, the average family in the top fifth ended the period with between $10,701 (Pennsylvania) and $27,323 (New Jersey) more than the best-off families in 1979. Smaller but significant gains were also made by upper-income Southern families, particularly in Virginia, South Carolina, Florida and Georgia.

In 28 states, the average income of families in the lowest fifth fell over the 1980s while the average income of the top fifth fell in only six states.

TABLE 7.5
Income Changes for Average Family, Bottom, Middle, and Top Fifth, 1979 to Late 1980s

Region/Division/State	Bottom Fifth	Middle Fifth	Top Fifth
Northeast			
New England			
Maine	$416	$5,460	$18,813
New Hampshire	2,268	9,485	21,024
Vermont	1,463	6,528	21,096
Massachusetts	787	8,907	24,220
Rhode Island	224	4,511	15,390
Connecticut	3,675	9,539	24,096
Mid-Atlantic			
New York	$ -858	$4,037	$19,735
New Jersey	1,860	7,898	27,323
Pennsylvania	-107	-546	10,701
Midwest			
East North Central			
Ohio	$ -1,413	$418	$8,181
Indiana	-2,519	-3,161	7,206
Illinois	-1,679	-250	10,276
Michigan	-1,483	-1,111	9,399
Wisconsin	-889	870	1,045
West North Central			
Minnesota	$ -56	$3,957	$8,917
Iowa	-1,999	-2,348	-1,249
Missouri	-33	336	9,872
North Dakota	334	1,427	-883
South Dakota	84	1,202	6,478
Nebraska	1,174	-1,060	6,269
Kansas	-140	906	6,175

TABLE 7.5 (continued)

Region/Division/State	Bottom Fifth	Middle Fifth	Top Fifth
South			
South Atlantic			
Delaware	$1,495	$2,942	$8,700
Maryland	134	5,038	5,560
Virginia	−1,578	5,122	23,429
West Virginia	−3,381	−2,789	3,914
North Carolina	−591	2,213	11,328
South Carolina	2,033	5,431	17,111
Georgia	−372	2,261	16,688
Florida	291	3,943	18,021
East South Central			
Kentucky	$−1,798	$−1,856	$4,910
Tennessee	−217	145	11,633
Alabama	116	1,059	10,598
Mississippi	−814	−2,839	3,140
West South Central			
Arkansas	$247	$−135	$3,972
Louisiana	−2,617	48	13,008
Oklahoma	−661	−392	7,592
Texas	−1,027	−1,331	3,742
West			
Mountain			
Montana	$666	$−3,331	$−1,591
Idaho	286	−2,060	4,385
Wyoming	−2,086	−1,498	−666
Colorado	−4,766	−4,923	−1,596
New Mexico	−885	−3,581	7,716
Arizona	−987	2,437	14,398
Utah	655	628	5,811
Nevada	−1,071	−2,789	−1,130
Pacific			
Washington	$1,490	$1,261	$4,659
Oregon	−127	898	8,836
California	−755	1,925	15,697
Alaska	1,100	−3,153	2,214
Hawaii	1,490	4,830	19,206

TABLE 7.6
Poverty Rates by Region and Division, 1980-1991

Region/Division	1980	1989	1991	Point Change 1980-89	Point Change 1989-91
Northeast	10.9%	10.0%	12.2%	−0.9	2.2
New England	9.5	7.2	10.4	−2.3	3.2
Mid-Atlantic	11.4	11.0	12.8	−0.4	1.8
Midwest	11.2%	11.9%	13.2%	0.7	1.3
East North Central	11.2	11.9	13.5	0.7	1.6
West North Central	11.1	11.7	12.6	0.6	0.9
South	16.3%	15.4%	16.0%	−0.9	0.6
South Atlantic	14.4	12.7	14.2	−1.7	1.5
East South Central	20.3	18.6	18.6	−1.7	0.0
West South Central	16.8	17.8	17.6	1.0	−0.2
West	11.4%	12.5%	14.3%	1.1	1.8
Mountain	12.0	13.1	13.9	1.1	0.8
Pacific	11.2	12.3	14.5	1.1	2.2
Total U.S.	13.0%	12.8%	14.2%	−0.2	1.4

330

Poverty

Although national poverty levels were about the same in 1980 and 1989 (the fact that poverty rates did not fall in response to the economic expansion over the 1980s is explored in Chapter 6), there were some notable regional differences, particularly involving child poverty. **Table 7.6** shows that in the Northeast, poverty fell 0.9 percentage points between 1980 and 1989 (data for our usual comparative peak year, 1979, are not available by division). However, given the dramatic rise in median family income in the Northeast (see Table 7.1), poverty rates might have been expected to show an even greater decline. This lack of response to growth at the median is driven by the heightened income inequality in the Northeast documented in Tables 7.4 and 7.5. Particularly in the Mid-Atlantic states, where poverty fell only 0.4 points (1880-1989), those families in the bottom fifth fared poorly, while those in the top fifth made significant gains. In both the Midwest and the West, poverty rates rose between 1980 and 1989, even while the national average fell very slightly, further emphasizing the uneven nature of the 1980s expansion.

Once again, the initial regional effects of the recession beginning in 1989 are notable, particularly in the Northeast. Table 7.6 shows that poverty grew at least twice as much in the Northeast (1.4 percentage points) as in the other regions in 1990. At the divisional level, the New England and Mid-Atlantic divisions show the most growth in poverty rates, of 2.0 and 1.2 points, respectively.

Child poverty rates (for persons under 18) grew over the 1980s (see Chapter 6), and, as presented in **Table 7.7**, show dramatic regional differences. Child poverty rates are generally higher for children in the South and are consistently higher for black children in all regions. However, child poverty fell in the South over the 1970s, driven by a 10.9 percentage point drop for black children. Over this same period, child poverty grew in the other three regions. Yet by 1987 (the latest year of available data) this trend of falling poverty rates for children in the South had been reversed, as poverty grew from 19.6% to 23.4% between 1979 and 1987. In fact, child poverty grew in all regions over this latter period, with the rates for white and black children growing by similar amounts, with the notable

Poverty grew at least twice as much in the Northeast (1.4 percentage points) as in the other regions in 1990.

331

TABLE 7.7
Child Poverty Rates by Race and Region, 1969-1987

Race/Region	1969	1979	1987	Point Change 1979-1987
All Races				
Northeast	10.9%	15.5%	16.9%	1.4
Midwest	10.6	13.0	18.4	5.4
South	23.5	19.6	23.4	3.8
West	12.9	14.2	18.9	4.7
Total U.S.	15.1%	16.0%	20.0%	4.0
White				
Northeast	8.4%	10.7%	13.5%	2.8
Midwest	8.3	9.6	13.6	4.0
South	15.0	12.7	15.7	3.0
West	11.2	10.8	16.9	6.1
Total U.S.	10.7%	11.0%	15.0%	4.0
Black				
Northeast	31.4%	37.1%	39.4%	2.3
Midwest	31.5	36.2	51.5	15.3
South	50.9	40.0	45.9	5.9
West	31.4	29.4	35.4	6.0
Total U.S.	42.0%	37.8%	45.1%	7.3

exception of black children in the Midwest, whose rates grew steeply, by 15.3 percentage points.

Wages and Taxes

The reasons for the recent growth in income inequality are analyzed on a national (and international, see Chapter 9) basis throughout this book. While data do not exist on a regional or state basis for each area explored in the national analysis, we do have data on two important causal factors of slow growth and growing inequality and poverty: wages and taxes.

The wage analysis in the next few tables shows the highly uneven nature of economic growth in the 1980s from a regional perspective. **Table 7.8** shows the percentage change, 1979-1991, in average hourly wages for wage and salary workers in each region, by gender and education level. The first panel has data for 1979-1989. Even in the prosperous Northeast, average hourly wages fell for most workers with up to three years of college. Male workers in the other three regions saw the biggest losses, and even college-educated men saw wage erosion in the Midwest (-4.4%) and the South (-0.5%), or flat growth in the West (1.6%). Wage loss was particularly dramatic for male high school dropouts in the Midwest and West; their wages fell by 21.4% and 23.9%, respectively. Female workers saw less wage erosion than males, 1979-1989, particularly those with at least some college education. However, in the Midwest, even female workers with some college saw their wages fall 3.0%.

The second panel of Table 7.8 shows the effect of the recession on regional hourly wages. (Recall from Chapter 3 that wage loss among the college educated predated the recession.) As noted above, the recession was particularly severe in the Northeast, where it was felt not only by less-educated persons, but by highly educated workers as well. A salient example is the case of college-educated men in the Northeast, whose average hourly wage grew by 4.6%, 1979-1989, and fell by 3.6%, 1989-1991, leaving it practically flat (0.9% growth) over the full 1979-1991 period (third panel, Table 7.8). In fact, the 4.4% growth in the Northeast for college-educated workers over the full period appears to have been driven primarily by female workers. College-educated workers also saw significant

During 1979-1989, even in the prosperous Northeast, average hourly wages fell for most workers with up to three years of college and even college-educated men saw wage erosion in the Midwest and the South.

TABLE 7.8
Percentage Change in Average Hourly Wages
by Gender, Education, and Region, 1979-1991

Year Region/Gender	Less Than High School	High School	College 1-3 Years	College 4 Years	College Plus 2 Years	All
1979-1989						
Northeast						
Male	−9.9%	−5.0%	−1.1%	4.6%	12.6%	2.9%
Female	−4.7	4.2	11.2	15.8	18.6	15.1
All	−9.6	−2.1	1.1	5.9	11.1	5.4
Midwest						
Male	−21.4%	−14.8%	−13.2%	−4.4%	8.2%	−9.1%
Female	−15.5	−6.7	−3.0	9.4	8.3	0.9
All	−21.7	−12.9	−12.3	−1.6	5.4	−7.8
South						
Male	−15.6%	−14.0%	−9.8%	−0.5%	8.3%	−5.5%
Female	−11.2	−4.1	4.5	12.5	13.1	5.9
All	−14.9	−11.0	−6.8	0.9	7.1	−3.0
West						
Male	−23.9%	−15.5%	−6.6%	1.6%	9.2%	−7.4%
Female	−14.9	−4.2	5.5	13.4	8.0	5.9
All	−21.1	−11.9	−3.8	2.3	6.2	−4.2
All						
Male	−18.2%	−12.7%	−8.3%	0.2%	9.7%	−5.2%
Female	−11.7	−3.2	3.8	12.6	12.6	5.6
All	−17.1	−9.9	−6.0	1.8	7.5	−2.8
1989-1991						
Northeast						
Male	−7.4%	−2.3%	−1.8%	−3.6%	2.6%	−1.2%
Female	1.8	−0.1	0.1	2.6	−0.2	1.8
All	−4.0	−1.5	−1.2	−1.5	1.5	−0.2
Midwest						
Male	7.2%	−3.4%	−1.6%	−0.6%	0.4%	−1.6%
Female	−4.6	−0.9	2.1	−0.5	−1.2	0.8
All	−6.2	−2.6	−0.2	−1.4	−0.1	−0.9
South						
Male	−4.6%	−4.9%	−0.8%	−2.5%	0.0%	−2.6%
Female	4.1	1.5	−2.9	−0.8	1.2	1.3
All	−2.3	−2.2	−1.8	−1.9	−0.4	−1.2
West						
Male	−6.1%	−4.2%	−1.3%	−3.1%	−1.7%	−2.3%
Female	0.1	1.0	0.4	3.0	2.6	1.8
All	−4.7	−1.9	−0.1	−0.8	−0.6	−0.7

TABLE 7.8 (continued)

Year Region/Gender	Less Than High School	High School	College 1-3 Years	College 4 Years	College Plus 2 Years	All
1989-1991 (continued)						
All						
Male	−6.2%	−3.8%	−1.3%	−2.5%	0.4%	−2.0%
Female	0.8	0.3	−0.3	0.8	0.6	1.4
All	−4.2	−2.1	−1.0	−1.5	0.2	−0.8
1979-1991						
Northeast						
Male	−16.5%	−7.1%	−2.9%	0.9%	15.5%	1.6%
Female	−3.0	4.2	11.2	18.8	18.4	17.2
All	−13.3	−3.5	−0.1	4.4	12.8	5.3
Midwest						
Male	−27.1%	−17.7%	−14.6%	−5.0%	8.6%	−10.6%
Female	−19.4	−7.5	−1.0	8.9	7.0	1.6
All	−26.6	−15.1	−12.4	−3.0	5.2	−8.7
South						
Male	−19.5%	−18.2%	−10.5%	−3.0%	8.2%	−7.9%
Female	−7.5	−2.7	1.5	11.6	14.4	7.2
All	−16.9	−12.9	−8.4	−1.0	6.7	−4.2
West						
Male	−28.5%	−19.1%	−7.7%	−1.6%	7.3%	−9.5%
Female	−14.8	−3.3	6.0	16.8	10.8	7.7
All	−24.9	−13.6	−3.9	1.4	5.5	−4.8
All						
Male	−23.2%	−16.1%	−9.5%	−2.3%	10.2%	−7.1%
Female	−11.0	−2.9	3.5	13.6	13.2	7.0
All	−20.5	−11.8	−6.9	0.3	7.8	−3.6

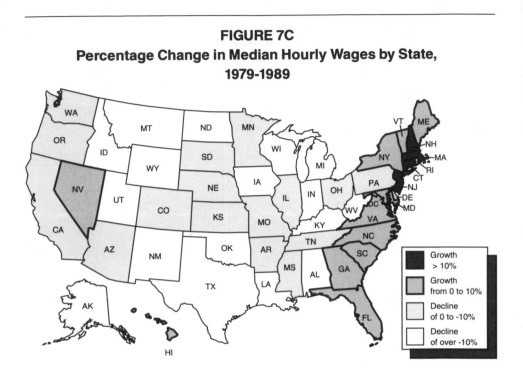

FIGURE 7C
Percentage Change in Median Hourly Wages by State,
1979-1989

Growth
> 10%

Growth
from 0 to 10%

Decline
of 0 to -10%

Decline
of over -10%

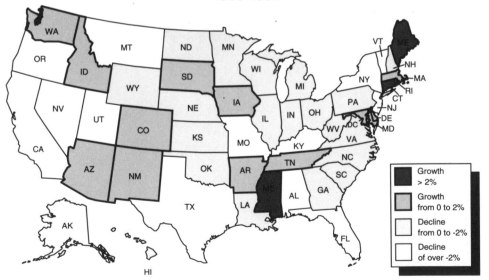

FIGURE 7D
Percentage Change in Median Hourly Wages by State,
1989-1991

Growth
> 2%

Growth
from 0 to 2%

Decline
from 0 to -2%

Decline
of over -2%

336

wage loss in the other regions, denoting the end of the 1980s "white-collar" boom and showing the white-collar nature of this recession (see Chapter 4). In the South and West, even workers with post-graduate educations saw a slight decline overall between 1989 and 1991.

In **Table 7.9** and **Figures** 7C and 7D, we shift to state level analysis, by gender (Table 7.9), and examine the percentage change in the real median hourly wage (half of all workers earn more than this wage, half earn less). Figure 7C shows that real median hourly wages fell in most (35) states. Four states saw median wage growth of greater than 10%; 12 saw wage growth of between 0% and 10%; 18 states saw their median hourly wage fall between 0% and 10%; and 17 states saw wages fall by more than 10%. The figure amply dramatizes the regional nature of economic growth over the 1980s, as only states on the Eastern seaboard (plus Nevada) saw growth in their median wage. Wages at the median fell in all other states.

The state data show that the large wage losses in the Midwestern and Western regions were mostly driven by the steep decline in male wages (Table 7.9). For example, men in Colorado and California saw their median wage fall by 19.9% and 11.6%, respectively, between 1979 and 1989; for women in those states, wage growth was either essentially flat (Colorado, -0.1%), or positive (California, 3.8%). However, women in Wyoming and Alaska did experience substantial wage loss. In the Northeast, wage growth was quite robust for both men and women between 1979 and 1989, though women's wages grew faster than those of men's in most Northeastern states (though the *level* of women's wages remained well below that of men's). There, median wages for women grew by as much as 21.9% (New Jersey), while the largest growth rate for males was 14.7% (New Hampshire).

Figure 7D shows that, with the rising unemployment beginning in 1989, the median hourly wage fell in 34 states, with notable differences in the eastern states. Wages grew in 16 states and the District of Columbia, although for 12 states and the District of Columbia, the growth was less than 2.0%; 20 states experienced a modest decline (0 to 2.0%); 14 states saw wages decline more than 2.0%.

The large wage losses in the Midwestern and Western regions were mostly driven by the steep decline in male wages.

337

TABLE 7.9
Percent Change in the Median Hourly Wages of Men and Women, by State, 1979-1991

| Division/State | Percent Change | | | |
| | 1979-1989 | | 1989-1991 | |
	Men	Women	Men	Women
New England				
Maine	2.5%	12.1%	1.7%	3.9%
New Hampshire	14.7	16.4	−1.5	2.8
Vermont	5.4	18.6	−2.6	−0.4
Massachusetts	9.8	21.8	−4.8	1.4
Rhode Island	−4.2	11.1	5.9	1.8
Connecticut	8.5	15.8	1.2	4.0
Mid-Atlantic				
New York	−0.8%	12.1%	−2.6%	3.2%
New Jersey	2.9	21.9	−5.3	1.0
Pennsylvania	−14.4	−0.6	0.1	3.3
East North Central				
Ohio	−14.1%	−0.8%	−0.6%	−0.2%
Indiana	−16.1	−3.8	0.6	−0.6
Illinois	−12.5	−3.1	−1.0	0.3
Michigan	−9.8	−6.4	−3.6	−0.7
Wisconsin	−14.7	−5.0	−3.9	−0.7
West North Central				
Minnesota	−17.7%	5.3%	0.1%	2.6%
Iowa	−15.0	−5.5	−3.1	−2.0
Missouri	−18.0	1.6	−3.1	−2.8
North Dakota	−19.2	−2.7	−5.2	−2.5
South Dakota	−16.5	−2.8	−3.7	3.7
Nebraska	−12.2	−6.5	−2.0	3.8
Kansas	−9.3	0.7	−5.3	0.9
South Atlantic				
Delaware	−8.3%	8.2%	−6.5%	2.0%
Maryland	−11.0	8.4	0.5	4.7
District of Columbia	−15.9	9.9	1.2	−6.3
Virginia	2.1	11.9	−7.4	1.0

338

TABLE 7.9 (continued)

Division/State	Percent Change			
	1979-1989		1989-1991	
	Men	Women	Men	Women
South Atlantic (continued)				
West Virginia	−24.8	−5.7	−2.6	−4.4
North Carolina	−2.7	1.4	1.8	2.2
South Carolina	4.2	2.2	1.7	2.0
Georgia	−2.2	4.7	−4.2	4.4
Florida	1.0	10.6	−8.0	−1.7
East South Central				
Kentucky	−14.1%	−5.3%	−3.7%	−3.6%
Tennessee	−13.8	−2.9	−3.9	5.0
Alabama	−13.0	2.3	−6.4	−3.6
Mississippi	−11.9	3.2	1.8	−1.7
West South Central				
Arkansas	−7.6%	−1.5%	2.0%	−5.0%
Louisiana	−12.1	−4.5	−10.1	4.7
Oklahoma	−15.3	−3.0	−1.8	−0.4
Texas	−14.7	4.5	−0.3	−2.1
Mountain				
Montana	−21.2%	−6.6%	−3.9%	−1.8%
Idaho	−21.5	−3.0	4.1	−2.6
Wyoming	−20.4	−13.0	−0.7	1.6
Colorado	−19.9	−0.1	4.7	−2.8
New Mexico	−19.8	−5.9	4.1	−1.4
Arizona	−13.6	1.0	−7.6	7.3
Utah	−13.5	0.0	−8.7	−4.7
Nevada	−8.2	4.1	−1.9	−2.9
Pacific				
Washington	−17.1%	−2.8%	2.7%	2.7%
Oregon	−17.4	−0.8	−4.0	0.0
California	−11.6	3.8	−2.1	2.0
Alaska	−23.6	−12.2	−0.6	−3.5
Hawaii	−5.5	6.7	−1.0	2.4
Total U.S.	−11.7%	5.4%	−1.4%	−2.8%

TABLE 7.10
State and Local Effective Tax Rates in the Ten Largest States as Percent of Income for Families of Four, 1985-1991

Region/State	Lowest Fifth		Middle Fifth		Top 15%		Top 4%		Top 1%	
	1985	1991	1985	1991	1985	1991	1985	1991	1985	1991
New York (NE)	14.4%	14.1%	13.4%	13.9%	13.4%	13.8%	13.1%	13.0%	12.0%	11.3%
Pennsylvania (NE)	15.6	15.9	9.9	9.8	8.6	8.3	8.2	7.3	6.4	5.5
New Jersey (NE)	13.3	15.2	9.3	10.8	8.4	10.7	8.3	10.7	6.8	9.7
Illinois (MW)	13.8%	16.5%	9.4%	10.8%	8.1%	9.0%	7.6%	7.7%	6.1%	6.0%
Ohio (MW)	12.3	13.4	9.5	10.0	9.3	9.6	9.6	9.8	9.7	9.6
Michigan (MW)	15.0	14.3	12.0	11.4	11.1	10.6	10.5	9.6	7.7	7.6
North Carolina (South)	10.2%	10.6%	8.6%	9.7%	8.5%	9.4%	8.4%	9.0%	8.1%	8.4%
Florida (South)	10.0	13.8	5.9	7.6	4.6	5.5	4.1	4.4	2.7	2.7
Texas (South)	12.4	17.1	6.2	8.4	5.0	6.4	4.5	5.1	3.0	3.1
California (West)	11.8%	14.1%	8.4%	8.8%	9.1%	9.7%	9.9%	10.7%	10.5%	10.6%

Point Change
1985-1991

Region/State	Lowest Fifth		Middle Fifth		Top 15%		Top 4%		Top 1%	
New York (NE)		−0.3		0.5		0.4		−0.1		−0.7
Pennsylvania (NE)		0.3		−0.1		−0.3		−0.9		−0.9
New Jersey (NE)		1.9		1.5		2.3		2.4		2.9
Illinois (MW)		2.7		1.4		0.9		0.1		−0.1
Ohio (MW)		1.1		0.5		0.3		0.2		−0.1
Michigan (MW)		−0.7		−0.6		−0.5		−0.9		−0.1
North Carolina (South)		0.4		1.1		0.9		0.6		0.3
Florida (South)		3.8		1.7		0.9		0.3		0.0
Texas (South)		4.7		2.2		1.4		0.6		0.1
California (West)		2.3		0.4		0.6		0.8		0.1

Most of the New England, Mid-Atlantic, and Southern states that experienced wage growth prior to the downturn saw their wages fall, 1989-1991.

The wage turnaround in the Northeast over the recent recession is also apparent in the state-level analysis of male median wages, 1989-1991 (Table 7.9). Males in five of the nine Northeastern states saw falling wages over the period, with men in New Jersey and Massachusetts posting large wage losses of 5.3 and 4.8%, respectively. However, except for Vermont, women in the Northeastern states made wage gains of between 1.0% and 4.0%. The wages of Midwestern male workers continued to fall over the recession, and by the end of the full period (full period data, 1979-1991, are not in the table), the median wage for males in every Midwestern state had fallen by between 13.1% (Michigan) and 23.4% (North Dakota). Males in Western states experienced similar wage declines over the full period, with median wages falling from between 5.6% (Hawaii) to 24.3% (Montana).

As noted in Chapter 2, state and local taxes tend to be regressive, meaning that the poor pay a larger proportion of their income in taxes than the wealthy. **Table 7.10** gives average effective tax rates in the ten most populated states for families of four in the bottom fifth; middle fifth; and, top 15%, 4%, and 1%. **Figure 7E** portrays the effective rates for the five most populated states. The data show that state and local taxes became even more regressive over the latter part of the 1980s (distributional data on the state and local tax burden are only available for these years). In California, the largest state (and one of the least regressive), the average family in the lowest fifth paid 14.1% of their income in state and local taxes in 1991, while the most wealthy families paid 10.6%. Furthermore, the poorest Californian families saw their tax burden rise by 2.3% of their income from 1985 to 1991, while those in the top 1% had only an extra 0.1% added to their burden.

Texas, Florida and Illinois also saw their already highly regressive state and local effective rates become more regressive (Table 7.10). In Texas in 1991, the poorest four-person families paid 17.1% of their income in taxes, while the most wealthy paid 3.1%. Similarly, in Florida, low-income families paid over five times the proportion of income paid by families in the top 1%.

State and local taxes became even more regressive over the latter part of the 1980s. In California the average family in the lowest fifth paid 14.1% of their income in state and local taxes in 1991, while the most wealthy families paid 10.6%.

341

FIGURE 7E
State and Local Effective Tax Rates in the
Five Most Populated States,
1991

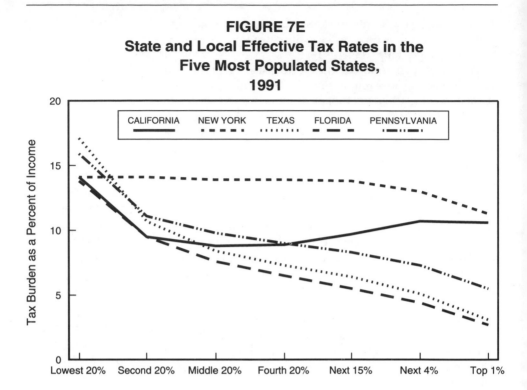

Employment

Table 7.11 shows annual rates of job growth by region and division, 1973-1990. With the exception of the Northeast, employment grew faster over the 1973-1979 business cycle than over the 1980s. In the West, employment grew one and one-half times faster, on an annual basis, between 1973 and 1979, than over the 1980s. However, even in light of the slowdown in employment growth, the Western region led the pack in the annual rate of job growth over the 1980s (2.7%). The Southern region had the second fastest growth, most due to the Atlantic division, where employment grew at an annual rate of 3.0%. In the Northeast, the job rate grew 2.3% annually in New England, and 1.5% in the Middle Atlantic states from 1979-1989.

Rates of job growth can be decomposed into two factors: growth due to a rising population, and growth due to an increase in the ratio of workers to the adult population. By these measures, the job growth in the Northeast and the West over the 1979-1989 period was driven by quite different factors. In Table 7.11, we find that of the 2.7% rate of Western job growth, 2.2 points, or about four-fifths of the total growth, came from that region's population growth, which was quite strong over the decade. Conversely, 70% of the Northeastern rate of 1.7% was generated by sending a larger proportion of the adult population into the workforce. This is most evident at the divisional level in the Mid-Atlantic, where of the 1.5% annual rate of job growth, 1.1 points (73%) are attributable to growth in the employment to population ratio. This finding suggests that much of the recent strong growth in family income in the Northeast (Table 7.1) is due to families sending more workers into the workforce, a theme explored in Chapter 1.

Interestingly, the recession beginning in 1989 appears to have primarily affected job growth in the Northeast, where growth turned negative, and did not affect other regions. While employment grew in New England at an annual rate of 2.3% between 1979 and 1989, it shrank at that same rate between 1989 and 1990 (the latest data available). Employment also fell slightly in the Mid-Atlantic states. Meanwhile, job growth actually accelerated in the Midwest, growing at an annual rate of 1.5%, 0.4 percentage points faster than the rate over the prior cycle (Table 7.11). In the

Of the 2.7% rate of Western job growth about four-fifths came from that region's population growth. Conversely, 70% of the Northeastern rate of 1.7% was generated by sending a larger proportion of the adult population into the workforce.

343

TABLE 7.11
Job Growth by Region and Division, 1973-1990

	Annual Rate of Growth of Employment			Employment Growth Due to: 1979-1989	
				Growth of Adult Population	Growth of Employment/ Adult Population
Region/Division	73-79	79-89	89-90		
Northeast	1.0%	1.7%	−0.7%	0.5%	1.2%
New England	1.9	2.3	−2.3	0.7	1.6
Middle Atlantic	0.6	1.5	−0.1	0.4	1.1
Midwest	1.8%	1.1%	1.5%	0.4%	0.7%
East North Central	1.6	1.0	1.4	0.4	0.6
West North Central	2.4	1.2	1.5	0.5	0.7
South	2.7%	2.3%	1.8%	1.9%	0.4%
South Atlantic	2.4	3.0	1.4	2.2	0.8
East South Central	2.0	1.5	1.4	1.1	0.4
West South Central	3.8	1.5	2.7	1.8	−0.3
West	4.2%	2.7%	2.4%	2.2%	0.5%
Mountain	4.6	2.6	2.8	2.4	0.2
Pacific	4.1	2.7	2.3	2.2	0.5
Total U.S.	2.4%	1.9%	1.3%	1.2%	0.7%

West, job growth slowed in the Pacific division, but grew in the Mountain division.

Using the official measure of unemployment (the ratio of those seeking work to the total workforce), the U.S. rate fell slightly (0.5 percentage points) from 1979 to 1989 (**Table 7.12** and **Figure 7F**). From a regional perspective, most of this decline was driven by a 2.1 point fall in the Northeast, which had the lowest 1989 unemployment rate, 4.5%. Unemployment fell significantly in all but one Northeastern state (New Hampshire). Conversely, unemployment grew slightly in the South (0.3 points), mostly due to rises in the West South Central division (plus Mississippi). The two other regions of the country saw unemployment rates fall slightly between 1979 and 1989, 0.1 points in the Midwest and 0.7 points in the West.

However, the rise in unemployment beginning in 1989 more than wiped out the progress made in lowering unemployment over the 1980s. Between 1989 and 1991, unemployment rose dramatically in certain Northeastern states. For example, in Massachusetts in 1989, unemployment, at 4.0%, was well below the national average of 5.3%, and even below the regional average of 4.5%. Yet in two years, unemployment in that state climbed 5.0 percentage points, to 9.0%, well above the national average of 6.7%. Of course, unemployment grew elsewhere as well, particularly in the South. Yet the Northeast, which started the recession with the lowest unemployment rates, had the country's highest rates by 1991. This is most evident in the Northeastern division of New England, which went from a 1989 rate of 3.9% to a 1991 rate of 8.0% (Figure 7F).

The Northeast, which started the recession with the lowest unemployment rates, had the country's highest rates by 1991.

Urban versus Rural

In this section, we examine geographic differences in certain economic indicators between urban, suburban and rural settings. We use the Census Bureau's definitions of these areas. Cities are areas with at least 50,000 residents that form an economic and population nucleus to the surrounding communities. A suburban area is an area close to a city, but with a smaller population than the city. The suburban economy is highly integrated with that of the nearby city. For some comparisons, it is useful to pool cities and

TABLE 7.12
Unemployment Rates by Region, Division, and State, 1979-1991

State/Division/Region	1979	1989	1991	Point Change 1979-89	Point Change 1989-91
Northeast	6.6%	4.5%	7.2%	−2.1	2.8
New England	5.5	3.9	8.0	−1.6	4.1
Maine	7.2	4.2	7.6	−3.0	3.4
New Hampshire	3.1	3.6	7.1	0.5	3.5
Vermont	5.3	3.6	6.4	−1.7	2.8
Massachusetts	5.5	4.0	9.0	−1.5	5.0
Rhode Island	6.7	4.0	8.6	−2.7	4.6
Connecticut	5.1	3.6	6.8	−1.5	3.1
Middle Atlantic	7.0%	4.7%	7.0%	−2.3	2.3
New York	7.1	5.1	7.2	−2.0	2.1
New Jersey	6.9	4.1	6.6	−2.8	2.5
Pennsylvania	6.9	4.5	6.9	−2.4	2.4
Midwest	5.5%	5.4%	6.4%	−0.1	1.0
East North Central	6.1	5.7	7.0	−0.4	1.3
Ohio	5.9	5.6	6.4	−0.4	0.8
Indiana	6.4	4.8	5.9	−1.7	1.2
Illinois	5.5	6.0	7.1	0.5	1.2
Michigan	7.8	7.1	9.2	−0.7	2.1
Wisconsin	4.5	4.4	5.4	−0.1	1.0
West North Central	4.0%	4.5%	5.0%	0.5	0.5
Minnesota	4.2	4.4	5.1	0.2	0.7
Iowa	4.1	4.3	4.6	0.2	0.3
Missouri	4.5	5.5	6.6	0.9	1.1
North Dakota	3.7	4.2	4.1	0.6	−0.1
South Dakota	3.6	4.2	3.3	0.6	−0.8
Nebraska	3.1	3.1	2.7	−0.1	−0.4
Kansas	3.3	4.0	4.4	0.7	0.4
South	5.4%	5.7%	6.6%	0.3	1.0
South Atlantic	5.5	4.8	6.4	−0.7	1.6
Delaware	8.2	3.6	6.0	−4.6	2.5
Maryland	5.9	3.7	5.9	−2.3	2.2
District of Columbia	7.3	5.1	7.8	−2.2	2.7
Virginia	4.7	3.9	5.8	−0.8	2.0

TABLE 7.12 (continued)

State/Division/Region	1979	1989	1991	Point Change 1979-89	Point Change 1989-91
South Atlantic (continued)					
West Virginia	6.7	8.6	10.5	1.9	1.9
North Carolina	4.8	3.5	5.8	−1.3	2.3
South Carolina	5.1	4.7	6.3	−0.3	1.5
Georgia	5.1	5.5	5.0	0.4	−0.5
Florida	6.0	5.6	7.3	−0.4	1.7
East South Central	6.1%	6.3%	7.3%	0.2	1.0
Kentucky	5.6	6.2	7.4	0.6	1.2
Tennessee	5.8	5.1	6.6	−0.7	1.5
Alabama	7.1	7.0	7.2	−0.1	0.2
Mississipppi	5.8	7.7	8.6	2.0	0.9
West South Central	4.7%	6.8%	6.7%	2.1	−0.1
Arkansas	6.2	7.2	7.3	1.0	0.1
Louisiana	6.7	7.9	7.1	1.2	−0.9
Oklahoma	3.4	5.6	6.7	2.1	1.1
Texas	4.2	6.7	6.6	2.5	−0.1
West	6.0%	5.3%	6.7%	−0.7	1.4
Mountain	5.0	5.5	5.6	0.5	0.1
Montana	5.1	5.9	6.9	0.8	1.0
Idaho	5.6	5.1	6.2	−0.5	1.0
Wyoming	3.1	6.3	5.0	3.2	−1.3
Colorado	4.8	5.8	5.0	1.0	−0.8
New Mexico	6.6	6.7	7.0	0.1	0.3
Arizona	5.0	5.3	5.6	0.2	0.4
Utah	4.3	4.7	5.0	0.4	0.3
Nevada	5.0	5.0	5.4	0.0	0.4
Pacific	6.4%	5.2%	7.1%	−1.2	1.9
Washington	6.8	6.2	6.3	−0.6	0.2
Oregon	6.8	5.7	6.0	−1.1	0.3
California	6.2	5.1	7.5	−1.1	2.5
Alaska	9.3	6.7	8.5	−2.6	1.8
Hawaii	6.4	2.7	2.7	−3.7	0.0
Total U.S.	5.8%	5.3%	6.7%	−0.5	1.5

347

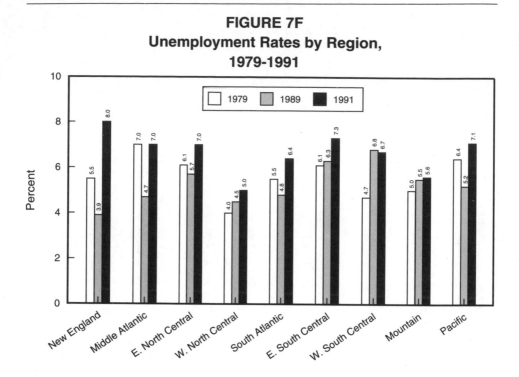

FIGURE 7F
Unemployment Rates by Region,
1979-1991

their suburbs into one area, which we will call "urban areas." Rural areas are, by definition, the areas outside of the urban areas; their economies are less closely integrated with cities.

Table 7.13 presents data on the proportion of families with low, middle and high incomes for city, suburban, and rural areas (similar to the analysis in Table 7.3). The rural areas had the largest lower-income group and the smallest upper-income group in each year. However, the lower-income class in cities has grown consistently since 1969; in both 1979 and 1989, it was only a few percentage points smaller than its rural counterpart. The middle-class shrinkage in the nation as a whole (see Chapter 1) appears to have taken place in each residential category between

The middle-class shrinkage in the nation as a whole has taken place in each residential category . . . with cities experiencing the largest decline.

TABLE 7.13
City/Suburb/Rural Comparisons of
Income Distribution, 1969-1989

Residence/Income Group*	1969	1979	1989	Point Change 1979-89
City				
Low	33.8%	39.6%	42.7%	3.1
Middle	54.9	49.8	44.5	−5.3
High	11.3	10.6	12.8	2.2
Total	100.0	100.0	100.0	0.0
Suburb				
Low	22.8%	25.1%	26.8%	1.7
Middle	62.7	58.7	53.7	−5.0
High	14.5	16.2	19.5	3.3
Total	100.0	100.0	100.0	0.0
Rural				
Low	44.1%	41.8%	46.8%	5.0
Middle	49.8	50.5	46.3	−4.2
High	6.1	7.7	6.9	−0.8
Total	100.0	100.0	100.0	0.0

*Low-income group refers to 0-0.75 of the median; middle-income group refers to 0.75-2.00 of the median; high-income group refers to 2.00 and above times the median.

TABLE 7.14
Poverty Rates by City, Suburban, and Rural Residence, 1973-1991

Year	City	Suburban	Rural	City/Rural Difference
1973	14.0%	6.4%	14.0%	0.0%
1979	15.7	7.2	13.8	1.9
1989	18.1	8.3	15.7	2.4
1991	20.2	9.6	16.1	4.1
Point Change				
1979-1989	2.4	1.1	1.9	0.5
1989-1991	2.1	1.3	0.4	1.7

FIGURE 7G
City, Suburban, and Rural Poverty Rates, 1973-1991

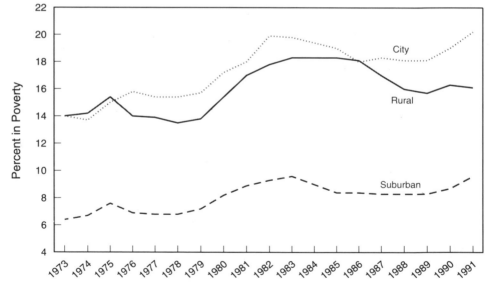

1979 and 1989, with cities experiencing the largest decline. However, in rural areas there occurred a major shift downward in the distribution of income. By 1989, 4.2% and 0.8% of the rural population had shifted from the middle- and upper-income classes to the lower.

A slightly different picture emerges when we compare recent poverty trends among city, suburban, and rural areas. In 1973, poverty rates for persons in rural areas and in cities were equal, at 14% (**Table 7.14**), while suburban rates were less than half as large, at 6.4%. As shown in **Figure 7G**, between 1973 and 1979, poverty declined in rural areas, and grew in cities and suburbs. From 1979 on, however, poverty grew in both rural and urban areas, and by the end of the recovery, in 1989, poverty had grown (since 1973) by 4.1 percentage points in cities and by 1.7 points in rural areas, (Table 7.14). As a result, by 1989, 2.4% more of the city population was poor relative to the rural population. Suburban poverty grew the least over the 1979-1989 period (up 1.1 percentage points), so that in 1989 the suburban poverty rate was well below the rates in both cities (9.8 points lower) and rural areas (7.4 points lower).

The economic downturn beginning in 1989 brought higher poverty rates to all types of residences. Poverty grew the most in the cities (2.1 points), and grew slightly (0.4 points) in rural areas. Suburban areas experienced dramatic growth of poverty over the recession, as poverty rates grew by more (1.3 points) between 1989 and 1991 than between the ten-year period, 1979-1989. This growth pattern further increased the distance between suburban rates and those of the other types of areas.

For recent years, 1988-1991, we can examine poverty rates by residence within the four regions. **Table 7.15** shows that in the Northeast and Midwest, poverty is highest in urban areas, while in the South, poverty is most common (i.e., proportionately) in rural areas. In 1989, over one-fifth of the persons living in Midwestern cities were poor. A similar proportion of rural Southerners (19.5%) were poor in that same year.

By 1991, urban poverty in Northeastern cities grew steeply, by 3.3 percentage points, driven by the falling incomes, declining wages, and rising unemployment experienced in that region as the recession began. Although other areas also saw rising poverty rates, 1989-1990, the

In 1973, poverty rates for persons in rural areas and in cities were equal at 14% . . . By 1989, 2.4% more of the city population was poor relative to the rural population.

351

TABLE 7.15
Poverty by Region and Residence, 1988-1991

Region/Residence	1988	1989	1991	Point Change 1989-1991
Northeast	10.1%	10.0%	12.2%	2.2
City	18.0	18.0	21.3	3.3
Suburban	5.6	5.3	7.0	1.7
Rural	10.2	10.9	12.3	1.4
Midwest	11.4%	11.9%	13.2%	1.3
City	19.8	20.8	23.1	2.3
Suburban	6.0	5.7	7.4	1.7
Rural	11.3	12.4	12.4	0.0
South	16.1%	15.4%	16.0%	0.6
City	19.7	18.6	20.0	1.4
Suburban	10.8	10.6	11.2	0.6
Rural	20.6	19.5	19.8	0.3
West	12.7%	12.5%	14.3%	1.8
City	14.6	15.1	16.9	1.8
Suburban	10.0	9.8	12.2	2.4
Rural	16.5	14.8	15.6	0.8

TABLE 7.16
Urban and Rural Employment Growth, 1979-1990

	Net Job Growth (000)		Annual Rate of Growth		Employment Growth Due to: 1979-1989	
					Growth of Population	Growth of Employment/ Population
	1979-89	1989-90	1979-89	1989-90		
Urban*	25,595	524	3.2%	0.6%	2.6%	0.6%
Rural	−5,198	48	−1.9	0.2	−2.3	0.4

*The urban category pools data from cities and suburbs.

352

rise of poverty in cities of the Northeast was by far the largest, 0.9 points greater than the next biggest increase: the 2.4 point rise in the suburban West.

Table 7.16 examines job growth by urban (including cities and suburbs) and rural setting, and shows that job creation in the 1980s was exclusively an urban phenomenon. Between 1979 and 1989, rural settings experienced a net loss of 5,198,000 jobs, 21% of the 1989 rural workforce. Over the same period, 25,595,000 new jobs were added to the urban workforce (28% of the 1989 urban workforce), at an annual growth rate of 3.2%. As the recession began in 1989, annual job growth in cities slowed to 0.6%, and turned positive (though practically flat) at 0.2% in non-urban areas.

Applying the same decomposition technique used above, it appears that changes in the annual rates of job growth were driven primarily by population changes in the adult population over the 1980s. In urban areas, 2.6 of the 3.2% growth rate can be attributed to population growth; the employment to population growth rate only accounted for the other 0.6 percentage points of job growth. In fact, the growth rate of employment to population was similar in both areas, 1979-1989 (the rural rate was 0.2 points lower than the urban), but the non-urban adult population fell at an annual rate of 2.3%, driving the negative job growth rate of 1.9%. Over the same period, urban population grew 2.6%, annually.

Job creation in the 1980s was exclusively an urban phenomenon. Between 1979 and 1989, rural settings experienced a net loss of 5,198,000 jobs.

TABLE 7.17
Unemployment Rates, Regular and Adjusted, Urban/Rural, 1979-1990

Year	Urban		Rural	
	Unemployment Rate	Adjusted Unemployment Rate*	Unemployment Rate	Adjusted Unemployment Rate*
1979	5.8%	8.0%	5.7%	8.5%
1980	7.0	9.5	7.3	10.7
1981	7.5	10.3	7.9	11.5
1982	9.5	13.1	10.1	14.9
1983	9.4	13.1	10.1	14.9
1984	7.3	10.4	8.1	12.2
1985	6.9	9.9	8.4	13.0
1986	6.6	9.5	8.3	12.8
1987	5.9	8.7	7.2	11.3
1988	5.3	7.9	6.2	10.1
1989	5.2	7.5	5.7	9.1
1990	5.4	7.9	5.9	9.4
Point Change				
1979-89	−0.6	−0.5	0.0	0.6
1989-90	0.2	0.4	0.2	0.3

*Unemployment rate adjusted to include discouraged workers and half of the involuntary part-time workers.

The rural job contraction noted above led to higher unemployment outside of cities over the 1980s (**Table 7.17** and **Figure 7H**). Unemployment rates, both as usually measured and adjusted to include discouraged workers (discouraged from seeking work by lack of previous job-seeking success) and half of the involuntary part-time workers (those who would prefer to work full-time, but are unable to find full-time work), were at similar levels in urban and rural settings in 1979. However, by 1990, the more comprehensive measure (the adjusted rate) was 9.4% in rural areas while the urban rate was 1.5 points lower at 7.9%. In fact, adjusted unemployment in rural areas was consistently higher than urban unemployment (Figure 7H), diverging by a high of 3.3 percentage points in 1986.

The rural job contraction led to higher unemployment outside of cities over the 1980s.

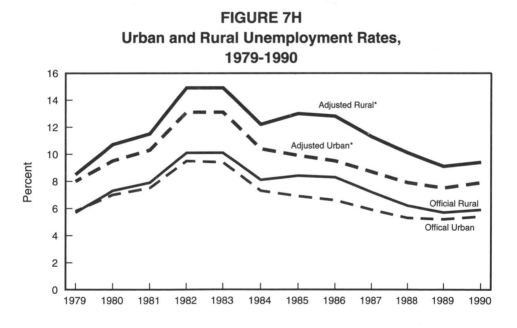

FIGURE 7H
Urban and Rural Unemployment Rates,
1979-1990

* Unemployment rate adjusted to include discouraged workers and
  half of the involuntary part-timers.

Conclusion

When we examine the economic problems that confronted American families over the 1980s, we find significant regional differences. While wage losses were common to some states in all regions, 1979-1989, the Midwest and the West saw big losses, while Northeastern states and Southern states on the Eastern seaboard saw wage growth at the median. Income inequality also grew over the 1980s, as the ratio of average family income in the top fifth to average income in the bottom fifth grew in 43 states.

The onset of the recession in 1989 saw unemployment rates rise in all but nine states. However, as stressed throughout the chapter, the early indicators included in this analysis suggest that the recession was much more acutely felt in the Northeast than in any other region.

Finally, our urban/rural analysis reveals that a downward shift in the rural income distribution occurred over the 1980s. Over the same period, poverty grew in all types of residences, but the largest increase was in cities. Employment growth was negative in rural settings, 1979-1989, leading to higher rural (versus urban) unemployment rates.

Early indicators suggest that the recession was much more acutely felt in the Northeast than in any other region.

Losing Access to Basic Necessities: Education, Housing, Health Care, and Child Care

So far, most of our research has defined well-being in terms of economic resources—primarily wealth, earnings, and income. This chapter adds another dimension, expanding our scope to include Americans' access to those basic necessities that have a vital impact on our living standard: education, housing, health care, and child care. We find that the same economic problems documented in earlier chapters—unequal growth, stagnant incomes for most families, and increased poverty—have had a negative impact on our educational and health-care systems, housing markets, and access to child care.

Unequal growth, stagnant incomes and increased poverty—have had a negative impact on our educational and health-care systems, housing markets, and access to child care.

Education

As a society, Americans place a high value on equal access to quality education for our children. Yet, as the following data show, we are far from providing it. An examination of test results from public elementary and high schools shows that minority and economically disadvantaged students do comparatively poorly in mathematics, science, and reading. The same students tend to have limited access to higher education. Finally, the U.S. devotes fewer public resources to public education than other countries; we also pay our public school teachers less than other equally well-educated professionals.

TABLE 8.1
Proficiency in Mathematics and Science, Age 9, 13, and 17 by Race/Ethnicity, 1970-1990: Average Scores

Age and Race/Ethnicity	Mathematics			Science		
	1973	1981	1990	1970	1981	1990
Age 9						
Race/Ethnicity						
White	225	224	235	236	229	238
Hispanic	202	195	214	n.a.	189	206
Black	190	204	208	179	187	196
As a Percentage of White Score						
Hispanic	89.8%	87.0%	91.1%	n.a.	82.5%	86.6%
Black	84.4	91.1	88.5	75.8%	81.7	82.4
Age 13						
Race/Ethnicity						
White	274	274	276	263	257	264
Hispanic	239	240	255	n.a.	217	232
Black	228	252	249	215	226	226
As a Percentage of White Score						
Hispanic	87.2%	87.6%	92.4%	n.a.	84.4%	87.9%
Black	83.2	92.0	90.2	81.7%	87.6	85.6
Age 17						
Race/Ethnicity						
White	310	304	310	312	293	301
Hispanic	277	272	284	n.a.	249	262
Black	270	277	289	258	235	253
As a Percentage of White Score						
Hispanic	89.4%	89.5%	91.6%	n.a.	84.8%	87.0%
Black	87.1	91.1	93.2	82.7%	80.1	84.1

Educational Proficiency: Low Scores for Minorities and the Poor

Scholastic achievement is a reasonable indicator of subsequent opportunity, regarding both college and future employment. Historically, achievement is highly influenced by family background: parental education, family income, community rank, and minority status. To the degree that schools can offset these factors, opportunity is somewhat equalized.

The next set of tables examines the performance of elementary and high school students in mathematics and science, by race/ethnicity, community, family background, and school quality. The findings suggest that, while minority students have shown some improvement in mathematics and science, inequalities exist in public schooling, and children from disadvantaged communities do worse relative to their affluent, white counterparts.

Tables 8.1 and 8.2 (as well as Table 8.4) present the National Assessment of Educational Progress (NAEP) findings in science, mathematics, and reading, using a proficiency scale from 0 to 500. Level 200 represents an understanding of simple principles; level 250, the application of general information; level 300, the analysis of procedures and data; and level 350, the integration of specialized information.

In **Table 8.1**, the mathematics and science scores for 9-, 13-, and 17-year-olds are given by race and Hispanic ethnicity, along with black and Hispanic scores relative to whites' scores, for the years 1970-1990. The levels show that while all races have improved marginally over the period in both subjects, only 17-year-old whites reach the 300 level (in mathematics). In addition, Hispanics and blacks show consistently poorer outcomes than whites.

However, black students showed marked improvement between the early 1970s and 1981, in their absolute scores. In addition, they also narrowed the gap relative to whites. For example, between 1973 and 1981, the ratio of black to white mathematics scores for 13-year-olds rose from 83.2 to 92.0%. Similar gains at a lower level were made by blacks in science. Yet between 1981 and 1990,

The findings suggest that, while minority students have shown some improvement in mathematics and science, inequalities exist in public schooling, and children from disadvantaged communities do worse relative to their affluent, white counterparts.

TABLE 8.2
Scholastic Aptitude Test Scores
By Race/Ethnic Group, 1976-1990

Verbal	1976	1980	1985	1990	Change 1976-90
American Indian	388	390	392	388	0
Asian American	414	396	404	410	−4
Black	332	330	346	352	20
Mexican American	371	372	382	380	9
Puerto Rican	364	350	368	359	−5
White	451	442	449	442	−9
All Students	431	424	431	424	−7
Math					
American Indian	420	426	428	437	17
Asian American	518	509	518	528	10
Black	354	360	376	385	31
Mexican American	410	413	426	429	19
Puerto Rican	401	394	409	405	4
White	493	482	490	491	−2
All Students	472	466	475	476	4

blacks made either slower gains or lost ground, relative to white students. Nine-year-old black students, having narrowed the gap with whites by 6.7 percentage points in mathematics between 1973 and 1981 (91.1% minus 84.4%), widened the gap by 2.6 points by 1990. The same students gained 5.9 points in science over the earlier period and made a smaller gain of 0.7 points over the 1980s.

Hispanic students also showed improvement over the period covered in Table 8.1. Except for nine-year-olds in mathematics, 1973-1981, their scores consistently improved in both subjects. Similarly, they also made progress toward closing the gap with whites between 1981 and 1990. For 13-year-old Hispanic mathematics students, the ratio to the score of whites was 92.4% in 1990, a 4.8 percentage point gain over their 1981 ratio of 87.6%.

Further evidence of black high-school students' improvement is seen in **Table 8.2**, Scholastic Aptitude Test (SAT) scores in selected years, 1976-1990 (unlike the other tables in this section, SAT scores range from 200 to 800). Over the period covered in the table, black students posted gains that are substantially larger than those of any other group. The average scores of blacks grew by 20 points between 1976 and 1990 in the verbal category and 31 points in mathematics. Mexican-Americans saw smaller gains in verbal skills, and all minority groups saw smaller gains (relative to blacks) in mathematics. However, even though white students scored lower in both areas in 1990 than in 1976, there still exists a substantial gap between the scores of whites and those of minorities, with the exception of Asian-Americans' scores in mathematics.

Even though white students scored lower in 1990 than in 1976, there still exists a substantial gap between the scores of whites and those of minorities.

TABLE 8.3
Proficiency in Mathematics and Science, Grades 4, 8, and 12
by Community, 1990: Average Scores

Test Subject	Mathematics	Science
Grade 4		
Advantaged Urban	231.0	251.6
Disadvantaged Urban	200.0	208.6
Rural	217.9	235.0
As a Percentage of Advantaged Urban		
Disadvantaged Urban	86.6%	82.9%
Rural	94.3	93.4
Grade 8		
Advantaged Urban	283.2	283.4
Disadvantaged Urban	251.7	242.2
Rural	261.1	257.4
As a Percentage of Advantaged Urban		
Disadvantaged Urban	88.9%	85.5%
Rural	92.2	90.8
Grade 12		
Advantaged Urban	308.4	304.1
Disadvantaged Urban	282.6	272.9
Rural	290.2	290.7
As a Percentage of Advantaged Urban		
Disadvantaged Urban	91.6%	89.7%
Rural	94.1	95.6

Table 8.3 presents a similar analysis as in Table 8.1 for 4th, 8th, and 12th graders by type of community in 1990. Advantaged urban areas are metropolitan areas where a high proportion of the students' parents are employed in professional or managerial positions. Disadvantaged urban areas are metropolitan areas where a high proportion of students' parents are receiving welfare or are frequently unemployed. Rural areas are those with populations below 10,000 and where many students' parents are farmers or farm workers.

The table shows that students from advantaged communities consistently score higher than those from disadvantaged or rural settings. The difference in achievement is most pronounced for 4th graders, with disadvantaged science students scoring 82.9% relative to those from advantaged communities. While the differences narrow with age, they still exist for high school seniors: disadvantaged mathematics and science students score 91.6% and 89.7%, respectively, relative to advantaged urban students.

Students from advantaged communities consistently score higher than those from disadvantaged or rural settings.

363

TABLE 8.4
Effects of Family Background on Scores
of 8th Graders, 1988

Test Subject and Score Group	Family Background		
	Disadvantaged	Average	Advantaged
Mathematics			
Lower Fourth	44.3%	23.8%	9.3%
Second Fourth	30.8	26.9	16.1
Third Fourth	17.0	27.0	26.2
Upper Fourth	7.9	22.3	48.5
Total	100.0	100.0	100.0
Reading			
Lower Fourth	44.0	24.2	11.1
Second Fourth	29.1	27.0	16.9
Third Fourth	18.5	25.8	29.4
Upper Fourth	8.4	23.0	42.5
Total	100.0	100.0	100.0
Science			
Lower Fourth	42.3	24.7	11.1
Second Fourth	29.2	25.5	16.9
Third Fourth	19.3	27.3	29.4
Upper Fourth	9.1	22.6	42.5
Total	100.0	100.0	100.0

Table 8.4 introduces family background, measured on a composite scale which factors in parental education, occupation, and income, for 8th graders in 1988 (the latest available data of this sort). The pattern in the table is strikingly similar for each subject: the higher the student's socio-economic status, the more likely he or she is to have a high score. Among those children with the most advantaged upbringing, between 42.5% and 48.5% were in the top fourth of all students in science, reading, and mathematics. Conversely, among the most disadvantaged students, between 42.3% and 44.3% of all students were in the lowest fourth of all students. Furthermore, less than 10% of students from disadvantaged families ever made it into the top fourth.

These racial, community, and family differences reflect a two-tiered system of public education provision. **Table 8.5** shows that when schools are sorted into thirds based on student performance, the gap between the top and bottom students is disturbingly wide. The average proficiency

The higher the student's socio-economic status, the more likely he or she is to have a high score.

TABLE 8.5
Average Proficiency of 4th, 8th, and 12th Graders by School Rank, 1990

| Test Subject | Average Proficiency | Pecentage of Students at or Above | | | |
		Level 200	Level 250	Level 300	Level 350
Grade 4					
Top One-Third Schools	232	90%	22%	0%	0%
Bottom One-Third Schools	198	46	3	0	0
Point Difference	34				
Grade 8					
Top One-Third Schools	284	100	88	29	1
Bottom One-Third Schools	246	94	44	4	0
Point Difference	38				
Grade 12					
Top One-Third Schools	312	100	97	66	10
Bottom One-Third Schools	273	100	77	18	1
Point Difference	39				

365

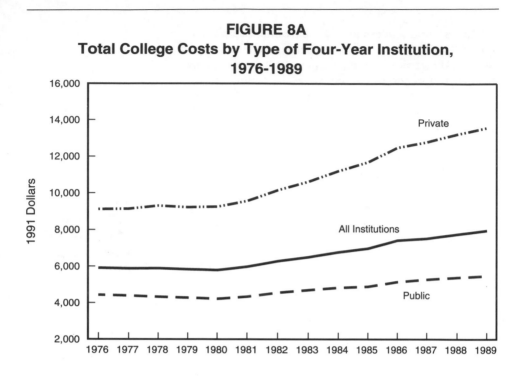

FIGURE 8A
Total College Costs by Type of Four-Year Institution, 1976-1989

TABLE 8.6
The Shrinking Federal Student Aid Grant,
School Years Beginning in 1977-1989
(1991 Dollars)

Year	Maximum Grant	Student Cost (Tuition, Room, and Board)	Maximum Grant as Percentage of Student Cost
1977	$3,017	$5,196	58.1%
1979	3,313	5,170	64.1
1981	2,524	5,274	47.9
1983	2,461	5,698	43.2
1985	2,658	6,183	43.0
1987	2,518	6,606	38.1
1988	2,533	6,757	37.5
1989	2,526	6,886	36.7

366

score difference between students in the top and bottom schools is 34 points for fourth graders and 39 points for high school seniors. In addition, fewer than half of the 4th graders from the bottom schools (46%) demonstrated a systematic grasp of basic grade-level principles (in this case, addition with whole numbers), while 90% of 4th graders from the top schools showed an understanding of these principles. A similar pattern exists at the 300 level for seniors, with 66% of those at the top schools performing "on-grade," as opposed to 18% of those from the lower-performing schools.

Access to College: Higher Costs, Less Aid

As **Figure 8A** shows, the real cost of attending college has increased since 1976. The figure shows an increase in the total cost, inclusive of room and board, of both public and private four-year institutions, from 1976 to 1989. The rate of increase appears especially precipitous for private colleges and universities; their average total cost of attendance had reached $13,563 (1991 dollars) by 1989. The figure also shows that, throughout the 1980s, the "affordability gap" between private and public institutions has grown, a result of the faster growth of private, relative to public, tuition.

However, it is frequently noted that the majority of middle- and low-income college students receive some form of government student aid, either from federal grants or loans, or from work-study. The next few tables include this factor in the cost burden of seeking higher education. The evidence shows that aid as a percentage of tuition has fallen over time, and that families with middle- and low-incomes are particularly hard-pressed to meet their expected contribution to their children's college education.

Table 8.6 presents the maximum grant, average student cost (an average of costs at all types of higher institutions), and the grant as a percent of student cost, from 1977-1989. The final column shows the dramatic drop in aid as a percentage of the total tuition. In 1977, the maximum grant accounted for 58.1% of student costs; by 1989, that percentage had dropped 21.4 points, to 36.7%.

Fewer than half of the 4th graders from the bottom schools (46%) demonstrated a systematic grasp of basic grade-level principles while 90% of 4th graders from the top schools showed an understanding of these principles.

TABLE 8.7
Costs of College: The Percent of Students with College Costs Covered by Expected Family Contribution and the Average Percent of Total Cost Met by Aid, by Family Income, 1987

Family Income	Percent of Students with Costs Covered by Expected Family Contribution		Average Percent Met by Aid	
	Public College	Private College	Public College	Private College
Less than $11,000	44.9%	37.6%	62.9%	64.1%
$11,000-17,000	47.8	35.4	64.5	69.9
$17,000-30,000	56.2	40.8	44.9	61.2
$30,000-50,000	80.5	52.7	23.0	40.3
More than $50,000	95.7	83.3	7.8	17.0

TABLE 8.8
Net Cost of College as a Ratio of Expected Family Contribution, by Family Income, 1987*

Family Income	Public College Average	Private College Average
Less than $11,000	1.99	3.58
$11,000-17,000	1.59	2.88
$17,000-30,000	1.34	1.95
$30,000-50,000	0.76	1.35
More than $50,000	0.35	0.68

*A ratio of one means that the cost of college is equal to the expected family contribution.

Table 8.7, introduces the concept of expected family contribution (EFC). Established by Congress, this formula takes into account a family's assets and expenses and then determines what the family is expected to contribute to their child's education.

Table 8.7 shows the average percent of total costs met by EFC and by aid (including grants, loans, and work-study) for students in different family income brackets in 1987. Less than half of low-income families (44.9%) were able to meet their expected contribution to public colleges; conversely, for wealthy families, the vast majority (95.7%) met their EFC. Moreover, the table shows that as family income rises, the percentage of families that can meet their children's college expenses rises. In the case of private college, even among families earning $30,000 to $50,000 in 1987, only about half (52.7%) were able to meet their EFC. The last two columns make the obvious point that aid is substantially more important to poor students relative to wealthy students. For students from families with incomes below $30,000 in 1987, the aid package covered an average of over 60% of total costs for private colleges. For the most wealthy students, this percentage was 17.0% for private college, 7.8% for public.

Table 8.8 demonstrates the difficulty less wealthy families have funding their children's college education. The table presents the ratio of the net cost of college (subtracting out grants, loans, and work-study) to the EFC. When this ratio exceeds one, it means that net costs of college attendance are higher than the EFC. In fact, this was the case for most income groups in the table. For public colleges, net costs exceeded the EFC (on average) for those families earning less than $30,000 in 1987. For those families with incomes below $11,000, net costs were about twice the EFC for public colleges; for private schools, the ratio was a substantially higher 3.58. In fact, for private colleges, only the most wealthy families had a ratio below one.

In 1977, the maximum grant accounted for 58.1% of student costs; by 1989, that percentage had dropped 21.4 points, to 36.7%.

369

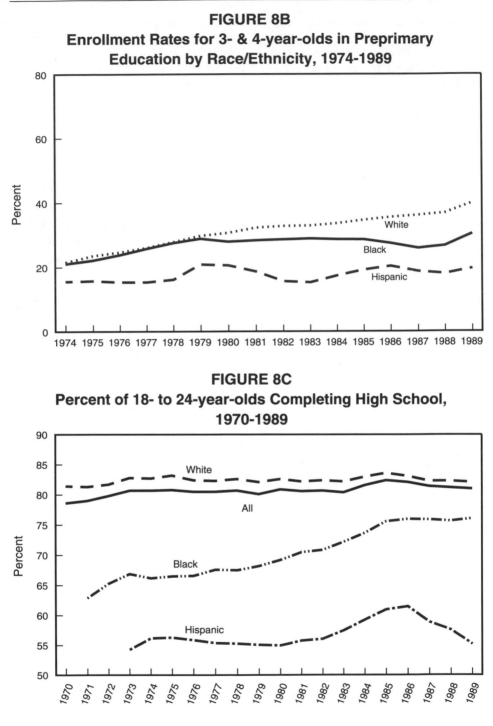

FIGURE 8B
Enrollment Rates for 3- & 4-year-olds in Preprimary Education by Race/Ethnicity, 1974-1989

FIGURE 8C
Percent of 18- to 24-year-olds Completing High School, 1970-1989

Minority Education: Uneven Results

Table 8.1 gave evidence of the disadvantage minority students face regarding educational proficiency. The following data suggest that minorities also suffer disadvantages regarding educational enrollment and attainment as well. However, at least in the case of high school completion rates, the position of blacks has improved.

Pre-kindergarten education for three- and four-year-olds (including Head Start), has been highly touted as the most important component of a national education goal: readiness to learn. However, as **Figure 8B** shows, preprimary enrollment has diverged for black and white children over the 1980s. From the beginning of the figure until about 1980, an approximately equal proportion of black and white children, between 21% and 30%, received preprimary instruction. Throughout the 1980s, the trend for white enrollment has continued to rise while black enrollment has flattened out. Hispanic enrollment has been relatively flat throughout the period, and has consistently been at the lowest level.

Figure 8C, covering the years 1970-1989, shows the percentage of 18- to 24-year-olds of a given race who have completed high school. The rate for whites has remained relatively constant, between 80 and 85 percent. However, the completion rate for blacks rose throughout the 1980s, and they can be seen to have gone a long way toward closing the gap with whites. Hispanics, however, show the lowest rates, and they began a downward trend in the late 1980s.

Pre-kindergarten education for three- and four-year-olds has been highly touted as a national education goal. However, pre-primary enrollment has diverged for black and white children over the 1980s.

371

FIGURE 8D
Percent of 18- to 24-year-olds in College, 1970-1989

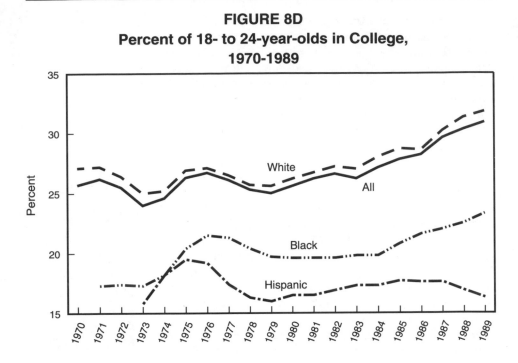

TABLE 8.9
Postsecondary Enrollment and Degree Attainment by Race/Ethnic Group, 1988-89
(U.S. Residents Only)

Group	Undergraduate Enrollment Fall 1988	Bachelor's Degrees 1988-89	Master's Degrees 1988-89	Doctorates* 1988-89
White, Non-Hispanic	80.2%	86.8%	87.9%	88.9%
Black, Non-Hispanic	9.4	5.9	5.1	3.8
Hispanic	5.7	3.0	2.6	2.2
Other**	4.7	4.3	4.3	5.1
Total (U.S. Residents)	100.0	100.0	100.0	100.0

*Ph.D., Ed.D., and comparable degrees.
**Other includes Asian/Pacific Islander and American-Indian/Alaskan Native.

The percentage of 18- to 24-year-olds enrolled in college is shown in **Figure 8D**, also for the years 1970-1989. Once again, blacks and Hispanics are at a distinct disadvantage relative to whites. And in this case, although blacks began to show an upward trend in the 1980s, the gap between them and whites remains. Hispanics have particularly low rates of college enrollment, and, as with high school completion rates, show a downward trend in the late 1980s.

Minorities and Advanced Degrees

In addition to their low rates of high school completion and college enrollment relative to whites, few minority college graduates go on to pursue advanced degrees. **Table 8.9** shows that in 1988, whites made up 80.2% of undergraduate enrollment, while blacks and Hispanics made up 9.4% and 5.7%, respectively (in this table, there are no Hispanics in the white and black categories). However, given this distribution of enrollment, whites are disproportionately represented among degree recipients, and this result becomes larger as the level of advancement increases. In 1988, blacks received 5.9% of bachelor's degrees, 5.1% of master's, and 3.8% of doctorates. Hispanics post a similar decline, at a lower level. Conversely, the percentages for whites were bachelor's: 86.8%, master's: 87.9%, and doctorates: 88.9%. (The high percentage of doctorates in the "Other" category, relative to blacks and Hispanics, was driven exclusively by Asian-Americans.)

Educational Expenditures: Less Investment than Other Countries and Greater Inequality Within the U.S.

One indicator of a government's commitment to public education is the percent of its gross domestic product (GDP) spent on education. Another indicator of society's commitment to education is seen in the degree to which teachers are remunerated relative to other professionals. On both of these indicators, the U.S. falls short.

Few minority college graduates go on to pursue advanced degrees.

TABLE 8.10
Public Expenditures on Education as
a Percent of GDP, 1986

Country	1986
Australia	5.3%
Austria	6.1
Belgium	5.4
Canada	6.7
Denmark	7.1
Finland	5.3
France	5.6
Greece	2.7
West Germany	4.3
Ireland	5.8
Italy*	5.1
Japan	5.0
Luxembourg	7.0
Netherlands	6.6
New Zealand	4.9
Norway	6.6
Portugal	4.1
Sweden	7.3
Switzerland	5.1
Turkey	2.0
United Kingdom	5.0
Yugoslavia	3.5
United States	**4.8**

*1986 data unavailable, figure is for 1984.

Table 8.10 gives public educational expenditures as a percent of GDP for the industrialized countries, for the year 1986, the latest available data. Public expenditures in the U.S. accounted for 4.8% of GDP, a figure that places the U.S. 18th out of 23 countries.

However, when private sector spending is factored into educational expenditures, as in Table 8.11, the U.S. rises to a middle position of those countries with valid data on private expenditures. This reflects the fact that the U.S., at 1.7% of GDP, has the highest proportion of private educational expenditures of the countries shown. Thus, those U.S. families with fewer resources of their own to devote to their children's education, i.e., the families that depend on public provision, are at a distinct disadvantage, relative to most other industrialized countries.

Public expenditures on education in the U.S. accounted for 4.8% of GDP, a figure that places the U.S. 18th out of 23 countries.

TABLE 8.11
Private and Total Educational Expenditures,
as a Percent of GDP, 1986*

Country	Private	Total, Public and Private
Australia	0.4%	5.7%
Canada	0.6	7.3
Denmark	0.1	7.2
Finland	0.5	5.8
France	1.0	6.6
Greece	0.2	2.9
West Germany	0.2	4.5
Ireland	0.3	6.1
Japan	1.4	6.4
Netherlands	0.2	6.8
Norway	0.2	6.8
Switzerland	0.1	5.2
United States	**1.7**	**6.5**

*Table includes only those countries with valid data on public and private expenditures.

TABLE 8.12
Public School Expenditures per Pupil, 1989-1990
Adjusted for Cost of Living Differences Between States

State	Adjusted Spending per Pupil 1989-90	Percent of U.S. Average
Highest Ten States:		
New York*	$6,994	141.2%
New Jersey*	6,708	135.5
Connecticut*	6,261	126.4
Pennsylvania*	6,033	121.8
Maine*	6,028	121.7
Rhode Island*	6,016	121.5
Wisconsin	5,978	120.7
Alaska	5,896	119.1
Vermont*	5,759	116.3
Wyoming	5,756	116.2
Lowest Ten States:		
South Carolina**	4,029	81.4
North Dakota	3,869	78.1
Tennessee**	3,779	76.3
Oklahoma	3,718	75.1
Hawaii	3,640	73.5
Alabama**	3,606	72.8
Arkansas**	3,600	72.7
Idaho	3,499	70.7
Mississippi**	3,454	69.8
Utah	2,928	59.1
U.S. Average	4,952	100.0

*Northeastern States
**Southern States

Resources are also distributed in a highly unequal manner within the U.S., i.e., between the states. **Table 8.12** shows that, even after adjusting for different costs of living, some states devote substantially more resources to education than others. The adjusted expenditures for the highest and the lowest ten states are given in the table, along with the percent of the U.S. average, for the school year 1989-1990. The wide disparity is seen in the range of percentages, from a low of 59.1% in Utah to a high of 141.2% in New York. Furthermore, the table highlights regional differences, as northeastern states are over-represented among the highest ten states, while southern states are over-represented among the lowest.

Finally, although much public rhetoric emphasizes the importance of well-trained teachers, society's economic valuation of teachers belies this emphasis. **Figure 8E** shows the average salaries of beginning public school teachers (in 1991 dollars), compared to the beginning salaries of college graduates in five other fields, from 1972 to 1991.

Resources are distributed in a highly unequal manner between the states.

FIGURE 8E
Beginning Teacher Salaries vs. Other College Graduates, 1972-1991

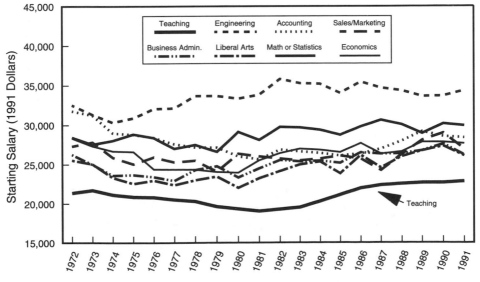

Legend: Teaching, Engineering, Accounting, Sales/Marketing, Business Admin., Liberal Arts, Math or Statistics, Economics

377

TABLE 8.13
Housing Costs, 1967-1990
(1989 Dollars)

Year	Owner Cost Annual After-tax Cash Cost	Renter Cost Monthly Gross Rent
1967	$5,801	$368
1973	6,825	368
1977	8,106	361
1979	9,171	360
1987	8,202	411
1989	8,599	409
1990	8,341	406

FIGURE 8F
After-Tax Home Owning and Rental Costs,
1967-1990

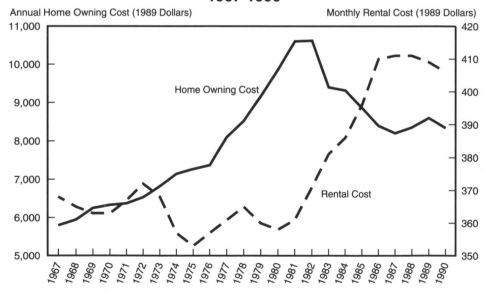

Annual Home Owning Cost (1989 Dollars) Monthly Rental Cost (1989 Dollars)

While the salaries of most professionals cluster together in the middle range (with engineers notably higher), teachers' salaries are consistently the lowest. Even though their real earnings grew in the mid-1980s (after falling in the late 1970s), there still remains a substantial pay gap between teachers and other college graduates.

Housing

Housing Costs: Rising Faster than Incomes

The affordability of housing, both for renters and owners, depends on trends in housing costs and trends in family income. The following tables and figures show that the cost of owning a home rose quickly in the late 1970s and early 1980s, both in real terms and as a percentage of income. Rental costs also grew throughout the 1980s. Oversupply of housing stock and falling mortgage rates in the latter part of the 1980s led to a fall in home ownership costs. However, stagnant income growth has kept the cost of housing as a percentage of income high, relative to earlier periods. Furthermore, large, low-income, and female-headed families continue to face inordinate difficulty in the housing market.

Table 8.13 and **Figure 8F** show the after-tax cost (mortgage payment less tax savings) of home ownership from 1967 to 1990, in 1989 dollars. Costs began to accelerate in about 1977, when they began a five-year climb, from $8,106 to $10,617 (Figure 8F). By the latter part of the 1980s, the trend had declined and flattened, but costs remained high relative to the beginning period in the figure.

Gross rental costs (inclusive of fuel and utility costs, taxes, and insurance), also plotted in Figure 8F, show a steep incline lasting until the mid-1980s. At $360 in 1979 (Table 8.13), gross rent peaked at $411 in 1987 and has fallen only slightly since then. As we show below, this rise in the cost of rental housing, in tandem with the particularly stagnant growth of renters' incomes, led to a steady incline in the housing burden for renters.

Stagnant income growth has kept the cost of housing as a percentage of income high, relative to earlier periods.

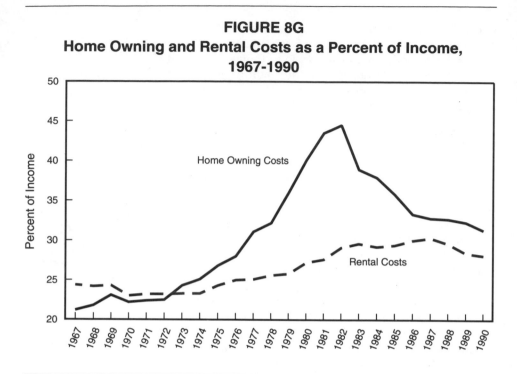

FIGURE 8G
Home Owning and Rental Costs as a Percent of Income, 1967-1990

TABLE 8.14
Burdens of Buying Homes and Renting, 1967-1989

	Housing Expenses as Percent of Income for:	
	Prime First-Time Home Buyers*	Renters
At Business Cycle Peaks:		
1967	21.2%	24.4%
1973	24.3	23.3
1979	36.0	25.8
1989	32.3	28.4
Period Averages:		
1967-73	22.5	23.7
1974-79	29.9	24.9
1980-89	37.2	29.0

*Married-couple renters aged 25 to 29.

380

Figure 8G and Table 8.14 introduce income growth into the analysis, by showing rental costs and first-time home purchasing costs as a percentage of income between 1967 and 1990. The housing cost burden for first-time home buyers is the expense of the median-priced home, expressed as a percentage of the median income of married-couple renters aged 25-29. These families are selected because they are especially likely to be considering the purchase of a first home. The cost burden for renters is the median gross rent as a percentage of the median renter's income.

Let us first consider first-time home buyers. Driven by the steep cost increases portrayed in Figure 8F, the housing cost burden rose from 21.2% of income in 1967 to 36.0% in 1979 (Table 8.14). As the housing market "softened," the burden fell, as seen in the decline toward the end of Figure 8G. However, as noted above, since family income at the median grew at a slower rate in the 1980s than in earlier periods, first-time home buyers were unable to reap the full benefits of the softer housing market in the late 1980s. While the cost burden fell from 36.0% in 1979 to 32.3% in 1989 (Table 8.14), the average over the 1980s, at 37.2%, was significantly higher than that of earlier periods, when it averaged 29.9% from 1974 to 1979, and 22.5% from 1967 to 1973.

With the exception of a slight decline at the end of the 1980s, renters saw a constant rise in their housing cost burden. Once again, the steep incline in gross rents over the 1980s (see Figure 8F) coupled with the previously mentioned sluggish income growth, led to the increased burden shown in the figure. Unlike first-time buyers, the cost burden for renters was higher at each peak year, as shown in Table 8.14, climbing from 24.4% in 1967 to 28.4% in 1989. Similarly, the average burden grew consistently over the period; for 1980-1989, the average cost burden for renters was 29.0%.

As earlier chapters have noted, the income growth over the 1980s has generated highly unequal outcomes, and certain types of families—larger families and female-headed families—were more vulnerable than others. These outcomes are, of course, evident in the housing market. Below we examine the housing experience of low-income fami-

The average housing cost burden over the 1980s, at 37.2%, was significantly higher than that of earlier periods.

381

TABLE 8.15
Percent of Owner and Renter Families
Who Could not Afford Median Priced Home, 1988

Family Type	Owners	Renters
All Families	30.9%	90.4%
Married Couple Families	25.5	86.5
With Children	32.2	90.7
Female-headed Families	61.0	97.2
With Children	71.5	97.2

TABLE 8.16
Shelter Poverty, by Household Size
1970-1989

A.   By Household Size

	Household Size					
Year	1	2	3	4	5	6+
1970	39.0%	27.1%	20.5%	26.6%	31.7%	43.5%
1979	28.9	24.4	24.6	28.8	37.7	51.8
1989	24.4	23.5	27.1	30.4	40.0	55.6
1991	26.7	25.3	29.5	32.2	43.3	57.6

B.   Small vs. Large Households

	All Households		
Year	Small (1-2 Persons)	Large (3+ Persons)	All Households
1970	30.3%	29.4%	29.7%
1979	25.6	34.2	31.5
1989	23.8	36.6	32.7
1991	25.7	38.9	34.9

lies, but **Table 8.15** shows the percentage of *all* owner and renter families in 1988 who would not have been able to purchase a median-priced home in that year, by family type. The table shows that the median home was out of reach for more than 90% of all families of renters in 1988. Among married couples with children who owned homes, the housing market and their family incomes were such that in 1988, 32.2% would have been unable to buy the median-priced home. The housing market was particularly inaccessible to female-headed families with children who rented in 1988, as 97.2% of these families could not afford the median home.

The high costs of housing in the 1980s has led analysts of the housing market to consider the amount of income families have left over for other necessities, after their housing expenditures. This work has led to the notion of "shelter poverty." A household is considered shelter poor if, after housing expenses, it does not have enough to pay for a minimum amount of non-housing necessities, as defined by the U.S. Bureau of Labor Statistics.

As shown in **Table 8.16**, 32.7% of all households (including both renters and homeowners) were "shelter poor" in 1989, higher than both the 1970 rate of 29.7% and the 1979 figure of 31.5%. In other words, in 1989, close to one-third of households were unable to buy enough food, clothing, and other necessities after paying for housing. Table 8.16 also shows that shelter poverty rates have risen over time for larger households and fallen for smaller households. For example, 21.7% of two-person households were shelter poor in 1970; by 1989, this rate had fallen to 23.5%. However, for households with four or more persons, shelter poverty rates have increased since 1970, and the larger the household size, the greater the increase. Well over half (55.6%) of the largest households—those with six or more persons—were shelter poor in 1989. As the figures for 1991 show, shelter poverty has risen for all households over the recent recession.

Home Ownership Rates: Falling for Young Families as a Result of Rising Costs

As would be expected, the rising costs of housing and sluggish income growth have depressed home ownership rates in the 1980s for those families entering the housing

In 1989, close to one-third of households were unable to buy enough food, clothing, and other necessities after paying for housing.

TABLE 8.17
Home Ownership Rates by Age of Household Head,
1973-1990

Age of Household Head	Home Ownership Rate in:				Point Change	
	1973	1980	1989	1990	1973-80	1980-89
Under 25	23.4%	21.3%	17.6%	15.3%	−2.1	−3.7
25-29	43.6	43.3	35.4	35.9	−0.3	−7.9
30-34	60.2	61.1	53.6	51.5	0.9	−7.5
35-39	68.5	70.8	63.9	63.1	2.3	−6.9
40-44	72.9	74.2	70.8	70.4	1.3	−3.4
45-54	76.1	77.7	75.3	76.1	1.6	−2.4
55-64	75.7	79.3	80.2	80.4	3.6	0.9
65-74	71.3	75.2	78.2	78.2	3.9	3.0
75+	67.1	67.8	70.3	71.0	0.7	2.5
Total	64.4	65.6	63.9	64.1	1.2	−1.7

market. **Table 8.17** shows home ownership rates, by the age of the household head, in selected years from 1973 to 1990. Overall, the percentage of households owning homes grew slightly (1.2 percentage points) between 1973 and 1980, and fell slightly (-1.7 points) over the 1980s.

However, more dramatic changes in ownership rates are evident when we examine changes by age group. Here we see that the percentage of home owners among all households headed by someone under 55 fell by at least 2.4 percentage points between 1980 and 1989. The biggest losses went to young households. In 1980, 43.3% of those household heads between the ages of 25 and 29 owned homes. By 1989, that percentage had fallen 7.9 points, to 35.4%. Households headed by a person aged 30-34 also did substantially worse over the period: their ownership rates fell by 7.5 points.

Ownership rates for older persons (55 and over) increased over both periods, though less so between 1980 and 1989. This increase is likely the result of older persons' incomes growing faster than those of younger persons over the period. Also, many older heads of households owned homes prior to the steep rise in housing prices shown in Figure 8F. The added wealth from the increased home equity realized by those households headed by an older person helped to insure that home ownership rates have remained high—above 75%.

The years 1983-1989 saw one of the longest expansions of the United States economy since World War II, yet housing costs as a percentage of income and shelter poverty were excessively high throughout the 1980s, and home ownership rates fell dramatically for most families. Once again, as we saw in Chapter 6, the uneven and unequal nature of the expansion is evident. There were some economic winners over the 1980s; many more lost.

Low-Income Housing: Reduction in Housing Stock and Deteriorating Conditions

Since 1970, the gap between the supply of, and the demand for, low-income housing has expanded (this is one factor leading to the high rates of shelter poverty noted above). In this section, we examine the housing problems of the poorest members of society. As Chapter 6 documented, poverty rates were high in the 1980s, partic-

Households headed by a person aged 30-34 also did substantially worse from 1980 to 1989: their ownership rates fell by 7.5 points.

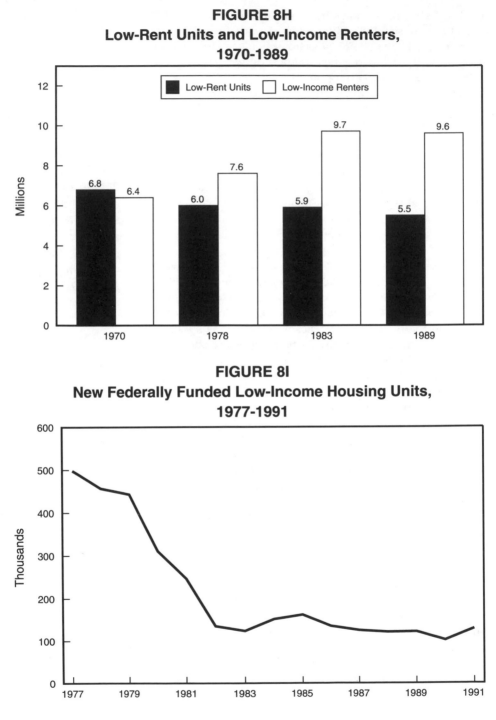

FIGURE 8H
Low-Rent Units and Low-Income Renters,
1970-1989

■ Low-Rent Units □ Low-Income Renters

1970: 6.8, 6.4
1978: 6.0, 7.6
1983: 5.9, 9.7
1989: 5.5, 9.6

Millions

FIGURE 8I
New Federally Funded Low-Income Housing Units,
1977-1991

Thousands

ularly when compared to other periods of economic growth. The following tables and figures show that the number of low-income units has fallen way behind the number of low-income households. We show that part of this development is a result of a diminished federal commitment to low-income housing over the 1980s. In addition, the housing conditions experienced by the poor are substantially worse than those of the non-poor.

Figure 8H shows that the number of low-rent units has fallen since 1970, while the number of low-income renters has increased. Low-income households in this figure are those whose annual income is $10,000 or less (1989 dollars), approximately the poverty line for a family of three in 1989. Low-rent units are those units renting for $250 a month or less, an expenditure of 30% of monthly income. There were 6.8 million units meeting this criterion in 1970. Since then, there has been a steady decline, until there were only 5.5 million units in 1989. However, on the demand side, the number of low-income renters has steadily grown, from 6.4 million in 1970 to 9.6 million in 1989.

The cause of this widening gap stems from the growth in poverty, as well as a reduced government commitment to house the poor. **Figure 8I** shows the net additional units of federally funded low-income housing from 1977 to 1991. In 1977, 498,000 units were added to the stock of low-income units. While the numbers of new units began to fall in the late 1970s, by 1982 there had been a radical drop in net additional units, reflecting the Reagan administration's reliance on existing housing stock. By 1990, net new units hit a low of 102,000.

Besides the shrinking supply of affordable housing, the poor also face significantly worse housing conditions than the non-poor. **Table 8.18** shows two indicators of housing conditions, by poverty status: deficient housing, defined as housing with moderate to severe physical or structural deficiencies, and overcrowded housing, defined as housing more than one person per room. In 1989, 17.9% of all poor households were housed in deficient structures, compared with 6.6% of non-poor households. Poor black households were in the worst condition: 29.2% of their structures were deficient in 1989.

In 1989, 17.9% of all poor households were housed in deficient structures, compared with 6.6% of non-poor households.

TABLE 8.18
Percent of Households Living in Deficient and
Overcrowded Housing, 1989

Households	Deficient Housing	Overcrowded Housing
Poor Households		
All Poor Households	17.9%	7.9%
Renters	19.4	10.0
Owners	15.8	4.7
Black	29.2	9.1
Hispanic	23.1	26.0
White	12.5	4.0
Non-Poor Households		
All Non-Poor Households	6.6	2.1
Renters	9.8	3 7
Owners	5.1	1.3
Black	13.0	3.3
Hispanic	12.0	11.3
White	5.6	0.2

TABLE 8.19
Estimates of Homelessness, 1987

Subject	Range
Estimated Range of Homeless Persons in a Given Month	496,000-600,000
Estimated Range of Homeless Children in a Given Month	35,000-90,000

The tight, low-income housing market documented above has led to overcrowded conditions for many poor households. In 1989, 7.9% of all poor households lived in overcrowded conditions, as opposed to 2.1% of non-poor households. Overcrowding is particularly severe for Hispanics. Poor Hispanics experienced the highest percentage of overcrowded households, with more than one-quarter (26.0%) overcrowded. In fact, *non-poor* Hispanic households had a higher rate of overcrowding (11.3%) than all non-Hispanic *poor* households.

Homelessness

The housing problems of the low-income population—high costs, low supply, deficient and overcrowded housing—have led to the highly visible increase in homelessness over the 1980s. The problem of homelessness has proven to be a difficult one to analyze. Due to the difficulty in both defining and counting the homeless, it is not easy to determine the number of homeless persons. This brief section presents the most recent data on homelessness, emphasizing the numbers and characteristics of the homeless. Unfortunately, the most recent data are from the year 1987. Most analysts agree that the magnitude of the problem has grown since that time. In fact, in a recent survey of major cities, 25 of the 28 cities in the survey report an average 13% rise in requests for emergency shelter over the course of 1991.

Table 8.19 gives a range of the number of homeless persons between about 500,000 and 600,000 in a given month, including 35,000 to 90,000 children. This estimate is an extrapolation from the number of homeless found to be using homeless services (soup kitchens and/or shelters) during the month of March 1987. There are many assumptions embedded in this estimate, including an estimate of the number of homeless not using services, given the number of known service-users. However, this estimate is well within the range of most studies of homelessness.

In a recent survey of major cities, 25 of the 28 cities in the survey report an average 13% rise in requests for emergency shelter over the course of 1991.

TABLE 8.20
Characteristics of Service-Using Homeless
Adults, in Percents, 1987

Characteristic	Percent
Gender	
Male	81%
Female	19
Race/Ethnicity	
White (Non-Hispanic)	46
Black	41
Hispanic	10
Other	3
Institutionalization*	
Mental Hospitalization	19
Detox or Alcohol/Drug Treatment Center	33
Jailed for 5 or More Days	52
State or Federal Prison	24
Length of Time Spent Homeless	
Less than 1 Month	8
2-3 Months	13
4-6 Months	19
7-12 Months	14
13-24 Months	16
25-48 Months	12
More than 48 Months	19

*These categories are neither exhaustive nor mutually exclusive.

The characteristics of those adults who use homeless services are given in **Table 8.20**. When examining the race of those homeless persons who use services, the largest percentage are white (46%), with blacks accounting for 41% and Hispanics, for 10%. An overwhelming majority, 81%, of the homeless are male. In addition, about one-fifth of homeless service users (19%) have been hospitalized for a psychiatric condition; over half have experienced some degree of imprisonment (possibly for being homeless).

A further important point is made regarding the length of time spent homeless. Recall that the estimates in Table 8.19 refer to the number of homeless in a particular month. Since, over the course of a year, there is a good deal of turnover in the homeless population, the number of homeless in a month will be substantially less than the number homeless during the course of a year. Table 8.20 shows that among the homeless adults using services, over half (54%) had been homeless one year or less, while a smaller group, comprising about one-fifth (19%) were homeless for over four years. Homeless analysts estimate that the number of homeless in a given year is about twice the number of homeless in a given month. This suggests, based on the data in Table 8.19, that there were approximately 1 million homeless persons in 1987.

There were approximately 1 million homeless persons in 1987.

391

TABLE 8.21
OECD Spending on Health, 1960-1989

Country	Total Health Expenditure as Percent of Gross Domestic Product in:				Rank in 1989 (out of 24)
	1960	1970	1980	1989	
Australia	4.6%	5.0%	6.5%	7.0%	17
Austria	4.6	5.4	7.9	8.2	7
Belgium	3.4	4.0	6.6	7.2	14
Canada	5.5	7.2	7.4	8.7	4
Denmark	3.6	6.1	6.8	6.3	21
Finland	3.9	5.7	6.5	7.1	15
France	4.2	5.8	7.6	8.7	3
West Germany	4.7	5.5	7.9	8.2	8
Greece	3.2	4.0	4.3	5.1	23
Iceland	1.2	4.3	6.4	8.6	5
Ireland	4.0	5.6	8.5	7.3	13
Italy	3.3	4.8	6.8	7.6	11
Japan	2.9	4.4	6.4	6.7	18
Luxembourg	n.a.	4.1	6.8	7.4	12
Netherlands	3.9	6.0	8.2	8.3	6
New Zealand	4.4	5.1	7.2	7.1	16
Norway	3.3	5.0	6.6	7.6	10
Portugal	n.a.	n.a.	5.9	6.3	20
Spain	2.3	4.1	5.9	6.3	19
Sweden	4.7	7.2	9.5	8.8	2
Switzerland	3.3	5.2	7.3	7.8	9
Turkey	n.a.	n.a.	n.a.	3.5*	24
United Kingdom	3.9	4.5	5.8	5.8	22
United States	**5.2**	**7.4**	**9.2**	**11.8**	**1**
U.S. Rank	2	1	2	1	
OECD Average (excluding Turkey, Portugal, and Luxembourg)	3.8	5.3	7.1	7.6	

*This percentage refers to 1987.

Health Care: Higher Costs, Poor Health Outcomes, and Many Uninsured

Americans spend more on health care than any other nation in the world, over $650 billion in 1990. This fact by itself is not necessarily cause for alarm. The question is: what are we getting for our money? Unfortunately, the picture that develops upon analysis of our health-care system is one of inflated costs, unsatisfactory results, and uneven insurance coverage.

U.S. Health-Care Costs:
Highest Among the OECD Countries

Total health-care expenditures as a percentage of Gross Domestic Product (GDP) are shown in **Table 8.21** for countries in the Organisation for Economic Co-operation and Development (OECD), an association that includes most of the advanced industrialized countries. Available data are for selected years from 1960 to 1989. The U.S. ranks either first or second in each year on health-care expenditures as a percent. In 1989, we spent 11.8% of our GDP on health care, the only nation to reach double-digits, and well above the OECD average of 7.6%. Sweden, the nation ranked second in the table, spent 8.8% percent of its domestic product on health care, a full 3% of GDP less than the U.S.

In 1989, we spent 11.8% of our GDP on health care, the only nation to reach double-digits, and well above the OECD average of 7.6%.

TABLE 8.22
The Main Components of Health-Care Expenditures in the U.S., per Capita, 1960-1990
(1991 Dollars)

Year	Hospital Care	Physicians' Services	Drugs and Other Medical Nondurables	Nursing-Home Care
1960	$225	$129	$101	$23
1970	429	208	135	76
1980	720	295	152	141
1989	994	485	216	204
1990	1,027	504	219	214
Percentage Change				
1960-1990	355.7%	291.5%	116.2%	828.5%
Annual Average Growth Rates				
1960-1990	5.1%	4.5%	2.6%	7.4%

FIGURE 8J
Per Capita National Health-Care Expenditures, 1960-1990

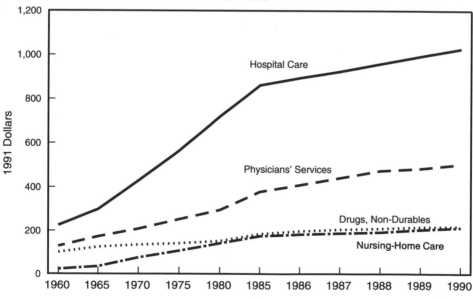

What has made medical spending grow so quickly in the U.S.? **Table 8.22** and **Figure 8J** show the per capita growth of the four largest components of our health-care bill: hospital care, physician services, drugs and other medical non-durables (e.g, bandages), and nursing-home care. As the figure shows, the costs of these services have risen sharply over time, with the fastest growth period occurring between 1970 and the mid-1980s. Hospital care, which cost $225 per capita in real terms in 1960, rose 355.7% by 1990, to $1,027. Physician services account for the second largest component of the growth of health-care expenditures, growing by 291.5% between 1960 and 1989. Nursing-home care, while representing a relatively small share of per capita expenditures, has had the most growth over the period, at an annual average rate of 7.4%. Demographic pressures—the aging of the population—will continue to create upward pressure on this component.

Hospital care rose 355.7% in real terms between 1960 and 1990.

An important reason why health care is so costly in our country has to do with medical inflation. As is well known, with the passage of time, prices rise. However, prices for certain items rise faster than others; such is the case with medical services throughout the 1980s. This means that we are spending more on medical care and getting less for our money, relative to other goods and services. **Figure 8K** plots the general price index we use to adjust prices throughout this text, the CPI-U-X1, against the price index for medical care. By about 1980, medical prices began to rise at a faster rate than the prices of the other items (one of which is medical care) used to compute the more general price index. Medical prices continued to accelerate, and as the figure shows, the price index for medical care has surpassed the general price index since 1983.

As health-care costs have risen, families have had to meet the rising costs from their budgets (businesses have also had to contend with rising health-care costs, as discussed

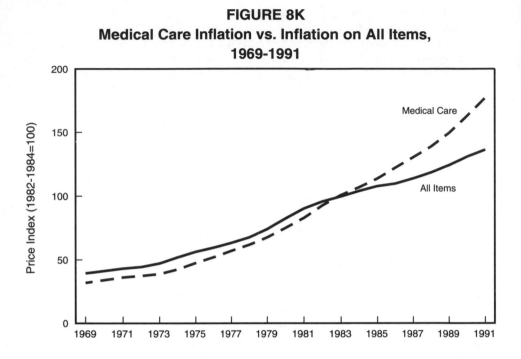

FIGURE 8K
Medical Care Inflation vs. Inflation on All Items,
1969-1991

below). However, health-care expenditures derive from a variety of sources. As **Table 8.23** shows, families have had to devote a greater proportion of their income (2.7% more) to health-care payments between 1980 and 1991. While fewer of these costs reflect out-of-pocket expenses, a greater proportion have been shifted to insurance and health-related taxes. As noted, the overall burden to the average family grew between 1980 and 1991, from 9.0% to 11.7% of family income (Table 8.23). In addition, costs in real terms grew in each category, with the average total family expenditure rising by 49.0%, or $1,412. The cost of Medicare premiums doubled, from $56 to $112 (Medicare is government sponsored health insurance, primarily for the elderly); insurance costs grew by 72.4%.

The overall burden to the average family grew between 1980 and 1991, from 9.0% to 11.7% of family income.

TABLE 8.23
The Family Health-care Burden, 1980 and 1991
(1991 Dollars)

Source of Payment	Expenditure				Expenditure and Percentage Point Changes, 1980 and 1991		
	1980	Percent of Total	1991	Percent of Total	Expenditure Changes	Point Change	Percent Growth
Average Family Expenditure	$2,885	100.0%	$4,297	100.0%	1,412	0.0	49.0%
Out-of-Pocket	1,082	37.5	1,362	31.7	280	−5.8	25.8
Insurance	429	14.9	739	17.2	310	2.3	72.4
Medicare Payroll	218	7.6	369	8.6	151	1.0	68.9
Medicare Premiums	56	2.0	112	2.6	56	0.7	100.0
General Taxes*	1,099	38.1	1,715	39.9	616	1.8	56.1
Average Family Income	33,201	9.0**	33,646	11.7**	4,445	2.7	13.8

*General taxes include federal contributions to Medicaid, government contributions to employer-sponsored insurance, and funding for other public health programs. Health payments cover the 1991 cost of all health services and supplies.

**Percent of family income spent of health care.

397

TABLE 8.24
Health Indicators in U.S. and OECD Average*

Indicator	Year	U.S. Rank (Out of 23)	U.S. Level	OECD Average	U.S. Level as Percent of OECD Average
Infant Mortality Rate**	1970	15	2.00	2.05	97.5%
	1980	17	1.26	1.14	110.1
	1989	19	0.97	0.80	121.3
Perinatal Mortality Rate**	1970	12	2.30	2.29	100.4
	1980	14	1.32	1.28	103.0
	1986	15	1.03	0.99	103.9
Female Life Exp. at Birth	1960	12	73.10	72.90	100.2
	1980	15	76.70	77.50	99.0
	1989	17	78.50	79.20	99.1
Male Life Exp. at Birth	1960	16	66.60	67.80	98.2
	1980	18	69.60	70.90	98.2
	1989	19	71.50	72.80	98.2

* Excluding Turkey.

**Infant mortality is deaths of infants less than one year old, as a percent of all live births. Perinatal mortality is fetal deaths occurring after 28 weeks of pregnancy, plus infant deaths occurring prior to 7 days after birth, as a percent of all live births and fetal deaths.

TABLE 8.25
Infant* and Neonatal** Mortality Rates, by Race, 1960-1988

Years	Whites			Blacks		
	Infant Mortality	Neonatal Mortality	Life Expectancy	Infant Mortality	Neonatal Mortality	Life Expectancy
1960	2.29%	1.72%	70.60	4.43%	2.78%	63.60
1970	1.78	1.38	71.70	3.26	2.28	64.10
1980	1.10	0.75	74.40	2.14	1.41	68.10
1988	0.85	0.54	75.60	1.76	1.15	69.20
Average Annual Rate of Change						
1960-1970	−2.5%	−2.2%	0.2%	−3.0%	−2.0%	0.1%
1970-1980	−4.7	−5.9	0.4	−4.1	−4.7	0.6
1980-1988	−3.2	−4.0	0.2	−2.4	−2.5	0.2

*The number of deaths in the first year of life as a percent of live births.
**The number of deaths in the first 28 days of life as a percent of live births.

Are We Getting Our Money's Worth?
Lagging Health Indicators

Clearly the U.S. is devoting a great deal more of our national resources to health care than the other OECD countries. But are we getting our money's worth? That is, given our extensive expenditures, how do our health indicators compare to those of other countries?

Table 8.24 shows that despite our high expenditure level, the U.S. ranks quite poorly on four basic health indicators: infant mortality rates, perinatal mortality rates, and male and female life expectancy at birth. Furthermore, our rankings have fallen over time. Column two shows the rank of the U.S. out of 23 OECD countries, all of whom spend a smaller proportion of their national product on health care. Regarding infant mortality rates (the deaths of all infants under one year old, as a percentage of all live births), the U.S. ranked 19 out of 23 in 1989, our worst ranking in the table. The U.S. perinatal mortality ranking was also high in 1986 (the latest year of data availability), and had risen over time. Regarding life expectancy, the U.S. rank was 17 for females and 19 for males in 1989 (again, out of 23). In both cases, the U.S. life expectancy—78.5 years for females, 71.5 for males—was below the OECD averages, 79.2 and 72.8, respectively.

There also exists a high degree of inequality in health indicators between whites and blacks *within* the U.S. **Table 8.25** has infant and neonatal (death within the first 28 days of life) mortality rates, and life expectancy from birth for selected years between 1960 and 1988, by race. All of the health indicators show blacks to have a poorer health status than whites. The black infant mortality rate in 1988 at 1.76%, was higher than that of whites, 0.85%. The black neonatal mortality rate, at 1.15% in 1988 is almost twice the white rate of 0.54%. Similar results are found for life expectancy; whites live longer, on average, than blacks.

Turning to average annual rates of change, both races show improvement over time, although the rates of improvement have slowed between 1980 and 1988. For both races, infant and neonatal mortality rates improved between 1960 and 1970, falling at an average annual rate between 2% and 3% for both races. The mortality rates fell significantly faster between 1970 and 1980, both for white and black infants; neonatal mortality rates fell at an annual

> *Regarding infant mortality rates (the deaths of all infants under one year old, as a percentage of all live births), the U.S. ranked 19 out of 23 in 1989, our worst ranking in the table.*

399

TABLE 8.26
Number and Percent of the Non-aged* Population
Without Health Insurance, 1987-1990

Non-aged Population	1987	1988	1989	1990
Number Uninsured (Million)	30.7	32.4	33.0	34.4
Percent Uninsured	14.4%	15.1%	15.3%	15.7%

*Persons under 65.

TABLE 8.27
Breaks in Health Insurance During a 28-Month Period, 1985-1987

Group	Percent Covered Less Than 28 Months	Percent with No Coverage Over 28 Months
All	28.1%	4.3%
Ethnicity		
White	26.4	4.0
Black	37.7	5.9
Hispanic*	52.0	11.3
Age		
Under 18	34.5	5.1
18-24	51.9	6.0
25-44	27.7	4.5
45-64	19.9	4.3
65 and over	0.7	0.1
Ratio of Income to Poverty Line		
Under 1.0	55.3	14.8
1.0 to 1.99	45.7	8.5
2.0 to 2.99	29.9	3.0
3.0 to 3.99	19.2	1.7
4.0 to 4.99	13.3	0.8
5.0 to 5.99	11.9	0.6
6.0 and over	8.9	0.5
Work Experience		
Worked Full-Period, Full-time	14.0	n.a.
Worked Full-Period, Part-Time	25.4	n.a.
Worked with Interruptions	44.7	n.a.

*Persons of Hispanic origin may be of any race.

400

rate of 5.9% for whites, 4.7% for blacks. However, the rate of improvement slowed down over the 1980s. Over the 1980s, the decline in the white infant mortality rate slowed from its 1970s average growth rate of -4.7% to -3.2% per year; for blacks, the rate's decline slowed from -4.1% to -2.4%.

Health Insurance Incomplete and Uneven Coverage

Despite the fact that we in the U.S. spend a great deal on health care, many Americans are without health insurance and are thus exposed to great medical and financial risks. Approximately 35.4 million Americans, 14.1% of the population, were without health insurance in 1991. Young adults, children, minorities, and workers with gaps in employment are the groups most likely to lack coverage. Also, workers in the service sector and in small firms are at greater risk of being uninsured.

As shown in **Table 8.26**, both the number and percentage of those lacking health insurance has grown in the recent past (earlier data are not comparable to these most recent findings). The findings in the table apply to the non-elderly (under 65) population, since these persons are not eligible for Medicare. In 1987, 14.4% of the non-elderly population were uninsured. This percentage has grown steadily, and reached 15.3%, or 33.0 million persons by 1989, the last non-recessionary year of data availability.

The data in Table 8.26 are from a "point-in-time" analysis, i.e., such data identify persons who lacked health insurance when that particular survey was administered. However, many persons experience gaps in their insurance over a given time period, possibly due to the loss of a job that provided insurance or a temporary loss of income. **Table 8.27** shows the result of a study that tracked the health insurance coverage of a representative group of persons over a 28-month period, between 1985 and 1987. Over 28% experienced a gap of at least one month in their coverage at some point over the 28-month period, showing that the point-in-time analysis understates the extent of the problem. On the other hand, only 4.3% of the overall population was uninsured for the entire period, suggesting that long-term lack of coverage is not a problem for most people.

Approximately 35.4 million Americans, 14.1% of the population, were without health insurance in 1991.

401

TABLE 8.28
Percent of U.S. Population Obtaining
Health Insurance from Specified Courses, 1990

Own Job	Family Member's Job	Medicare	Medicaid	Other	Uninsured	Total
29.4%	29.7%	11.2%	6.8%	9.0%	13.9%	100.0%

TABLE 8.29
Persons without Health Insurance: Their Attachment
to the Workforce, 1988-1990

	1988		1989		1990	
	Total* (000)	Percent of Uninsured	Total (000)	Percent of Uninsured	Total (000)	Percent of Uninsured
Non-worker	6,017	16.3%	4,975	14.9%	4,958	14.3%
Full-Year/Full-time Worker	12,973	35.2	11,573	34.7	17,059	49.3
Part-time Workers**	17,840	48.5	16,837	50.4	12,612	36.4
Total	36,830	100.0	33,385	100.0	34,629	100.0

*Other than non-worker category, totals include workers and their dependents.
**Includes full-year/part-time, part-year/full-time, and part-year/part-time workers.

Those most likely to experience a gap in health insurance coverage tended to be minority, young, low-income, and with a tenuous connection to the workforce. More than half of Hispanics (52.0%) and 37.7% of blacks were covered for less than the full period; 11.3% of Hispanics had no coverage at all for the full 28 months. For young adults between the ages of 18 and 24, 51.9% experienced a gap in coverage, while 6.0% were without insurance over the full period. Poor persons (those whose ratio of family income to the poverty line was less than one) were the most likely to be without coverage, both for at least one month (55.3%) and for the entire 28 months (14.8%). Those whose income to poverty ratio was above 4.00, were less likely to be without coverage; less than one percent were without coverage for the whole period.

The last panel of Table 8.27 shows that the likelihood of experiencing a gap in coverage rises for those who either worked part-time or with employment interruptions. **Table 8.28** confirms that most persons (59.1%) receive their health insurance either through their own or a family member's job. The rest of the insured population (27.0%) depend on government sponsored or privately purchased insurance.

However, having a job, even a full-time job, does not guarantee the provision of health insurance. In fact, as shown in **Table 8.29**, in 1990 almost one-half of the uninsured had some connection to the full-time/full-year workforce, and a minority of uninsured persons in each year were non-workers. The table shows the numbers and percentages of workers and their dependents without health insurance by their attachment to the labor force, 1988-1990. In 1988, 35.2% of the uninsured were full-year, full-time workers or their dependents. By 1990, this percentage had risen by 14.1 points, to 49.3%. Of the population of persons lacking health insurance in 1990, approximately 29.7 million persons, 85.7% of the uninsured, had some connection to the workforce.

Having a job does not guarantee the provision of health insurance . . . in 1990 almost one-half of the uninsured had some connection to the full-time/full-year workforce.

TABLE 8.30
Health Insurance Coverage of Workers, by Industry, 1989

	Percent Receiving Insurance from:			
Industry	Own Job	Other Source	Not Insured	Total
Agriculture, Forestry, and Fisheries	17.8%	54.0%	28.2%	100.0%
Personal Services, Including Household	22.7	52.8	24.5	100.0
Entertainment and Recreation Services	29.0	49.4	21.6	100.0
Retail Trade	31.8	47.9	20.3	100.0
Business and Repair Services	41.0	37.5	21.5	100.0
Construction	43.9	28.8	27.3	100.0
Professional and Related Services	55.6	35.7	8.7	100.0
Wholesale Trade	60.3	26.5	13.2	100.0
Finance, Insurance, and Real Estate	61.8	29.7	8.5	100.0
Manufacturing, Nondurable Goods	68.8	18.8	12.4	100.0
Transportation, Communications, and Public Utilities	73.5	16.6	9.9	100.0
Public Administration	73.9	21.1	5.0	100.0
Mining	76.0	14.1	9.9	100.0
Manufacturing, Durable Goods	77.1	14.2	8.7	100.0

TABLE 8.31
Employer Health Care Burden for the Average Business, 1980 and 1991

Health Care	1980	Percent of Total	1991	Percent of Total	Expenditure Change	Point Change	Percent Growth
Insurance	71,605	58.4	131,360	55.3	59,755	−3.1	83.5
Medicare Payroll Tax	19,437	15.9	39,204	16.5	19,767	0.6	101.7
General Taxes*	21,630	17.6	47,965	20.2	26,335	2.6	121.8
Other**	9,930	8.1	19,112	8.0	9,182	−0.1	92.5
Total Burden	$122,602	100.0%	$237,641	100.0%	$115,039	0.0	93.8%

*General taxes include federal contributions to Medicare and Medicaid, government contributions to employer-sponsored insurance, and other public health programs.

**Worker's compensation, temporary disability, and industrial health benefits.

One factor contributing to the high rates of those who are employed and uninsured is the job growth in industries that are less likely to provide their employees with health insurance. **Table 8.30** has the percentages of covered workers by industry, for the year 1989. Service sector firms, such as those in personal services, entertainment and recreation services, and retail trade have low rates of coverage (22.7%, 29.0%, and 31.8%, respectively) and correspondingly high rates of uninsured workers (24.5%, 21.6%, and 20.3%). As noted in Chapter 3, the employment share of these industries rapidly expanded over the 1980s. Manufacturing, an industry with a shrinking employment share, has traditionally high rates of coverage—77.1% for durable goods manufacturing in 1989, the highest rate of coverage in the table.

Another factor influencing the lack of coverage through employment is the rising health-care burden faced by businesses. Whereas Table 8.23 examines the family health-care burden, **Table 8.31** shows a similar analysis for businesses. Between 1980 and 1991, the total real cost of health-care provision rose by 93.8% for the average business, from $122,602 to $237,641. The largest growth came from the growth of health-care-related taxes, which grew 121.8%, and from increased contributions to the Medicare program, which grew 101.7%. Insurance costs, while representing a smaller share of the average 1991 business health-care burden (compared to 1980), grew by 83.5%. **Figure 8L** plots the growth of the total cost to employers of health insurance provision, 1965 to 1990. In real 1991 dollars, these costs grew from $23.7 billion in 1965 to $144.8 billion in 1990. The rising health-insurance expenditures reflect both the expanding size of the insured workforce and the rising costs of health insurance.

The health-care burden on families and businesses is greater in the United States than in the other OECD countries primarily due to our lack of public commitment to health-care provision. **Table 8.32** gives the percentage of public health expenditures in the 24 OECD countries, in 1989. At 42%, the U.S. has the second lowest level of public expenditures as a percent of all health-care spending. In Germany, public spending accounts for 72% of its health care budget; in France, 75%. Countries with well-developed national health plans have an even larger public commitment: the Swedish public sector covers 90% of that coun-

One factor contributing to the high rates of those who are employed and uninsured is the job growth in industries that are less likely to provide their employees with health insurance.

405

FIGURE 8L
Employer Spending on Private Health Insurance, 1965-1990

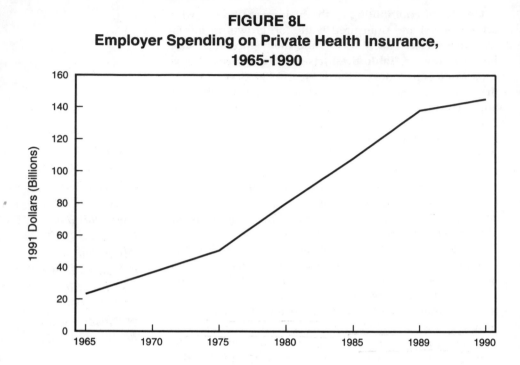

TABLE 8.32
Public Health Expenditures as a Percentage of
Total Health Expenditures, OECD Countries, 1989

Country	Public Spending 1989
Australia	70%
Austria	67
Belgium	89
Canada	75
Denmark	84
Finland	79
France	75
West Germany	72
Greece	89
Iceland	88
Ireland	84
Italy	79
Japan	73
Luxembourg	92
Netherlands	73
New Zealand	85
Norway	95
Portugal	62
Spain	78
Sweden	90
Switzerland	68
Turkey	37
United Kingdom	87
United States	**42**
Average	76

FIGURE 8M
Women in the Labor Force by Presence of Children, 1947-1991

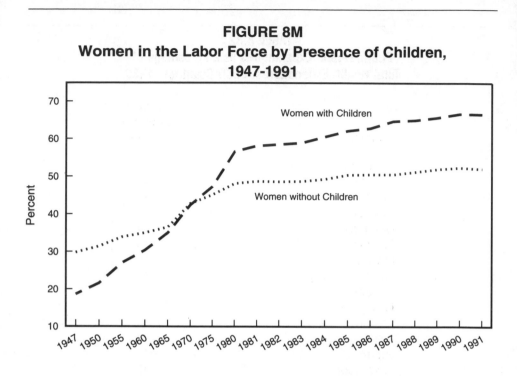

TABLE 8.33
Percent of Women with Children in the Labor Force, by Age of Child, 1950-1991

| Year | Total | Age of Child | |
		Under Age 6	Age 6 to 17
1950	21.6%	13.6%	32.8%
1960	30.4	20.2	42.5
1970	42.4	32.2	51.6
1980	56.6	46.8	64.3
1990	66.7	58.2	74.7
1991	66.6	58.4	74.4

try's health costs; the United Kingdom, 87%. Furthermore, it cannot be argued that the smaller proportion of private expenditures compromise the quality of health care in these countries with a greater public commitment. Each one of the five countries cited above surpasses the U.S. on the health indicators listed in Table 8.24.

Child Care: A Constraint on Working Parents

Earlier in this text, we documented the increasingly important role played by working spouses in maintaining family incomes. As more mothers enter the workforce, there has been a growing need for an essential corollary to mothers' workforce participation: child care. Along with this increased demand are a variety of concerns regarding the availability, the quality, and the costs of child care. Lack of affordable, high-quality child care can be a constraint, keeping mothers either out of the workforce or working for fewer hours than they would prefer (i.e., underemployed), or simply cutting into a family's resources and adding stress to family life. This constraint can be particularly severe for low-income families, who both need the extra earnings, and tend to earn less than better-educated, more experienced women. In fact, we will show that these low-income families tend to spend a higher proportion of their incomes on child care than wealthier families, and are therefore left with fewer resources to pay for other necessities.

Figure 8M demonstrates the important social and economic trend alluded to above: the dramatic increase of mothers in the labor force. Although a larger percentage of women without children than mothers worked (or sought work) in 1947, by 1970 the situation began to reverse. Over the course of the 1980s, the percentage of working mothers continued to grow, reaching two-thirds by 1991 (**Table 8.33**). Those mothers with children over age 6 have had the highest participation rates, as close to three-quarters of them were in the labor force in 1991. Clearly, a shrinking minority of mothers has come to provide full-time care for their children.

Since the primary responsibility for child care typically falls on women, research has focused on the impact of child-care constraints on mothers. This research has found

Mothers out-of-work due to child care were disproportionately poorly educated, lowering their potential to earn a wage that might have allowed them to purchase the very child care they needed to go out and work. Thus, they were stuck in a vicious cycle.

TABLE 8.34
Child-care Problems as a Constraint on Work, Women 21 to 29 Years Old, 1986

	Main Reason for Work Status			
	Child-care Problems		Other Problems	
Work Status	Number (000)	Percent	Number (000)	Percent
Never Employed	726	65.5%	1,519	42.0%
Underemployed*	383	34.5	2,098	58.0
Total	1,109	100.0	3,617	100.0

*Employed less than full-time or full-year even though preferring more hours of work.

TABLE 8.35
Mothers, 21 to 29 Years Old, Not in the Labor Force, by Selected Characteristics, 1986'

	Total, All Mothers Not in the Labor Force (000)	Mothers Not in the Labor Force Because of Child-care Problems	
Characteristics		Number (000)	As a Percent of All Mothers Not in the Labor Force
Total	4,726	1,109	23.5%
Race or Hispanic Origin*			
Hispanic Origin	433	176	40.6
Black	860	250	29.0
White	3,433	683	19.9
Total Number of Children			
One	1,854	376	20.3
Two	1,912	428	22.4
Three or More	961	305	31.8
Poverty Status			
At or below Poverty Line	1,217	414	34.0
Above Poverty Line	2,763	509	18.4
Educational Attainment			
No High School Diploma	1,157	372	32.2
High School Graduate	3,547	727	20.5

*In this table, race and Hispanic origin are mutually exclusive categories.

that for over one million mothers, difficulties attributable to child care kept them either under- or unemployed ("under-employed" refers to less than full-time/full-year workers who would have preferred to work more hours). **Table 8.34** shows the result of a national survey that asked mothers for the main reason why they were not working or were underemployed at any period in 1986, the year the survey was conducted. For mothers between the ages of 21 and 29, 1,109,000 answered that child-care problems restricted their labor force participation. The majority of these women (65.5%) never worked at all in the survey year and 34.5% were underemployed.

As **Table 8.35** shows, these women who were struggling to balance employment with day-care constraints, represent almost one-quarter of all mothers of this age range not in the 1986 labor force. Mothers who were kept out of the workforce by child-care problems in 1986 tended to be poor, minority, and with large families (3 or more children). Of those mothers not in the workforce because of child care, 34.0% were poor (about twice as many as those who were non-poor). Among non-working minority mothers, 40.6% of Hispanics and 29.0% of blacks reported child-care problems as keeping them out of the workforce. The percentage for whites, 19.9%, was substantially lower. Furthermore, mothers out-of-work due to child care were disproportionately poorly educated, lowering their potential to earn a wage that might have allowed them to purchase the very child care they needed to go out and work. Thus, they were stuck in a vicious cycle.

Child care can also present problems for women who *are* working, from lateness and absenteeism to job loss. **Table 8.36** shows that in 1988 a total of 3.7% of mothers missed work in a given month due to child-care problems. As might be expected, that proportion is higher for families with infants in child care (5.3%), since infants are likely to require more parental care. Wealthy parents (those earning an annual income of $50,000 or more in 1988), also lost more work than average, suggesting that child care is not exclusively a low-income problem. The final column of Table 8.36 shows that 2.3% of working mothers in 1988 actually left the labor force (voluntarily or otherwise) due to child-care problems. Again, loss of work is more common for women with infants (3.0%), as well as for women from low-income families.

Wealthy parents (those earning an annual income of $50,000 or more in 1988), also lost more work than average, suggesting that child care is not exclusively a low-income problem.

411

TABLE 8.36
Child-care Related Constraints on Women's Employment, 1988

	Mother (23-31) Missed Work w/in Last 4 Weeks Due to Child-care Problems	Mother (21-31) Dropped Out of Labor Force Because of Child-care Problems
Total	3.7%	2.3%
Age of Youngest Child		
Birth to 1 Year	5.3	3.0
2-4 Years	2.8	2.0
5 Years	3.4	2.0
Net Family Income (in 1988 Dollars)		
$0-14,999	3.7	4.2
$15,000-24,999	3.4	2.6
$25,000-49,999	3.1	1.6
$50,000 and more	4.7	0.3

FIGURE 8N
Distribution of Child-Care Choices for Preschool Children, 1965-1990

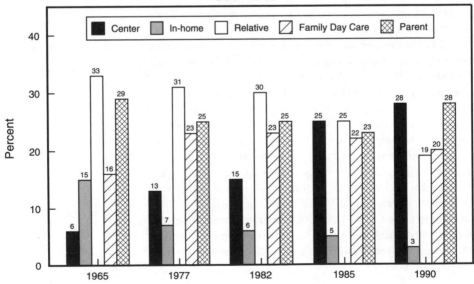

Child-Care Arrangements

Even in the context of the child-care induced constraint on women's labor force participation, Figure 8M shows that mothers have continued to enter the workforce. Families continue to find ways to see that their children are cared for when no family caretakers are available. The following section examines the different types of child-care arrangements, how they are utilized, and what they cost.

Child care is provided in a number of formats: child-care centers, family day-care homes (care for a small number of children in a care-giver's home), in-home care (care provided by a non-relative in the child's home), and care provided by a relative. **Figure 8N** shows the trend in the use of these different venues in selected years since 1965, for pre-schoolers (under age 5) in families with an employed mother. Each bar represents the proportion of families using a specific arrangement in the given year.

One of the most pronounced trends in Figure 8N is the increased proportion of families reliant on child-care centers, from 6% in 1965 to 28% in 1990, resulting from the increased proportion of working mothers with young children (see Table 8.33, column two). An associated trend is the fall in in-home care, from 15% to 3% over the period, and the fall in care provided by a relative, from 33% to 19%. A surprising trend is the recent increase in parent care. Given the known increase in labor force participation of mothers, this trend probably reflects the increased involvement of fathers in child care, as well as more flexible work scheduling by both parents.

Regarding availability, the demand for child care appears to have led to a growth in providers, although there is little reliable data on nation-wide availability. Nevertheless, the anecdotal evidence suggests that many parents have difficulty finding affordable, high-quality child care (costs are discussed below). A 1990 poll of mothers whose children were in child-care centers reported that more than half said they would have chosen another program had one been available. Infant care, which is both more costly and more labor intensive than average, appears to be in particularly short supply. From the late 1970s to 1990, the proportion of children under one year old in child-care centers went from 1% to 4%; for one- to two-year-olds, the proportion grew from 3% to 5%. In New York City in 1987, licensed providers could accommodate only 6% of the children

In New York City in 1987, licensed providers could accommodate only 6% of the children aged two or younger who needed care.

413

TABLE 8.37
Average Percentage of Family Income Spent on Child Care,
by Family Income, 1990*
(1990 Dollars)

	Percent Paying For Care	Average Weekly Cost	Percent of Income Spent on Care
Total	57.0%	$63.2	10.4%
Poverty Status			
Below Poverty	n.a.	37.3	23.2
Above Poverty	n.a.	65.5	8.7
Annual Family Income			
Less than $15,000	42.0	37.9	24.8
$15-24,999	48.0	50.7	13.2
$25-34,999	52.0	50.7	8.8
$35-49,999	54.0	64.5	10.2
$50,000 or more	68.0	85.1	6.2

*Data is for employed mothers with youngest child under five.

aged two or younger who needed care. In Connecticut in 1990, fewer than one-third of the licensed centers or family day-care homes would accept infants.

There is also a lack of hard data on the quality of the child care provided in the various settings noted above. Although those centers and family day-care homes that are licensed are required to meet state regulations, the Children's Defense Fund estimates that as many as 43% of the children in child-care situations outside their homes are in unregulated settings. Such settings are likely to be understaffed, with poor health standards and poorly trained staffs.

Moreover, simply the fact that a child-care setting is regulated does not insure quality care. Research on individual sites has found that in certain locales, regulations are so lax that even licensed providers deliver below-standard care. A study on licensed centers in Atlanta, Georgia found preschoolers to be ignored 79% of the time; infants, 61% of the time. Other states' regulations do not require children to be immunized against contagious diseases, or allow for excessively low staff to child ratios. A national study examining trends between the mid-1970s and 1990 found that the average number of children enrolled in centers increased by 39% over that period, while staffs increased by an average 25%. This trend has lowered the staff to child ratio in licensed centers. In addition, thirty-five states require no training for child-care staff members.

The Costs of Child Care

The costs of child care for employed mothers with preschoolers are examined in **Table 8.37**. Most families with children under five (57%) were paying for child care in 1990, and wealthy families were paying a smaller percentage of their income than middle- and low-income families. In fact, low-income families spent as much as one-quarter of their income for child care, significantly constraining their family budgets.

The likelihood of purchasing child care rises with income both because wealthier families have more resources to purchase child care, and because they work more hours. Less than half (42%) of the families with low incomes purchased child care while over two-thirds (68%) of wealthy families did so in 1990. Although families with

For a single parent working full-time at the minimum wage, with a one-year-old, child care uses between 44.4% and 69.6% of their income.

415

TABLE 8.38
Child-Care Cost Burden, as Percentage of Income for Low- and Middle-Income Families: Licensed Centers in Four Cities, 1990

Cities	One-year-old Child				Four-year-old Child			
	Low Income*		Middle Income**		Low Income*		Middle Income**	
	Single Parent	Two Parents	Single Parent	Two Parents	Single Parent	Two Parents	Single Parent	Two Parents
Oakland, CA	60.8%	32.8%	27.5%	13.7%	50.9%	27.5%	23.0%	11.5%
Boulder, CO	69.6	37.5	33.7	17.0	47.1	25.4	22.8	11.5
Dallas, TX	41.1	22.2	22.4	11.4	35.6	19.2	19.4	9.9
Orlando, FL	44.4	23.9	24.4	12.5	32.9	18.1	18.1	9.3

*One (in the case of single parents) or both parents working full-time/full-year at the minimum wage.
**One (in the case of single parents) or both parents working full-time/full-year at the state-specific median wage.

416

incomes over $50,000 spent more in absolute terms on child care than other families, their expenditures, on average, amounted to only 6.2% of their income. Conversely, the least well-off families, those with incomes under $15,000, spent 24.8% of their annual income on child care.

In addition, costs vary by regional location, by the age of the child under care, and by child-care setting. **Table 8.38** has the percentage of family income required to send a one- or four-year-old child to a licensed center in four different cities in 1990, for one- and two-parent families. For a single parent working full-time at the minimum wage, with a one-year-old, child care is clearly prohibitive, using up between 44.4% and 69.6% of their income. The situation is not much better if the child is four (thereby requiring less expensive care); the expenditure still calls for between 32.9% and 50.9% of income. Even for middle-income single parents (working full-time at the median wage in that state) with a one-year-old, child-care costs between 22.4% and 33.7% of income. For two low-income parents, child-care costs require approximately one-fifth to one-third of family income. Only for two middle-income parents, both working full-time, do child-care expenditures potentially leave enough income left over for other necessities. For such a family in Dallas or Orlando, child care for a four-year-old requires slightly less than 10% of family income. However, if this family had a one-year-old in Boulder, the expenditure would call for 17.0% of family income.

In sum, as the proportion of mothers entering the workforce has risen, so has the use of child care become a necessity for the majority of families with young children. While the supply of child-care services has grown in response to the demand, anecdotal data suggest that there are problems with the availability and quality of child care. Furthermore, expenditures on child care are regressive: though low-income families pay less in absolute terms than wealthy families, in relative terms (proportion of income) they pay substantially more. Finally, child care can serve as a constraint on the workforce participation of mothers. Both low- and high-income families report that child-care problems have cost them time at work.

For two low-income parents, child-care costs require approximately one-fifth to one-third of family income.

Conclusion

Our examination of those services vital to a rising standard of living reveal a trend of decreased access for most families. Our education system is found to be two-tiered: disadvantaged students score poorly on tests of basic skills compared to their more wealthy counterparts. Further, blacks and Hispanics account for well under 10% of the advanced degrees in 1989 (Table 8.9). The housing market over the 1980s has been characterized by rising costs as a proportion of income for persons trying to enter the market, leading to home ownership rates that fell as much as 8 percentage points for young families (Table 8.17). Regarding health care, the American system is the most costly in the world, yet our health indicators show us behind most industrialized countries. Our health-care system also leaves a substantial number of persons uninsured or partially insured. Finally, the sharp rise of mothers in the workforce has led to a growing need for child care. However, the costs of child care are prohibitive for many mothers; even middle-class families report that child care is a constraint on their workforce participation.

> *Our examination of those services vital to a rising standard of living reveal a trend of decreased access for most families.*

Why not greater supply of child care?

418

Chapter 9

International Comparisons: The United States is Falling Behind

Introduction

In this chapter we examine how American workers and their families have fared in comparison to their foreign counterparts. While Americans still have the highest per capita income as measured by relative purchasing power, many indicators of economic well-being still show the U.S. to be falling behind. Compared to other countries, U.S. productivity growth has been relatively stagnant. Likewise, wage growth (which is related to productivity) has been sluggish, while other countries have seen strong growth. Finally, though the U.S. economy seemed to have a faster rate of job growth than other countries over the 1980s, taking account of population growth, other countries have had higher rates of job creation.

The growth of U.S. income inequality documented throughout this text is also notable in an international context. Poverty in the U.S. is both higher and more persistent than in other countries. Furthermore, the U.S. tax and transfer system has become *less* effective at poverty reduction over the 1980s, while the systems of other countries have grown *more* effective.

Incomes and Productivity: Sluggish Growth in the U.S.

One widely accepted measure of living standards is per capita Gross Domestic Product (GDP): the total value of

While Americans still have the highest per capita income as measured by relative purchasing power, many indicators of economic well-being still show the U.S. to be falling behind.

TABLE 9.1
Per Capita GDP Growth in Ten Countries, 1979-1989, Broken Down into Growth of Employment and Productivity

Country	Growth Rate of Real per Capita GDP, 1979-1989	Percent of Growth Due to		
		More Workers	Higher Productivity	Total
Australia	1.8%	48%	52%	100%
Canada	2.0	42	58	100
France	1.6	−24	124	100
West Germany	1.6	34	66	100
Italy	2.2	9	91	100
Japan	3.3	16	84	100
Netherlands	1.0	74	26	100
Sweden	1.8	34	66	100
United Kingdom	2.1	19	81	100
United States	**1.8**	**40**	**60**	**100**
Weighted Average*	2.1	24	76	100

*Weighted by each country's population, which is taken to be the average of the populations of 1979 and 1989.

goods and services produced in the domestic economy divided by the population. Growth of per capita GDP is considered an essential component of rising living standards. Such growth comes from two sources: greater output per worker (i.e., higher productivity), and sending more workers into the workforce (i.e., expanding the ratio of employment to the population). Since sending more workers into the workforce (and/or working longer hours) can lower living standards, it is important to decompose GDP growth into these two factors. **Table 9.1** does so by examining the growth of GDP over the 1980s for the seven major industrialized countries, as well as for three others for whom there are comparable data.

Column one of Table 9.1 shows the annual growth rates of real per capita GDP for the years 1979-1989. Although GDP per person in the United States rose over the decade, it grew at a below average pace (1.8% versus 2.1%), meaning other countries' per capita incomes were rising faster than ours. At 1.8%, the growth rate for the U.S. was below the growth rates sustained by Canada (2.0%), Italy (2.2%), and the United Kingdom (2.1%), and was almost half of Japan's rate (3.3%).

Of equal importance is whether per capita growth of GDP is generated through higher productivity or through an increase in the proportion of the population in the workforce. In general, if productivity growth is strong and wages rise accordingly, families can live better without sending more workers into the workforce; if it is weak, living standards can rise only if more people work (or those working put in longer hours). Columns two and three of Table 9.1 show that a relatively large part of our per capita income growth (40%) comes from more workers—increasing the proportion of the employed population. Only three countries have a higher percentage of their growth rate coming from this source. The U.S. rate of growth attributable to more workers is also well above the ten-country average of 24%. Conversely, the U.S. percentage of growth attributable to higher productivity (60%) is well below the average of 76%.

Although GDP per person in the United States rose over the decade, it grew at a below average pace, meaning other countries' per capita incomes were rising faster than ours.

421

TABLE 9.2
Living Standards vs. Productivity Growth, 1979-1989

Country	Indices of 1979-89 Growth Rates (Weighted Average = 100)	
	Real per Capita GDP	Productivity (GDP/Worker)
Australia	88	61
Canada	98	75
France	77	127
West Germany	77	67
Italy	105	126
Japan	159	176
Netherlands	46	16
Sweden	86	76
United Kingdom	99	106
United States	**86**	**67**
Weighted Average*	100	100

*Weighted by each country's population, which is taken to be the average of the populations of 1979 and 1989.

TABLE 9.3
Productivity Growth Rates, 1960-1989

Country	1960-1967	1967-1973	1973-1979	1979-1989	Cumulative 1960-1989*
Australia	n.a.	2.8%	1.7%	1.0%	1.7%
Canada	2.7%	2.6	1.2	1.2	1.8
France	5.1	4.2	2.4	2.0	3.1
West Germany	4.6	4.3	2.9	1.1	2.8
Italy	7.1	5.0	2.8	2.0	3.8
Japan	9.1	7.7	3.4	2.8	5.1
Netherlands	n.a.	n.a.	0.0	0.2	0.2
Sweden	4.7	2.8	0.6	1.2	2.1
United Kingdom	2.7	3.3	1.3	1.7	2.1
United States	**3.1**	**1.0**	**−0.1**	**1.1**	**1.2**

*Netherlands: 1973-1989; Australia: 1967-1989.

Table 9.2 provides a direct comparison of per capita GDP and productivity growth rates. Column one shows that the U.S. per capita income grew at 86% of the average rate, as suggested by the data in Table 9.1. However, our productivity rate grew at an even slower relative pace, at 67% of the average. Japan, on the other hand, saw its per capita income grow at 159% of the average rate, fueled by productivity growth that was 176% of the average. In fact, only two countries—Australia and the Netherlands—posted lower productivity growth rates than the U.S.

The above tables have emphasized the importance of worker productivity (GDP per worker) to our standard of living. **Table 9.3** presents the average annual growth rates of this important statistic for various periods, 1960-1989. The growth rates for the U.S. are relatively low; for the cumulative period the U.S. rate is the second lowest in the table. U.S. productivity was at its highest between 1960 and 1967, when it grew at an annual rate of 3.1%. Since that time, it has fallen precipitously and was even negative between 1973 and 1979.

The rates for other countries have also slowed down over the period, though all but the growth rate of the Netherlands remain higher than that of the U.S. (**Figure 9A**). Japan's productivity fell from an average annual rate of 9.1% between 1960 and 1967, to 2.8% over the most recent period. Similarly, West Germany's rate fell from 4.6% to 1.1%. However, even in the context of this general slowdown, the majority of the other countries still had faster productivity growth rates than those of the U.S. since 1973.

Only two countries— Australia and the Netherlands— posted lower productivity growth rates than the U.S.

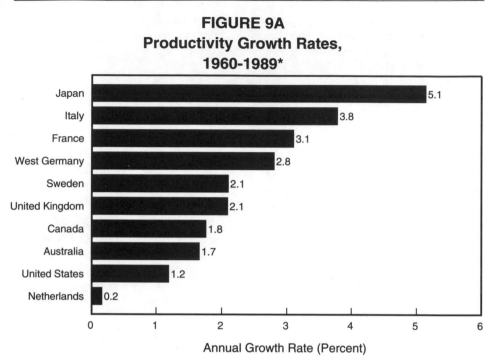

FIGURE 9A
Productivity Growth Rates, 1960-1989*

Annual Growth Rate (Percent)

*Netherlands: 1973-1989; Australia: 1967-1989.

TABLE 9.4
Hourly Manufacturing Compensation Growth, 1979-1989

Country	Growth Rate of Compensation in Manufacturing, 1979-1989	
	All Employees	Production Workers
Canada	0.4%	0.5%
Denmark	−0.1	0.3
France	1.7	2.1
West Germany	2.4	1.8
Italy	0.9	0.6
Japan	1.8	1.3
Netherlands	0.8	0.9
Sweden	0.5	0.9
United Kingdom	2.0	1.7
United States	**0.2**	**−0.6**

Wages: Falling for Production Workers

Given that wage growth is in part dependent on productivity growth, we would expect to see U.S. wages reflect the relatively stagnant growth of productivity presented above. In fact, **Table 9.4** and **Figure 9B** reveal that the U.S. annual growth rate for hourly manufacturing compensation (wages plus fringe benefits) is well behind that of most comparable nations. (The only comparative data are from the manufacturing sector.)

Between 1979 and 1989, real hourly manufacturing compensation in the U.S. grew at an average annual rate of 0.2%. Only Denmark had a lower growth rate, at -0.1%. Meanwhile, compensation in West Germany grew at an average rate of 2.4% a year, ten times the U.S. growth rate. Furthermore, what little growth U.S. manufacturing wages experienced benefitted only supervisors and managers.

What little growth U.S. manufacturing wages experienced benefitted only supervisors and managers. Production workers saw their compensation fall at a rate of 0.6% a year.

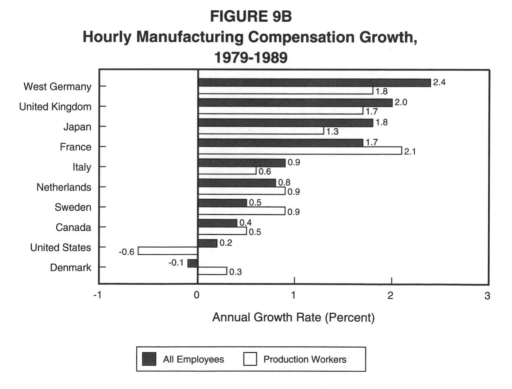

FIGURE 9B
Hourly Manufacturing Compensation Growth, 1979-1989

TABLE 9.5
Manufacturing Hourly Compensation Compared, 1979, 1989, and 1990
(Using Purchasing Power Parity Exchange Rates)

Country	1979	1989	1990
All Workers			
Canada	81	84	86
Denmark	68	64	65
France	86	94	93
West Germany	82	94	96
Italy	80	77	79
Japan	48	55	57
Netherlands	96	98	97
Sweden	83	79	78
United Kingdom	62	69	71
United States	**100**	**100**	**100**
Average*	68	73	74
Production Workers			
Canada	82	92	97
Denmark	76	77	80
France	69	85	85
West Germany	94	111	113
Italy	92	93	94
Japan	51	61	63
Netherlands	95	106	104
Sweden	82	89	90
United Kingdom	64	75	77
United States	**100**	**100**	**100**
Average*	71	80	83

*Averages are weighted by hours worked; they exclude the United States.

Production workers saw their compensation fall at a rate of 0.6% a year. The U.S. was the only country whose production workers experienced wage loss during this period.

Whereas Table 9.4 examined the growth rates of manufacturing compensation, the next two tables compare the actual levels of compensation, indexed to the U.S. In order to make such comparisons, we first converted wages from their national currency into dollars, using two different exchange rate series: Purchasing Power Parity exchange rates (PPP's) and market exchange rates. PPP's are currency values intended to measure the cost of buying the same "basket" of goods and services in all countries. Market exchange rates represent the value of the dollar relative to other currencies in world financial markets. While both exchange-rate-measures have their drawbacks, the PPP's are commonly considered an indicator of the relative price of consumption. Market exchange rates reflect the relative value of American goods, services (including labor), and assets in international markets.

When we use PPP's to adjust for currency differences, as in **Table 9.5**, U.S. compensation ranks the highest. However, by 1989, France, West Germany, and the Netherlands had compensation levels that were 94%, 94%, and 98%, respectively, of the U.S. levels for all workers. Moreover, other countries gained on the U.S. throughout the 1980s, as seen by the rise in the "All Workers" averages (averages in this and the next table exclude the U.S.), from 68% of U.S. compensation to 74%. Given the findings in Table 9.4 regarding the falling compensation of U.S. production workers, it is not surprising that production workers in two countries have surpassed the U.S. in this category (**Figure 9C** shows the PPP adjusted wages). By 1989, production workers in West Germany and the Netherlands had higher levels of compensation than their American counterparts, by 11% and 6%, respectively.

When we use market exchange rates (**Table 9.6**), the story changes significantly: American workers no longer lead the pack. Since 1979, workers in many countries (and production workers in *most* countries) have received higher hourly compensation than U.S. workers. The average hourly compensation for non-managerial (i.e., production) workers was only 6% below that of the U.S. in 1989. By

By 1989, production workers in West Germany and the Netherlands had higher levels of compensation than their American counterparts, by 11% and 6%, respectively.

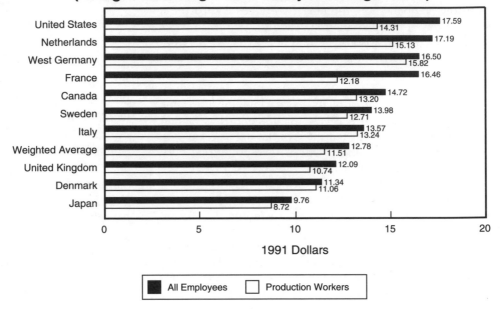

FIGURE 9C
Comparative Manufacturing Compensation, 1989
(Using Purchasing Power Parity Exchange Rates)

Country	All Employees	Production Workers
United States	17.59	14.31
Netherlands	17.19	15.13
West Germany	16.50	15.82
France	16.46	12.18
Canada	14.72	13.20
Sweden	13.98	12.71
Italy	13.57	13.24
Weighted Average	12.78	11.51
United Kingdom	12.09	10.74
Denmark	11.34	11.06
Japan	9.76	8.72

1991 Dollars

■ All Employees   □ Production Workers

TABLE 9.6
Manufacturing Hourly Compensation Compared, 1979, 1989, and 1990
(Using Market Exchange Rates)

Country	1979	1989	1990
All Workers			
Canada	83	93	96
Denmark	105	84	99
France	105	98	113
West Germany	110	104	123
Italy	69	77	93
Japan	57	80	77
Netherlands	127	100	115
Sweden	127	110	123
United Kingdom	60	62	77
United States	**100**	**100**	**100**
Average*	78	85	93
Production Workers			
Canada	84	103	108
Denmark	117	101	121
France	85	89	103
West Germany	125	123	146
Italy	79	92	111
Japan	61	88	86
Netherlands	126	109	123
Sweden	126	123	142
United Kingdom	62	67	84
United States	**100**	**100**	**100**
Average*	82	94	104

*Averages are weighted by hours worked; they exclude the United States.

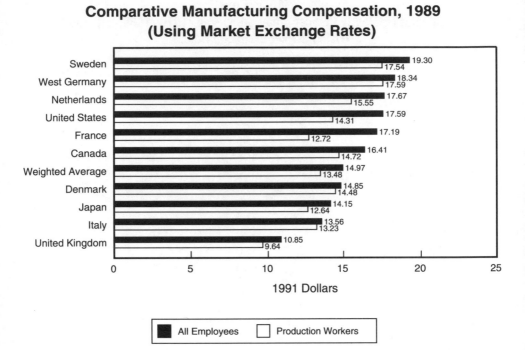

FIGURE 9D
Comparative Manufacturing Compensation, 1989
(Using Market Exchange Rates)

1991 Dollars

All Employees   Production Workers

1990, the U.S. was 4% *below* the average; production workers in West Germany and Sweden were earning 146% and 142% of the U.S. production worker's earnings, respectively (**Figure 9D** shows the wages adjusted by market exchange rates). As market exchange rates reflect the relative attractiveness of U.S. products in international markets, the comparisons in this table further underscore the charge that the U.S. is becoming a low-wage country (see Chapter 3).

These wage data make two important points regarding the economic position of the U.S. in international markets. Firstly, we have had to let the market value of the dollar decline in order to offset our competitive decline. This has caused the earnings of U.S. workers to fall relative to workers of other countries. Secondly, these data suggest that the trade imbalances we have with many of these countries cannot be blamed on an overpaid U.S. workforce.

Poverty: Highest and Most Persistent in the U.S.

In discussions of America's relative prosperity, much is often made of our high per capita income. **Table 9.7** shows per capita income adjusted by PPP's and indexed to the U.S. Indeed, our per capita income was the highest in 1979 and 1989, although the rising averages (exclusive of the U.S.) show the other countries to be gaining on us. However, a per capita income comparison contrasts the "average" person in each country. Given different degrees of income inequality, this average measure reveals little about how persons in the different countries are faring.

To make such comparisons, we need to examine evidence of how income is distributed throughout each economy. In **Table 9.8**, the after-tax income distributions of nine industrialized countries are presented, with the percentage of the poor and near-poor, the middle class, and the well-to-do given for each country. These data, from the mid-1980s, show the U.S. to have the most unequal distribution, after taxes and transfers. At one end of the scale, we find that the middle class in the U.S. is the smallest (53.7%); the low-income class is the largest (24.2%). West Germany and the Scandinavian countries have much greater income equality, with relatively large middle classes and smaller low-income and wealthy classes. At the other end of the scale, the U.S. has the third largest wealthy class.

These data suggest that the trade imbalances we have with many of these countries cannot be blamed on an overpaid U.S. workforce.

TABLE 9.7
Per Capita Income Compared to U.S., 1973-1989

Country	Per Capita Incomes Adjusted for Purchasing Power (U.S. = 100)		
	1973	1979	1989
Australia	74	75	74
Canada	80	88	90
Denmark	76	77	77
France	77	81	79
West Germany	79	85	83
Italy	63	70	73
Japan	63	67	78
Netherlands	75	77	71
Norway	58	70	73
Sweden	78	79	79
Switzerland	107	97	97
United Kingdom	70	71	73
United States	**100**	**100**	**100**
Weighted Average*	71	75	78

*Weighted by population, excluding U.S.

TABLE 9.8
Income Distribution: International Comparisons, Mid-1980s

All Persons	Poor and Near-Poor	Middle Class	Well-to-Do	Total
Australia	21.4%	56.0%	22.6%	100.0%
Canada	21.0	58.5	20.6	100.0
West Germany	12.6	70.1	17.3	100.0
Netherlands	14.2	62.5	23.3	100.0
Norway	13.2	73.4	13.4	100.0
Sweden	10.5	79.0	10.5	100.0
Switzerland	15.9	67.2	16.9	100.0
United Kingdom	21.4	58.5	20.2	100.0
United States	**24.2**	**53.7**	**22.1**	**100.0**
Average	17.2	64.3	18.5	100.0

*Income is post-tax and transfer, and is adjusted for family size. Poor and near-poor have income up to 62.5% of the median income for that country. Middle class is between 62.5% and 150%; well-to-do is above 150% of median income.

This means that, relative to these other countries, American incomes are distributed much more unevenly, with a greater proportion of Americans having relatively low incomes, proportionately fewer with middle-class incomes, and with a larger group of well-off families relative to most other countries.

Another important measure of income inequality is the extent of poverty. Chapter 6 presented an analysis of the problem of poverty in the U.S. In this section, we introduce an international perspective and examine both the extent of poverty in other countries, and how those countries have responded. We find that American poverty rates are the highest, and that our system of social protection is the weakest.

The next three tables examine poverty rates in the late 1970s and the mid-1980s, the years of available data. The poverty lines used are 40% of median income in each country, a relative definition of poverty (Chapter 6 discusses this approach to measuring poverty), producing a poverty threshold close to the official U.S. poverty lines in the mid-1980s. Since the levels of income and wealth vary significantly between countries, a relative threshold is essential to international comparisons. Like the official U.S. definition, these rates take cash transfers into account and are adjusted for family size, but unlike the U.S. definition, these data also account for taxes and the value of food stamps.

Table 9.9 has the poverty rates from eight industrialized countries, for all persons, all adults (age 18-64), and children (17 and under). The U.S. poverty rates are by far the highest for each category. In the broadest category, 13.3% of all Americans were poor in 1986, nearly twice the percentage as in the next highest country (Canada), and 2.3 times the average level of 5.9%. As noted in Chapter 6, American child poverty is particularly high. At 20.4%, the U.S. child poverty rate is almost three times the average rate of 7.4%.

The next table, **Table 9.10**, examines the impact of the tax and transfer systems of the various countries, for the same categories as in the previous table. The "Pre" columns give the poverty rates generated by the market, prior to the introduction of taxes and transfers. Thus, these percentages represent the degree of poverty that would exist with no government intervention.

The U.S. poverty rates are by far the highest for each category.

433

TABLE 9.9
International Poverty Statistics

| Country | Poverty Rates in the Mid-1980s | | |
	All Persons	All Adults (18-64)	All Children (17 or under)
Australia	6.7%	6.16%	9.0%
Canada	7.0	7.0	9.3
France	4.5	5.2	4.6
West Germany	2.8	2.6	2.8
Netherlands	3.4	3.9	3.8
Sweden	4.3	6.6	1.6
United Kingdom	5.2	5.3	7.4
United States	**13.3**	**10.5**	**20.4**
Average	5.9%	5.9%	7.4%
Ratio of U.S. to Average	2.3	1.8	2.8

TABLE 9.10
The Impact of Taxes and Transfers on
International Poverty Rates, Mid-1980s

| Country | All Persons | | | Adults (18-64) | | | Children (17 or under) | | |
	Pre*	Post*	Point Change	Pre*	Post*	Point Change	Pre*	Post*	Point Change
Australia	19.1%	6.7%	−12.4	12.9%	6.1%	−6.8	16.4%	9.0%	−7.4
Canada	17.1	7.0	−10.1	11.5	7.0	−4.5	15.7	9.3	−6.4
France	26.4	4.5	−21.9	17.6	5.2	−12.4	21.1	4.6	−16.5
West Germany	21.6	2.8	−18.8	9.8	2.6	−7.2	8.4	2.8	−5.6
Netherlands	21.5	3.4	−18.1	17.4	3.9	−13.5	14.1	3.8	−10.3
Sweden	25.9	4.3	−21.6	13.4	6.6	−6.8	7.9	1.6	−6.3
United Kingdom	27.7	5.2	−22.5	18.1	5.3	−12.8	27.9	7.4	−20.5
United States	**19.9**	**13.3**	**−6.6**	**12.8**	**10.5**	**−2.3**	**22.3**	**20.4**	**−1.9**
Average	22.4%	5.9%	−16.5	14.2%	5.9%	−8.3	16.7%	7.4%	−9.3

*"Pre" refers to pre-tax, pre-transfer income; "post" refers to post-tax, post-transfer income.

434

The extent of market-generated poverty in these eight industrialized countries is quite alarming (**Figure 9E**). On average, over one-fifth of all persons were poor prior to government intervention. In France, the United Kingdom, and Sweden, that proportion rises to over one-fourth. To some degree, these high overall rates are driven by exceptionally high poverty rates of elderly persons (not shown), but the rates for adults and particularly children are also disturbingly high. Interestingly, by this measure, the U.S. rates are relatively low (with the notable exception of child poverty). The U.S. pre-tax and transfer poverty rate for all persons, 19.9%, is higher only than Canada and Australia, and below the average rate of 22.4%.

However, the post-tax and transfer column tells quite a different story. Here, the U.S. rates are the *highest in all cases*. Clearly, our market outcomes, while leaving one-fifth of all persons impoverished, generate relatively less poverty than most other countries. Nevertheless, it is equally clear that our system of taxes and transfers is much less

Our system of taxes and transfers is much less effective in reducing poverty than that of any other country.

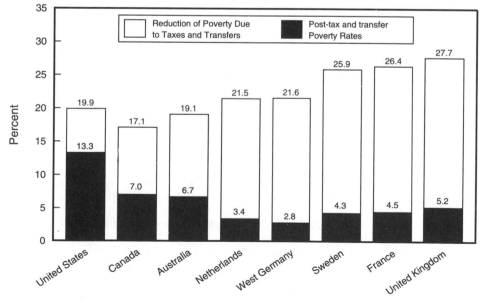

FIGURE 9E
Impact of Taxes and Transfers on Poverty Rates, Mid-1980s

435

TABLE 9.11
Tax and Transfer System Effectiveness, Early to Mid-1980s

	United States			Average of Other Nations*		
	1979	1986	Point Change	Period 1	Period 2	Point Change
All Persons						
Pre**	18.5%	19.9%	1.4	20.6%	21.6%	1.0
Post**	10.8	13.3	2.5	5.7	6.0	0.3
Point Change	−7.7	−6.6	1.1	−14.9	−15.6	−0.7
Percentage of Poverty Reduced	41.6%	33.2%		72.3%	72.2%	
Adults (18-64)						
Pre**	11.2%	12.8%	1.6	12.6%	13.6%	1.0
Post**	8.3	10.5	2.2	5.6	6.0	0.4
Point Change	−2.9	−2.3	0.6	−7.0	−7.6	−0.6
Percentage of Poverty Reduced	25.9%	18.0%		55.6%	55.9%	
Children (17 or Under)						
Pre**	19.0%	22.3%	3.3	13.7%	15.1%	1.4
Post**	14.7	20.4	5.7	6.5	7.4	0.9
Point Change	−4.3	−1.9	2.4	−7.2	−7.7	−0.5
Percentage of Poverty Reduced	22.6%	8.5%		52.6%	51.0%	

*Average of Canada, Australia, Sweden, Germany, Netherlands, and France. Period 1 is either 1979 or 1981, except for Netherlands (1983). Period 2 is either 1986 or 1987, except for France and Germany (1984).

**"Pre" refers to pre-tax, pre-transfer income; "post" refers to post-tax, post-transfer income.

effective in reducing poverty than that of any other country.

The effect of taxes and transfers is shown in the point change columns of Table 9.10, and in the lighter area in the bars of Figure 9E. For example, in the United Kingdom, the market economy of the mid-1980s left 27.7% of all persons poor. However, after taxes and benefits, the U.K. poverty rate fell to 5.2%, a change of 22.5 percentage points. By this measure of poverty reduction, the U.S. is an extreme laggard. For all persons, our redistribution system lowered poverty by only 6.6 points, well below the average reduction of 16.5 points. For adults, poverty was reduced by a lesser amount, 2.3 points (note, however, that all countries show less poverty reduction for adults). For U.S. children, poverty barely fell at all (1.9 points). This is in stark contrast to the child poverty reduction of the other countries, where poverty was reduced between 5.6 and 20.5 points.

Table 9.11 introduces changes over time into the analysis, examining changes between two periods (see table for the description of the time periods). The table compares the U.S. to the average of the other countries in the study, omitting the U.K. due to lack of data from the earlier year. The first point that may be seen in the table is that poverty worsened over the 1980s in all countries for each category, both in pre- and post-transfer terms. However, turning to a comparison of the U.S. and the average of the other countries, we find that poverty reduction is not only less effective in the U.S., as shown in the previous table, it has become even worse over time. In contrast, poverty reduction in other countries has grown more effective.

This point is made in the point change column of Table 9.11. For example, in the U.S. in 1986, the market left 1.4% more persons in poverty than in 1979. After taxes and transfers, 2.5% more persons were poor in 1986 compared to 1979. Thus, poverty reduction was 1.1 (2.5 minus 1.4) percentage points less effective in 1986 as in 1979. Similarly, U.S. poverty reduction was slightly less effective for adults (0.6 points) and significantly less effective for children (2.4 points). Turning to the average of the other countries, we observe an opposite trend. For all persons, poverty was reduced by an extra 0.7 percentage points for all persons in Period 2 as compared to Period 1. For adults and children, poverty reduction was 0.6 and 0.5 points, respectively, more effective in the latter period. Thus, although

Poverty reduction is not only less effective in the U.S., it has become even worse over time. In contrast, poverty reduction in other countries has grown more effective.

437

TABLE 9.12
Poverty Rates and Transitions Out of Poverty
for Families with Children, Mid-1980s

Country	Poverty Rate*	Transition Rate**	Percent of Families Poor in All 3 Years of a 3-year Period
Canada	17.0%	12.0%	11.9%
France-Lorraine	4.0	27.5	1.6
West Germany			
All	7.8	25.6	1.5
German	6.7	26.9	1.4
Foreign	18.0	20.0	4.0
Ireland	11.0	25.2	n.a.
Luxembourg	4.4	26.0***	0.4
Netherlands	2.7	44.4	0.4
Sweden	2.7	36.8	n.a.
United States			
All	20.3	13.8	14.4
White	15.3	17.0	9.5
Black	49.3	7.7	41.5

*Percent of families with income below 50% of that country's median income in year one.

**Percent of families who were poor in year one who had more than 60% of median income in year two.

***Based on 10-30 cases.

438

markets were generating more poverty abroad, the tax and transfer systems lessened the ultimate outcomes so that poverty rose only slightly.

A more encompassing measure is shown in Table 9.11 as the percentage of poverty reduced. If we consider pre-tax and transfer poverty to be the total amount of poverty that the redistributive system can effect, then the percentage of poverty reduced is the ratio of the point change to the poverty induced by the market, expressed as a percent. The table shows a smaller *percentage* reduction of pre-tax and transfer poverty in the U.S. than in other countries. In addition, this percentage fell over time in the U.S., while holding constant elsewhere. For all Americans in 1979, 41.6% of the pre-transfer poor were lifted out of poverty by taxes and transfers, but in 1986, this percentage fell to 33.2%. In the other nations, the percentage of poverty reduced was both much higher than the U.S. and essentially the same in both periods. For example, in the average foreign nation, child poverty was reduced 52.6% in Period 1 and 51.0% in Period 2. In the U.S., child poverty was reduced a much smaller 22.6% in 1979, and an even smaller 8.5% in 1986.

In the average foreign nation, child poverty was reduced 52.6% in Period 1 and 51.0% in Period 2. In the U.S., child poverty was reduced a much smaller 22.6% in 1979, and an even smaller 8.5% in 1986.

Comparing Economic Mobility Between Countries

In Chapter 6, we note that poverty is a dynamic, rather than a static, phenomenon. Research on the length of time spent poor has found a great deal of transition into and out of poverty. In **Table 9.12** and **Figure 9F**, we present the results of an international study of the economic mobility of poor families with children in the mid-1980s, enabling us to compare U.S. economic mobility to that of other countries. As above, a relative definition of poverty is applied; however, in this analysis, the poverty lines are set at 50% of median income (the previous tables used 40% of the median income as the standard; again, income is post-tax and transfer and adjustments are made for family size).

The first column of Table 9.12 gives the poverty rates for families with children in the countries in this study. Once again, the U.S. rates are the highest; this is particularly the case for black families, whose poverty rate was 49.3%.

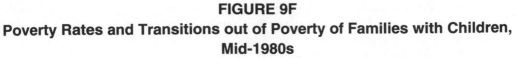

FIGURE 9F
Poverty Rates and Transitions out of Poverty of Families with Children, Mid-1980s

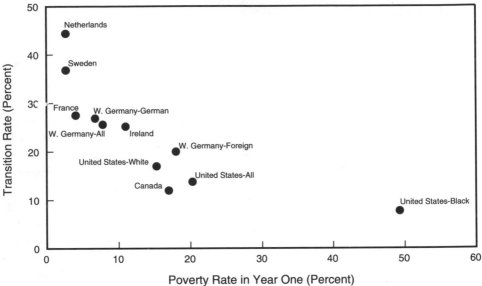

TABLE 9.13
Absolute Poverty Among
Children, Adults, and the Elderly, 1979-1982

Absolute Poverty	Poverty Rates in Poor Families			
	Children	Adults	Elderly	Overall
Australia	16.9%	10.5%	19.2%	13.2%
Canada	9.6	7.5	4.8	7.4
West Germany	8.2	6.5	15.4	8.3
Norway	7.6	7.1	18.7	8.6
Sweden	5.1	6.7	2.1	5.6
Switzerland	5.1	6.2	6.0	5.8
United Kingdom	10.7	6.9	37.0	11.8
United States	**17.1**	**10.1**	**16.1**	**12.7**

However, it is the second and third columns in which we are most interested, as here (column two) we find the percent of poor families in year t, who escaped poverty by year t + 1 ("t" refers to year one or two of the study; t + 1 refers to years two or three), and the percent of families who were poor for three consecutive years (column three).

The horizontal axis of Figure 9F is the percent of families who were poor in year t of the study (column one, Table 9.12). The vertical axis is the percentage of poor families who escaped poverty by year t+1. Therefore, as the data points in the figure move out to the lower right (higher poverty in year t, a lower probability of escape by year t+1), the economic situation worsens.

Most of the countries in Figure 9F show relatively low poverty rates and relatively high "escape" rates. France, for example, has a family poverty rate of 4% in year t, and 27.5% of the poor in that year had escaped poverty by the next year (Table 9.12). However, the U.S. position in the figure reveals high poverty and low mobility. The U.S. overall poverty rate (20.3%) is the highest in the table, and the escape rate of 13.8% is the second lowest. The situation for U.S. blacks is particularly severe. As noted above, the poverty rate for American black families was 49.3% in the mid-1980s, the highest in the table. Blacks also had the lowest probability of escaping poverty; only 7.7% of the poor in year t were non-poor in year t+1. Only the Canadian poor are less likely than the U.S. poor to leave poverty. In fact, even foreigners within Germany, who have higher poverty rates than U.S. whites, have higher escape rates than the U.S. poor.

Column three of Table 9.12 shows further evidence of low economic mobility in the U.S. compared to the other countries in the table. The probability of a poor family with children remaining poor for the full length of the three-year period of the study was highest in the U.S., at 14.4%. While the rate for Canada was slightly lower (11.9%), the other countries in the study had much lower persistent poverty rates than the U.S. Black families were most likely to experience persistent poverty, as 41.5% were poor for the full period.

As noted, the previous tables use a relative definition of poverty, based on the median income in each country. By this measure, the U.S. has been found to have the highest rates of poverty. However, some might argue that absolute

The poverty rate for American black families was 49.3% in the mid-1980s, the highest in the table. Blacks also had the lowest probability of escaping poverty.

441

TABLE 9.14
Jobs Created in Ten Countries, 1979-1989

Country	Total Created 1979-89 (000)	New Jobs as Percent of 1979 Employment
Australia	1,617	26.5%
Canada	2,091	20.1
France	160	0.8
West Germany	1,690	6.6
Italy	840	4.2
Japan	6,460	12.0
Netherlands	720	13.5
Sweden	364	8.7
United Kingdom	1,460	5.9
United States	**18,518**	**18.7**

TABLE 9.15
Contributions to Employment Growth in Ten Countries
1979-1989

Country		Breakdown of Employment Growth into Sum of	
	Employment Growth Rate, 1979-1989	Population Growth Rate, 1979-1989	Employment/ Population Ratio Growth Rate, 1979-1989
Australia	2.4%	1.5%	0.9%
Canada	1.8	1.0	0.8
France	0.1	0.5	−0.4
West Germany	0.6	0.1	0.5
Italy	0.4	0.2	0.2
Japan	1.1	0.6	0.5
Netherlands	1.3	0.6	0.7
Sweden	0.8	0.2	0.6
United Kingdom	0.6	0.2	0.4
United States	**1.7**	**1.0**	**0.7**

poverty rates, i.e., a fixed income threshold, adjusted for family size, should show American poverty to be relatively low. That is, despite our relative inequalities, our high per capita income should leave fewer Americans than foreigners with purchasing power below an absolute poverty line. In fact, the last analysis of this question, which took place in 1979-1982, found the opposite to be true.

Table 9.13 shows that the proportion of Americans in absolute poverty, 12.7%, is only surpassed by Australia's poverty rate, 13.2%. The situation is similar for children and adults; in fact, American children have the highest absolute poverty rates in the table, 17.1%. Only elderly persons in the U.S. have less absolute poverty than their foreign counterparts. These data mean that even when using a poverty standard set by the U.S., with its relatively high purchasing power, the percentage of persons who cannot afford the basic necessities is higher in this country than in most industrialized nations. Furthermore, a number of factors, including the rising average of per capita GDP exclusive of the U.S. (Table 9.7), high absolute poverty rates over the 1980s (Chapter 6), and our high relative rates shown above, suggest that high U.S. absolute poverty rates relative to other countries have most certainly risen over the 1980s.

The U.S. annual employment growth rate (1.7%) turns out to be due more to population growth (1.0%) than to a rising employment/ population ratio (0.7%).

Job Growth and the Public Commitment to Job Training and Unemployment Compensation

We have already shown (Chapter 4) that most of the net job growth over the 1980s occurred in low-paying service industries. Here we examine job growth from an international perspective, and find that other countries have had faster job growth and lower unemployment than the United States.

Table 9.14 shows that from 1979 to 1989 thousands more jobs were created in the U.S. than in other countries (column one). However, the U.S. should be expected to have the largest absolute number of jobs, as it is by far the largest country. A better indicator is the *rate* of job creation. Column two of Table 9.13 shows that U.S. employment in 1989 was 18.7% greater than in 1979, compared to increases of 26.5% in Australia and 20.1% in Canada over the same period.

443

TABLE 9.16
Hours Worked Per Employee in Manufacturing, Indexed to the United States, 1970-1989

Country	1970	1979	1989
Canada	100	98	95
Denmark	96	86	82
France	98	90	83
West Germany	99	91	82
Italy	100	92	95
Japan	119	114	111
Netherlands	98	88	83
Sweden	91	80	79
United Kingdom	104	100	95
United States	**100**	**100**	**100**

TABLE 9.17
Paid Vacation in European Countries

Country	Weeks Mandated by Law
Austria	5
Belgium	4
Finland	5
France	5
Greece	4
West Germany	3
Iceland	5*
Ireland	3
Luxembourg	5
Malta	4
Netherlands	4
Norway	4*
Portugal	30 Days
Spain	30 Days
Sweden	5
Switzerland	4
United States**	**16.1 Days**

*Iceland has 4 weeks, 4 days; Norway, 4 weeks, 1 day.
**Estimated average, not mandated.

Another reason that simple job counts are misleading is that they do not take into account population growth, a factor that limits both the number of jobs created and the rate of job growth. Some countries (e.g., West Germany) have had very little population growth while most others have grown at a much slower rate than the U.S. Without population growth the only manner in which additional job growth can be achieved is by raising the percentage of the population with employment, which is always a slow process. On the other hand, countries with fast growing populations have the possibility of creating substantial growth in employment.

To address this issue, **Table 9.15** breaks down the growth in employment into growth of population, on the one hand, and of the employment/population ratio on the other. The U.S. annual employment growth rate (1.7%) turns out to be due more to population growth (1.0%) than to a rising employment/population ratio (0.7%). By a more appropriate standard, the employment/population ratio, the U.S. has still done well in creating employment, but not orders of magnitude better than the other countries. And as shown above, we have accomplished this at the expense of wage growth.

Workers in the U.S. have also been putting in more hours than workers in most other countries, in part, to compensate for falling wages. **Table 9.16** shows the hours worked per employee in manufacturing (the only data of this type available), indexed to the U.S. While two countries had average hours of work in 1970 that exceeded ours, by 1989 only Japan had more hours of work per average manufacturing employee. Furthermore, American workers had less generous vacation benefits than European workers (**Table 9.17**). The majority of European workers receive four or five weeks of paid vacation, mandated by law. American workers typically get slightly over two weeks of paid vacation. Furthermore, American workers' lesser vacation time only partially explains our extra hours of work.

Another way in which European countries are more generous to their workers is in the provision of publicly provided job training, placement and job creation. Such programs are vital to an economy like the United States, both as we shift from manufacturing to services, and as the armed forces reduce their workforce. When compared to the U.S., only Japan and Australia devote *less* of their national

Workers in the U.S. have been putting in more hours than workers in most other countries . . . American workers have also had less generous vacation benefits than European workers.

445

TABLE 9.18
Public Spending on Training and Placement, Direct Job Creation and Subsidies, as Percent of GDP, 1989

Country	Training and Placement	Direct Job Creation and Subsidies	Total
Australia	0.20%	0.04%	0.24%
Belgium	0.49	0.63	1.12
Canada	0.49	0.02	0.51
Denmark	1.32	0.03	1.35
Finland	0.53	0.45	0.98
France	0.69	0.04	0.73
West Germany	0.83	0.19	1.02
Italy*	0.80	0.00	0.80
Japan	0.07	0.10	0.17
Luxembourg	0.33	0.02	0.35
Netherlands	1.03	0.05	1.08
Norway	0.72	0.16	0.88
Spain	0.30	0.50	0.80
Sweden	1.43	0.13	1.56
United Kingdom	0.63	0.03	0.66
United States	**0.24**	**0.01**	**0.25**

*1988

resources to promote these programs. As shown in **Table 9.18**, in 1989 the U.S. government spent only 0.24% of GDP on job training and placement, and much less (0.01%) on job creation and subsidies.

As Chapter 4 points out, unemployment rates provide only a partial measure of labor force supply and demand, as they fail to capture the under-employed and discouraged workers. However, a general sense of the performance of the U.S. labor market from an international perspective is given in **Table 9.19**. In 1979, U.S. unemployment, at 5.8%, was well above the average of 4.9% for the major industrialized countries. By 1989, unemployment had fallen in the U.S. to 5.2%; among the seven major countries, only Japan's rate was lower. Among the smaller countries, the Scandinavian countries had less unemployment than the U.S.

When compared to the U.S. only Japan and Australia devote less of their national resources to promote job training and placement programs.

TABLE 9.19
Unemployment in OECD Countries, 1973-1989

Country	Unemployment Rate		
	1973	1979	1989
Canada	5.5	7.4	7.5
France	2.7	5.9	9.4
West Germany	0.8	3.2	5.6
Italy	6.2	7.6	10.9
Japan	1.3	2.1	2.3
United Kingdom	3.0	5.0	7.1
United States	**4.8**	**5.8**	**5.2**
Seven Major Countries	3.4	4.9	5.7
Smaller Countries			
Australia	2.3	6.2	6.1
Belgium	2.7	8.2	8.0
Finland	2.3	5.9	3.4
Netherlands	2.2	5.4	8.3
Norway	1.5	2.0	4.9
Spain	2.5	8.5	16.9
Sweden	2.5	2.1	1.4
Total OECD	3.3	5.1	6.2

447

TABLE 9.20
Unemployment and Unemployment Compensation, 1989

Country	Percent of GDP Spent on Unemployment Compensation	1989 Unemployment Rate	Percent of GDP per Percent of Unemployment
Australia	0.87%	6.1%	0.14%
Canada	1.57	7.5	0.21
France	1.27	9.4	0.14
West Germany	1.20	5.6	0.21
Italy*	0.40	10.9	0.04
Japan	0.34	2.3	0.15
Netherlands	2.42	8.3	0.29
Sweden	0.55	1.4	0.39
United Kingdom	0.84	7.1	0.12
United States	**0.47**	**5.2**	**0.09**

*The figure in column one for Italy is from 1988.

Most other countries are also more generous than the U.S. in the provision of unemployment compensation. **Table 9.20** shows that the U.S. spends only 0.47% of GDP on compensating those who are out of work; only Italy and Japan spend less. However, this figure does not take the level of unemployment into account. That is, a country might devote very few resources to unemployment compensation because of low unemployment. Therefore, column two gives the unemployment rates for the various countries in the table, and the third column is the ratio of compensation to unemployment, a measure of relative generosity given the country's unemployment rate. The numbers in this column tell us the percent of GDP that would be spent on compensation if unemployment rose by 1%. The U.S. spent 0.09% of GDP per 1% of unemployment in 1989; every country except Italy spent more. West Germany had unemployment rates similar to the U.S., yet their expenditure on unemployment compensation was over 2.5 times that of the U.S.

Conclusion

Compared to other industrialized countries, the U.S. is falling behind on many important economic indicators. Our comparatively sluggish productivity growth and declining competitiveness are limiting our wage growth, while most other countries are experiencing rising wages (for an explanation of additional factors causing wage decline, see Chapter 3). This development, in tandem with the diminished effectiveness of our tax and transfer system, has left the U.S. with the highest and most persistent poverty rates among the industrialized countries examined in this chapter. The stagnant wages and productivity in the U.S., along with the diminished effectiveness of our system of taxes and transfers, have begun to seriously undermine the U.S. standard of living, once considered the highest in the world.

The stagnant wages and productivity in the U.S., along with the diminished effectiveness of our system of taxes and transfers, have begun to seriously undermine the U.S. standard of living, once considered the highest in the world.

Table Notes:

Frequently Cited Sources

The following abbreviations are used throughout the Table Notes.

ERP:	President of the United States. *Economic Report of the President*, 1992.
Green Book:	U.S. House of Representatives. *Green Book*. Various years.
P-60 Series:	U.S. Department of Commerce, Bureau of the Census. *Series P-60*. Various dates.
SCB:	U.S. Department of Commerce. *Survey of Current Business*. Monthly.
Employment and Earnings:	U.S. Department of Labor. *Employment and Earnings*. Monthly and historical supplements.
NIPA:	U.S. Department of Commerce. *National Income and Product Accounts*. Revisions as of Spring 1992.

Table Notes:

Introduction

A. *Incidence of Labor Market Distress*. Based on tabulations of the March 1990 Current Population Survey (CPS) provided by Edie Rasell. The sample is all civilians ages 25-64, excluding the unincorporated self-employed. Poverty level wage earners are those who *averaged* $6.09 per hour or less over the year (based on annual wages and usual weekly hours and weeks worked). This is the four-person poverty level ($12,675) in 1989 divided by 2080 hours. We excluded zero or negative earners from our count. Involuntary part-timers are those who could not find full-time work and worked part-time involuntarily or those who because of slack work were working part-time involuntarily. Discouraged workers are those who did not work or look for work at some time during the year because they believed no work was available. Most discouraged workers fell into an additional category of distress. We did not count 16-24 year olds, or those involuntary part-time or unemployed for less than four weeks so our measure focused on unmistakably serious distress among the prime-age workforce.

451

1.1   *Median Family Income. P-60 Series,* No. 97, p. 30; *P-60 Series,* No. 166, p. 11; *P-60 Series,* No. 174, p. 201; *P-60 Series,* No. 180, Table 13.

1.2   *Annual Growth of Median Family Income.* Yearly dollar change is annual average of total dollar change in period. Size-adjusted median family income is weighted by families and adjusted for family size using the poverty equivalence scale. This is actually the average income in the middle fifth, not the median. Based on data in Table 1.1 and from the *Green Book* (1992), p. 1446.

1.3   *Growth of Median Family Income by Age of Householder.* 1991 from *P-60 Series,* No. 180, Table 13; 1989 from *P-60 Series,* No. 174, p. 52; 1979 from *P-60 Series,* No. 129, p. 32; 1973 from *P-60 Series,* No. 97, pp. 49-51; 1967 from *P-60 Series,* No. 59, pp. 32-34 (through telephone conversation with Ed Welniak on June 15, 1990).

1.4   *Growth of Median Family Income by Race/Ethnic Group.* 1991 from *P-60 Series,* No. 180, Table 13; 1989 from *P-60 Series,* No. 174, pp. 53-55; 1979 from Fisher (1986): Table 1B; 1947-1973 from *P-60 Series,* No. 129, pp. 42-43.

1.5   *Income Growth by Type of Family.* For 1991 from *P-60 Series,* No. 180, Table 13. Other data from Department of Commerce unpublished historical tables (1991c): Table 13.

1.6   *Shares of Family Income Going to Various Fifths, and to Top 5%. P-60 Series,* No. 174, p. 216, and *P-60 Series,* No. 180, Table B-7.

1.7   *Real Family Income Growth by Fifth. P-60 Series,* No. 174, p. 216 and, for 1947, Department of Commerce unpublished historical tables (1991c): Table 10, and *P-60 Series,* No. 180, Table B-7.

1.8   *Income Growth by Fifth and Family Type. Green Book* (1992): Table 45, pp. 1371-72.

1.9   *Income Growth Among Top Fifth and by Fifth.* From House of Representatives, Ways and Means Committee (1991).
          Persons are placed into fifths and percentiles based on adjusted family income; the numbers in the table, however, are average *unadjusted* family incomes for the families in each group. The numbers of persons in each fifth are the same, though the numbers of families differ. Averages are weighted by families, not by persons. "All" includes families with zero or negative incomes, but the bottom fifth excludes these families.

1.10   *Changes in Family Income Shares.* House of Representatives, Ways and Means Committee (1991). See note to Table 1.9. Shares for groups add up to slightly more than 100% because families with negative incomes are excluded from the lowest fifth but included in "All." Maximum income thresholds are for a family of four as presented in *Green Book* (1992), p. 1515. The actual income thresholds depend on family size, and we use the four-person threshold for illustrative purposes.

1.11 *Change in Family Income by Income Level Using Tax Return Data*. From U.S. Treasury (1992): Table A2. These are "constant law" adjusted gross incomes.

1.12 *Shares of Consumption*. From Cutler and Katz (1992): Table 1.

1.13 *Shares of Aggregate Income Growth*. See note to Table 1.10. Shares for groups add up to slightly more than 100% because families with negative incomes are excluded from the lowest fifth but included in "All" and, therefore, affect the aggregate growth.

1.14 *Source of Family Income for Each Fifth of Families*. From unpublished Congressional Budget Office (CBO) tabulations, "Shares and Sources of Family Income: All Families, 1977, 1980, 1985, 1988, 1989," provided by Frank Sammartino. Market-based income is total income less transfer and other (e.g., alimony, pension) income.

1.15 *Real Income Growth by Type of Personal Income. NIPA*. Table 2.1. The earliest data available are for 1959.

1.16 *Shares of Market-Based Income by Type*. From *NIPA*, Table 2.1. The earliest data available are for 1959.

1.17 *Shares of Income by Type, by Sector*. Based on *NIPA*, Table 1.15. The "Corporate and Business" sector includes "corporate," "other private business" and "rest of world." The "government/nonprofit" sector includes the household, government enterprise, and government sectors, all of which generate no capital income.

1.18 *Distribution of Labor and Capital Incomes*. See note to Table 1.14.

1.19 *Sources of Income Growth of Top Fifth*. Data derived from shares of income by type of income from unpublished Congressional Budget Office (CBO) data (see note to Table 1.14) and from income levels from Table 1.9.

1.20 *Shares of Income Growth by Type of Income for Top Fifth*. Based on data in Table 1.19.

1.21 *Distribution of Persons, Households and Families by Income Level*. Based on a Census Bureau analysis presented in *Green Book* (1992): Table 90, p. 1455.

1.22 *Distribution of Prime Age Adults by Relative Income Level*. Based on a Census Bureau analysis presented in *Green Book* (1992): Table 93, p. 1458.

1.23 *Changes in Incomes of Married Couple Families with Children by Source*. Joint Economic Committee (1992): Table 1.

1.24 *Husbands' and Wives' Hours of Work*. Joint Economic Committee (1992): Tables 3 and 4. The hours for employed wives and husbands are corrected numbers from tabulations provided by the JEC.

1.25 *Change in Hourly Wages of Husbands and Wives.* Joint Economic Committee (1992): Table 2.

1.26 *Role of Higher Wives' Earnings and Hours on Family Income Growth.* Based on the hours, wages and income data presented in Tables 1.23, 1.24 and 1.25 and Joint Economic Committee (1992): Tables 1 and 7. The hypothetical calculations use the hours, wages and incomes in 1979 as a base and ask what if the hours or earnings of wives remained at the 1979 levels but other dimensions of income changed as they did over the 1979-1989 period. For the hypothetical calculations of income changes without higher wives' hours, the 1989 hourly wage levels of wives are used.

1.27 *Effect of Wives' Earnings on Income Shares Among Married Couples with Children.* Derived from data presented in Joint Economic Committee (1992): Table 8.

1.28 *Changes in Hours Worked in All Families and in Married-Couple Families.* Based on Congressional Research Service computations of March Current Population Survey (CPS) data, presented in *Green Book* (1992): Table 70, pp. 1424-1425.

1.29 *Effect of Wives' Earnings on Income Inequality Among All Families and Married Couples.* From Cancian, Danziger, and Gottschalk (1992): Table 7.

1.30 *Effect of Second Earner on Household Expenditures.* Democratic Study Group (1990): Table 1, pp. 8-9.

1.31 *Child-Care Expenditures and Family Income for Employed Women With Children.* Democratic Study Group (1990): Table 3.

1.32 *Hours Worked by Employed Parents by Gender.* Leete-Guy and Schor (1992): Table 9.

1.33 *Income Growth by Cohort.* From unpublished Census Bureau historical tables, Table 15.

1.34 *Distribution of Individuals in Final Year by Family Income Fifth in Starting Year.* Sawhill and Condon (1992): Table 1.

1.35 *Transitions Into or Out of Middle Income for Families with Children.* Based on research by Duncan et al. (1991) as presented in *Green Book* (1992): Table 99, p. 1467.

Chapter 2

2.1 *Federal vs. State and Local Tax Burdens.* From *NIPA* Tables 1.1, 3.2, 3.3. 1991 data from Survey of Current Business (SCB) (February 1992).

2.2 *Tax Revenues in OECD Countries.* From Organisation of Economic Co-operation and Development (OECD) (1990a), p. 71.

2.3 *Average After-Tax Family Income.* U.S. House of Representatives (1991), pp. 67-68.

2.4. *Shares of After-tax Income for All Families.* U.S. House of Representatives, (1991), p. 71.

2.5 *The Effects of Tax and Income Changes on After-tax Income Shares.* 1977 and 1989 actual effective rates were applied to 1989 average before-tax incomes—from *U.S. House of Representatives* (1991), p. 67. The resulting average after-tax incomes were multiplied by the number of families in each group (provided by Frank Sammartino, Congressional Budget Office (CBO)) to get total after-tax incomes per group. Then these were converted to shares by dividing each group's total by the sum over the groups. Shares in the second and fourth column differ somewhat from corresponding shares in Table 2.4 because of rounding error in *U.S. House of Representatives* (1991) tables—particularly for the number of families in the top 1%—and because total income for all families in Table 2.5 necessarily excludes families with zero or negative incomes, while in Table 2.4 such families are included.

2.6 *Effective Average Tax Rates.* U.S. House of Representatives (1991), p. 73.

2.7 *Effect of Federal Tax Changes on Family Tax Payments.* Average pre-tax family income is from *U.S. House of Representatives* (1991), p. 67. See note to Table 2.6 for effective rates.

2.8 *Effective Tax Rates for Selected Federal Taxes.* Data provided by Frank Sammartino, Congressional Budget Office (CBO).

2.9 *Changes in Effective Federal Taxes.* See note to Table 2.8.

2.10 *Taxed and Untaxed Corporate Profits.* Figures are from *NIPA*: Tables 1.1 and 1.16. Taxes include federal, state, and local combined. Actual profits are taxed profits plus net interest (interest paid minus interest received) and the difference between the allowance for inventory investment and capital depreciation allowed in the tax code, on the one hand, and actual inventory investment and capital depreciation, on the other. The idea for this analysis is based on Thomas Karier (1990). Only nonfinancial corporations are included because banks do not pay net interest—they *receive* net interest.

2.11 *Corporate Profits Tax Rates. NIPA:* Tables 1.1 and 1.16.

2.12 *Total State and Local Taxes in 1991 (Effective Rates) as Shares of Income for Families of Four.* McIntyre, et al. (1991), p. 18. Any tax analysis of this nature must make a number of assumptions regarding tax incidence. For example, in this study half of the property tax paid on rental units is allocated to the owners of the property, and half is assigned to the renters in the form of higher rents. We consider the assumptions in this study to be reasonable and unbiased. The methodology of the study is discussed on pp. 70-72.

2.13 *Federal vs. State and Local Taxes, 1991, as Percent of Revenue at Each Level. NIPA:* Tables 3.2, 3.3.

2.14 *The Composition of Taxes as Percent of GDP. NIPA:* Tables 1.1, 3.2, 3.3.

Chapter 3

3.1 *Trends in Average Wages and Average Hours.* Unpublished tabulations from Kevin Murphy from an update of Murphy and Welch (1989), based on March Current Population Survey (CPS) files, 1963-1990. Hours of work derived from differences between annual, weekly and hourly wage trends. Unfortunately, the data include self-employed as well as wage and salary workers. We suspect that the wage growth from 1982 to 1989 is overstated in their series (particularly the hourly wage). Productivity data for 1959 to 1989 are from *ERP* (1992): Table B-44, p. 348 for the non-farm business sector. 1990 productivity data from Joint Economic Committee *Economic Indicators* (June 1992a), p. 16.

3.2 *Changes in Hourly Wages, Benefits and Compensation.* Based on employment cost levels from the Bureau of Labor Statistics (BLS) Employment Cost Index series for March 1987 to March 1992 for private sector workers. We categorize pay differently than the BLS, putting all wage related items (including paid leave) into the hourly wage. Benefits, in our definition, only include payroll taxes, pensions, insurance and "other" benefits. See Mishel and Bernstein (1992): Appendix A for further discussion.

It is important to use the current-weighted series rather than the fixed-weighted series because composition shifts have a large effect, as we show in Table 3.26. Data for 1966, 1972 and 1977 are based on BLS surveys of employer expenditures for employee compensation (EEEC) in the private non-farm economy, provided by BLS economist Albert Schwenk.

3.3 *Hourly and Weekly Earnings of Production and Nonsupervisory Workers. Employment and Earnings* (March 1992): Table C-1, p. 133; and for 1947, Supplement to *Employment and Earnings* (March 1985), p. 5.

3.4 *Changes in Wages and Compensation.* See note to Table 3.2. Our analysis in which we tried to match occupational data from the earlier employer expenditures for employee compensation (EEEC) data to the Employment Cost Index (ECI) data yielded nonsensical results, perhaps based on changes in definitions.

3.5 *Wages for All Workers by Wage Percentile.* Based on analysis of Current Population Survey (CPS) wage data described in the Appendix. These data differ slightly from those in Mishel and Bernstein (1992) because of some corrections to the 1989 data.

3.6 *Wages for Male Workers by Wage Percentile.* See note to Table 3.5.

3.7 *Wages for Female Workers by Wage Percentile.* See note to Table 3.5.

3.8 *Changes in the Gender Wage Differential.* Based on data from Tables 3.6 and 3.7.

3.9   *Distribution of Total Employment by Wage Level.* Based on analysis of Current Population Survey (CPS) wage data described in the Appendix. The poverty level wage was defined as the four-person poverty threshold in 1979 divided by 2080 hours and deflated by CPI-U-X1 to obtain levels for other years. We calculated more intervals than we show but aggregated for simplicity of presentation (no trends were lost).

3.10   *Distribution of White Employment by Wage Level.* See note to Table 3.9. These are non-Hispanic whites.

3.11   *Distribution of Black Employment by Wage Level.* See note to Table 3.9. These are non-Hispanic blacks.

3.12   *Distribution of Hispanic Employment by Wage Level.* See note to Table 3.9. Hispanics may be of any race.

3.13   *Employer Hourly Benefit Costs, by Type.* Based on employer expenditures for employee compensation (EEEC) and Employment Cost Index (ECI) as described in note to Table 3.2. Inflation in medical care services from *ERP* (1992): Table B-58, p. 364, and from Consumer Price Index (CPI) news release with seasonally adjusted data for the first three months of 1992.

3.14   *Changes in Private Sector Benefit Coverage.* Based on tabulations of the March 1980 and March 1990 Current Population Survey (CPS) data files, provided by Edie Rasell. The sample includes wage and salary workers ages 18-64 in the private sector who worked at least 20 hours weekly and for at least 26 weeks. Health insurance coverage is where the employer offers coverage and pays for at least some of the costs. Pension coverage is where worker's employer has a plan in which the employee participates. Unfortunately, the 1979 data are based on 1970 Census weights.

3.15   *Changes in Private Sector Benefit Coverage by Wage Fifth.* See note to Table 3.14.

3.16   *Trends in Days Off With Pay.* Based on unpublished Bureau of Labor Statistics data, provided by Bill Gullickson, on the ratio of hours at work to hours paid, for production and nonsupervisory workers in nonagricultural business (limited to 1981-1989) and in manufacturing (1947-1989). The days off of paid leave is computed from one less the ratio of hours at work to hours paid times 260 days (assumes a five-day week for 52 weeks). Data for non-farm business for 1966, 1972 and 1977 derived from employer expenditures for employee compensation (EEEC) data (see note to Table 3.2) from the ratio of hourly compensation per hour paid to hourly compensation per hour worked.

3.17   *The Joint Effect of Education and Experience on Wages.* Based on tabulations of Current Population Survey (CPS) wage data described in the Appendix. The basic data are the hourly wages and employment shares of workers by experience (five-year categories starting with 1-5 years, and going to 31-35 years, and a 35 plus years category) and education (less than high school, high school graduate, some college, college graduate, more than college) for all workers, men and women. The decomposition is based on three terms: (1) the initial wage times the difference in employment shares; (2) the initial employment share times the difference in wages; and (3) the change in shares times the change in wages. The first column represents the first term, the second column the second term and the third term is not presented, but can be derived from the difference between the last column and the first two columns.

3.18   *The Separate Effects of Education and Experience on Wages.* Same data and analysis as in Table 3.17, but we separate the education and experience effects.

3.19   *Change in Real Hourly Wage by Education.* Based on tabulations of Current Population Survey (CPS) wage data described in the Appendix. The group with 17 years of schooling (college plus one) is omitted for simplicity of presentation.

3.20   *Change in Real Hourly Wage of Men by Education.* See note to Table 3.19.

3.21   *Change in Real Hourly Wage for Women by Education.* See note to Table 3.19.

3.22   *Change in Real Hourly Wage by Work Experience.* Based on tabulations of Current Population Survey (CPS) wage data described in the Appendix.

3.23   *Entry-Level Wages and Employment Shares.* Based on tabulations of Current Population Survey (CPS) wage data described in the Appendix. Following Katz and Murphy (1990) we examine the wages of workers with 1-5 years of work experience (traditionally defined).

3.24   *Employment Growth by Sector. Employment and Earnings,* (March 1990): Table B-1 with 1989 data as revised in *Employment and Earnings* (June 1991).

3.25   *Changes in Employment Share by Sector.* Based on data in Table 3.24.

3.26   *Effect of Structural Employment Shifts on Pay Levels.* This comparison is based on two computations of pay levels in March 1989. One is the current weighted pay levels from the Employment Cost Index. See note to Table 3.2. The other is from the underlying, unpublished data used to compute quarterly changes in hourly wages and compensation, which is based on 1980 Census weights. The major difference between the pay levels in these computations is the weighting scheme. Because the data with current weights are based on an employer survey, and the data with 1980 weights are based on a household survey, the difference in the weighted and unweighted pay levels also incorporates differences in how households and employers classify the workforce by occupation.

Household data yields a larger share of executives, managers and sales workers and a lesser share of administrative and service workers. We correct for this by calculating the effect of the difference between household (CPS) data and employer (Occupational Employment Statistics) survey data on pay levels in 1990 using a shift-share analysis. Pay levels are wages or compensation from the Employment Cost Index (ECI) for 1990. The Current Population Survey (CPS) household employment data are from *Employment and Earnings* (January 1991): Table 21, p. 184. The OES employer data are from Silvestri and Lukasiewic (1991): Table 1, p. 65.

3.27 *Pay in Expanding and Shrinking Industries.* Costrell (1988): Tables A4 and A5.

3.28 *Effect of Industry Employment Shifts on Pay.* Based on Costrell (1988) as shown in Mishel (1989): Table 3.

3.29 *Industry Employment Shifts and Production Worker Weekly Wages.* Based on Costrell (1988) as shown in Mishel (1989): Table 4.

3.30 *Trade Induced Changes in Labor Supply.* From Borjas et al. (1991): Table 1.

3.31 *Immigration and Labor Supply.* From Borjas et al. (1991): Tables 2 and 3.

3.32 *Effect of Trade on Labor Supply of High School and College Workers.* From Borjas et al. (1991): Table 5.

3.33 *Effect of Trade and Immigration on Education Wage Differential.* From Borjas et al. (1991): Table 6.

3.34 *Comparison of Union and Nonunion Hourly Wages and Benefits.* Employment Cost Index pay level data in U.S. Department of Labor (1989a): Table 10.

3.35 *Effect of Deunionization on Male Occupation and Education Differentials.* From Freeman (1991): Table 2.

3.36 *Impact of Deunionization on Changes in Average Hourly Earnings.* From Blackburn et al. (1991): Appendix Table 4.

3.37 *Effect of Unions on Wages, By Wage Fifth.* From Card (1991): Table 8. The effect of deunionization is the change in union coverage times the union wage premium.

3.38 *Effect of Unions on Male Wage Inequality.* From Card (1991): Table 9 and from Freeman (1991): Table 6.

3.39 *Value of Minimum Wage.* Historical values of minimum wage from Shapiro (1987), p. 19. Wages for 1990 and 1991 are based on legislated increases to

$3.80 on April 1, 1990 and to $4.25 on April 1, 1991. Inflation projection for 1992 from a Merrill Lynch (May 4, 1992) forecast.

3.40 *Amount by Which Earnings of a Full-Time, Full-Year Minimum Wage Worker are Above (Below) the Poverty Line*. See note to Table 3.39 for source of minimum wage levels and 1992 inflation projection. Annual earnings are based on 2,080 paid hours of work, and assuming no additional income. Poverty lines are from *P-60 Series*, No. 166, p. 88. This source gives poverty lines adjusted by the CPI-U, which is the official method. We convert these poverty lines back to actual (nominal) poverty lines for each year using the CPI-U, take the difference between these lines and the actual salary of a minimum wage worker, and adjust this "gap" for inflation using the CPI-U-X1.

3.41 *Minimum Wage Workforce Demographic Composition*. Based on tabulations of Current Population Survey (CPS) wage data described in the Appendix. Because of the change in the legislated minimum wage in April 1991 the definition of a minimum wage worker differs between the first three and the last nine months.

3.42 *Distribution of Wage Earners by Minimum Wage Status and Family Income*. Based on tabulations of March 1990 Current Population Survey (CPS) data file prepared by Bill Spriggs.

3.43 *Distribution of Workers Before and After Minimum Wage Increases*. Based on tabulations of 1990 and 1991 CPS Outgoing Rotation Group files prepared by Bill Spriggs.

3.44 *Effects of Computer Usage on Wage Structure*. Derived from Krueger (1991): Tables 1 and 8. The computer-use wage premium is based on the coefficients of the computer-use variable (a) and its interaction (b) with schooling (S) as exp (a+bS)-1.

3.45 *Executive Pay Levels. The Economist* (December 23, 1989), using data on gross and net income in dollars.

3.46 *Real Growth in Executive Pay*. Based on data in Table 3.40, converted from dollars to national currency using exchange rates from *ERP* (1990): Table C-109, p. 418 and then converting to constant currency values using an index for domestic consumer prices from International Monetary Fund, *International Financial Statistics*, except the Personal Consumption Expenditures (PCE) index was used for the U.S.

3.47 *Comparative Pay Levels for Workers and CEOs*. Towers, Perrin and Company (October 1988): Exhibits 8 and 9, pp. 18-19.

3.48 *The Gap Between Executives and Production Workers*. Hourly compensation of production workers from U.S. Department of Labor (1989c). CEO pay from Towers, Perrin and Company (October 1988).

3.49 *Black-White Wage Differentials Among Young Workers*. From Bound and Freeman (1991): Table 3. The data were transformed from log points to percentage changes.

3.50 *Employment Opportunity and Wage Growth*. From Blackburn et al. (1991): Tables 1 and 3. The wage growth in the last column is for 1979-1988.

3.51 *The Effect of Occupation and Industry Employment Shifts on Skill and Education Requirements*. From Teixeira and Mishel (1992): Table 2.

3.52 *The Effect of Occupation and Employment Shifts on Pay*. From Teixeira and Mishel (1992): Table 2.

Chapter 4

4.1 *Unemployment Rates. Employment and Earnings* (January 1990): Table 3, pp. 162-64; Table 39, p. 206; and, *Employment and Earnings* (January 1992): Table 40, p. 209; Table 3, pp. 164-66.

4.2 *Rates of Underemployment*. For 1973 and 1979, U.S. Department of Labor (1985): Table 1, p. 6; Table 4, p. 14; Table 21, p. 58. For 1989, *Employment and Earnings* (January 1990): Table 1, p. 160; Table 31, p. 199; Table 35, p. 202.

4.3 *Changes in Unemployment in Postwar Recessions*. Unemployment rates for all but the 1990s recession from Meisenheimer et al. (1992): Table 4. 1990 data from *Employment and Earnings* (January 1992): Table A-43, p. 54. 1992 data from July 2, 1992 Bureau of Labor Statistics (BLS) release on unemployment data. Unemployment rate due to "permanent job loss" is based on "other job loser" category with "other reasons" including layoffs, job leaves, re-entrants and new entrants."

The permanent job loser unemployment rate was derived from the aggregate unemployment rate and from data on the percentage of the unemployed that were "other job losers" from U.S. Department of Labor (1982): Table E-23, p. 417 for 1967-1981; from Bureau of Labor Statistics (BLS) economist Gloria Green for 1982; from *Employment and Earnings* (January 1991): Table A-52, p. 60 for 1990; and, from the July 2, 1992 Bureau of Labor Statistics (BLS) release on unemployment for 1992. Length of recessions are based on National Bureau of Economic Research (NBER) dating, as presented in Henwood (1991), p. 9.

We assume the trough of the early 1990s' recession was in May 1992. As of this writing there has been no "officially declared" end of the recession. Although output increased in most of 1991 and in 1992, there was a continued growth of unemployment, especially in the first six months of 1992.

Last, in contrast to the Bureau of Labor Statistics (BLS) analysis, we identified 1990:2 and not 1990:3 as the peak quarter because of the 0.3% rise in unemployment in the 1990:2 period. The other peak quarters identified by Bureau of Labor Statistics (BLS) were output peaks, not unemployment peaks. However, choosing the unemployment peak, as we did for 1990, would only affect the 1980:1 peak and not other peaks.

4.4 *Changes in Labor Force Levels and Participation in Recessions.* Labor force size and participation data for 1969 to 1981 from U.S. Department of Labor (1982): Table E-1, p. 300; Table E-2, p. 316; for 1982 from Bureau of Labor Statistics (BLS) economist Gloria Green; and, for 1990 from *Employment and Earnings* (January 1991): Table A-43, p. 53. Rates of change are annual rates (but not log annual rates).

4.5 *Change in Unemployment Rate by Occupation, Gender, Race, and Industry.* For 1990 from *Employment and Earnings* (January 1991): Table A-50. For 1992 from Bureau of Labor Statistics (BLS) economist Leo Rydzewski.

4.6 *Changes in Employment and Unemployment in Recessions by Occupation.* Data through 1982 from unpublished tabulation, provided by Bureau of Labor Statistics (BLS) economist Joseph Meisenheimer, of data used in Meisenheimer et al. (1992): Table 5. For 1990 from *Employment and Earnings* (April 1992): Table A-46 and for 1992 from (July 2, 1992) Bureau of Labor Statistics (BLS) release on unemployment.

4.7 *Proportion of the Unemployed Who Receive Some Unemployment Insurance Payment.* Center on Budget and Policy Priorities (1992): Table 1.

4.8 *Employment Growth in Expansions.* Length of expansion from National Bureau of Economic Research (NBER) dating reported in Henwood (1991), p. 9. Employment data are from the establishment survey as presented in U.S. Department of Labor (1991a), pp. 2, 6, and 689.

4.9 *Employment Growth.* For full-time equivalent, *NIPA*: Table 6.5C. For hours, *NIPA*: Table 6.9C (earliest year is 1948 so growth rate for earliest period adjusted accordingly). For Labor Force Participation, Working Age Population and Civilian Employment, *Employment and Earnings* (January 1992): Table 1, p. 162. Note the slowdown in labor force participation is even greater when the measure is decline in non-participation.

4.10 *Composition of Non-Agricultural Employment.* For 1973 and 1979 from U.S. Department of Labor (1989b): Table 23, p. 121. For 1989 from *Employment and Earnings* (January 1990): Table 32, p. 199. For 1991 from *Employment and Earnings* (January 1992): Table 32, p. 201.

4.11 *Age and Gender Composition of the Labor Force and Rate of Part-time Employment.* From Tilly (1991): Table 1.

4.12   *Industry Composition of the Labor Force and Rate of Part-time Employment.* From Tilly (1991): Table 3.

4.13   *Rate of Voluntary and Involuntary Part-time Work by Industry.* From Tilly (1991): Table 4.

4.14   *Wage Differences Between Part-Time and Full-Time Workers by Gender and Selected Occupation.* From analysis of Current Population Survey (CPS) wage data as described in the Appendix.

4.15   *Difference in Fringe Benefits, for Full-Time and Part-Time Workers, By Gender or Marital Status and Occupations.* Blank (1990): Table 4, p. 30.

4.16   *Growth of Multiple Jobholding, All Workers.* All figures are from May of the given year. 1973 and 1989 are from U.S. Department of Labor (1989d). 1985 is from Stinson (1986). 1979 is from Sekscenski (1980). 1991 is from U.S. Department of Labor (1991b).

4.17   *Growth of Multiple Jobholders, by Gender.* See note to Table 4.16.

4.18   *Distribution of Multiple Jobholders Experiencing Economic Hardship.* See note to Table 4.16.

4.19   *Hours Worked by Multiple Jobholders, by Gender.* Unpublished data provided by Bureau of Labor Statistics (BLS) economist John Stinson.

4.20   *The Use of Various Types of Contingent Labor.* The two surveys are the Conference Board survey (1989) and the Bureau of National Affairs survey (1986). For details see Carre (1992).

4.21   *The Growth of Personnel Services Industry Employment.* Standard Industrial Classification (SIC) 736 from *Employment and Earnings* (Supplements for 1982 and earlier years; for 1989, March 1990: Table B-2; and for 1991, March 1992: Table B-2). 1989 and 1991 data for women were obtained from Bureau of Labor Statistics (BLS) by telephone.

4.22   *Growth in Temporary Help Industry Employment.* Employment in Standard Industrial Classification (SIC) 7362 from same sources as Table 4.21.

4.23   *Elements of the Marginal Workforce.* Carre (1992).

4.24   *The Growth of Self-Employment.* U.S. Department of Labor (1989b): Table 21, pp. 112-13; *Employment and Earnings*, (January 1990): Table 23, p. 189; and *Employment and Earnings*, (January 1992): Table 23, p. 191; Table 19, p. 18.

4.25   *Self-Employment and Paid Employment Earnings.* Haber et al. (1987): Table 4, p. 20.

Chapter 5

5.1   *Growth of Household Wealth.* Assets and debts are year-end outstanding
        values from balance sheet data for households, personal trusts and nonprofit
        organizations from Board of Governors (1992), pp. 14-17 for 1967-1991;
        and (1990), pp. 19-24 for 1949 data. Nonprofit organizations, a small compo-
        nent judging from the breakout on tangible assets, were included because
        the Federal Reserve System does not give the breakout for financial assets.
        Data converted to real dollars using the Personal Consumption Expenditures
        fixed-weight price index from *NIPA*. The growth rates in the table are assets
        net of debt per adult. The number of adults from *ERP* (1992): Table B-29,
        and for 1991 from telephone conversation with the Census Bureau's Popula-
        tion Estimates Department. Adult population includes the Army.

5.2   *Distribution of Wealth.* From 1989 Survey of Consumer Finance (SCF) tabu-
        lations in Wolff (1992b): Table 2. Net financial assets breakdown from Wolff
        over the telephone.

5.3   *Selected Holdings of Assets by Family Wealth Level.* 1989 Survey of Con-
        sumer Finance (SCF) data from Wolff (1992b): Table 6.

5.4   *Share of Total Household Wealth Held by Richest One Percent of Individuals.*
        From Wolff (1992a): Table 1.

5.5   *Composition of Aggregate Household Wealth.* 1989 Survey of Consumer
        Finance (SCF) data from Wolff (1992b): Table 5.

5.6   *Changes in Distribution of Net Worth and Family Income.* 1983 and 1989
        Survey of Consumer Finance (SCF) data from Wolff (1992b): Table 2.

5.7   *Sources of Wealth Growth.* Reported in Wolff (1992b), p. 21.

5.8   *Change in Net Worth by Wealth Class.* Computed from data in Wolff (1992b):
        Table 2.

5.9   *Change in Wealth by Income Class.* From Census Bureau study of Survey of
        Income and Program Participation (SIPP) data presented in Eargle (1990):
        Table H, p. 8.

5.10   *Household Debt Burden.* Asset and debt data from Federal Reserve Board bal-
        ance sheet data (see note to Table 5.1). Personal income data for 1959 to
        1989 from *ERP* (1992): Table B-23; for 1991 from Joint Economic Commit-
        tee, *Economic Indicators* (May 1992), p. 5.
            Because current *NIPA* data start in 1959, personal income data for 1949 are
        taken from earlier *NIPA* data, Table 2.1.

5.11   *Ratio of Household Income and Wealth Between Non-White and White Fam-
        ilies.* From Wolff (1992b): Table 8.

5.12 *Net Worth by Race and Household Characteristics*. From Wolff (1992b): Table 9.

Chapter 6

6.1 *Percent and Number of Persons in Poverty with Averages Over Peak Years*. Actual poverty rates are from *P-60 Series*, No. 176, p. 16. Predicted rates are from unpublished data provided by Rebecca Blank. The Blank model is described in Blank (1991).

6.2 *Consumption-Based Poverty Measures*. Ruggles (1992), p. 7.

6.3 *Poverty Rates when (Nonmedical) Non-cash Benefits are Included*. Green Book (1992), p. 1305.

6.4 *Percent of Persons with Low Relative Income Adjusted for Family Size*. P-60 Series, No. 177, p. 8. Equivalence factors (to adjust for family size) are from Ruggles (1990). Unrelated individuals treated as one-person families.

6.5 *Poverty Gap: Aggregates and Means*. Center for Budget and Policy Priorities (1992), p. 33.

6.6 *Persons Below 50% of the Poverty Level*. Center for Budget and Policy Priorities (1992), p. 37.

6.7 *Distribution of Poverty Spells for Nonelderly Persons Entering Poverty*. Bane and Ellwood (1986), p. 12.

6.8 *Events Leading to Poverty Spells, and Average Spell Length*. Bane and Ellwood (1986), p. 18.

6.9 *Length of Poverty Spells for Children Age 1-10, by Race, in Percent*. Green Book (1992), p. 1177.

6.10 *Poverty by Race/Ethnicity*. Center for Budget and Policy Priorities (1992), p. 3.

6.11 *Percent of Children in Poverty, by Race*. P-60 Series, No. 175, p. 24.

6.12 *Poverty Among the Elderly and All Persons Before and After Transfers*. Danziger and Weinberg (1992): Tables 2 and 7.

6.13 *Changing Family Structure and Poverty*. Current Population Survey (CPS) P-60 Series, No. 174, p. 58. Number of persons in female-headed families in 1959 is an estimate based on the number poor and in such families, together with the poverty rate among such families.

6.14 *Changing Family Structure and Poverty*. See note to Table 6.13. This type of demographic decomposition assumes the changes in population shares occur independently of changes in the poverty rates of each specific group.

The interaction term in column three reflects the extent to which changing demographics are causally linked to changes in poverty rates.

6.15   *Poverty Rates for Female-Headed Families*. Center for Budget and Policy Priorities (1992), p. 5.

6.16   *Increase in Poverty in Female-Headed Families, by Race*. Center for Budget and Policy Priorities (1992), p. 6.

6.17   *Marital Status of Female Family Heads*. Women without dependents are not included. 1973, 1979 are for women aged 14 and over, while 1989 is restricted to women aged 15 and over. 1973 numbers are from U.S. Department of Commerce *Series P-20*, No. 255, pp. 25-26; 1979 data come from U.S. Department of Commerce, *Series P-20*, No. 349, pp. 31-32; 1989 data are from U.S. Department of Commerce, *Series P-20* (1989), p. 55.

6.18   *Expected Lifetime Births, by Marital Status and Race*. Jencks (1991), p. 86.

6.19   *Poverty Rates Using Different Income Definitions*. *Green Book* (1991). All persons: p. 1164. Single parent families: p. 1168. Married-couple families: p. 1170.

6.20   *AFDC Participation Rates of Female-Headed Families with Children*. Moffitt (1992), p. 9.

6.21   *Shares of Workers Earning Enough to Maintain a Family of Four at 0.75 of Poverty and up to the Poverty Line, by Gender and Race*. Authors' tabulations of Current Population Survey (CPS) wage data; see the Appendix for description of analytic methods.

6.22   *Wage Trends Relevant to the Poor and Near-Poor*. Same source as Table 6.21.

6.23   *Work Experience of the Poor*. 1979 from *P-60 Series*, No. 130, p. 58; 1989 from *P-60 Series*, No. 168, p. 65.

6.24   *Percentage of Half-Time and Full-Time Worker Equivalents' in Poor Families with Children*. *Green Book* (1992), pp. 1282-83. Families include unrelated subfamilies.

6.25   *Hours Worked by Family Type in the Bottom Fifths*. *Green Book* (1992), pp. 1424-25.

Chapter 7

7.1   *Median Family Income, by Region*. U.S. Department of Commerce, unpublished historical data (1991c): Table 12.

7.2   *Median Income for Four-Person Families, by State*. U.S. Department of Commerce (1992): Table 1.

7.3 *Percent of Families with Low, Middle, and High Relative Income, by Region.* *P-60 Series*, No. 177, p. 18-19.

7.4 *Ratio of Average Income of the Top Fifth to Average Income of Bottom Fifth.* Barancik and Shapiro (1992), p. 22.

7.5 *Income Changes for Average Family, Bottom, Middle, and Top Fifth.* Barancik and Shapiro (1992), pp. 50-51.

7.6 *Poverty Rates by Region and Division.* 1990 from *P-60 Series*, No. 175, p. 155; 1989 from *P-60 Series*, No. 171, p. 149; 1980 from *P-60 Series*, No. 175, pp. 219-21; and Bureau of Economic Analysis diskettes, released April 22, 1992 and September 6, 1991 (for population).

7.7 *Child Poverty Rates, by Race and Region.* Children's Defense Fund (1991), p. 147.

7.8 *Percentage Change in Average Hourly Wages by Gender, Education, and Region.* Authors' tabulation of Current Population Survey (CPS) wage data, see Appendix.

7.9 *Percent Change in the Median Hourly Wages of Men and Women, by State.* Authors' tabulation of Current Population Survey (CPS) wage data, see Appendix.

7.10 *State and Local Effective Tax Rates in the Ten Largest States as Percent of Income for Families of Four.* McIntyre et al. (1991), pp. 23, 28, 32, 41, 49, 51, 52, 54, 57, 62. Any tax analysis of this nature must make a number of assumtions regarding tax incidence. For example, in this study half of the property tax paid on rental units is allocated to the owners of the property, and half is assigned to the renters in the form of higher rents. We consider the assumptions in this study to be reasonable and unbiased. The methodology of the study is discussed on pp. 70-72.

7.11 *Job Growth by Region and Division.* Calculated from employment and population figures in Bureau of Economic Analysis diskettes, released April 22, 1992 and September 6, 1991.

7.12 *Unemployment Rates by Region, Division, and State.* Bureau of Labor Statistics diskette (1992).

7.13 *City/Suburb/Rural Comparisons of Income Distribution.* *P-60 Series*, No. 177, p. 18-19. "Cities" refer to the Census Bureau terminology "central cities," "Suburbs" to "not central cities," (but within metropolitan), and "Rural" to "not metropolitan."

7.14 *Poverty Rates by City, Suburban, and Rural Residence.* Center on Budget and Policy (1992), p. 20.

7.15   *Poverty by Region and Residence. P-60 Series*, No. 175, p. 154; *P-60 Series*, No. 171, pp. 149, 315.

7.16   *Urban and Rural Employment Growth.* Department of Agriculture (Winter 1991/92), pp. 14-15.

7.17   *Unemployment Rates, Regular and Adjusted, Urban/Rural.* See note to Table 7.16.

Chapter 8

8.1   *Proficiency in Mathematics and Science, Age 9, 13, and 17 by Race/Ethnicity.* U.S. Department of Education (1991a), p. 64.

8.2   *Scholastic Aptitude Test Scores by Race/Ethnic Group.* U.S. Department of Education (1991a), p. 123.

8.3   *Proficiency in Mathematics and Science, Grades 4, 8, and 12, by Commu-nity.* Mathematics: U.S. Department of Education (1991b), pp. 485, 497, 511. Science: U.S. Department of Education (1992), pp. 145-47.

8.4   *Effects of Family Background on Scores of 8th Graders.* U.S. Department of Education (1989), p. 118. Family background, or "socioeconomic status," is based on a composite score of parental education and occupations, family income, and household characteristics. The "disadvantaged" group is the lowest fourth; the "average" is the middle one-half; the "advantaged" group is the top fourth.

8.5   *Average Proficiency of 4th, 8th, and 12th Graders by School Rank.* U.S. Department of Education (1991b), p. 13.

8.6   *The Shrinking Federal Student Aid Grant.* Pell grant data are from The College Board (1991), p. 10. Cost data are for all institutions and are from U.S. Department of Education (1991a), p. 296. Figures for 1985 and 1987 are estimates.

8.7   *Costs of College: The Percent of Students with College Costs Covered by Expected Family Contribution and the Average Percent of Total Cost Met by Aid, by Family Income.* U.S. Department of Education, *The Condition of Education* (1991), pp. 113-14.

8.8   *Net Cost of College as a Ratio of Expected Family Contribution, by Family Income.* U.S. Department of Education, *The Condition of Education* (1991), p. 114.

8.9   *Postsecondary Enrollment and Degree Attainment by Race/Ethnic Group.* U.S. Department of Education (1991a), pp. 200, 264, 267, 270.

8.10   *Public Expenditures on Education as a Percent of GDP.* Organisation of Economic Co-operation and Development (OECD) (1990b), p. 87.

8.11 *Private and Total Educational Expenditures, as a Percent of GDP.* See note to Table 8.10.

8.12 *Public School Expenditures per Pupil. Adjusted for Cost of Living Differences Between States.* U.S. Department of Education (1991), p. 28.

8.13 *Housing Costs.* Apgar et al. (1991), p. 24. See note from Table 8.14 for description of the methodology used to calculate housing costs.

8.14 *Burdens of Buying Homes and Renting.* Apgar et al. (1991), p. 24. Incomes: 1970 is from the 1970 Census of Populations; 1967-1969 are from the Panel Survey of Income Dynamics (PSID); 1971-1972 are interpolated from the PSID and 1970 Census of Population; 1973-1983 are from the American Housing Survey (AHS); 1983-1989 are from the AHS, adjusted by the Current Population Survey.

Prime first-time home buyers are married-couple renters ages 25 to 29. House prices are the AHS median values of houses purchased by first-time home buyers ages 25 to 29 in 1977, indexed by the Census Department's Construction Reports C-27 Constant Quality Home Price Index. Mortgage rates equal Federal Home Loan Bank Board contract mortgage rate. Yearly payments are calculated based on a 30-year mortgage with a 20% down payment.

Also included in yearly home costs are property taxes, insurance, fuel and utilities, and maintenance.

The tax benefits are deducted. Rent is median 1977 contract rent from AHS, indexed by the Consumer Price Index (CPI) residential rent index, with depreciation adjustments. Also included in rental costs are fuel and utilities, property taxes, and insurance.

8.15 *Percent of Owner and Renter Families Who Could Not Afford Median Priced Homes.* U.S. Department of Commerce, *Series P-20* (1991), p. 11. In this analysis, "family" refers to a group of two or more persons related by birth, marriage or adoption who reside together. Affordability calculations were made using a conventional fixed-rate 30-year mortgage. The interest rate used is the average contract interest rate on loans made in the months of February through May 1988. The cost of the median home is specific to each of the four Census regions. Income includes wages, salaries, wealth and other types of "permanent" income.

8.16 *Shelter Poverty, by Household Size.* Stone (1993), pp. 419, 420, 422, 423. Averages for panel B use 1979 weights for the number of households in each category, so that changes in shelter poverty are not a function of the shift to smaller households over the 1980s. The data for 1991 are estimates based on predicted family incomes, housing costs, unemployment, and changes in the number of households.

8.17 *Home Ownership Rates by Age of Household Head.* Apgar et al. (1991), p. 9.

8.18 *Percent of Households Living in Deficient and Overcrowded Housing.* Lazere et al. (1991), pp. 24-25. The specific physical and structural defficiences, as defined by the Bureau of the Census and the Department of Housing and Urban Development, are given on p. 22 of the report.

8.19 *Estimates of Homelessness.* Burt and Cohen (1989), p. 2. Estimate of children, p. 28. Upper-bound for children is from *Green Book* (1992), p. 1183.

8.20 *Characteristics of Service-Using Homeless Adults, in Percents. Green Book* (1992), p. 1187.

8.21 *OECD Spending on Health.* Schieber and Poullier (1991), p. 109.

8.22 *The Main Components of Health-Care Expenditures in the U.S., per Capita. Green Book* (1992), p. 289.

8.23 *The Family Health-Care Burden.* Families USA Foundation (1991): Tables 4A and 4B. The costs of health services and supplies come from the Office of National Cost Estimates. Direct sources of financing health expenditures include out-of-pocket expenditures, health insurance, and public programs. These financing sources were split into public and private sources; private sources were then divided into household and business contributions. See methodology section in the Families USA Foundation report for further description of data sources involved in these calculations.

8.24 *Health Indicators in U.S. and OECD Average.* Health Care Financing Administration (1989), pp. 177-78, 185-86 for data from 1970-1986. Data for 1989 are from OECD (1992b), pp. 46-47. Turkey is excluded from OECD averages as it has the health statistics and living standards of a Third World country and would skew the averages.

Infant mortality is deaths of infants less than one-year-old, as a percent of all live births. Perinatal mortality is fetal deaths occurring after 28 weeks of pregnancy, plus infant deaths occurring prior to seven days after birth. 1986 perinatal mortality for Belgium, France, Italy, and Spain are actually from 1984, and for Ireland, from 1985. Canadian life expectancies in 1960 and 1980 are actually from 1961 and 1981, respectively. Portuguese life expectancies in 1980 are from 1981.

8.25 *Infant and Neonatal Mortality Rates, by Race.* National Center for Health Statistics. United States (1990), p. 107.

8.26 *Number and Percent of the Non-aged Population without Health Insurance. Green Book* (1992), p. 318.

8.27 *Breaks in Health Insurance During a 28-Month Period.* Nelson and Short (1990). Sample is those numbers of the Survey of Income and Program Participation 1985 panel (interviewed February 1985-August 1987) for whom 28 months of continuous information was available.

8.28   *Percent of U.S. Population Obtaining Health Insurance from Specified Sources. Green Book* (1992), p. 312.

8.29   *Persons without Health Insurance: Their Attachment to the Workforce. Green Book* (1992, 1991, 1990), pp. 315, 311, 291, respectively.

8.30   *Health Insurance Coverage of Workers, by Industry. Green Book* (1991), p. 312.

8.31   *Employer Health Care Burden for the Average Business.* See note for Table 8.23; Tables 5A and 5B.

8.32   *Public Health Expenditures as a Percentage of Total Health Expenditures, OECD Countries. Green Book* (1992), p. 330.

8.33   *Percent of Women with Children in the Labor Force, by Age of Child. Green Book* (1992), p. 935.

8.34   *Child-care Problems as a Constraint on Work, Women 21 to 29 Years Old.* Cattan (1991), p. 5.

8.35   *Mothers, 21 to 29 Years Old, Not in the Labor Force, by Selected Characteristics.* Cattan (1991), p. 6.

8.36   *Child-care Related Constraints on Women's Employment.* Veum and Gleason (1991), p. 16.

8.37   *Average Percentage of Family Income Spent on Child Care by Family Income. Green Book* (1992), p. 944.

8.38   *Child-care Cost Burden, as Percentage of Income for Low- and Middle-Income Families: Licensed Centers in Four Cities.* Cost data are from Children's Defense Fund (1991), p. 43. State specific median wages are from Current Population Survey (CPS) wage data; see Appendix. The value of the Earned Income Tax Credit was added to the income of both family types. The value of the Dependent Care Tax Credit was added to the income of two-parent families only, since the income of single-parent families was too low to qualify for this non-refundable credit. Since these are the only effects of the tax system factored into these estimates (i.e., no tax liabilities are accounted for), the percentages are underestimates of the actual child-care burden.

Chapter 9

9.1   *Per Capita GDP Growth in Ten Countries.* GDP stands for "Gross Domestic Product," and is essentially the total of all money received for goods and services produced in the economy in a single year. It is not exactly the same thing as Gross National Product, or GNP, which is total money received from all productive sources, because GNP also includes net investment income from abroad. However, the differences between GDP and GNP are usually very small, which is why GDP per capita is commonly used as an indicator of national living standards.

Real GDP comes from Organisation of Economic Co-operation and Development (OECD) (1992c); civilian employment comes from U.S. Department of Labor, Monthly Labor Review (July 1986), p. 96 and (June 1992), p. 113; and total population comes from OECD (1992c), pp. 156-57. Ideally, this type of decomposition would only use the adult population since this is the relevant population when examining labor market participation. However, international data on adult populations were not readily available. At any rate, the findings would be similar.

9.2 *Living Standards vs. Productivity Growth.* Growth rates for real per capita GDP and for productivity (GDP per civilian worker) were computed, and a straightforward weighted average of these rates was computed. Then the growth rates were converted to indices, with the weighted average growth rates equal to 100. The weighted averages were weighted by the populations of the countries; a country's population was taken to be the arithmetic average of the populations in 1979 and 1988. These countries were selected because the Bureau of Labor Statistics regularly compiles information about their employment levels. Civilian employment levels come from U.S. Department of Labor, Monthly Labor Review (June 1992), p. 112. Real GDP comes from Organisation of Economic Co-operation and Development (OECD) (1992c).

9.3 *Productivity Growth Rates.* Civilian employment levels are from U.S. Department of Labor, Monthly Labor Review (June 1992), p. 112. Real GDP comes from Organisation of Economic Co-operation and Development (OECD) (1992c).

9.4 *Hourly Manufacturing Compensation Growth.* The consumer price index listed in the International Monetary Fund (1991) was used to deflate hourly compensation in all countries except the U.S. We deflated U.S. compensation growth using the CPI-U-X1. Data for all employees is from U.S. Department of Labor (1992), p. 3; data for production workers in manufacturing is from U.S. Department of Labor (1990b).

9.5 *Manufacturing Hourly Compensation Compared, (Using Purchasing Power Parity Exchange Rates).* Exchange rates are from Organisation of Economic Co-operation and Development (OECD) (1992), p. 156-57. Data for all workers are from U.S. Department of Labor (1992), p. 3. Data for production workers are from U.S. Department of Labor (1990b), and from U.S. Department of Labor (1992), p. 8.

9.6 *Manufacturing Hourly Compensation Compared, (Using Market Exchange Rates).* See note to Table 9.5.

9.7 *Per Capita Income Compared to U.S.* Organisation of Economic Co-operation and Development (OECD) (1992c), pp. 146-47.

9.8 *Income Distribution: International Comparisons. Green Book* (1992), p. 1293.

9.9 *International Poverty Statistics.* Smeeding (1992), p. 31. The poverty thresholds used are 40% of the median income in the relevant country, adjusted for family size. Income is post-tax and post-transfer, and includes the value of food stamps.

9.10 *The Impact of Taxes and Transfers on International Poverty Rates.* Smeeding (1992), p. 33.

9.11 *Tax and Transfer System Effectiveness.* Smeeding (1992), p. 34.

9.12 *Poverty Rates and Transitions Out of Poverty for Families with Children.* Duncan et al. (1991): Table 1.

9.13 *Absolute Poverty Among Children, Adults, and the Elderly.* U.S. Department of Labor, Monthly Labor Review (July 1986), p. 96, and (June 1992), p. 112.

9.14 *Jobs Created in Ten Countries.* Civilian employment from U.S. Department of Labor, Monthly Labor Review (July 1986), p. 96, and (June 1992), p. 112.

9.15 *Contributions to Employment Growth in Ten Countries.* See note Table 9.14. Population from Organisation of Economic Co-operation and Development (OECD) (1992), pp. 156-57. Ideally, this type of decomposition would only use the adult population since this is the relevant population when examining labor market participation. However, international data on adult populations were not readily available. At any rate, the findings would be similar.

9.16 *Hours Worked per Employee in Manufacturing, Indexed to the United States.* Leete-Guy and Schor (1992), p. 16.

9.17 *Paid Vacation in European Countries.* Leete-Guy and Schor (1992), p. 19.

9.18 *Public Spending on Training and Placement, Direct Job Creation and Subsidies, as Percent of GDP.* Organisation of Economic Co-operation and Development (OECD) (1991), pp. 238-49.

9.19 *Unemployment in OECD Countries.* Organisation of Economic Co-operation and Development (OECD) (1992a), p. 192.

9.20 *Unemployment and Unemployment Compensation.* See notes to Tables 9.18 and 9.19.

473

Figure Notes

3D   *Employment at or Below Poverty Level Wages, By Race, 1973-1991.* See notes to Table 3.10, Table 3.11, and Table 3.12.

3E   *Change in Real Hourly Wage by Education, 1973-1991.* See note to Table 3.19.

3F   *Real Entry-Level Wages for High School Graduates, 1973-1991.* See note to Table 3.23.

3G   *Real Entry-Level Wages for College Graduates, 1973-1991.* See note to Table 3.23.

3H   *Pay in Expanding and Shrinking Industries, 1948-1987.* See note to Table 3.27.

3I   *Trade Induced Changes in Labor Supply, 1967-1985.* See note to Table 3.30.

3J   *Union Pay Premiums, 1989 Dollars.* See note to Table 3.34.

3K   *Value of Minimum Wage, 1960-1992.* See note to Table 3.39.

3L   *Real Growth in Executive After-Tax Pay, 1979-1989.* See note to Table 3.46.

3M   *Black-White Wage Differentials Among Young Workers, 1973-1989.* See note to Table 3.49.

3N   *Growth in Skill and Education Requirements, 1970-2000.* See note to Table 3.51.

4A   *Real Rates of Underemployment, 1973-1991.* See note to Table 4.2.

4B   *Duration of Recessions, 1948-1992.* See note to Table 4.3.

4C   *Civilian Employment Growth, 1947-1991.* See note to Table 4.9.

4D   *Part-Time Employment Rates, 1973-1991.* See note to Table 4.10.

4E   *Partially or Fully Paid Medical Benefits Offered to Employees, by Full- or Part-time Status, 1991.* Hewitt Associates survey as in Callaghan and Hartmann (1991): Figure 13, p. 16.

4F   *Multiple Jobholding Rates, 1979-1991.* See note to Table 4.16.

4G   *Temporary and Personnel Services Industry Employment, 1973-1991.* See note to Table 4.21.

5A   *Growth of Household Wealth Per Adult, 1949-1989.* See note to Table 5.1.

5B   *Distribution of Income and Wealth, 1989.* See note to Table 5.2.

5C   *Distribution of Wealth, 1983-1989.* See note to Table 5.6.

5D   *Change in Net Worth by Wealth Class, 1983-1989.* See note to Table 5.8.

5E   *Distribution of Net Worth Growth by Wealth Class, 1983-1989.* Based on data in Table 5.8, last column, adjusted to sum to 100%, as table data does not sum to 100 due to negative growth for the middle and second quartiles.

6A   *Predicted vs. Actual Poverty Rates, 1959-1991.* See note to Table 6.1.

6B   *Poverty Rates by Price Index, 1974-1991.* CPI-U-X1 rates to 1989 from *P-60 Series*, No. 171; 1990 figure from authors' communication with the Bureau of the Census; for CPI-U rates see note to Table 6.1.

6C   *Persistent Poverty in Industrialized Countries: Households With Children, Mid-1980s.* McFate (1991): Figure 2.

6D   *Poverty Before and After Transfers: Elderly vs. All Persons, 1967-1990.* See note to Table 6.12.

6E *Expected Lifetime Births by Marital Status and Race, 1960-1987.* See note to Table 6.18.

6F *Poverty Before and After Transfers: Families with Children, 1967-1990.* See note to Table 6.12.

6G *Demographic and Benefit-Sum Trends, 1960-1989.* Moffit (1992): Figure 4. Data brought forward to 1989 from *P-60 Series*, 1981-1989 (headship); U.S. National Center for Health Statistics, *Monthly Vital Reports*, 1981-1989 (divorce); U.S. National Center for Health Statistics, *Advance Report of Final Natality Statistics*, 1981-1989 (out-of-wedlock births). Added data for benefit sum are from *Green Book,* (1992), pp. 1210-11.

6H *AFDC Participation Rates, 1967-1987.* See note to Table 6.20.

7A *Percentage Point Change in Middle Class by Region, 1969-1989.* See note to Table 7.3.

7B *Distribution of Changes in States' Income Inequality, 1979-1989.* See note to Table 7.4.

7C *Percentage Change in Median Hourly Wages by State, 1979-1989.* Authors' tabulations of Current Population Survey (CPS) wage data, see Appendix.

7D *Percentage Change in Median Hourly Wages by State, 1989-1991.* Authors' tabulations of Current Population Survey (CPS) wage data, see Appendix.

7E *State and Local Effective Tax Rates in the Five Most Populated States, 1991.* See note to Table 7.10.

7F *Unemployment Rates by Region, 1979-1991.* See note to Table 7.12.

7G *City, Suburban, and Rural Poverty Rates, 1973-1991.* See note to Table 7.14.

7H *Urban and Rural Unemployment Rates, 1979-1990.* See note to Table 7.17.

8A *Total College Costs by Type of Four-Year Institution, 1976-1989.* U.S. Department of Education (1991), pp. 296-97.

8B *Enrollment Rates for 3- & 4-year-olds in Primary Education by Race/Ethnicity, 1974-1989.* U.S. Department of Education (1992), p. 18.

8C *Percent of 18- to 24-year-olds Completing High School, 1970-1989.* Carter and Wilson (1992): Table 1. Series for blacks and Hispanics smoothed with three-year moving average to reveal trend.

8D *Percent of 18- to 24-year-olds in College, 1970-1989.* Carter and Wilson (1992): Table 1. Series for blacks and Hispanics smoothed with three-year moving average to reveal trend.

8E *Beginning Teacher Salaries vs. Other College Graduates, 1972-1991.* Educational Research Service, (editions since 1973-1974).

8F *After-Tax Home Owning and Rental Costs, 1967-1990.* See note to Table 8.13.

8G *Home Owning and Rental Costs as a Percent of Income, 1967-1990.* See note to Table 8.14.

8H *Low-Rent Units and Low-Income Renters, 1970-1989.* Lazere, et al. (1991), p. 5.

Appendix: Wage Analysis Computations

This appendix provides background information on our analysis of wage data from the Current Population Survey (CPS), which is prepared by the Bureau of the Census for the Bureau of Labor Statistics (BLS). Specifically, we analyze computer tapes provided by the BLS which have a full year's data on the outgoing rotation groups (ORG) in the CPS. We believe that the CPS ORG files allow for a more timely, up-to-date, and more accurate analysis of wage trends than the traditionally used March CPS files (which, for 1991, will not be available until the end of 1992) while keeping within the familiar labor force definitions and concepts employed by the CPS.

The ORG files provide data on those CPS respondents in either the fourth or eighth month of the CPS (i.e., in groups four or eight, out of a total of eight groups). Therefore, in any given month the ORG file represents a quarter of the CPS sample. For a given year, the ORG file is equivalent to three months of the entire CPS (one quarter of the 12 monthly surveys). For our analysis, we use the full year ORG samples, with sample sizes ranging from 155,265 in 1979 to 171,296 in 1991.

Changes in annual or weekly earnings can result from changes in hourly earnings or from more working time (either more hours per week or more weeks per year). Our analysis is centered around the hourly wage, which represents the pure price of labor (exclusive of benefits), because we are interested in changing pay levels for the workforce and its subgroups. We do this to be able to clearly distinguish changes in earnings resulting from more (or less) work rather than more (or less) pay. Our analysis, therefore, does not take into account that weekly or annual earnings may have changed because of longer working hours or lesser or greater opportunities for employment.

In our view, the ORG files provide a better source of data for wage analysis than the traditionally used March CPS files. In order to calculate hourly wages from the March CPS, analysts must make calculations using at least two of three retrospective variables: the annual earnings, weeks worked, and usual weekly hours worked in the year prior to the survey. Limiting the March sample to full-time, full-year workers is increasingly unsatisfactory since this is only two-thirds of wage earners and there can be a significant variation of hours worked in this group over time and year by year. In contrast, respondents in the ORG are asked a set of questions about hours worked, weekly wages, and (for workers paid by the hour) hourly wages in the week prior to the survey. In this regard, the data from the ORG are likely to be more reliable than data from the March CPS. The ORG files are also more current and have a much larger sample size.

Our sub-sample includes all wage and salary workers with valid wage and hours data, whether paid weekly or by the hour. Specifically, in order to be included in our sub-sample, respondents had to meet the following criteria:
— Aged 18 to 64;
— Employed in the public or private sector (self-employed were excluded);

479

—Hours worked within the valid range in the survey (0-99 hours per week); and,

—Either hourly or weekly wages within the valid survey range (top-coding problems discussed below).

For those who met these criteria, an hourly wage was calculated in the following manner. If a valid hourly wage was reported, that wage was used throughout our analysis. For salaried workers (those who only report a weekly wage), the hourly wage was their weekly wage divided by their hours worked. CPS weights were applied to make the sample nationally representative.

For the survey years 1979, 1987, and 1988, the weekly wage is top-coded at $999.00. Particularly for the later years, this truncation of the wage distribution creates a downward bias in the mean wage. This is especially problematic for comparisons between 1987 and 1988 to later years, when the top code was raised to $1,923.00. Fortunately, the 1987 and 1988 ORG files have an unedited field that allowed us to impose the new higher top-code present in the ORG files for 1989 and beyond. This unedited field in the 1987 and 1988 ORG files includes reported weekly wages up to the new top-code of $1,923. There are no imputations in that data field.

If a weekly wage from the edited field (with the lower top-code) was top-coded, and a valid wage existed in the unedited field, we used the wage with the higher top-code. At the top of the wage distribution, this procedure yielded substantially higher mean hourly wages. For example, in 1988, for males with more than six years of education beyond high school the mean hourly wage increased by $1.65, from $16.36 to $18.01, when using the field with the higher top-code.

We extended our analysis back to 1973 by pooling the 1973 and 1974 May CPS. The 1974 data were deflated to 1973 dollars using the Personal Consumption Expenditures (PCE) (1972 base year).

Demographic variables are also used in the analysis. Education refers to years of school completed. Our race variable is comprised of four mutually exclusive categories:

—White, non-Hispanic;
—Black, non-Hispanic;
—Hispanic, any race;
—All others.

Inflation Adjustment

To adjust for inflation we used the CPI-U-X1, which corrects the more commonly used Consumer Price Index (CPI) for allegedly overstating inflation in the 1970s (starting in 1983 the two indices are the same). This is the deflator we use throughout the book.

Time Period

Our analysis tracks wages from 1979 onward by examining trends from one cyclical peak, 1979, to another, 1989, and then from 1989 to the most recent year, 1991. The post 1989 wage trends are influenced by the cyclical downturn and may partially reflect short-term, recession-induced developments. We believe, however, that the 1989-1991 wage trends primarily reflect longer- term trends. For one, the use of hourly wages (especially person-weighted) as our measure moderates the impact of the cycle. Two, the trends we observe from 1989 to 1991 prevailed before the recession. This can be seen in the year-by-year wage trends from 1987 to 1991.

We do analyze a number of trends from 1987 onwards. There are several reasons why this particular time period is analyzed. In order to show that the wage trends we identified preceded the onset of the recession it was necessary to examine some pre-recession years. However, for technical reasons—the ORG data has a different top-code (and no unedited field with the new top code) in 1986—we could not examine trends prior to 1987. Therefore, the wages of high-wage workers, such as college-educated workers, are not comparable between 1986 and 1987 (although there is a comparability between 1979 and 1987 because the old top-code in 1979 was hardly binding).

Bibliography

American Federation of Teachers. *Survey & Analysis of Salary Trends, 1989*. Washington, DC: AFT, 1989.

Apgar, William C., Jr., Denise DiPasquale, Jean Cummings and Nancy McArdle. "The State of the Nation's Housing: 1991." Cambridge, MA: Joint Center for Housing Studies of Harvard University, 1991.

Bakija, Jon, and C. Eugene Steuerle. "Individual Income Taxation Since 1948." *National Tax Journal*, Vol XLLIV, No. 4, Part 2, December 1991, pp. 451–475.

Bane, Mary Jo and David T. Ellwood. "Slipping Into and Out of Poverty: The Dynamics of Spells." *The Journal of Human Resources*, Vol. XXI, No. 1, Winter 1986, pp. 1–23.

Barancik, Scott, and Isaac Shapiro. *Where Have all the Dollars Gone: A State by State Analysis of Income Disparities in the 1980s*. Washington, DC: Center on Budget and Policy Priorities, 1992.

Blackburn, McKinley L., David E. Bloom, and Richard B. Freeman. "Changes in Earnings Differentials in the 1980s: Concordance, Convergence, Causes, and Consequences." Working Paper No. 3901. Cambridge, MA: National Bureau of Economic Research, 1991.

Blank, Rebecca M. "Are Part-Time Jobs Bad Jobs?" In Gary Burtless, ed., *A Future of Lousy Jobs*? Washington, DC: Brookings Institution, 1990.

Blank, Rebecca M. "Why Were Poverty Rates So High in the 1980s?" Working Paper No. 3878. Cambridge, MA: National Bureau of Economic Research, 1991.

Board of Governors, Federal Reserve System. *Balance Sheets for the U.S. Economy: 1945–1989*. Washington, DC: FRS, April 1990.

Board of Governors, Federal Reserve System. *Balance Sheets for the U.S. Economy: 1960–91*. Washington, DC: FRS, March 1992.

Borjas, George J., Richard B. Freeman, and Lawrence F. Katz. "On the Labor Market Effects of Immigration and Trade." Working Paper No. 3761. Cambridge, MA: National Bureau of Economic Research, 1991.

Bound, John, and Richard B. Freeman. "What Went Wrong? The Erosion of Relative Earnings and Employment Among Young Black Men in the 1980s." Unpublished, 1991.

Burt, Martha R., and Barbara E. Cohen. "America's Homeless: Numbers, Characteristics, and Programs that Serve Them." *Urban Institute Report 89–3*. Washington, DC: Urban Institute Press, 1989.

Callaghan, Polly, and Heidi Hartmann. *Contingent Work: A Chart Book on Part-Time and Temporary Employment*. Washington, D.C.: Economic Policy Institute, 1991.

Cancian, Maria, Sheldon Danziger, and Peter Gottschalk. "The Changing Contributions of Men and Women to the Level and Distribution of Family Income, 1968–1988." Prepared for the Jerome Levy Economics Institute Conference: *Economic Inequality at the Close of the Twentieth Century*, Bard College, June 1991.

Card, David. "The Effect of Unions on the Distribution of Wages: Redistribution or Relabelling?" Working Paper No. 287. Department of Economics, Princeton: Princeton University, 1991.

Card, David. "The Effect of Unions on the Distribution of Wages: Redistribution or Relabeling?" Working Paper No. 287. Department of Economics, Princeton: Princeton University, 1991.

Carre, Françoise J. "Temporary Employment in the Eighties." In Virginia L. DuRivage, ed., *New Policies for the Part-Time and Contingent Workforce*. Economic Policy Institute Series. Armonk: M.E. Sharpe, Inc., 1992.

Carter, Debroah J., and Reginald Wilson. *Minorities in Higher Education*. Washington, DC: American Council on Education, 1992.

Cattan, Peter. "Child-care Problems: An Obstacle to Work." *Monthly Labor Review*, October 1991, pp. 3–9.

Center on Budget and Policy Priorities. *1990 Poverty Tables*. Washington, DC: CBPP, 1992.

Children's Defense Fund. *The State of America's Children: 1991*. Washington, DC: CDF, 1991.

Children's Defense Fund. *The Health of America's Children: Maternal and Child Health Data Book*. Washington, DC: CDF, 1989.

College Board. *Trends in Student Aid: 1981 to 1991*. New York: College Board Publications, 1991.

Congressional Budget Office. "Shares and Sources of Family Income: All Families, 1977, 1980, 1985, 1988, 1989." Unpublished, 1992.

Costrell, Robert M. *The Effects of Industry Employment Shifts on Wage Growth: 1948–87*. A study prepared for the Joint Economic Committee, Washington, DC: JEC, August 1988.

Cutler, David M., and Lawrence F. Katz. "Rising Inequality? Changes in the Distribution of Income and Consumption in the 1980s." Presented at the American Economic Association Meetings, January 1992.

Danziger, Sheldon H., and Daniel H. Weinberg. "Market Income, Income Transfers and the Trend in Poverty." Paper presented at the conference *Poverty and Public Policy: What Do We Know? What Should We Do?* Institute for Research on Poverty. Madison: University of Wisconsin, May 28–30, 1992.

Democratic Study Group. "They Didn't Come to the Party: A Tough Decade for Families in the Middle." Special Report, No. 101–32. Washington, DC: U.S. House of Representatives, 1990.

Duncan, Greg, et al. "Poverty and Social Assistance Dynamics in the United States, Canada and Europe." Paper presented at the conference *Poverty and Public Policy*, Washington, DC: Joint Center for Political and Economic Studies, September, 1991.

Duncan, Greg J., Timothy Smeeding and Willard Rodgers. *W(h)ither the Middle Class: A Dynamic View?* Survey Research Center. Ann Arbor: University of Michigan, 1991.

Eargle, Judith. *Household Wealth and Asset Ownership: 1988*. Current Population Reports, Series P-70, No. 22, U.S. Bureau of the Census, Washington, DC: U.S. Government Printing Office, 1990.

The Economist. "Bosses Get Rich." December 23, 1989, pp. 92–93.

Educational Research Service. *Salaries Paid Professional Personnel in Public Schools*. Reston: ERS, various dates.

Educational Research Service. *Salaries Paid Support Personnel in Public Schools*. Reston: ERS, various dates.

Families USA Foundation. *Health Spending: The Growing Threat to the Family Budget*. Washington, DC: Families USA Foundation, December 1991.

Faux, Jeff. *Family Incomes in Trouble*. Briefing Paper. Washington, DC: Economic Policy Institute, 1986.

Fisher, Gordon M. *Trends in Money Income and Poverty*. Unpublished. U.S. Census Bureau, November 1986.

Freeman, Richard B. "How Much Has De-unionization Contributed to the Rise in Male Earnings Inequality?" Working Paper No. 3826. Cambridge, MA: National Bureau of Economic Research, 1991.

Haber, Sheldon E., Enrique L. Lamas, and Jules H. Lichtenstein. "On Their Own: The Self-employed and Others in Private Business." *Monthly Labor Review*, May 1987.

Harrison, Bennett, and Barry Bluestone. *The Great U-Turn*. New York: Basic Books, 1988.

Health Care Financing Administration. *Health Care Financing Review: 1989 Annual Supplement*. Washington, DC: U.S. Government Printing Office, December 1989.

Henwood, Doug. *Left Business Observer*. Supplement No. 1. New York: Henwood, September 1991.

International Monetary Fund. *International Financial Statistics*. Washington, DC: IMF, monthly.

Jencks, Christopher. *"Is the American Underclass Growing?"* In Christopher Jencks and Paul E. Peterson, eds., *The Urban Underclass*. Washington, DC: Brookings Institution, 1991.

Jerome Levy Economics Institute Conference on *Economic Inequality at the Close of the Twentieth Century*, Bard College, June 1991. Revised January, 1992.

Joint Economic Committee. *Economic Indicators*. Washington, DC: JEC, Monthly.

Joint Economic Committee. *Families on a Treadmill: Work and Income in the 1980s*. Washington, DC: JEC, January 1992.

Karier, Thomas. "What Happened to the Corporate Profit Tax?" Working Paper No. 37. Annandale-on-Hudson: Jerome Levy Economics Institute, May 1990.

Katz, Lawrence F., and Kevin M. Murphy. "Changes in Relative Wages, 1963–1987: Supply and Demand Factors." Unpublished. Cambridge: Harvard, 1990.

Krueger, Alan B. "How Computers Have Changed the Wage Structure: Evidence from Microdata, 1984–89." Presented at National Bureau of Economic Research Labor Studies Workshop, July 1991.

Lazere, Edward B., et al. *A Place to Call Home: The Low Income Housing Crisis Continues*. Washington, DC: Center on Budget and Policy Priorities, 1991.

Leete-Guy, Laura, and Juliet B. Schor. *The Great American Time Squeeze: Trends in Work and Leisure, 1969–1989*. Washington, DC: Economic Policy Institute, 1992.

Levit, Katharine R., and Cathy A. Cowan. "Business, Households, and Governments: Health Care Costs, 1990." *Health Care Financing Review*, Vol. 13, No. 2, Winter 1991, pp.83–91.

Levit, Katharine R., Mark S. Freeland, and Daniel R. Waldo. "Health Spending and Ability to Pay: Business, Individuals, and Government." *Health Care Financing Review*, Vol. 10, No. 3, Spring 1989.

McFate, Katherine. *Poverty, Inequality and the Crisis of Social Policy*. Washington, DC: Joint Center for Political and Economic Studies, 1991.

McIntyre, Robert S., et al. *A Far Cry From Fair*. Washington, DC: Citizens for Tax Justice, April 1991.

Meisenheimer II, Joseph R., Earl F. Mellor, and Leo G. Rydzewski. "The Labor Market in 1991." *Monthly Labor Review*, Vol. 115, No. 2, February 1992, pp. 3–17.

Merrill Lynch. *Weekly Economic and Financial Commentary*. May 18, 1992.

Mishel, Lawrence. *The Polarization of America: The Loss of Good Jobs, Falling Incomes and Rising Inequality*. Washington, DC: Industrial Union Department, AFL-CIO, October 1986.

Mishel, Lawrence, and Jacqueline Simon. *The State of Working America*. Washington, DC: Economic Policy Institute, 1988.

Mishel, Lawrence R. "The Late Great Debate on Deindustrialization." *Challenge*, January/February 1989.

Mishel, Lawrence, and Jared Bernstein. "Declining Wages for High School and College Graduates." Washington, DC: Economic Policy Institute, 1992.

Mishel, Lawrence, and David Frankel. *The State of Working America, 1990–91 edition*. Economic Policy Institute Series. Armonk: M.E. Sharpe, Inc., 1991.

Mishel, Lawrence, and Ruy Teixeira. *The Myth of the Coming Labor Shortage: Jobs, Skills, and Incomes of America's Workforce 2000*. Washington, DC: Economic Policy Institute, 1991.

Moffit, Robert. "Incentive Effects of the U.S. Welfare System: A Review." *Journal of Economic Literature*, Vol. XXX, No. 1, March 1992, pp. 1–61.

Murphy, Kevin, and Finis Welch. "Recent Trends in Real Wages: Evidence From Household Data." Paper prepared for the Health Care Financing Administration of the U.S. Department of Health and Human Services. Chicago: University of Chicago, January 1989.

Nelson, Charles, and Kathleen Short. *Health Insurance Coverage: 1986–88*. Current Population Reports, Household Economic Studies, Series P-70, No. 17. Washington, DC: U.S. Government Printing Office, 1990.

Nelson, F. Howard. *An Interstate Cost-of-Living Index*. Washington, DC: American Federation of Teachers, November 1989.

OECD. *Revenue Statistics of OECD Member Countries: 1965–1989*. Paris: Organisation for Economic Co-operation and Development, 1990a.

OECD. *Education in OECD Countries: 1987–88*. Paris: Organisation for Economic Co-operation and Development, 1990b.

OECD. *Employment Outlook*. Paris: Organisation for Economic Co- operation and Development, 1991.

OECD. *OECD Economic Outlook*. No. 51. Paris: Organisation for Economic Co-operation and Development, 1992a.

OECD. *OECD in Figures*. 1992 Edition. Paris: Organisation for Economic Co-operation and Development, 1992b.

OECD. *National Accounts: Main Aggregates*. Paris: Organisation for Economic Co-operation and Development, 1992c.

President of the United States. *Economic Report of the President*. Washington, DC: U.S. Government Printing Office, annual.

Rasell, M. Edith, and Lawrence Mishel. *Shortchanging Education: How U.S. Spending on Grades K-12 Lags Behind Other Industrial Nations*. Washington, DC: Economic Policy Institute, 1990.

Ruggles, Patricia. *Drawing the Line: Alternative Poverty Measures and Their Implications for Public Policy*. Washington, DC: Urban Institute, 1990.

Ruggles, Patricia. "Measuring Poverty." *Focus*. Vol. 14, No. 1, Spring 1992, pp. 1–9.

Sawhill, Isabel V., and Mark Condon. "Is U.S. Income Inequality Really Growing?" *Policy Bites*, No. 13. Washington, DC: Urban Institute, June 1992.

Schieber, George J., and Jean-Pierre Poullier. "International Health Spending: Issues and Trends." *Health Affairs*, Vol. 10, No. 1, Spring 1991, pp. 106–116.

Sekscenski, Edward S. "Women's Share of Moonlighting Nearly Doubles During 1969–79." *Monthly Labor Review*, Vol. 103, No. 5, May 1980.

Shapiro, Isaac. "No Escape: The Minimum Wage and Poverty." Washington, DC: Center on Budget and Policy Priorities, June 1987.

Shapiro, Isaac, and Marion Nichols. *Far From Fixed: An Analysis of the Unemployment Insurance System*. Washington, DC: Center on Budget and Policy Priorities, March 1992.

Sivestri, George, and John Lukasiewicz. "Occupational Employment Projects." *Monthly Labor Review*. Vol. 114, No. 11, November 1991.

Smeeding, Timothy M. "Why the U.S. Antipoverty System Doesn't Work Very Well." *Challenge*, January-February 1992, pp. 30–35.

Smeeding, Timothy, Barbara Boyle Torrey, and Martin Rein. "Patterns of Income and Poverty: The Economic Status of Children and the Elderly in Eight Countries." In Palmer, Smeeding, and Torrey, eds., *The Vulnerable*. Washington, DC: Urban Institute, 1988.

Stinson, John F., Jr. "Moonlighting by Women Jumped to Record Highs." *Monthly Labor Review*, Vol. 109, No. 11, November 1986.

Stone, Michael E. *Shelter Poverty: New Ideas on Housing Affordability*. Philadelphia: Temple University Press, forthcoming 1993.

Swartz, Katherine, and Timothy D. McBride. "Spells Without Health Insurance: Distributions of Durations and Their Link to Point-in-Time Estimates of the Uninsured." *Inquiry*. Vol. 27, Fall 1990, pp. 281–88.

Tax Foundation. *Tax Burden by Income Class: 1986–1987*. Washington, DC: Tax Foundation, 1989.

Teixeira, Ruy, and Lawrence Mishel. *Myth of Rural Labor Shortage*. Washington, DC: Economic Policy Institute, 1992.

Tilly, Chris. "Continuing Growth of Part-Time Employment." *Monthly Labor Review*, Vol. 114, No. 3, March 1991, pp. 10–18.

Towers, Perrin and Company. *Worldwide Total Remuneration, 1988*. October 1988.

U.S. Department of Agriculture, Economic Research Service. *Rural Conditions and Trends*. Vol. 2, No. 4. Washington, DC: ERS, Winter 1991/92.

U.S. Department of Commerce, Bureau of Economic Analysis. *Survey of Current Business*. Washington, DC: U.S. Government Printing Office, various dates.

U.S. Department of Commerce, Bureau of the Census. "Marital Status and Living Arrangements." *Current Population Reports: Series P-20*. Washington DC: U.S. Government Printing Office, various dates.

U.S. Department of Commerce, Bureau of the Census. *Current Population Reports: Series P-60*. Washington, DC: U.S. Government Printing Office, various dates.

U.S. Department of Commerce, Bureau of the Census. *Current Population Reports: Series P-70*. Washington, DC: U.S. Government Printing Office, various dates.

U.S. Department of Commerce, Bureau of the Census. *Who Can Afford to Buy a House?* Current Housing Report, Series H121/91–1. Washington, DC: U.S. Government Printing Office, 1991a.

U.S. Department of Commerce, Bureau of the Census. *Trends in Relative Income: 1964 to 1989*. Current Population Reports, P-60 Series, No. 177. Washington, DC: U.S. Government Printing Office, 1991b.

U.S. Department of Commerce, Bureau of the Census. "Historical Tables." Unpublished, 1991c.

U.S. Department of Commerce, Bureau of the Census. "Estimates of Median Four-Person Family Income, by State: 1974–89." Current Population Reports: TP-61. Washington, DC: U.S. Government Printing Office, 1992.

U.S. Department of Commerce, Bureau of Economic Analysis. *National Income and Product Accounts*. Washington, DC: U.S. Government Printing Office, 1992.

U.S. Department of Education, National Center for Education Statistics. *The Condition of Education*. Washington, DC: U.S. Government Printing Office, various dates.

U.S. Department of Education, National Center for Education Statistics. *Digest of Education Statistics, 1989*. Washington, DC: U.S. Government Printing Office, 1989.

U.S. Department of Education, National Center for Education Statistics. *Digest of Education Statistics, 1991*. Washington, DC: U.S. Government Printing Office, 1991a.

U.S. Department of Education, Office of Educational Research and Improvement. *The State of Mathematics Achievement: NAEP's 1990 Assessment of the Nation and the Trial Assessment of the States.* Prepared by Educational Testing Service. Washington, DC: U.S. Government Printing Office, 1991b.

U.S. Department of Education, Office of Educational Research and Improvement. *Trends in Academic Progress.* Prepared by Educational Testing Service. Washington, DC: U.S. Government Printing Office, 1991c.

U.S. Department of Education, Office of Educational Research and Improvement. *The 1990 Science Report Card.* Prepared by Educational Testing Service. Washington, DC: U.S. Government Printing Office, 1992.

U.S. Department of Health and Human Services. National Center for Health Statistics. *Health United States: 1989.* Washington, DC: U.S. Government Printing Office, 1990.

U.S. Department of Health and Human Services. National Center for Health Statistics. Advanced Report of Final Natality Statistics . Washington, DC: U.S. Government Printing Office, various years.

U.S. Department of Health and Human Services. National Center for Health Statistics. Monthly Vital Reports . Washington, DC: U.S. Government Printing Office, various years.

U.S. Department of Labor, Bureau of Labor Statistics. *Employee Compensation in the Private Nonfarm Economy, 1974.* Bulletin 1963. Washington, DC: U.S. Government Printing Office, 1977.

U.S. Department of Labor, Bureau of Labor Statistics. *Labor Force Statistics Derived From the Current Population Survey: A Databook*, Bulletin 2096, Washington, DC: U.S. Government Printing Office, September 1982.

U.S. Department of Labor, Bureau of Labor Statistics. *Supplement to Labor Force Statistics Derived From the Current Population Survey: A Databook*, Bulletin 2096–1. Washington, DC: U.S. Government Printing Office, May 1984.

U.S. Department of Labor, Bureau of Labor Statistics. Handbook of Labor Statistics, Bulletin 2217. Washington, DC: U.S. Government Printing Office, June 1985.

U.S. Department of Labor, Bureau of Labor Statistics. "Employer Costs for Employee Compensation, March 1989." USDL:89–295, Washington, DC, 1989a.

U.S. Department of Labor, Bureau of Labor Statistics. Handbook of Labor Statistics, Bulletin 2340. Washington, DC: U.S. Government Printing Office, August 1989b.

U.S. Department of Labor, Bureau of Labor Statistics, Office of Productivity and Technology. *Hourly Compensation Costs for Production Workers; 40 Manufacturing Industries; 34 Countries, 1957 and 1978–88.* Washington, D.C: U.S. Government Printing Office, August 1989c.

U.S. Department of Labor, Bureau of Labor Statistics. *Multiple Jobholding Reached Record High in May 1989*. USDL: 89–529, Washington, DC, November 6, 1989d.

U.S. Department of Labor, Bureau of Labor Statistics, *Comparative Real Gross Domestic Product, Real GDP Per Capita, and Real GDP Per Employed Person: Fourteen Countries: 1950–1989*. Washington, DC: Office of Productivity and Technology, June 28, 1990a.

U.S. Department of Labor, Bureau of Labor Statistics, Office of Productivity and Technology. *Hourly Compensation Costs for Production Workers, All Manufacturing, 34 Countries, 1975 and 1979–89*. Washington, DC: U.S. Government Printing Office, September 1990b.

U.S. Department of Labor, Bureau of Labor Statistics. *Employment, Hours, and Earnings, United States*. Volume I, 1909–90. Bulleting 2370. Washington, DC: U.S. Government Printing Office, 1991a.

U.S. Department of Labor, Bureau of Labor Statistics. *Multiple Jobholding Unchanged in May 1991*. USDL No. 91–547, *News*, October 28, 1991b.

U.S. Department of Labor, Bureau of Labor Statistics, Office of Productivity and Technology. *Underlying Data For Indexes of Output Per Hour, Hourly Compensation, and Unit Labor Costs in Manufacturing, Twelve Industrial Countries, 1950–1990 and Unit and Labor Costs in Korea and Taiwan, 1970–1990*. Washington, DC: U.S. Government Printing Office, February 5, 1992.

U.S. Department of Labor, Bureau of Labor Statistics. *Employment and Earnings*. Washington, DC: U.S. Government Printing Office, monthly.

U.S. Department of Labor. *Monthly Labor Review*. Washington, DC: Bureau of Labor Statistics, monthly.

U.S. House of Representatives, Committee on Ways and Means, Subcommittee on Human Resources. *Background Material on Family Income and Benefit Changes*. Washington, DC: U.S. Government Printing Office, 1991.

U.S. House of Representatives. *Green Book: Background Material and Data on Programs Within the Jurisdiction of the Committee on Ways and Means*. Washington, DC: U.S. Government Printing Office, various years.

U.S. Department of Treasury. "Treasury Report on Income Mobility." *Tax Notes*. Special Supplement. Vol. 55, No. 9, June 1, 1992.

Willer, Barbara, et al. *The Demand and Supply of Child Care in 1990*. Washington, DC: National Association for the Education of Young Children, 1991.

Wolff, Edward N. "Changing Inequality of Wealth." Presented at American Economic Association Meetings, January 1992a.

Wolff, Edward N. "Trends in Household Wealth During the 1980s." Economic Policy Institute, preliminary draft, June 1992b.

491

World Bank. *World Development Report 1992*. Oxford: Oxford University Press, 1992.

Veum, Jonathan R. and Philip M. Gleason. "Child-care: Arrangements and Costs." *Monthly Labor Review*, Vol. 114, No. 10, October 1991, pp. 10–17.

EPI Book Series

Unions and Economic Competitiveness
Lawrence Mishel and Paula B. Voos, *editors*
0-87332-828-0 (paper) $16.95
0-87332-812-4 (cloth) $37.50

The State of Working America, 1990–1991
Lawrence Mishel and David Frankel
0-87332-812-4 (cloth) $29.95
0-87332-813-2 (paper) $14.95

Beyond the Twin Deficits: *A Trade Strategy for the 1990s*
Robert Blecker
1-56324-090-4 (cloth) $42.50
1-56324-091-2 (paper) $17.95

New Policies for the Part-Time and Contingent Workforce
Virginia L. duRivage, *editor*
1-56324-164-1 (cloth) $45.00
1-56324-165-x (paper) $17.95

To order Economic Policy Institute books, contact

M.E. Sharpe, Inc.
80 Business Park Drive
Armonk, NY 10504

or call toll-free **1-800-541-6563.**

EPI Study Series

America's Industrial Policy Successes: *The Forgotten History of Picking Winners and Losers*
Robert Cohen
0-944826-47-4   (Vol. 36) $12.00

Does America Need Cities?: *An Urban Investment Strategy for National Prosperity*
Joseph Persky, Elliott Sclar,
and Wim Wiewel, with the assistance
of Walter Hook
0-944826-47-4   (Vol. 35) $12.00

Short Hours, Short Shrift: *Causes and Consequences of Part-time Work*
    Chris Tilly
    0-944826-29-6   (Vol. 25) $10.00

Export Controls: *Industrial Policy in Reverse*
    Robert Kuttner
    0-944826-39-3   (Vol. 24) $12.00

One-Third of A Nation: *A New Look at Housing Affordability in America*
    Michael E. Stone
    0-944826-31-8   (Vol. 23) $12.00

Job Displacement and the Rural Worker
    Michael Podgursky
    0-944826-14-8   (Vol. 22) $10.00

Capital Flight and the Latin American Debt Crisis
    Manuel Pastor
    0-944826-19-9   (Vol. 21) $12.00

Are Americans on a Consumption Binge?: *The Evidence Reconsidered*
    Robert A. Blecker
    0-944826-22-9   (Vol. 20) $12.00

Flying Blind: *The Failure of Airline Deregulation*
    Paul Stephen Dempsey
    0-944826-23-7   (Vol. 19) $12.00

Modernizing Manufacturing: *New Policies to Build Industrial Extension Services*
    Philip Shapira
    0-944826-24-5   (Vol. 18) $12.00

Beyond Free Trade and Protectionism: *The Public Interest in a U.S. Auto Policy*
    Daniel Luria
    0-944826-08-3   (Vol. 17) $10.00

Shortchanging the Workforce: *The Job Training Partnership Act and the Overselling of Privatized Training*
    John Donahue
    0-944826-18-0   (Vol. 16) $12.00

The State of Working America, 1988–1989
Lawrence Mishel and Jacqueline Simon
0-944826-04-0 (Vol. 6) $12.00

Manufacturing Numbers: *How Inaccurate Statistics Conceal U.S. Industrial Decline*
Lawrence Mishel
0-944826-03-2 (Vol. 5) $12.00

Prisons for Profit: *Public Justice, Private Interests*
John Donahue
0-944826-02-4 (Vol. 4) $10.00

The Limits of Privatization
Paul Starr
0-944826-01-6 (Vol. 3) $10.00

Economic Competitiveness: *The States Take the Lead*
David Osborne
0-944826-00-8 (Vol. 2) $12.00

No Longer Leading: *A Scorecard on U.S. Economic Performance*
Lucy Gorham
0-944826-32-6 (Vol. 1) $12.00

Special Offer

A complete set of EPI Studies (Volumes 1–36) is available at a reduced price of $299.00 (a 25% savings on the full price). When ordering by phone use the order code EPIPS-FALL.

Public Interest Publications also offers EPI's Studies through a standing order plan. Please call **1-800-537-9359** for more detailed information.

EPI Working Paper Series

No. 101
Better Jobs or Working Longer For Less
Lawrence Mishel   0-944826-25-3 $10.00

No. 102
Trading Away Jobs: *The Effects of the U.S. Merchandise Trade Deficit on Employment*
Faye Duchin and Glenn-Marie Lange
0-944826-26-1 $10.00

No. 103
Family Incomes in the 1980s: *New Pressure on Wives, Husbands, and Young Adults*
Stephen Rose and David Fasenfest
0-944826-28-8 $10.00

No. 104
Trade Protectionism and Industrial Revitalization: *American Steel in the 1980s*
Robert E. Scott, Thea M. Lee, and Robert Blecker $10.00

No. 105
Reconsidering the Benefits and Costs of Trade Protection: *The Case of Textiles and Apparel*
Robert E. Scott and Thea M. Lee
0-944826-41-5 $10.00

EPI Seminar Series

Employee Rights in a Changing Economy: *The Issue of Replacement Workers*
Julius Getman, William Gould IV,
Cynthia Gramm, Ray Marshall, Lawrence
Mishel, Brian Shell, William Spriggs,
Jeff Faux   0-944826-40-7 $12.00

Macroeconomic Policy
Barry Bosworth, Paul Davidson,
Robert Eisner, James Galbraith,
Hyman Minsky, Lawrence Summers,
Edward Yardeni, Jeff Faux   0-944826-20-2 $12.00

Declining American Incomes and Living Standards
Frank Levy, Barry Bluestone,
Lester Thurow, Ralph Whitehead, Jr.,
Jeff Faux   xerox $12.00

EPI Briefing Paper Series

The Effect of George Bush's NAFTA On American workers: *Ladder Up or Ladder Down*
Jeff Faux and Thea Lee   (BP31) $5.00

The Myth of the Coming Labor Shortage in Rural Areas
Ruy A. Teixeira and Lawrence Mishel   (BP30) $5.00

Unprepared for Recession: *The Erosion of State Unemployment Insurance Coverage Fostered by Public Policy in the 1980s*
Marc Baldwin and Richard McHugh   (BP29) $5.00

The Great American Time Squeeze: *Trends in Work and Leisure, 1969–1989*
Laura Leete-Guy and Juliet B. Schor   (BP28) $5.00

A Report Card on the Greenspan Fed
Gary Dymski, Gerald Epstein,
James Galbraith, Robert Pollin   (BP27) $5.00

Investment-Led Stimulus: *A Plan for Short-Term Recovery and Long-Term Economic Growth*
Jeff Faux   (BP26) $5.00

New Policies for the Part-Time and Contingent Workforce
Virginia L. duRivage   (BP25) $5.00

500

Other

Poster:
**A Statement of Warning from 327 Economists
About Public Investment—America's
"Third Deficit"** $1.50

Policy Memorandum:
Excise Taxes: Not Regressive? *Comments on the CBO
Study, Federal Taxation of Tobacco, Alcoholic Beverages,
and Motor Fuel*
    Max B. Sawicky $5.00

Lawrence Mishel is the Research Director of the Economic Policy Institute. He is the author of the previous two editions of *The State of Working America* (1988-1989 with Jacqueline Simon, 1990-1991 with David M. Frankel), *The Myth of the Coming Labor Shortage* (with Ruy Teixeira), *Manufacturing Numbers* and *Shortchanging Education* (with M. Edith Rasell). He holds a Ph.D. in economics from the University of Wisconsin and has published a variety of academic and non-academic journals.

Jared Bernstein, a jazz bassist and former social worker, is an economist at the Economic Policy Institute. Mr. Bernstein is completing his dissertation in pursuit of the Doctor of Social Welfare degree at Columbia University.

The Economic Policy Institute was founded in 1986 to widen the debate about policies to acheive healthy economic growth, prosperity, and opportunity in the difficult new era America has entered.

Today, America's economy is threatened by stagnant growth and increasing inequality. Expanding global competition, changes in the nature of work, and rapid technological advances are altering economic reality. Yet many of our policies, attitudes, and institutions are based on assumptions that no longer reflect real world conditions.

Central to the Economic Policy Institute's search for solutions is the exploration of the economics of teamwork—economic policies that encourage every segment of the American economy (business, labor, government, universities, voluntary organizations, etc.) to work cooperatively to raise productivity and living standards for all Americans. Such an undertaking involves a challenge to conventional views of market behavior and a revival of a cooperative relationship between the public and private sectors.

With the support of leaders from labor, business, and the foundation world, the Institute has sponsored research and public discussion of a wide variety of topics: trade and fiscal policies; trends in wages, incomes, and prices; the causes of the productivity slowdown; labor market problems; U.S. and Third World debt; rural and urban policies; inflation; state-level economic development strategies; comparative international economic performance; and studies of the overall health of the U.S. manufacturing sector and of specific key industries.

The Institute works with a growing network of innovative economists and other social science researchers in universities and research centers all over the country who are willing to go beyond the conventional wisdom in considering strategies for public policy.

The research committee of the Institute includes:

Jeff Faux—EPI President
Lester Thurow—Dean of MIT's Sloan School of Management
Ray Marshall—former U.S. Secretary of Labor, currently a Professor at the LBJ School of Public Affairs, University of Texas
Barry Bluestone—University of Massachusetts-Boston
Robert Reich—JFK School of Government, Harvard University
Robert Kuttner—Author; columnist, *New Republic,* and *Business Week;* co-editor, *New Republic*

EPI Reports, Working Papers, Briefing Papers, and Seminars are distributed by *Public Interest Publications.* For a publications list or to order, call 1-800-537-9359.

Other **EPI Books** are available from ME Sharpe at 1-800-541-6563.

For additional information contact the Institute / 1730 Rhode Island Ave., NW, Suite 200 / Washington, DC 20036 / 202-775-8810.